LANDPOWER IN THE LONG WAR

AUSA Books

SERIES EDITOR: Joseph Craig

LANDPOWER IN THE LONG WAR

PROJECTING FORCE AFTER 9/11

EDITED BY JASON W. WARREN

FOREWORD BY DANIEL P. BOLGER

UNIVERSITY PRESS OF KENTUCKY

Editorial and Sales Offices: The University Press of Kentucky
663 South Limestone Street, Lexington, Kentucky 40508-4008
www.kentuckypress.com

Cataloging-in-Publication data is available from the Library of Congress.

ISBN 978-0-8131-7757-1 (hardcover : alk. paper)
ISBN 978-0-8131-7759-5 (pdf)
ISBN 978-0-8131-7760-1 (epub)

This book is printed on acid-free paper meeting
the requirements of the American National Standard
for Permanence in Paper for Printed Library Materials.

Manufactured in the United States of America.

 Member of the Association
of University Presses

LANDPOWER IN THE LONG WAR

PROJECTING FORCE AFTER 9/11

EDITED BY JASON W. WARREN

FOREWORD BY DANIEL P. BOLGER

UNIVERSITY PRESS OF KENTUCKY

Editorial and Sales Offices: The University Press of Kentucky
663 South Limestone Street, Lexington, Kentucky 40508-4008
www.kentuckypress.com

Cataloging-in-Publication data is available from the Library of Congress.

ISBN 978-0-8131-7757-1 (hardcover : alk. paper)
ISBN 978-0-8131-7759-5 (pdf)
ISBN 978-0-8131-7760-1 (epub)

This book is printed on acid-free paper meeting
the requirements of the American National Standard
for Permanence in Paper for Printed Library Materials.

Manufactured in the United States of America.

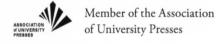

Member of the Association
of University Presses

In memory of Lieutenant Colonel John F. Guilmartin Jr., PhD

CONTENTS

Abbreviations

9/11	11 September 2011
AAR	After Action Report
AQI	Al Qa'ida in Iraq
CJCS	Chairman Joint Chiefs of Staff
CSA	Chief of Staff Army
COIN	counterinsurgency operations
DoD	Department of Defense
DoS	Department of State
GWOT	Global War on Terrorism
ISAF	International Security Assistance Force
Surge	Iraq "Surge"
ISIS	Islamic State of Iraq and Syria or Islamic State in the Levant
NATO	North Atlantic Treaty Organization
OEF	Operation Enduring Freedom
OIF	Operation Iraqi Freedom
RMA	Revolution in Military Affairs
SOF	special operations forces
USAREUR	US Army Europe
USAFRICOM	US African Command
USCENTCOM	US Central Command
USEUCOM	US European Command
USPACOM	US Pacific Command
USSOUTHCOM	US Southern Command

Foreword

Daniel P. Bolger

The numbers always went our way. That is for sure. We had more troops, more planes, more ships, more ammunition, and way more money. We killed more of them—a lot more. We dug more wells, built more schools, and paved more roads. We even ran elections, helped introduce constitutions, and taught human rights. Day after day, week after week, year after year, we piled up achievements crowded onto reams of PowerPoint slides. The statistics looked terrific. But you know what they say in the NFL. Statistics are for losers. What matters is the final score.

On that stark basis, our military has much to answer for. We backed into misbegotten, multi-year, American-led counterinsurgencies in both Afghanistan and Iraq. Our numbers might have looked good. But those gritty guerrillas outlasted us. We pulled the plug. Rump governments hang on in both unhappy countries, backed by small US and allied contingents narrowly constrained in what little they can do. Our insurgent, terrorist adversaries are as numerous as ever. Some show up on our doorstep now and then, bent on payback. Ugh.

Where does American landpower go from here? While our well-trained soldiers chased cranky goatherds and poked through trash piles looking for booby traps, the Chinese and the Russians rearmed and kept chipping away at the expense of weak neighbors. Dangerous regional troublemakers—North Korea, Iran, Venezuela, and others—did as they wished. We cannot afford to spend too much time on recriminations. Our opponents are on the move.

So we need to figure out what we just did to ourselves, why we did it, and what to do about it. That is what this book is all about. In compiling this volume and hosting the affiliated conference and research, the US Army War College continues in the tradition that underscored American victories in two world wars, the Cold War, and many lesser confrontations. It would be easy to avoid the troubling developments and frustrating results since the horrific Al Qa'ida attacks of 9/11. Some want to do just that.

Fortunately, for our fellow citizens, the US Army is not built that way, and the Army War College has taken a leading role in this painful but necessary self-assessment. The authors in this lineup seek understanding. They ask the hard questions. They do not always have answers. Some problems cannot be solved by landpower. Those might just be the most important lessons of all.

As unsatisfying as the major ground campaigns in Afghanistan and Iraq turned out to be, we must be careful not to confuse rightful disquiet over indecisive wars of attrition with a misguided hope that we can give up on landpower as a fundamental facet of America's superpower. People live on land, not in the skies or seas. Economic sanctions, offshore blockades, and the smartest of smart bombs only do so much. At some point, you have to take and hold the key ground. That takes landpower. And we must get it right. This book shows us the way.

Introduction

Jason W. Warren

What will we do when we lose the war? Prepare for the next one.
—Sam Peckinpah, *Cross of Iron*

In his observations of the US Air Force's support of American landpower, William Waddell asserts that the gods of the air domain must descend from Mt. Olympus's heights to better support their brethren on the ground.[1] Yet Ares, the god of war often depicted with sword and shield, has always been a creature of the land domain.[2] His sword appears to have been blunted, however, in the campaigns of the so-called War on Terror. As such, this volume calls for the reformation of the United States' ability to project landpower. Ares's business in the modern era is often related to Carl von Clausewitz's maxim that war is a continuation of policy and politics by other means.[3] The policy surrounding the employment of US landpower, as the Army defines it, "the ability—by threat, force, or occupation—to gain, sustain, and exploit control overland, resources, and people,"[4] is tied intimately to the preroga-tives of the District of Columbia "Beltway." This often focuses landpower inward rather than outward, dulling Ares' instrument of power. War-win-ning becomes a secondary objective to domestic agendas, which the concept of a "Long War" serves.[5]

This volume explores landpower from several perspectives, not only ground operations in Iraq and Afghanistan.[6] Thus, it is a comprehensive con-sideration of the critical aspect of US foreign policy—the threat or ability to use landpower underpins diplomacy. Even the most decisive of naval and air battles, from Salamis and Trafalgar to the Blitz and Midway, have required Plataea, Waterloo, D-Day, and Manilla to achieve victory. No war has been won without effective landpower because the land "domain" is where people reside.

For edited volumes it is especially important to define what the schol-arship is not. *Landpower* is not a reconsideration of what iconoclast profes-sor Andrew Bacevich has identified as a bipartisan consensus of America's foreign policy. This volume assumes that the relationship between American Exceptionalism and the means and will to operationalize this ideology through power projection that underlay Bacevich's "Washington Rules"[7] will remain constant. This is not primarily a consideration of why Americans fight, but how. The volume is also not in the main an archival history, as many primary sources have not appeared. The apparent lack of success of US landpower, however, begs immediate reconsideration of its current doctrinal tenets and the reformation of its employment. As the contributors to this volume demonstrate, the conceptualization of landpower must move beyond the limited operational definition offered by Army doctrine better to encompass social changes, trauma, the rule of law, acquisition of equipment, civil-military relationships, headquarters manning, and bureaucratic decision-making. It should be a useful concept for warfighters and the government agencies that rely on it. Defeat at the hands of Napoleonic France forced a reconsideration of Prussian ground capabilities, catapulting reformers like Clausewitz to temporary influence; poor results of US landpower projection must spark a similar change in the modern context.

Former commander of forces in Afghanistan Lieutenant General Daniel Bolger (Ret.) emphasizes in the book's foreword the rarity of post-9/11 landpower successes, a view many other scholars and commentators reinforce.[8] This unless one considers the employment of landpower through the prism of the Beltway incentive-driven standpoint. The concept of a "Long War" developed, as much as a result of these bureaucratic incentives as any leader's intentional design, to protect the interests of an updated version of President Dwight Eisenhower's paradigm: a massive military-*informational* complex. Theories of bureaucratic friction have their modern origin in the failure of Vietnam, and discussing these is now considered passé.[9] Perhaps this volume will serve as a primer for political scientists to revisit the topic. Protecting Beltway prerogatives, particularly at the DoD, retarded the warfighting that was occurring "downrange" in a host of global hot spots.[10] Even with the Iraq War on the line and the Surge of troops into the region (accompanied by the intellectual surge of thinking about counterinsurgency operations [COIN]), the bureaucrats remained unmoved: "you go to the Pentagon and there's no sense of a war on-going, there's no sense of everybody surging."[11]

The Beltway's bureaucracy is not a monolith. Rather, it operates via agencies competing for power and scarce resources, which is at its root a disincentive for winning wars. Victory—the term even has largely been stripped from government lexicon, although a 2018 Army recruiting video mentions "win"—requires a cohesive interagency approach. The United States continues a Long War because there is little institutional incentive to end it. Multiple briefings at the highest levels focus on preparing to meet the needs of the headquarters above them or Congress, instead of a single-minded effort toward war-winning.

Contractors like those employed by the infamous Blackwater became major players in military operations as an attempt to outsource soldier-related costs. Although covered briefly later but a topic deserving of book-length treatment, contractors overly influence military operations.[12] It is no coincidence, then, that the wealthiest counties in the nation, inhabited by the vast contractor-related workforce, now surround Washington, DC, or that the populist movement on both sides of the political spectrum during the 2016 presidential election focused on economic disparities, in part exemplified by the Beltway and its environs.[13] I touch on the outcomes of bureaucratic friction here as a framework for the following chapters, which do so tangentially.

When ISIS accomplished Osama bin Laden's goals under its banner with the recreation of the Caliphate in Muslim lands, it appeared that the United States and its allies had faltered. Viewed through the perspective of bureaucratic growth, however, America had succeeded. The nation has seen this saga before, when clear victory is achieved, leading to inevitable military drawdowns, and hence a decrease in Beltway power.[14] This was easier to swallow in earlier times, as a largely amateur mass-produced army was disbanded after the victory parade, leaving a small kernel of a professional force. The advent of the Cold War altered this paradigm, as the standing professional force required continual maintenance and employment.

As an anecdote that circulated around social media at the outset of the 2003 Iraq invasion related, "killing is my business, and business is booming." The flippant military unit that posted this sign at the entrance to its forward operating base gave a more forthright assessment of the bureaucracy's goals than any political speech.[15] War also quickly became the business of an insurgent enemy in Iraq in the aftermath of Saddam Hussein's takedown, and the United States and its allies soon learned that two could make a killing.

As the war effort spun out of control with an inability to end dynamic insurgencies, the government's propaganda machine went into overdrive. Headquarters assured military success. Metrics sometimes took the form of the all-too-familiar body count of the Vietnam era, but also other suspect measurements like the sheer number of *shuras* (meetings) with local Iraqi and Afghan leaders. One battalion commander from the pre-Surge days in Iraq claimed: "While bloated multinational commands produced massive Power-Point presentations that attempted to link political and military challenges, while always demonstrating 'progress' in the campaign, frontline soldiers in combat battalions strove to achieve the impossible task of implementing tactical solutions to an ambiguous, if not outright illusory, strategic framework."[16]

The haphazard employment of landpower within this framework is a result of systemic factors rather than intentional design. I learned about the law of perverse incentives as an officer in charge of regional training in Afghanistan when, for DoD budget compliance, higher headquarters canceled Mine Resistant Ambush Protected (MRAP) vehicle training. This was eerily similar to the issue of vulnerable unarmored Humvees in Iraq, when then Secretary of Defense Donald Rumsfeld quipped that the United States must fight with the army that it has. My command had no choice but to make do with a "work-around" for the MRAPs, but imagine these situations multiplied across the US Army's global footprint, and the friction between war winning and Beltway objectives comes more clearly into focus. Later, Major General Fastabend (Ret.), a major contributor to the Iraq campaign, examines challenges with the Army's procurement system, which was exemplified by the MRAP debacle.

Events were more complicated, however, than the hindrances of a faceless bureaucratic system, as political managers like Rumsfeld interfered with military objectives. Retired Army Lieutenant Colonel and strategist Donald Travis and Colonel Frank Sobchak point out that Rumsfeld undermined the early war effort through arbitrary force caps and by truncating the careers of leaders like General Eric Shinseki as a signal to the others to fall in line with his plans "or else." Despite Shinseki's good faith attempt to ameliorate this incident, probably to prevent further harm to the civilian-military relationship, the damage was done.[17] This undermined sound military planning that would have dictated more soldiers on the ground.

As a key component of landpower, mass has a value all its own, and the Army War College's John Bonin argues that the Army lacked the necessary headquarters structure adequately to command the war. But Rumsfeld was out to prove the second Bush administration's point that military force could be wielded without mass, collateral damage, or nation-building. This was the conclusion of the Revolution in Military Affairs (RMA) decade that General David Petraeus's former executive officer Colonel Peter Mansoor (now a professor at The Ohio State University) describes as distracting from sound strategy. None have answered for their misconceptions, as the rows of headstones at Arlington continue to advance, standing sentinel in judgment of the Beltway.

Within the Army, the primary purveyor of landpower, a narrow Cold War mentality continues to value Ares's tactical level of war above the strategic. Lukas Milevski in the opening chapter details the United States' lack of a grand strategy that should inform military strategy. Officers are promoted for tactical prowess, and it is assumed that combat experience will counter a lack of civilian graduate education and an absence of institutional landpower knowledge. The Army's officer corps is professional in name only, not adhering to standards that undergird other professions, such as law and medicine, that demand a baseline of knowledge (in the Army's case doctrine, regulations, standard operating procedures, military history, etc.) and continued learning. In fact, any reference to intellect is frowned on in "field" units within a pervasive anti-intellectual atmosphere.

The Army even attempted to eliminate a West Point Rhodes Scholar because after graduation he went straight to Oxford University instead of the field—only CSA Mark Milley's personal intervention saved the young officer. He is not alone.[18] Many more promising officers did not receive a stay of execution, as the Army incredibly eliminated nearly forty more field grade officers (some of them friends)—teachers, mentors, coaches to the cadets—than would be expected due to normal attrition *during* the fall semester of 2016, undermining temporarily the academic and military credentials of the US Military Academy.[19] On the fraud, waste, and abuse front, the American taxpayers had just funded graduate school for these officers so that they could serve at West Point, yet they were eliminated from government service mainly for undertaking the very broadening opportunity the Army offered them instead of yet another deployment to USCENTCOM. As these cases signify, the Army officer corps has increasingly and narrowly defined itself as desiring technicians who dislike the more cerebral demands of officership that warfare requires to deal with strategic issues and complexity. The Army's best and brightest often eschew the Army War College—the self-described home of strategic landpower—for fellowships at Ivy League institutions that focus on the intricacies of networking, not ground-power projection. Promising Army officers also attend the other services' war colleges, which are less steeped in landpower. Officers have become the surgical techs of landpower, not the doctors.[20]

Lieutenant Colonel J. P. Clark argues that generational antagonism has resulted between the three generations of officers fighting the Long War.[21] A larger problem, however, has been the increasing Army bureaucratization since the Progressive Era, which Clark credits as a driving factor in the increased professionalization of the officer corps early last century. This ultimately came at a price, as the birth of the DoD in the aftermath of victory in the Second World War accelerated bureaucratization that has choked war-winning efforts since 1945.[22]

Too many civilian secretaries and undersecretaries and their inflated staffs now interpose their bureaucratic will on what had been the domain of generals and admirals like George Marshall, Chester Nimitz, and John J. "Black Jack" Pershing. This has pushed politics further into the ranks (and, as Edward A. Gutiérrez points out later, into the intelligence agencies) and focused the efforts of senior admirals and generals on tactics and operations instead of strategy. This was the fear of then Navy Secretary Admiral James Forrestal, who during the debate over the creation of DoD "[m]ost of all . . . did not want any new cabinet secretary to intervene between himself and the president."[23] The United States has not left the field in victory since the creation of the Defense Department with the exception of the Gulf War, which featured a threat that mirrored the Army's tactical preoccupation. Even if the DoD disappeared, the officer corps is no longer capable of producing the leaders of yesteryear to act with this renewed autonomy.[24]

Budget incentives continue to reflect a Cold War mentality, where the Army's biggest political items are rotations of heavy combat brigades through the National Training Center (NTC) for over $30 million dollars a turn.[25] Some training for "the big one" is a worthwhile endeavor for deterrence, but so is training for current wars. The efficacy in pushing every available combat brigade through these rotations is questionable, given the character of current operations and the announcement of troop increases in Afghanistan.[26] This too is a government incentive, with a greater ease in making a case for budgeting for these rotations like the other services do with aircraft carriers and F-35 fighters. Brigade commanders who are deemed successful at these largely canned tactical exercises (the training is confined to a particular battlespace, timeframe, and opposing force, often with predictable missions) join the running for general officer, where it is assumed—despite the preconditions for a lack of professional discourse—they will now be capable of serving at the higher levels of war.[27] Unfortunately for the strategic prospects of the nation, winning at NTC has not equated to victory.

As showcased in this book, the Army institution did not get it all wrong since 9/11, however, as it rapidly shifted from an inflexible Cold War structure to a less rigid modular model with new doctrine and leadership to right a war in Iraq that had gone terribly wrong. This too was a case of incentives, where government leaders understood that defeat would undermine their power, in this case the administration of George W. Bush. The Army accomplished between 2005 and 2009 what no global institution could. Once it was incentivized, the institution rapidly changed its structure, training, and doctrine, all while fighting globally. As three Army strategists relate in their chapter, humanitarian missions have been largely successful since 9/11, projecting less force and more good will. The Army did not achieve success alone. Mark Balboni and Paul Westermeyer detail a Marine Corps task force's accomplishments in Afghanistan as a microcosm of that service's contribution to this newfound success, while special operations forces (SOF) also played a larger role in a shift to a COIN model.

Influential anti-COIN advocate Colonel Gian Gentile (Ret.) has argued that the civil war in Iraq generated "positive" statistics in what appeared to be landpower progress, and that many frontline troops had already employed some version of COIN prior to the Surge.[28] Even so, the Army institution changed rapidly while maintaining effectiveness. Population-centric COIN is a massive undertaking at all levels of war, requiring an understanding of the local factors. Some have even referred to it as the graduate level of war.[29] The Army's attempt to master COIN demonstrated a major (albeit temporary) shift from its Cold War mentality of conventional battle, the latter of which Gentile points out also requires elements of a graduate level understanding. Unfortunately, by the time the Army shook off its Cold War malaise, America's domestic politics had moved beyond Iraq. Sobchak argues that an Obama administration-led pullout squandered gains in Iraqi stability. He and Ibrahim Al-Marashi note how ISIS and Iran filled the void. Sobchak helped author the Army's controversial Iraq War report, and his chapter here provides a synopsis.

The Iraq pullout and the concomitant surge in Afghanistan also illustrated that Clausewitz's maxim was only half of the equation. War is also a continuation of worldview or *weltanschauung,* an idea that policy only partially encompasses. The Obama administration's view was different in some ways from that of the George W. Bush administration. The former believed that a smaller overseas landpower footprint and a change in tone of diplomacy would lead to more stability. Its naivete in terminating and preventing conflicts matched its predecessor administration's naivete in initiating wars to spread democracy. The Bush administration had previously attempted to grapple with the neo-conservative paradox of achieving democracy through aggressive landpower projection. The ideology behind the Washington Rules undergirded the post-9/11 foreign policy misadventures of both the Bush and Obama administrations. Donald Travis highlights the civil-military challenges in negotiating these often amorphous interests that complicate strategy.

The Army, blowing with the political winds, shunted aside the institutional progress of 2005–2009 to the point where members of my unit in Afghanistan were disallowed in 2012–2013 from referencing COIN. A Cold War mentality quickly reemerged as perceived threats requiring heavy forces allowed the institution to prepare for its favored NTC rotations. The modular brigade structure, which brought the Army into the twenty-first century, is now in danger of lapsing back into the rigid divisional model. Army generals' lack of institutional history and force structure knowledge, and the incentives of the Beltway, create a void of understanding that risks the reestablishment of a division-based Army emblematic of the military-industrial complex of Ike's day. Prisoners of tactical experience and victims of the Beltway's systemic disincentives, Army leadership is rapidly moving back to the future. Landpower in the near term will likely resemble that of 10 September 2001.

As I write this, SOF-backed local forces supported by US airpower are poised to topple ISIS. With success they will appear to have vindicated the Rumsfeld doctrine. Closer consideration reveals a hefty conventional footprint underreported to the American people, however, in support of this campaign from large bases across the Middle East. One must also realize the cost of this late triumph (events in Afghanistan continue to go poorly). The human toll since 9/11 has been enormous, especially considering the fallout from the Arab Spring, the impetus for which at least partially derived from the War on Terror. Professor Lawrence Tritle describes the combat trauma experienced by American forces, and one can imagine the traumas experienced by the populations of the Middle East and Southwest Asia.[30] Professor Jacqueline Whitt describes the social changes the DoD undertook to help offset casualties and the related recruiting gap caused by post-9/11 operations. How foreign to most Americans today, with less than one half of one percent serving in the armed forces, does President John F. Kennedy's famous urging seem: "Ask not what your country can do for you—ask what you can do for your country?"[31]

Huge swaths of what had been the flower of many empires now lay in ruin, from the Babylonian and Roman to the Ottoman. Mosul fell recently, but the city was completely destroyed.[32] Tacitus's infamous refrain about poor maintenance of empire has rarely been more apt: "They make a desolation and call it peace."[33] This belated and costly progress indicts the US government with a lack of landpower efficacy during this era, and, given its necessity for continuing American interventionism, begs for its reformation. The chapter authors have collectively given voice to a new conception of strategic landpower. Landpower, governed by universal legal norms and reflective of cultural frameworks, assists in achieving national policy through the strategic employment of overland force unencumbered by bureaucratic inertia; it redirects the will of host populations toward this end while recognizing human limitations through considerations of trauma and social conditions; its purveyors consider global effects and follow-on consequences. This volume demonstrates how these components of strategic landpower relate to each other, which is often the most important aspect of its projection.

Clausewitz would be comfortable operating in this contemporary space, as he had experienced Prussian landpower's degradation from the highpoint of Frederick the Great's earlier reign to the kingdom's humiliating defeat at Jena-Auerstedt, and Napoleon's subsequent occupation of Berlin. He too called for reformation, and his voice was heard and promoted (with the help of his wife) by a conservative ruler, who risked a measure of liberalization to regain his kingdom. Washington is not in danger of occupation other than the bureaucratic kind, and thus perhaps the United States has not experienced enough failure to force such needed transformation. Hopefully this volume's reconsideration of landpower will spark critical change. Ares's sword is in need of whetting.

Notes

1. I owe a debt of gratitude to Andrew Bacevich, Daniel Bolger, John Bonin, Antonio Echevarria, Edward A. Gutiérrez, Andrea Jacobs, Donald Travis, and Lawrence Tritle for their guidance on the introduction.

2. See for instance Peter Paul Reubens, "Consequences of War" (also known as "Horror of War," executed during the Thirty Years' War), 1638–1639, Palazzo Pitti, Florence, Italy.

3. According to leading Clausewitz scholar Antonio Echevarria, Clausewitz meant this maxim to help describe the nature of war, not the political events of any singular time period (email correspondence July 2017). Carl von Clausewitz, *On War*, ed. and trans. Michael Howard and Peter Paret (Princeton, N.J.: Princeton Univ. Press, 1976), 87.

4. *Army Doctrine Reference Publication 3-0, Operations* (Washington, DC: Headquarters Department of the Army, 16 November 2016), 1-9/1-51.

5. Andrew J. Bacevich, ed., *The Long War: A New History of U.S. National Security Policy since World War II* (New York: Columbia Univ. Press, 2007), ix–xi.

6. There have been a number of solid accounts of fighting in Iraq and Afghanistan, including Michael Gordon and General Bernard Trainor, *Cobra II* (New York: Vintage Books, 2007), and more recently Beth Bailey and Richard Immerman, eds., *Understanding the U.S. Wars in Iraq and Afghanistan* (New York: New York Univ. Press, 2015). Michael O'Hanlon has written a brief critique of landpower employment and a more lengthy prognostication of its future implementation: *The Future of Land Warfare* (Washington, DC: Brookings Institution, 2015). While a timely and worthy endeavor, O'Hanlon treats landpower in a much more narrow sense than does this volume.

7. Andrew Bacevich, *Washington Rules: America's Path to Permanent War* (New York: Holt, 2010), 12–15.

8. There is a vast literature on post-9/11 failures. For example, Tom Ricks argued in *The Generals* (New York: Penguins Books, 2013) that there has been no accountability for failed military operations in but one of many commentators' accounts

criticizing various aspects of the post-9/11 war-making. On the political front, the Republicans were not punished for policy missteps in Iraq and Afghanistan until the midterm elections of 2006 and Barack Obama's election in 2008, many years into the conflicts of 9/11. Also see Tom Ricks, *Fiasco* (New York: Penguin Press, 2006); Dexter Filkens, *The Forever War* (New York: Vintage Books, 2008); and Andrew Bacevich's monographs *The New American Militarism* (New York: Oxford Univ. Press, 2005), *The Limits of Power* (New York: Holt, 2008), *Washington Rules* (New York: Holt, 2010), *Breach of Trust* (New York: Holt, 2013), and *America's War for the Greater Middle East* (New York: Random House, 2016). Peter Mansoor's *Surge* (New Haven, Conn.: Yale Univ. Press, 2013) details near military collapse under the Army leadership of Generals George Casey and John Abizaid.

9. Long War George H. Quester, "The Politics of Conventional Warfare," in *The Long War*, 119–122.

10. I have chosen to highlight the role of the bureaucracy in impeding land-power to better round out this volume. Fred Kaplan, *The Insurgents* (New York: Simon and Schuster, 2013), highlights the military bureaucracy that General David Petraeus and his allies had to circumvent to save the war effort in Iraq. Bacevich, *The Long War,* viii, describes the bureaucratic "army" that underpinned the massive security apparatus of the Cold War era. It was not disbanded after the collapse of the Soviet Union.

11. As quoted in Tom Rick's *The Gamble: General David Petraeus and the American Military Adventure in Iraq, 2006–2008* (New York: Penguin Press, 2009), 235.

12. I have witnessed influential contractors advise flag officers to make decisions that, to an outsider, *appear* to further contracts for their respective businesses.

13. Rebecca Lerner, "The Top 10 Richest Counties in America," *Forbes,* 13 July 2017, https://www.forbes.com/sites/rebeccalerner/2017/07/13/top-10-richest-counties-in-america-2017/#6229de9d2ef3.

14. See Jason W. Warren, ed., *Drawdown: The American Way of Postwar* (New York: New York Univ. Press, 2016).

15. Interestingly, veterans of other wars remember the circulation of a similar quote. Tritle, then an Army lieutenant, remembers a similar desk placard during the Vietnam era.

16. Quote from Colonel Kevin Farrell (Ret.), Ph.D., who commanded 1-64 Armor Battalion in Iraq from 2005 to 2006, in Warren, *Drawdown,* 293.

17. General Shinseki's 10 June 2003 End of Tour Memorandum.

18. Jim Perkins, "This Isn't About Me: A Personnel Story," https://warontherocks.com /2016/11/this-isnt-about-me-a-personnel-story/ (accessed 31 March 2018).

19. This number was obtained from West Point. The source's name and department have been redacted.

20. Jason W. Warren, "The Centurion Mindset and the Army's Strategic Leader Paradigm," *Parameters* 45, no. 3 (autumn 2015): 27–38.

21. J. P. Clark, *Preparing for War: The Emergence of the Modern U.S. Army, 1815–*

1917 (Cambridge, Mass.: Harvard Univ. Press, 2017); J. P. Clark, "Organizational Change and Adaptation in the US Army," *Parameters* 46, no. 3 (autumn 2016).

22. Warren, "The Centurion Mindset," 32.

23. As quoted in Anna Kasten Nelson, "The Evolution of the National Security State," in *The Long War*, 268.

24. Warren, "The Centurion Mindset."

25. Michelle Tan, "Combat Training Rotations Will Increase to 18 Days," *Army Times*, 6 February 2015, https://www.armytimes.com/story/military/careers/army/2015/02/06/army-extends-ctc-rotations/22948785/.

26. President Donald Trump speech, 21 August 2017.

27. Warren, "The Centurion Mindset."

28. Ricks, *The Gamble*, 217–219.

29. Mansoor, *Baghdad at Sunrise* (New Haven, Conn.: Yale Univ. Press, 2008), 345. Gentile has countered this idea in a number of talks for the Society of Military History's annual conference, arguing conventional warfare also requires a graduate level understanding of war.

30. Hassan Blasim's morbid award-winning historical fiction *The Corpse Exhibition,* trans. Jonathon Wright (New York: Penguin Books, 2009), details some of the destruction and misery in Iraq after its wars with the United States and Iran.

31. No author, https://www.jfklibrary.org/Research/Research-Aids/Ready-Reference/JFK-Quotations/Inaugural-Address.aspx (accessed 21 August 2017). There is a growing disconnect between the military and the average citizen. See David Zucchino and David Cloud, "US Military and Civilians Are Increasingly Divided," *Los Angeles Times,* 24 May 2015, http://www.latimes.com/nation/la-na-warrior-main-20150524-story.html. A front-page article in the *Army Times* 78, no. 4 (2017) debated bringing back the draft because of the perceived civil disconnect with the all-volunteer military.

32. Igor Kossov, "Mosul Is Completely Destroyed," *The Atlantic,* 10 July 2017, https://www.theatlantic.com/international/archive/2017/07/mosul-iraq-abadi-isis-corruption/533067/.

33. Tacitus, *Agricola*, 30.5. Tritle contextualizes this famous quote as not only a Roman elite's perception of empire and its subjects, but also more broadly as a Roman Way of War in "Deserts Called Peace: Toward a Roman Way of War," San Francisco, Society of Classical Traditions conference, 2015.

PART I

The Strategic Underpinnings of US Landpower

Chapter 1

Variable Heroism
Landpower in US Grand Strategy since 9/11

Lukas Milevski

The history of US landpower since 9/11, of its utility and use, has been a story of change. At times policymakers sought to impose change upon landpower itself. At other times, policy was altered and landpower had to adapt. Sometimes the context in which both policy and strategy were made evolved, forcing everything else to adapt to it. Landpower could be considered the primary instrument to accomplish policy goals, only to be found unnecessary for the achievement of desired political effects at other times.

To understand variations in the contextual utility and employment of landpower over the past decade and a half, one must first grapple with the question of whether or not the American use of landpower throughout US strategic history may be described with a singular "big idea." This question has become salient in the debate on the American Way of War, as various scholars have argued either case. Most apprehend enduring patterns, whether Russell Weigley's emphasis on attrition versus annihilation or Brian McAllister Linn's three archetypes of American military officers—Guardians, Heroes, and Managers. Others, most notably Antulio Echevarria, decry this notion and suggest that the American use of force has been overwhelmingly pragmatic, without particular attachment to one specific idea.[1] Yet regardless of whether or not abstract big ideas dominate the whole of American military history, due to temporary trends in strategic and political thought and practice, big ideas may temporarily govern the employment of US landpower for extended periods.

Since the end of the Cold War, the United States has been unsure of its role in the world, an uncertainty that has been reflected in its varied use of landpower. A sequence of four alternating phases marked by varying heroism characterizes US grand strategy and its reliance on landpower: a first post-heroic phase, then a heroic phase, the re-emergence of a post-heroic phase, and finally today's security environment, which appears to require a greater readiness to behave heroically once again. Heroism and post-heroism, according to Edward Luttwak, refers to a political and strategic willingness, or lack thereof, to incur costs and casualties to achieve policy goals with force. In each phase, the basic assumptions and characteristics of landpower have fluctuated in their relevance to the policy at hand.

Grand Strategy and Landpower

Grand strategy has had many, frequently mutually incompatible, definitions. Not all of these definitions are equally valuable, however, as their inherent practicability varies. The realistically practicable definitions, those that can be transferred to the real world of action, are those emphasizing the multi-instrumental nature of grand strategy, which remains nonetheless subordinate to policy and politics.[2] Ironically, this basic interpretation of grand strategy is the least understood. Lawrence Freedman's assessment remains apt: "The view that strategy is bound up with the role of force in international life must be qualified, because if force is but one form of power then strategy must address the relationship between this form and others, including authority."[3] Grand strategy can fill this role. Defining grand strategy in terms of a multiplicity of instruments of power is both practicable and worthwhile. A vital distinction therefore exists between policy and grand strategy. Policy is the articulated goal, the given direction toward which strategists must work, combined with limits on what is deemed politically acceptable action. Grand strategy is the specific consideration given to the multiplicity of national instruments, military, and nonmilitary, to fulfill policy along indicated guidelines. Yet how does one actually study grand strategy, so defined?

One must start with *assumptions*—beliefs or understandings, usually unspoken and implicit, which underpin decisions, actions, and behaviors. Assumptions are both fundamental and crucial: "Given the complexity of international politics, assumptions are quite obviously inevitable (or, and more correctly, unavoidable) and frequently play a central role in decision making. . . . Second, there is a practical requirement for those assumptions to be right, or to eliminate as much error in judgment as is possible. That this is an imperative is due to the stakes being so great."[4] The assumptions that matter are not, however, assumptions about any particular enemy or the international system. Rather, the assumptions of interest for understanding the role of landpower in grand strategy are those that are implicit and underpin each of the various forms of power within grand strategy—that is, about the instrument itself. Landpower is understood based on a set of assumptions distinct from those of seapower, airpower, economic power, and so forth. These assumptions matter because they relate directly to how these various forms of power achieve effect, the potential scale of their effect, the times-cale on which effect is achieved, and the cost with which that effect can be achieved. They are assumptions about the nature of power itself in its manifold manifestations.

The assumptions concerning military power, and especially *land*power, have been apparent (albeit not often explicitly discussed) for at least a century, ever since the German military historian Hans Delbrück distinguished between two types of military strategies: annihilation (*Niederwerfungsstrategie*) and exhaustion/attrition (*Ermattungsstrategie*).[5] Of the two, the strategy for annihilation is most significant. The ideal strategy for annihilation results in a swift campaign crowned with an overwhelming victory in which the enemy's army is destroyed as a fighting force and the enemy's political will to continue the war is broken. What Delbrück's distinction in types of strategies reveals about the assumptions that underpin military power is telling, as no form of nonmilitary power has engendered such a distinction. There is an assumption, reasonably supported by history, that military power has the unique capability of achieving swift success. It does not necessarily always do so in reality, but in principle it *can*. No other form of power makes such a promise. These types of assumptions matter for grand strategy, as they determine the relative value of various forms of power when faced with an adversary in a particular context.

What is landpower? Landpower is the ability to exert control—of territory, of people, of outcomes, etc.—within the land environment. The distinct assumptions and real and potential costs that underpin and characterize its use stem from the nature of the instrument itself. The relevance to the value of landpower of these assumptions, costs, and characteristics in any particular strategic circumstance is necessarily contingent on the specific application of landpower in context. The basic assumptions and characteristics of landpower are immersion, control, vulnerability, and political contentiousness.

Unlike airpower or seapower, landpower is fundamentally and permanently completely *immersed* within its geographical medium. Planes must eventually land and ships must eventually return to port, but armies, in action or at rest, remain within the land environment. The sole exceptions are when landpower must traverse other geographies to come to grips with foes in distant lands. This basic fact is salient for both the basic potential value and the costs of landpower. Humanity lives on land and not on the sea or in the air: "Belligerents in war are therefore territorially defined and so it is land that, of all the environments, has the highest *symbolic and physical value.*

Because of this, in the end the highest order security interests of political actors tend to be associated inextricably with territory."[6] Landpower not only exists within the most fundamental physical geography of strategy and politics, but requires no special effort, no explicit expenditure of technology to do so—unlike airpower or seapower, which are platform-based forms of power.

Due to its ability to persist freely within the inherently most valuable geographical context, landpower has the general ability, unique within grand strategy, to *control* the broad pattern of a war. The naval historian and strategic theorist Herbert Rosinski perhaps best defined control, in two important but separate statements. First, he noted that "*it is this element of control which is the essence of strategy: Control being the element which differentiates true strategic action from a haphazard series of improvisations.*" Second, "comprehensive control of a field of action means a concentration upon those minimum key lines of action or key positions from which the entire field can be positively controlled."[7] To have control is to have the freedom of action to pursue actively one's desired objectives, whereas not to have control is to suffer limitations on one's freedom of action, such that one cannot deliberately seek to accomplish positive objectives but must improvise in order to regain the ability to do so. The field of action in which one's freedom of action may be forcefully manipulated is both physical and mental—what one may or may not be able to do physically matters, as does whether or not one is mentally or morally prepared to make an attempt from the remaining options.

Although other forms of military power may be able to exert positive control within its own geographical domains, landpower is the only one that may impose and exercise control on the pattern of the war as such—because it exists within the land environment. The prizes that are at stake on land tend to garner greater attention than those that are elsewhere. Moreover, landpower has the additional generic opportunity to achieve control quickly by pursuing a strategy for annihilation. Strategists have on occasion achieved the ideal outcome of destroying or incapacitating the opposing army to such an extent that the enemy can no longer act in a strategically effective manner—one may think of Napoleon's classic campaigns, or the Prussian victory over the Austrians in 1866.

Of course, this option of annihilation and swift victory is not always available, due not only to the adversarial logic of war through which the enemy also has significant input into the unfolding of events and their consequences, but also to the strategic and political value of the land environment, which makes landpower so potent. Any given territory "is usually an organic part of your enemy's country, or otherwise of so much importance to him that he will be willing to use unlimited effort to retain it." Furthermore, "there will be no strategical obstacle to his being able to use his whole force to that end."[8] An enemy may redouble his own efforts to succeed in war despite crushing loss simply because the consequences of defeat on land may be so grave. For every Königgrätz—where the Prussians inflicted a crushing defeat on the Austrians that swiftly led to a peace treaty advantageous to Prussia— there may be a Cannae—where Hannibal annihilated a Roman army, a victory to no political effect and actually to disadvantageous strategic effect.

The innate dangers of employing landpower also stem from its basic nature. Landpower is the most inherently *vulnerable* military instrument. Not only is it the most organizationally complex and the densest in terms of moving parts—the smallest unit in landpower ultimately is the individual soldier—but to achieve control this organization must actively put itself into danger. There is no entry requirement for being tactically active in the land environment, which allows even individuals with secondhand weapons to become fighters. Although it may be difficult to defeat an army, it is not difficult to attack one. The result is that landpower is bound to take casualties in any adversarial situation, and this is a fundamental assumption that must be understood by those who seek to employ landpower.

Partly for this reason, landpower is often the most politically contentious of all instruments of national power, both internationally and with regard to the domestic audience. Politicians consider the US public to be notoriously casualty-averse, although the veracity of this claim is under dispute.[9] This supposed cultural aversion to casualties stems from the experience of the Vietnam War. Its popular narrative claims that the US strategy gradually fell afoul of domestic pressures exerted by a disaffected American society growing increasingly unconvinced by the reasons for intervention, as well as by the intervention's actual effectiveness. As the war went on, the average American became increasingly unwilling to sacrifice American—and Vietnamese— lives for little appreciable effect. The US Army eventually responded to this popular narrative with the restrictive dicta of the Weinberger Doctrine (later Weinberger-Powell), which stipulated strict requirements for employing US landpower, including ensuring the full support of American public opinion, in order to circumvent its inevitable political contentiousness. Related to the question of political contentiousness is the expense of landpower. It is notably both expensive and difficult to maintain and sustain operations. This is especially true of US landpower, the operations of which typically take place overseas at vast distances from their ultimate bases of supply.

Since 9/11, American grand strategists seeking to bring to fruition their nation's policies would have had to consider these fundamental assumptions and characteristics of landpower and, in each individual case, answer the question: Is landpower the appropriate instrument for the task, or might other—possibly even nonmilitary—instruments be more effective in the present context?

Landpower and the Evolving Assumptions of American Interventionism

The story of landpower in US grand strategy since 9/11—that is, the tale of the compatibility of the assumptions underpinning landpower with US policy—is essentially a narrative of the variable attractiveness of landpower over a decade and a half. The overarching storyline is one of post-heroic strategic conduct, followed by a period of heroic strategy, before finally experiencing a return to post-heroism. Present day security challenges may, however, require the ability to return to a heroic mind-set should they ever escalate to a new war.

Post-Heroism in US Strategy and Landpower

To understand the full story of US landpower since 9/11, one must consider American strategy during the 1990s. This decade began with the Gulf War and the climax of the Revolution in Military Affairs (RMA), which demonstrated an apparent American ability to wage major war in a nearly casualty-free manner through the application of overwhelming military power, including landpower. Somalia swiftly derailed this optimism, which essentially heralded a decade of post-heroic strategy. This style of strategic conduct relied primarily on airpower to achieve effects, avoiding the use of landpower whenever possible, and otherwise emphasizing the personal safety of members of the US armed forces. Such restrained conduct gave rise to the "post-heroic" moniker demonstrated most notably in Bosnia and Kosovo.[10]

During this decade, non-landpower intervention was in vogue in the Clinton administration, although landpower was not. The result was that although the United States could usually achieve its policy goals through airpower when it decided to intervene, it was never achieved in a timely manner. The world's most powerful military alliance required seventy-eight days—rather than the expected handful—to coerce Serbia into abandoning its ethnic cleansing in Kosovo, despite a sustained bombing campaign, and even in this case the exact reasons for the Serb withdrawal were debatable. Some credit the looming threat of an actual land-based intervention by NATO.[11] It was exactly the political contentiousness of landpower that inhibited its use, but the wars that occurred during the breakup of Yugoslavia attested to the continuing relevance of landpower, even if only to the threat of its use, because control on the ground was vital to the outcomes of each of these wars. Features of the RMA—precision-guided munitions and stealth technology—primarily sustained airpower's ability to achieve results during this period.

As the 1990s became the 2000s, the George W. Bush administration was sworn in and Donald Rumsfeld returned to the DoD after nearly thirty years since his first tenure as secretary of defense. Bush and Rumsfeld came with an agenda of transformation (the RMA) and Rumsfeld aimed to remodel the US armed forces, especially the Army. The transformation advocate Max Boot wrote in his paean on the subject: "Spurred by dramatic advances in information technology, the US military has adopted a new style of warfare that eschews the bloody slogging matches of old. It seeks a quick victory with minimal casualties on both sides. Its hallmarks are speed, maneuver, flexibility, and surprise. It is heavily reliant upon precision firepower, special forces, and psychological operations. And it strives to integrate naval, air, and land power into a seamless whole."[12]

One of the implicit purposes of transformation was to adapt the US Army for the post-heroic age, to revise permanently the basic assumptions that underpinned the very concept of landpower so as to minimize its vulnerabilities without sacrificing its effects. Transformation sought to reduce the potential costs of landpower through maneuver, through the precise application of joint land and air power, as well as through nonmilitary instruments.

This was in keeping with the neo-conservative policy preference for maintaining global American unipolarity.[13] The more cheaply American landpower could be used, in both domestic political and resource terms, the greater the United States' ability to maintain primacy over the longer term, and the more amenable such interventions would be to the American public. The goal of transformation was a natural continuation of the United States' strategic trends during the 1990s, except finally applied to land warfare—post-heroic landpower. Ideally, it would be so effective, both in terms of achieving strategic objectives and in reducing costs, that the Weinberger-Powell Doctrine would become redundant, rendering landpower politically uncontentious.

Yet, even with such an anticipated revision of US landpower, the Bush administration understood that the constant employment of landpower was a nonstarter. Rumsfeld emphatically stated that in considering intervention, he would "rule nothing out—including ground forces. The enemy must understand that we will use every means at our disposal to defeat them, and that we are prepared to make whatever sacrifices are necessary to achieve victory." But he also emphasized that it was "our policy in this war of accepting help from any country" and that "wars can benefit from coalitions of the willing."[14]

The new American Way of War heralded by transformation seemed to work, and the experience of invading Afghanistan in 2001 and Iraq in 2003 testified to its apparent effectiveness. In both wars, it was fast, it was cheap, and it was all but bloodless.

Of the two, Afghanistan in 2001 was not specifically a triumph of post-heroic landpower. American landpower hardly featured, as opposed to the forces of the Northern Alliance, US airpower, and SOF. Rumsfeld had been quite pleased by the Northern Alliance, whose active role minimized the need for US landpower in the initial invasion of Afghanistan. This intervention was not, however, entirely distinct from previous strategic practice, despite this reliance on allies, airpower, and special operations forces. As Stephen Biddle noted in late 2002, "the Afghan campaign of last fall and winter was actually much closer to a typical 20th century mid-intensity conflict, albeit one with unusually heavy fire support for one side."[15] Concurrently, Biddle also warned that it would be unwise to premise defense policy based on the experience of the Afghan campaign. The unique constellation of local allies may not necessarily always exist elsewhere, thereby requiring a much more significant dedication of US landpower than in Afghanistan.

Operation Iraqi Freedom (OIF) in 2003 was such a scenario. It was an entirely different mission from Afghanistan, one that centered on the application of US landpower in an offensive from Kuwait to Baghdad itself, although by the end of March, local allies had begun joining in the destruction of the Saddam regime. The US Army displayed its operational skill throughout a campaign that was the antithesis of Desert Storm in 1991. In the war plan, "mass would be sacrificed for speed, information, and precision killing power." This emphasis overrode all other considerations: "Throughout the campaign the Coalition focused on getting to Baghdad as fast as possible," risking both logistical troubles and enemy action in the rear areas.[16] Iraqi strategy aided this emphasis, which led to a dispersal of Iraqi military forces throughout Iraq to maintain stability rather than concentration to resist a major US land invasion. Nevertheless, the assumptions of post-heroic landpower appeared vindicated during the invasion.

The successes of the experiment in fundamentally revising the vulnerabilities of landpower did not endure. The lack of serious US landpower was already felt in Afghanistan in 2002. The positive results from the campaign in 2001 led to a belief that the Afghanistan experience represented a radical break in strategic conduct and effectiveness, only to be repudiated by the Tora Bora campaign of December 2001. In this operation, America's Afghan allies proved unwilling to break into Al Qa'ida's cavern defenses despite significant US airpower support: "many now see this ground force hesitancy as having allowed Osama bin Laden and much of his command structure to escape capture and flee into neighboring Pakistan."[17] The implication was that professional US landpower might have succeeded in erasing Al Qa'ida as a functional entity in 2002. Perhaps this alternative belief is erroneous, but we can never know. Nevertheless, the assumptions of the new American Way of War were already undercutting US strategic effectiveness. In Afghanistan, local allies supported by US airpower and SOF were insufficient to attain full control in war. Al Qa'ida and the Taliban both escaped to relative sanctuary with the resolve to fight again another day. As soon as the enemy becomes unreachable, the degree of control to which he may be subjected substantially decreases.

The United States' political and strategic assumptions also proved deleterious soon after the fall of Baghdad. Five assumptions underpinned the US invasion of Iraq, of which three specifically pertained to the expected post-invasion societal and political climate in Iraq. First, "our leaders were repeatedly told by exiles that the United States would be seen as liberators," claims which the Bush administration believed. Second, "the Iraqi people hungered for democracy and human rights and . . . this hunger would suppress the urge to settle scores or to think in narrow tribal or sectarian terms." Third, US security forces "would receive great help from the Iraqi police, the army, and the ministries, all of which were seen by many experts as salvageable, malleable, and professional."[18] These basic assumptions poisoned the administration against the advice of landpower experts such as CSA General Shinseki, who had claimed before the invasion that several hundred thousand troops would be required to provide security and stability to Iraq afterward. This was unwelcome input for those who held to the strategic assumptions of post-heroic landpower and the political assumptions that enabled it.

Heroic Landpower in the Middle East and Central Asia

New and unfolding adversarial interactions swiftly demonstrated the inaptness of US political and strategic assumptions concerning consequences of post-heroic landpower and the nature of the reception of US intervention in targeted countries. Insurgency sprang up in Iraq in 2003, although it would take a longer period for the Taliban to make its comeback in Afghanistan. American policy adapted, albeit slowly, reluctantly, and painfully, to the shifting circumstances. No longer could the United States assume a painless postwar period and an easy transition to local national governments. Rather, war was renewed, although against a different adversary in Iraq. The policy goal became to protect the United States' attempts at rebuilding the political order in Iraq and, later, in Afghanistan.

With this shift of policy, the assumptions of post-heroic landpower became obsolete. Although smooth cooperation among the various branches of the military and the ability to strike precisely identified enemies, among other qualities, remained desirable if not vital, the overriding emphasis on celerity in operations was no longer apt and the minimization of casualties as a primary objective grew increasingly unrealistic. Instead, the employment of landpower returned to its natural assumptions. Landpower persisted permanently within the operating environment and, to fulfill US policy, had to stand in the way of the insurgent enemy—between the adversary and the new political order under fire. It was a return to heroic landpower, to landpower as it had been understood throughout the twentieth century and indeed throughout most of history. It was the only way to contest control within Iraq and Afghanistan.

One assumption did not change immediately, and this was that landpower remained the indispensable tool of policy. In much the same way that landpower was the only instrument which through maneuver could conquer Baghdad and topple Saddam Hussein, it was similarly the only means with which the United States could preserve its preferred political order in Iraq and Afghanistan. No other instrument within the broad means of US grand strategy could possibly achieve the desired effects in Iraq or Afghanistan. The resulting dearth of security would have simply precluded the effects of any other means from taking hold.

Nevertheless, alongside landpower, the relative significance of nonmilitary instruments grew. The invasions of Afghanistan and Iraq were too short for nonmilitary means to have any real effect, but their import changed once the two conflicts became prolonged counterinsurgent and state-building efforts. Circumstances forced a rebalancing of US grand strategy away from a focus on the achievements of landpower, supported by other military power, to a broader array of national power, including nonmilitary forms of power.[19] Such a rebalance in itself is neither good nor bad, but rather indicates shifting circumstances and an American attempt to adapt to those changes.

The Return of Post-Heroic Strategy

US policy continued to adapt to the changing strategic conditions of the Long War. Al Qa'ida became a franchise as jihadi groups throughout the Islamic world associated themselves with it. The group Al Qa'ida in Iraq, an early stalwart of the insurgency and sectarian violence in that country, was only one of the first. It was followed by Al Qa'ida in the Arabian Peninsula, the Islamic Maghreb, and Al-Shabaab, among others. With the proliferation of such groups claiming allegiance to or alliance with Al Qa'ida, and with the enduring quagmires of Iraq and Afghanistan, US policymakers were forced to reconsider the respective roles of landpower versus other instruments of grand strategy.

Although landpower remained the mainstay of US grand strategy in Iraq and Afghanistan, the salience of other national instruments—both military and nonmilitary—to the conduct of the Long War increased. These instruments included widespread use of unmanned aerial vehicles (UAVs), SOF, diplomacy and sanctions, and reliance on allies as the primary vehicle to address certain threats.

To reach the many affiliates of Al Qa'ida, the United States sought to rely more heavily on UAVs and SOF. However, neither appears to have been strategically very successful, despite tactical success in striking desired targets. The best known SOF operation occurred in 2011, when it finally located and killed Osama bin Laden a decade late.[20] Similarly, known independent UAV operations take place in only three countries—Yemen, Somalia, and Pakistan—and relatively infrequently despite the media coverage.[21] The disparity between effectiveness and use stems from the far more lenient assumptions of UAV and SOF employment as opposed to any other form of military power. Independent UAV and SOF operations cannot achieve control, but US policy is no longer interested in achieving control.

The United States has had to rely on a different set of instruments to deal with Iran, which is another significant issue area for US policy, both for Iran's sponsorship of terrorist groups throughout the Middle East as well as for its nuclear program. Iran has long been a potential target for invasion by those wishing to impose their control. Thus far, however, the US grand strategy emphasis has been on diplomacy, economic and later financial sanctions, and cyber power—at least to limit the Iranian nuclear program. Sanctions had already long been placed on Iran in an attempt both to interfere with its ability to sustain its nuclear program and to pressure the country into giving up that program. Pressure on the Iranian nuclear program and economy had proven indecisive, leading to the use of cyber means—the Stuxnet attacks—in an attempt to sabotage the Iranian nuclear program. It succeeded on a tactical level in dealing physical damage to Iranian centrifuges in Natanz, but this success merely delayed the Iranians, rather than definitively setting back their progress.[22] The strategic failure of Stuxnet led to a continuation of diplomacy and the United States and the European Union's imposition of new, this time financial, sanctions in 2010. They eventually proved to be crippling and were arguably decisive in leading to the final diplomatic agreement in 2015, which limited the Iranian nuclear program.[23]

When the Arab Spring flared up across North Africa and the Middle East in 2011, only two of the affected countries fell into civil war: Libya, then Syria. The West's intervention in Libya indicated the direction in which US policy was already heading, particularly regarding the employment of landpower. Specifically, after the initial air strikes the US sought to lead from behind, logistically and electronically supporting what were primarily British and French air operations against Gaddafi's armed forces, which in turn were supporting rebel forces ostensibly under the control of the National Transitional Council based in Benghazi.[24] Landpower was still necessary to unseat Gaddafi, but it was rebel Libyan landpower rather than US landpower, and it would never have caused the downfall of the regime if not for NATO airpower. Libya marked a full return to the same style of post-heroic strategy that had distinguished American interventionism during the 1990s.

US policy throughout the Syrian Civil War has only further confirmed the disinclination to employ landpower in favor of airpower and nonmilitary pressure. In response to the chemical attack at Ghouta in August 2013, the United States and its allies considered a military intervention, albeit without a landpower element, before finally accepting a diplomatic solution pioneered by Russia. Throughout the civil war, the United States has supported Syrian rebel groups and, since its rise, any group that fights ISIS, especially the Kurds, including with airpower. The United States, however, has been relying largely on the landpower of local groups, such as the Kurds, to prosecute the war against ISIS. The fight against ISIS is similarly landpower focused, but in Iraq it is the Iraqi army that has been conducting the various campaigns to eject ISIS, with relatively little direct US combat support.

US grand strategic reliance on allies also grew, and for more than simple considerations of international legitimacy. Rather, allies were expected to assume part of the burden of the Long War. This began with Libya but occurred elsewhere as well. It was the French, for instance, who raised the profile of the conflict in Mali to an international security issue and who eventually intervened—with French landpower—to address in a reasonably successful manner the security problem that they had identified.[25] In 2015, the Gulf states, particularly Saudi Arabia and the United Arab Emirates, took a similarly proactive approach to the strife in Yemen and intervened of their own accord in an attempt to roll back Iranian influence on the Arabian Peninsula. Their success in the war has been mixed, however, and "a plausible outcome of the intervention is a failed state at their border, in which the Houthis survive as a key military actor dominating a vast territory, and in which the conditions for radicalisation and jihadi recruitment are ideal."[26]

Sanctions have also been employed by the United States and the European Union to attempt to coerce Russia and its proxies in the Donbas to adhere to the second Minsk agreement. They remain in force, as the separatists and Russian mercenaries in the breakaway territories in the Donbas have not yet fully implemented the tenets of the agreement.[27] Years of sanctions have not had the effect for which the West has hoped, but sanctions were the only instrument whose basic assumptions were amenable to overall US policy, which at the same time was also seeking to court Russia in the contexts of the Syrian Civil War, nuclear nonproliferation, and Iran.

The increasing use of instruments other than landpower over the past decade indicates that the assumptions and characteristics that underpin landpower became increasingly incompatible with US policy under the Obama administration. The growing popularity of these other instruments sometimes occurred despite their relative lack of strategic utility, enabled because the geopolitical problems to which they are applied are minor. Landpower itself, the ultimate source of control, remains vital to the achievement of many US policy goals—it was crucial in Libya, in Syria against ISIS, in Iraq against ISIS, in Mali against the Islamists, and so forth. However, under the Obama administration no longer was it *American* landpower that was inserted into trouble spots. Instead, allies were expected to take control on the ground. In Libya, it was the National Transitional Council; in Syria, the Kurds; in Iraq, the Iraqis; and in Mali, the French. They were all supported through airpower, logistical support, cyber power, and other instruments of national power. For the Obama administration, America's preferred style of strategic conduct became post-heroic.

Landpower and Contemporary Security Challenges

Global geopolitics never stagnates, and new security challenges emerge. As administrations change, approaches to dealing with threats may also alter. The most salient strategic question is: To what extent is it necessary, desirable, or even *possible* to impose United States' control on contemporary security challenges? It is the intersection of these three aspects—necessity, desirability, and possibility—that will influence the potential use and utility of landpower as an element in US grand strategy.

The United States has increasingly pondered the possibility of war with China. Due to the sheer geographical realities of war in the western Pacific— as the United States is unlikely to embark upon a land invasion of China— landpower would necessarily play a minimal role compared to seapower and airpower. Any armed clash would likely occur for command of the commons in East Asia, especially for control of the disputed seas around China.[28] The intersection of geography and politics alone renders landpower largely inapt for such a conflict. North Korea, however, is a strategic challenge in East Asia that has had a significant US landpower component since 1950 and will certainly require an even greater infusion of landpower should the situation ever escalate to war.

In contrast with the Chinese scenario, the reemergence of Russia as a security threat to the Western-led world order has created a situation in which landpower must play a leading role, both in peace and in any potential war. Landpower is a central element in the United States' attempts to deter Russia, and both NATO as a whole and the United States individually have already stationed small forces in the Baltic States as well as Poland. Yet if war comes, RAND analysts predict that these forces are insufficient for the task of defending the Baltic States. They suggest that a deployment to the Baltic States of seven brigades, of which three are heavily armored, is necessary to practice safely a policy for deterrence by denial.[29] Much as in Iraq and Afghanistan, landpower in such conditions is necessarily heroic, standing between the adversary and one's allies to protect the latter. So far, however, the forces dedicated are insufficient to maintain control, should it actually be challenged.

Since 2014, the role of landpower in US grand strategy has been slowly growing again, due especially but not entirely to the reemergence of Russia as a danger to NATO. The changeover to the Trump administration may be accelerating this rise in priority. This clearly illustrates that even though the assumptions underpinning landpower are difficult to change, the policies to which those assumptions and characteristics must be matched can and do change— due to altered geopolitical situations, new administrations, and so forth.

Conclusion

Landpower is the strongest instrument, military or nonmilitary, in grand strategy.[30] Despite this strength, it must necessarily always remain contextual, as must all forms of power, the suitability of its fundamental assumptions and characteristics being contingent on external factors. The history of US landpower since 9/11, as one instrument of national power among many, reflects this contingent suitability.

This recent period began with an attempt to revise the basic assumptions of landpower, which ultimately faltered upon the jagged rocks of adversarial interaction in war. Transformation could not be sustained and the experiment in post-heroic landpower failed. Changing strategic circumstances forced landpower into a heroic posture for the better part of a decade in Iraq and a full decade in Afghanistan. Yet even as these two conflicts dragged on, more security threats affiliated with Al Qa'ida emerged in the Islamic world, and the United States felt compelled to respond, thereby geographically expanding the Long War. Yet this occurred not through the employment of landpower, but through the reapplication of post-heroic strategies premised upon airpower and other comparatively low-cost (but also less effective) alternatives, including use of UAVs, SOF, economic and financial instruments, and reliance on allies. The implicit assumptions that underpinned these other instruments, from their inexpensiveness to their relative secrecy to their footprint in other countries, all compared favorably with the assumptions of landpower.

Landpower's star declined significantly during the Obama administration, which was unwilling further to apply it to terrorism and saw little role for it in the Pacific against a rising and competitive, but not adversarial, China. The reemergence of Russia as a potential threat to NATO led to a renewed emphasis on landpower, the only possible decisive instrument in any conflict with Russia. The changeover from one administration to the next also changes the strategic and political calculus, which weighs the various instruments of grand strategy.

While the future is unpredictable, it necessarily emerges out of the past and the ongoing present. One may reasonably anticipate that, despite the flirtation with post-heroic landpower in the early years of the 2000s, landpower in the near future will remain staunchly heroic, as it has been since the insurgency began in Iraq. However, exactly because of this heroism, its potential use may be limited to the relatively greatest threats, which require the strongest response. Over the past fifteen years, US policy and strategy have wavered between post-heroism and heroism, with landpower inextricably caught up in these fluctuating policies and contexts. It would seem that there is no prospect of improved consistency on this score as the future turns into history.

Notes

1. See Russell F. Weigley, *The American Way of War: A History of United States Military Strategy and Policy* (Bloomington: Indiana Univ. Press, 1973); Brian McAllister Linn, *The Echo of Battle: The Army's Way of War* (Cambridge, Mass.: Harvard Univ. Press, 2007); Antulio J. Echevarria II, *Reconsidering the American Way of War: US Military Practice from the Revolution to Afghanistan* (Washington, DC: Georgetown Univ. Press, 2014).

2. Lukas Milevski, "Can Grand Strategy Be Mastered?" *Infinity Journal* 5, no. 4 (summer 2017): 33–36.

3. Lawrence Freedman, "Strategic Studies and the Problem of Power," in *War, Strategy, and International Politics: Essays in Honour of Sir Michael Howard,* ed. Lawrence Freedman, Paul Hayes, and Robert O'Neill (Oxford: Clarendon Press 1992), 290.

4. Ben Lombardi, "Assumptions and Grand Strategy," *Parameters* 41, no. 1 (spring 2011), 29.

5. Gordon A. Craig, "Delbrück: The Military Historian," in *Makers of Modern Strategy: From Machiavelli to the Nuclear Age,* ed. Peter Paret (Oxford: Clarendon Press 1986), 341–344.

6. Christopher Tuck, *Understanding Land Warfare* (London: Routledge 2014), 15, emphasis in original.

7. Herbert Rosinski, quoted in Henry E. Eccles, *Military Concepts and Philosophy* (New Brunswick, N.J.: Rutgers Univ. Press, 1965), 46, 47, emphasis in original.

8. Julian S. Corbett, *Some Principles of Maritime Strategy* (Annapolis, Md.: Naval Institute Press, 1988), 54–55.

9. Christopher Gelpi, Peter D. Feaver, and Jason Reifler, "Success Matters: Casualty Sensitivity and the War in Iraq," *International Security* 30, no. 3 (winter 2005–2006): 7–46.

10. Edward Luttwak. "Toward Post-Heroic Warfare," *Foreign Affairs* 74, no. 3 (May–June 1995): 109–122.

11. On the debate surrounding Serbia's giving up in Kosovo, see Benjamin S. Lambeth, *NATO's Air War for Kosovo: A Strategic and Operational Assessment* (Santa Monica, Calif.: RAND, 2001), chapter 4.

12. Max Boot, "The New American Way of War," *Foreign Affairs* 82, no. 4 (July–August 2003): 42.

13. See for example Charles Krauthammer, "The Unipolar Moment," *Foreign Affairs* 70, no. 1 (January 1991): 23–33; and Charles Krauthammer, "The Unipolar Moment Revisited," *National Interest* 70 (winter 2002–2003): 5–18.

14. Donald H. Rumsfeld, "Transforming the Military," *Foreign Affairs* 81, no. 3 (May/June 2002): 31.

15. Stephen Biddle, *Afghanistan and the Future of Warfare: Implications for Army and Defense Policy* (Carlisle, Pa.: Strategic Studies Institute, 2002), vii.

16. Williamson Murray and Robert H. Scales Jr., *The Iraq War: A Military History* (Cambridge, Mass.: Belknap Press of Harvard Univ. Press, 2003), 95, 245.

17. Biddle, *Afghanistan and the Future of War,* 40.

18. Joseph J. Collins, "Choosing War: The Decision to Invade Iraq and Its Aftermath," Institute for National Strategic Studies, Occasional Paper 5 (April 2008), 17, 19, 20.

19. David Lake, "The Practice and Theory of US Statebuilding," *Journal of Intervention and Statebuilding* 4, no. 3 (2010): 265–280.

20. Nicholas Schmidle, "Getting Bin Laden: What Happened That Night in Abbottabad," *New Yorker,* 8 August 2011, http://www.newyorker.com/magazine/2011/08/08/getting-bin-laden (accessed 19 March 2017).

21. Jacqueline L. Hazelton, "Drone Strikes and Grand Strategy: Toward a Political Understanding of the Uses of Unmanned Aerial Vehicle Attacks in US Security Policy," *Journal of Strategic Studies* 40, nos. 1–2 (2017): 81.

22. Lukas Milevski, "Stuxnet and Strategy: A Special Operation in Cyberspace?" *Joint Force Quarterly* 63 (October 2011): 64–69.

23. Daniel Drezner, "Targeted Sanctions in a World of Global Finance," *International Interactions* 41, no. 4 (2015): 758–759.

24. Christopher S. Chivvis, "Libya and the Future of Liberal Intervention," *Survival* 54, no. 6 (2012): 69–92.

25. Bruno Charbonneau and Jonathan M. Sears, "Fighting for Liberal Peace in Mali? The Limits of International Military Intervention," *Journal of Intervention and Statebuilding* 8, nos. 2–3 (2014): 196–200.

26. Emile Hakeem and David B. Roberts, "The War in Yemen," *Survival* 58, no. 5 (2016): 180.

27. Viljar Veebel and Raul Markus, "At the Dawn of a New Era of Sanctions: Russian-Ukrainian Crisis and Sanctions," *Orbis* 60, no. 1 (winter 2015–2016): 128–139.

28. Stephen Biddle and Ivan Oelrich, "Future Warfare in the Western Pacific: Chinese Antiaccess/Area Denial, U.S. AirSea Battle, and Command of the Commons in East Asia," *International Security* 41, no. 1 (summer 2016): 7–48.

29. David A. Shlapak and Michael W. Johnson, "Reinforcing Deterrence on NATO's Eastern Flank: Wargaming the Defense of the Baltics" (Santa Monica, Calif.: RAND, January 2016).

30. Lukas Milevski, "Fortissimus Inter Pares: The Utility of Landpower in Grand Strategy," *Parameters* 42, no. 2 (summer 2012): 6–15.

2

The Revolution in Military Affairs and Strategic Thought in the US Military, 1991–2003

Peter R. Mansoor

Lieutenant Colonel Ernest "Rock" Marcone's soldiers of 3-69 Armor had just blitzed their way through the Karbala Gap when they descended on Objective Peach, a vital highway bridge spanning the Euphrates River. Substituting speed and situational awareness for mass, they quickly overwhelmed their opponents from the 14th Mechanized Brigade of the Iraqi Republican Guard Corps' Medina Division. Engineers then conducted an assault river crossing to seize the crucial span. Aided by air strikes, attack helicopters, and artillery, 3-69 Armor troopers smashed a nighttime counterattack by the Medina Division's 10th Armored Brigade and the 22nd Armored Brigade from the Nebuchadnezzar Division, destroying them in the process. The road to Baghdad was open. Three days later, Colonel David Perkin's 2nd Brigade of the 3rd Infantry Division made the first of two "Thunder Runs" into the Iraqi capital, effectively sealing the fate of Saddam Hussein's regime.[1]

The rapid advance of the US Army's 3rd Infantry Division and the 1st Marine Division from Kuwait to Baghdad and the destruction of much of the Iraqi army along the way seemed to validate the concept of "rapid, decisive operations," or RDO—an outgrowth of the Revolution in Military Affairs (RMA) that gripped the attention of the US defense establishment in the previous decade.[2] The promoters of the precision-information RMA posited that guided munitions, robust intelligence/surveillance/reconnaissance (ISR) assets, and networked information systems would substitute for mass, enabling military forces to see farther, move faster, and overwhelm their opponents more quickly than in the past, and without the extensive logistical trail required by an industrial age army. Yet beneath the shiny veneer of victory in the spring of 2003 lay fundamental issues concerning force structure, doctrine, and strategic outlook that would haunt the US Army in the aftermath of major combat operations.[3]

A recurring theme of post–World War II US military history is the fixation of American policymakers, both uniformed and civilian, on technological solutions to strategic challenges. This has led to so-called "offset" strategies to leverage US technological capabilities and substitute high-tech weapons for manpower. The first offset strategy was the reliance in the Eisenhower administration on massive retaliation by nuclear weapons in lieu of adequate conventional ground capabilities to halt Communist expansion throughout the world. This policy left the Army unprepared to face challenges in Europe, Asia, and in the Third World as the wars of decolonization gripped Asia and Africa.[4] To make matters worse, the Army attempted to gain a greater share of the defense budget by refashioning its forces for a nuclear battlefield, another example of military innovation gone off the rails by lack of grounding in historical reality and contemporary feasibility. Although the "Pentomic Army" was a disaster, the force was never put to the test in combat, saving the United States a strategic setback.[5]

The second attempt at an offset strategy was more successful. As the United States poured blood and treasure into fighting the war in Vietnam, the Soviet Union commenced a massive conventional buildup in Europe that left NATO forces ill-equipped to deter a Warsaw Pact assault without resorting to the use of nuclear weapons.[6] US defense policymakers realized that the lack of conventional capabilities in US Army Europe and NATO put deterrence at risk. Their attention once again fixed on the massive Soviet conventional armies positioned in East Germany, defense planners sought technological solutions to even the odds. The 1973 Yom Kippur War demonstrated the lethality of a modern battlefield, where guided antitank weapons such as the TOW (tube-launched, optically tracked, wire-guided antitank missile) devastated entire fleets of armored vehicles. In just three weeks, the Israeli, Syrian, and Egyptian armies lost a combined 2,650 tanks, and although not all of these were casualties of antitank missiles, the lethality of guided weapons was apparent.[7] Defense planners worried that similar loss rates would doom NATO's ability to turn back a Warsaw Pact assault into Western Europe.

US Army doctrine in 1976 featured Active Defense, a scheme of lateral reinforcement that could theoretically defeat a Soviet-style attack.[8] The problem was that the US Army in Europe could only defeat an initial attack into West Germany; subsequent Red Army and Warsaw Pact echelons arrayed in depth would eventually arrive to overwhelm US and NATO forces. To overcome this liability, the US Army would have to develop doctrine to defeat echeloned Soviet forces in both time and space. While Army doctrine writers worked on a new operating concept, research and development progressed on a new generation of guided weapons.

Although guided munitions were first employed in battle in 1943, they only became a staple of the United States' approach to warfare after the end of the conflict in Vietnam.[9] The advent of technologically sophisticated guided weapons made possible new concepts, such as Assault Breaker—a "system of systems" devised in the mid-1970s by the Office of the Secretary of Defense and the Defense Advanced Research Projects Agency (DARPA). If realized, Assault Breaker would marry guided munitions with advanced ISR systems to attack Red Army formations in depth—before they had the opportunity to engage in the close fight with NATO forces. All-weather precision-guided munitions coupled with long-range target acquisition radars would give NATO forces the capability to strike enemy formations with power commensurate with that of tactical nuclear weapons, but without causing collateral damage or fallout from radiation.[10]

While research and development ensued in an attempt to make Assault Breaker a reality, Army officers worked on a new conception to take advantage of its possibilities and restore offensive maneuver to US Army doctrine. In 1982, the Army published an updated version of its capstone operational doctrine, *Field Manual 100-5: Operations.* Active Defense was jettisoned in favor of the maneuver-based AirLand Battle. NATO followed suit two years later with its embrace of follow-on forces attack, a new concept to improve alliance capabilities to defeat Soviet conventional forces without use of tactical nuclear weapons. US and alliance commanders were now called on to think of the battlefield in four dimensions—not just in terms of space, but also in time. NATO forces would focus not just on the close fight, but also on using guided munitions to disrupt Soviet follow-on echelons before they could arrive on the battlefield. These doctrinal concepts justified the expense of producing a new generation of guided munitions.[11]

The intellectual ferment and technological development surrounding guided munitions and AirLand Battle paid enormous dividends in the final decade of the Cold War. The US military acquired projectiles that could be fired from aircraft, helicopters, cannons, and howitzers. Advanced weaponry and command and control systems included the M172 Copperhead—the world's first cannon-launched, fin-stabilized, terminally guided munition designed to hit point targets with the assistance of a laser designator in the hands of a forward observer; the AGM-114 Hellfire missile, a laser-guided weapon designed for use by the Army's new AH-64 Apache attack helicopter; the Joint Surveillance Target Attack Radar System (JSTARS); and the Army

Tactical Missile System (ATACMS) and Multiple Launch Rocket System (MLRS). Dr. William Perry, the undersecretary of defense for research and engineering (and a future secretary of defense), boasted, "It [the Copperhead munition] will deny the Russians the opportunity of massing tanks because we're going to tear the hell out of them with these kind of systems. [Precision-guided munitions] have a greater potential for revolutionizing tactical warfare than the introduction of radar in World War II."[12] He was wrong about the Copperhead, but right about guided munitions in general. They would in time revolutionize armored warfare.

Although initially developed with a European battlefield and Soviet forces in mind, high-tech ISR systems and guided munitions came to dominate the United States' approach to warfare after the Gulf War of 1991.[13] During Operation Desert Storm, guided munitions launched from attack helicopters, warships, and stealth fighters devastated the Iraqi air defense network, command and control system, air forces, and transportation nodes, and caused serious attrition to armored forces in the Kuwaiti Theater of Operations.[14] General Norman Schwarzkopf captivated the media and public during his briefings by showing video footage of guided munitions hitting key targets as far away as Baghdad. The future of warfare was at hand.

Guided munitions had an outsized effect for the numbers employed. In six weeks, US Army and Marine Corps helicopters fired 3,035 Hellfire missiles and US and coalition aircraft dropped 10,468 guided bombs and fired 5,508 guided missiles. While constituting just 10 percent of the munitions tonnage expended during the campaign, these guided weapons were "credited with causing approximately 75 percent of the serious damage inflicted upon Iraqi strategic and operational targets."[15] Attacks on bridges connecting the Kuwaiti theater with Iraq effectively isolated the battlefield—and with far less time and effort than would have been required using conventional bombs.[16]

US military leaders had every right to believe that guided munitions—particularly laser-guided bombs and missiles—were a game changer. The authors of the Gulf War airpower survey concluded, "Laser-guided bombs were particularly effective because their employment came as something of a surprise to the Iraqis," adding wryly, "Their reaction is understandable, because the LGB [laser-guided bomb] performance also surprised the United States."[17] Guided munitions attained the holy grail of airpower advocates—the ability to destroy a single target with a single munition. The ramifications of this emerging reality were revolutionary.

After the Gulf War, the DoD's Office of Net Assessment under Dr. Andrew Marshall led the intellectual charge into the future. Marshall believed that guided weapons and high-tech ISR systems constituted an RMA—the integration of new technology with innovative doctrine and force structure that alters how war is waged. Under Marshall's tutelage, defense analyst Andrew Krepinevich delved into the changes wrought by advanced information systems enabled by the microprocessor, advanced ISR systems, and guided munitions. His report confirmed that a RMA was in the process of fundamentally changing the character of war.[18] The Gulf War was a harbinger of wars to come.

If valid, Krepinevich's analysis meant the US Army had to rethink the way it fought. Army forces would no longer need to mass on the battlefield, since much of the destruction of enemy forces would occur via targeting enemy formations with long-range, precision fires. Furthermore, concentrated troop formations would present an inviting target to an enemy equipped with advanced ISR systems, guided munitions, and the capability to deliver them on the battlefield. War would devolve into a targeting exercise, in which the side with better and more information would win.[19]

An accomplished military historian, Krepinevich understood the limitations of the RMA. He warned that, given US battlefield dominance, nonpeer and nonstate adversaries would fight US forces asymmetrically to counter its strengths in conventional warfare: "Low-intensity warfare, comprising primarily but not exclusively insurgency, terrorism, and subversion, has been the most prevalent form of conflict in the post–World War II era. It seems likely that these conflicts, which are characterized by unconventional operational concepts, will continue as a dominant form of warfare in the post–Cold War era. It also is highly probable that non-peer competitors will engage in low-intensity warfare, employing the unconventional operational concepts characteristic of those kinds of conflicts, albeit modified somewhat by the infusion of more advanced military systems, as a means of frustrating peer competitor adversaries."[20] Regrettably, this warning was lost on US Army leaders, who spent much of the ensuing decade focused on "digitizing" ground forces. Although Force XXI experimentation throughout the 1990s and early 2000s had much to commend it, senior Army leaders lost sight of the connection between strategy and military operations and virtually ignored any type of war other than the one for which the Army's powerful conventional forces were designed. The US Army, in the words of Army strategist Jason Warren, had "become a more ethical version of the Wehrmacht"—a supremely competent tactical and operational force that lost two world wars due to its failure to think strategically.[21]

Two other points are in order here. The first is that by the time US military leaders realized a RMA was underway, it had already run much of its course.[22] In the 1990s, US military forces would add impressive new capabilities to their arsenal, such as GPS-guided weapons, the Blue Force Tracker command and control system, and the Apache Longbow attack helicopter with its advanced fire control radar. But US forces at the dawn of the twenty-first century were essentially improved versions of those that fought the Gulf War using a similar doctrinal concept. The question that went unanswered was what would come next.

The second point is that while the arguments of RMA advocates for smaller, more nimble, and better-networked ground forces were valid on the tactical and operational levels of war, they largely ignored the purposes for which wars are fought and how wars are really won in the aftermath of fighting.[23] Large numbers of troops would be required in postconflict operations to stabilize shattered societies and rebuild deposed governments.[24] Furthermore, stability and counterinsurgency operations (COIN) are troop-intensive affairs. Army leaders did not even have to understand history to get the point; they merely had to look at the peacekeeping and stability operations undertaken in the Balkans from 1996 onward to realize the difficulty of these operations and the need for a robust force structure to prosecute them.[25]

Although the US Marine Corps advocated a more holistic warfighting doctrine with the concept of a "three block war," Army leaders largely bought into the high-tech model of war propounded by such RMA advocates as Admiral Bill Owens.[26] In his turn-of-the-century book *Lifting the Fog of War*, Owens argued that technology had evolved to the point where a commander could enjoy near-complete situational awareness from a computer screen in his command post. "I believe the technology that is available to the US military today and now in development can revolutionize the way we conduct military operations," Owens wrote. "That technology can give us the ability to see a 'battlefield' as large as Iraq or Korea—an area 200 miles on a side—with unprecedented fidelity, comprehension, and timeliness; by night or day, in any kind of weather, all the time."[27] Gone were the "hoary dictums about the fog and friction of war, and all the tactics, operational concepts, and doctrine pertaining to them."[28] Information and precision firepower would substitute for boots on the ground, reducing the need for expensive ground forces in future conflicts. In other words, to borrow a phrase from a stinging critique penned by historian Williamson Murray, Clausewitz was out; the computer was in.[29]

The problem with this conception of the precision-information RMA was its complete lack of grounding in the history of military affairs. The adage that those military leaders who study the past war are invariably unprepared to fight the next has definitively been shown to be untrue. Historians have observed, rather, that effective military innovation is thoroughly grounded in the study of past conflicts, is focused on real problems presented by potential enemies, and is tested under realistic conditions.[30] By pinning innovation on an unproven theory of warfare without realistic testing, the US military had established a warfighting doctrine ideally suited to fighting a mirror-imaged enemy.

On the eve of the Iraq War in 2003, US Army leaders and RMA advocates believed that high-tech ISR systems and guided weapons would enable US forces to achieve "rapid dominance" in a conflict waged with "shock and awe."[31] Technological determinism dominated the thinking of Secretary of Defense Donald Rumsfeld and military planners in devising the concept of operations and force structure for the Iraq War. Despite warnings by CSA Eric Shinseki in congressional testimony that several hundred thousand troops would be required to stabilize Iraq in the wake of major combat operations, Rumsfeld whittled down the US force structure for the invasion to fewer than 150,000 troops.[32] The secretary of defense was intent on validating a theory of transformation predicated on smaller forces operating at a higher tempo than their adversaries and overcoming them with precision firepower made possible by information superiority.[33] Little thought was given to what would happen the day after Saddam Hussein fell from power. "The persistent belief in near-certainty in future war," wrote historian and future US national security advisor H. R. McMaster, "elevated anticipated capabilities of information technologies to the level of strategy, encouraged linear thinking, and undermined the positive features of the new concepts."[34]

According to the most recent US Army doctrinal publication, landpower is "the ability—by threat, force, or occupation—to gain, sustain, and exploit control over land, resources, and people."[35] If this is so, then the Iraq War showed that landpower is only truly decisive if all three aspects (gain, sustain, and exploit) are achieved. The force structure and concept of operations employed for OIF was sufficient to conduct regime change, but not to sustain or exploit control over Iraq, its resources, and its people—no matter how benign US intentions might have been in that regard. Despite the brilliant performance of US ground forces in the "march up" to Baghdad, no amount of tactical virtuosity could substitute for adequate troop strength to stabilize Iraq. In the aftermath of major combat operations, Army leaders learned the limitations of the information-precision RMA as massive looting destroyed Iraq's infrastructure and a budding insurgency began to grip the country.[36]

Although technology can give US forces an enormous edge in tactical combat and perhaps as well in operational maneuver, weapons and tactics are not a substitute for strategic thinking. In the aftermath of regime change in Iraq, US commanders struggled to develop an operational concept suitable to achieve the strategic goal of creating a stable, democratic Iraq that was not a threat to its people or its neighbors and that would be a US ally in the broader war against terror. Designing such a construct required of US military commanders a number of attributes that all too many lacked: historical vision, cultural awareness, and knowledge of what Iraqis believed and desired. Instead, commanders exhorted their troops to stay on the offensive against the remnants of a defeated regime while the Coalition Provisional Authority worked to remake Iraq in a more Western image.[37]

The resulting descent of Iraq into a virulent insurgency and the inability of US ground forces to stabilize the country until the surge of forces and the adoption of a fully resourced COIN campaign in 2007–2008 need not be recounted here. The point is that US Army leaders were unprepared to fight such a conflict in 2003 because of their nearly single-minded focus on high-end combat operations over the previous thirty years. Having shunted aside other types of conflict as "military operations other than war" or "low intensity conflict," Army leaders proved incredibly resistant to embracing COIN in Iraq until defeat stared them in the face.[38] Whether that experience will lead to a more balanced appraisal of and preparation for future war remains to be seen.

The US military's experience with COIN warfare and stability operations has never been particularly blissful, but these types of conflicts are far more prevalent in the landscape of American military history than massive existential wars.[39] Army leaders cannot simply ignore them because they are not the type of combat they are looking for. The wars in Iraq and Afghanistan have shown the fallacy of combating unconventional enemies with a doctrine finely tuned to fighting near-peer competitors. Some aspects of the precision-information RMA, such as armed drones, have proven useful in these wars, but absent an appropriate doctrine to counter irregular enemies, leaders more broadly educated in a wider range of military affairs, and a strategy to achieve America's goals, US landpower has proven a blunt and ineffective instrument of policy in the twenty-first century. The Iraq War spiraled downward for four years before the US Army and Marine Corps revised their COIN doctrine, by which time a great deal of damage had been done to America's strategic interests in the Middle East and the American people had grown tired of a war seemingly without end. The United States can do better.

Whether or not the world is in the midst of an ongoing RMA, the US Army needs to be prepared for the broad array of enemies it will face in the years ahead. This necessity means integrating information networks, ISR systems, and guided munitions into a broader warfighting framework that military leaders can adapt to whatever type of enemies they may face. Peer competitors might adopt similar resources and methods, but weaker opponents or nonstate groups might rely instead on other forms of power, such as nuclear weapons, hybrid warfare, or the weapons of the weak: terrorism and guerrilla warfare. But whatever type of conflicts US land forces are involved in, getting the strategy right is paramount. As historians Allan Millett and Williamson Murray conclude based on their three-volume study of military effectiveness from 1914 to 1945:

> No amount of operational virtuosity . . . redeemed fundamental flaws in political [and strategic] judgment. Whether policy shaped strategy or strategic imperatives drove policy was irrelevant. Miscalculations in both led to defeat, and any combination of politico-strategic error had disastrous results, even for some of the nations that ended the war as members of the victorious coalition. Even the effective mobilization of national will, manpower, industrial might, national wealth, and technological know-how did not save the belligerents from reaping the bitter fruit of [strategic] mistakes. This is because it is more important to make correct decisions at the political and strategic level than it is at the operational and tactical level. Mistakes in operations and tactics can be corrected, but political and strategic mistakes live forever.[40]

This is advice that US Army leaders would do well to heed today to ensure that landpower is both decisive in its application and strategic in its effects. Any attempt to reach for a third offset strategy, one perhaps featuring robotic air and ground vehicles, must not yet again result in the substitution of technological savvy for strategic thinking. Keeping US forces at the cutting edge of the technological revolution is fine, provided the technology used and operating concept employed are grounded in a thorough understanding of the past and the requirements of the contemporary battlefield against real-world adversaries. Only then will the next offset strategy serve the needs of strategy, rather than becoming an end unto itself.

Notes

1. For the fighting on Objective Peach, see James Lacy and Williamson Murray, "Objective Peach," in *Moment of Battle: The Twenty Clashes that Changed the World* (New York: Bantam, 2013).
2. For an overview of the RDO concept, see U.S. Joint Forces Command J9

Futures Lab, "A Concept for Rapid Decisive Operations," RDO Whitepaper version 2.0, www.globalsecurity.org/military/library/report/2001/RDO.doc.

3. On 1 May 2003 the president landed on the aircraft carrier USS *Abraham Lincoln* and spoke under a banner declaring "Mission Accomplished." The premature declaration of victory would come to haunt the Bush administration.

4. Upon his retirement, CSA General Maxwell D. Taylor wrote an indictment of the Eisenhower administration's "New Look" defense policy. General Maxwell D. Taylor, *The Uncertain Trumpet* (New York: Harper, 1960).

5. A. J. Bacevich, *The Pentomic Era—The U. S. Army between Korea and Vietnam* (Washington, DC: National Defense Univ. Press, 1986).

6. For an examination of the history of US Army Europe during this period, see Ingo Trauschweizer, *The Cold War U.S. Army: Building Deterrence for Limited War* (Lawrence: Univ. Press of Kansas, 2008).

7. Richard W. Stewart, ed., *American Military History*, vol. 2 (Washington, DC: Center of Military History, 2005), 377, http://www.history.army.mil/books/amh-v2/amh/0v2/chapter12.htm.

8. For an examination of the development of the active defense doctrine, see Paul H. Herbert, *Deciding What Has to Be Done: General William E. DePuy and the 1976 Edition of FM 100-5, Operations* (Fort Leavenworth, Kans.: Combat Studies Institute, 1988).

9. The first guided weapon used in combat was the Fritz-X, a German radio-guided bomb that debuted against Italian, American, and British warships off the coast of Italy during the Allied invasion of Salerno in September 1943.

10. Barry D. Watts, *Six Decades of Guided Munitions and Battle Networks: Progress and Prospects* (Washington, DC: Center for Strategic and Budgetary Assessments, 2007), 11; Comptroller General, "Report to the Congress: Decisions to Be Made in Charting the Future of DOD's Assault Breaker," 28 February 1981, i, http://www.gao.gov/assets/140/132235.pdf.

11. Office of Technology Assessment, *Technologies for NATO's Follow-On Forces Attack Concept* (Washington, DC: Government Printing Office, July 1986), 1; Robert Tomes, "The Cold War Offset Strategy: Assault Breaker and the Beginning of the RSTA Revolution," *War on the Rocks*, 20 November 2014, http://warontherocks.com/2014/11/the-cold-war-offset-strategy-assault-breaker-and-the-beginning-of-the-rsta-revolution/.

12. William Currie, "New 'Smart' Weapons Make 'Star Wars' Appear Tame," *Chicago Tribune*, 21 January 1979, http://archives.chicagotribune.com/1979/01/21/page/32/article/new-smart-weapons-make-star-wars-appear-tame.

13. In this sense, the US approach came to mirror the Soviet approach to the use of guided munitions. For more on the Soviet approach to the precision-information RMA, see Dima Adamsky, *The Culture of Military Innovation: The Impact of Cultural Factors on the Revolution in Military Affairs in Russia, the US, and Israel* (Palo Alto, Calif.: Stanford Univ. Press, 2010).

14. Thomas A. Keaney and Eliot A. Cohen, *Gulf War Air Power Survey Summary Report* (Washington, DC: Government Printing Office, 1993), http://www.dtic.mil/dtic/tr/fulltext/u2/a273996.pdf.

15. Ibid., 109, table 8 on page 203; Richard P. Hallion, "Precision Guided Munitions and the New Era in Warfare," APSC Paper 53, Air Power Studies Centre, 1995, http://fas.org/man/dod-101/sys/smart/docs/paper53.htm.

16. By comparison, the transportation campaign in France that isolated the Normandy beachhead before D-Day in 1944 used the combined resources of the US Eighth and Ninth Air Forces and RAF Bomber Command in a three-month effort to destroy the French rail network, upon which German forces relied for operational mobility.

17. Keaney and Cohen, *Gulf War Air Power Survey*, 226.

18. Andrew F. Krepinevich Jr., "The Military-Technical Revolution: A Preliminary Assessment," Office of Net Assessment, July 1992, reprinted at Center for Strategic and Budgetary Assessments, http://www.csbaonline.org/wp-content/uploads/2011/03/2002.10.02-Military-Technical-Revolution.pdf.

19. Ibid., 17–18.

20. Ibid., 31.

21. Jason W. Warren, "The Centurion Mindset and the Army's Strategic Leader Paradigm," *Parameters* 45, no. 3 (autumn 2015): 27–38, 28.

22. Krepinevich believed the RMA was in its infancy, closer to the birth of mobile, combined arms warfare in 1920 than to the apex of "blitzkrieg" during the battle for France in 1940. For the argument that the precision-information RMA was essentially consummated, see Williamson Murray and MacGregor Knox, "The Future Behind Us," in *The Dynamics of Military Revolution, 1300–2050*, ed. MacGregor Knox and Williamson Murray (Cambridge: Cambridge Univ. Press, 2001), 189–190.

23. This is a point made by Isaiah Wilson in *Thinking beyond War: Civil-Military Relations and Why America Fails to Win the Peace* (New York: Palgrave Macmillan, 2007).

24. This has historically always been the case. For examples, see Matthew Moten, ed., *Between War and Peace: How America Ends Its Wars* (New York: Free Press, 2011), and Nadia Schadlow, *War and the Art of Governance: Consolidating Combat Success into Political Victory* (Washington, DC: Georgetown Univ. Press, 2017).

25. R. Cody Phillips, *Bosnia-Herzegovina: The U.S. Army's Role in Peace Enforcement Operations 1995–2004* (Washington, DC: Center of Military History, 2005).

26. Marine Corps commandant General Charles C. Krulak coined the phrase "three block war" in 1997 to describe the multiple demands placed on ground forces at the turn of the century: combat, peacekeeping, and humanitarian operations, often in the same area. See A. Walter Dorn and Michael Varey, "The Rise and Demise of the 'Three Block War,'" *Canadian Military Journal* 10, no. 1 (2009): 38–45; and Charles Krulak, "The Strategic Corporal: Leadership in the Three Block

War," *Marine Corps Gazette* 83, no. 1 (January 1999): 18–23. Owens was the vice chairman of the Joint Chiefs of Staff from 1994–1996.

27. Admiral Bill Owens with Ed Offley, *Lifting the Fog of War* (New York: Farrar, Straus, and Giroux, 2000), 14.

28. Ibid., 15.

29. Williamson Murray, "Clausewitz Out, Computer In: Military Culture and Technological Hubris," *National Interest,* no. 48 (1 June 1997): 57–64.

30. Williamson Murray and Allan R. Millett, eds., *Military Innovation in the Interwar Period* (New York: Cambridge Univ. Press, 1996).

31. Harlan Ullman, James Wade Jr., et al., *Shock and Awe: Achieving Rapid Dominance* (Washington, DC: Institute for National Strategic Studies, National Defense University, 1996), http://www.dodccrp.org/files/Ullman_Shock.pdf.

32. For Iraq War planning, see Michael R. Gordon and Bernard E. Trainor, *Cobra II: The Inside Story of the Invasion and Occupation of Iraq* (New York: Pantheon, 2006).

33. For a critique of rapid, decisive operations, see Antonio J. Echevarria II, "Rapid Decisive Operations: An Assumptions-Based Critique," U.S. Army War College Strategic Studies Institute, November 2001, http://www.strategicstudiesinstitute.army.mil/pdffiles/pub218.pdf.

34. H. R. McMaster, "Crack in the Foundation: Defense Transformation and the Underlying Assumption of Dominant Knowledge in Future War," Center for Strategic Leadership, US Army War College, November 2003, 74, http://www.au.af.mil/au/awc/awcgate/army-usawc/mcmaster_foundation.pdf.

35. *ADRP 3-0, Unified Land Operations* (Washington, DC: Department of the Army, November 2016), Glossary-5.

36. For a critique of US military operations in the Iraq War, see Peter R. Mansoor, *Surge: My Journey with General David Petraeus and the Remaking of the Iraq War* (New Haven, Conn.: Yale Univ. Press, 2013).

37. For an examination of the first critical year of the occupation of Iraq, see Peter R. Mansoor, *Baghdad at Sunrise: A Brigade Commander's War in Iraq* (New Haven, Conn.: Yale Univ. Press, 2008).

38. David Ucko, *The New Counterinsurgency Era: Transforming the U.S. Military for Modern Wars* (Washington, DC: Georgetown Univ. Press, 2009).

39. Max Boot, *The Savage Wars of Peace: Small Wars and the Rise of American Power* (New York: Basic Books, 2002).

40. Allan Millett and Williamson Murray, "Lessons of War," *National Interest,* no. 14 (winter 1988/1989): 83–95, 85.

3

Strategic Landpower
Application at the Nexus of Deviant Globalization and Nonstate Actors

Joel Hillison

Landpower is arguably the oldest component of the military instrument of power. While Carl von Clausewitz would suggest that the nature of war never changes, the nature of landpower has changed over time. Globalization has caused significant changes in the geostrategic environment in which landpower is employed and has empowered nonstate actors to challenge the authority and stability of states. As a result, these changes have influenced the application of landpower, especially in the aftermath of 9/11. This chapter examines the impact of deviant globalization on the application of landpower, examining how nonstate actors are exploiting changes in the nature of power brought about by globalization. It will also consider how landpower has been used to address the challenges posed by those nonstate actors. Finally, it will address how landpower has been used to support efforts related to the rule of law and discuss other implications for the use of strategic landpower. While fighting and winning the nation's wars remains the central task of landpower, the application of landpower in crisis management and cooperative security missions will increasingly deal with the effects of deviant globalization and the empowerment of nonstate actors this phenomenon enabled. If landpower does not adapt, it may continue to win tactical victories, but it will often fall short of the desired strategic outcomes.

Globalization has largely been a force for good. The growing interdependence and interconnectedness of mankind has led to a significant increase in trade and a major reduction in poverty. We are living in perhaps the most peaceful and least violent era in human history.[1] Globalization has been enabled by advances in technology, such as the Internet, mobile devices, and global positioning. Today, it is easier, faster, and cheaper to contact people and to retrieve and send data than ever before. Increased mobility has enabled the cheaper, and more efficient, movement of people (for example, air travel) and material goods (for example, containerized shipping). Globalization has not only empowered developing nations and corporations, but it has also significantly increased the agency of the individual. In *The Road to Global Prosperity*, Professor Michael Mandelbaum argues that, on average, globalization has led to economic improvement globally, though unequally.[2]

Globalization also has a dark side, and theorists sometimes refer to it as deviant globalization.[3] The increased mobility has created a permissive environment for nefarious actors to acquire and utilize unparalleled power for nonstate actors.[4] For example, a solitary hacker can bring multinational corporations and even countries to their knees. Deviant globalization reflects "the proliferation of illicit trade within the global commons, enabled by . . . technological advances and increased global mobility."[5] This illicit trade encompasses illegal goods and services, human trafficking, and the use of legal goods and services to launder illicit profits. The diffusion of power from traditional state actors to nonstate actors and the increased interconnectedness caused by globalization have facilitated the growth of and increased capabilities of both transnational criminal networks and international terrorist networks.[6] This trend poses some challenges for landpower.

The Army definition of landpower is the "ability, by threat, force, or occupation, to gain, sustain, and exploit control over land, resources, and people."[7] Strategic landpower is the active pursuit of US national interests by employing ground forces, or the potential capability of those forces, to achieve strategic effects. It is one of the many tools available to a state and perhaps one of the more decisive ones. Because land is the primary human domain, landpower has a unique place in strategy formulation and execution.

The institutional Army naturally likes to focus on high-end, combined arms operations. These are arguably the most dangerous scenarios—but also the least likely. In the 1990s, many argued that there was a Revolution in Military Affairs (RMA) that empowered US land, air, and sea forces to dominate conventional warfare like never before. The RMA was evident in Operation Desert Storm when coalition forces quickly overwhelmed Iraqi forces. The notion of RMA led landpower advocates to buy into the idea of complete situational awareness and full spectrum dominance.[8] However, many contemporary threats reside in the lower end of the spectrum of conflict, where deviant globalization has empowered nonstate actors. This is the strategic environment where it is difficult to discern clear objectives, who the actors are, and what their intentions might be. Because of this ambiguity, landpower has not proved itself especially decisive.

Prominent defense analyst Michael O'Hanlon takes a different view of landpower. In his 2015 book, *The Future of Land Warfare*, O'Hanlon questions the wisdom of relegating landpower to the provision of special operations forces and relying on other high-tech means of military power.[9] He argues that a substantial conventional land force is still necessary, not only to deter other great powers, but also to manage regional crises and to combat terrorist threats. Even with the rise of hybrid and asymmetric warfare, landpower has an important role to play. The modern land domain is increasingly contested by state and nonstate actors. Deviant globalization has resulted in the diffusion of power away from traditional states and their military forces toward these actors.

The End of Power

Moisés Naím's groundbreaking *The End of Power* explains the changing nature of power. He argues that globalization has made the acquisition of power easier for nonstate actors and networks. Conversely, globalization has made it increasingly difficult for state actors and institutions to maintain sovereignty. Governments from Venezuela to the Philippines have lost control of national territory to insurgent groups.[10] Deviant globalization has exacerbated the problems that countries such as Mexico and Pakistan have in projecting authority into their peripheries where sovereignty has always been challenged. A monopoly on the legitimate use of power used to reside within the state. Naím uses four typologies of power to explain the diffusion of power that has eroded state control: muscle, pitch, code, and reward.[11]

Force or the threat of force is the best example of "muscle power." Globalization has ensured nonstate actors' access to more lethal weapons, unmanned aerial vehicles, sophisticated communications, and encryption gear. They can also use the Internet and social media to gather intelligence and to facilitate messaging. In some situations, even where states retain an advantage in muscle power, sovereignty is constrained by political boundaries (for example, cross-border sanctuaries) or norms on the protection of human rights and the rule of law. Nonstate actors, unfettered by these constraints, can often leverage muscle power more quickly and effectively. According to Naím, large conventional land armies will play a decreasing role in the exercise of state power. Recent experience seems to bear this out. Since 9/11, landpower has more often than not been used to address threats such as insurgencies or terrorists and to support humanitarian operations. While the operational tempo for land forces seems to be increasing, the reliance on massed forces seem to be declining.

Globalization has also increased the power of "pitch" for nonstate actors: "Pitch is just the capacity to persuade others to see the situation in a way that leads them to advance the persuader's goals or interests."[12] According to the *Economist,* the so-called Islamic State of Iraq and Syria (ISIS) terrorist group created "sophisticated online propaganda, which it uses to recruit, promote its ideology, and trumpet its social and military achievements. It puts as much attention into digital marketing as any big company."[13] Not only can nonstate actors transmit quickly and to a wide audience, they can sometimes do so more rapidly than governments and the traditional media, both of which are constrained by bureaucratic review processes.

Even where landpower gives state actors a comparative advantage in muscle power, the ability to use pitch can often turn positive tactical results into negative strategic messages. The Taliban and other nonstate actors best exemplify this by using civilian causalities caused by friendly strikes to promote their narratives to delegitimize the government. Military forces must remain cognizant of how adversaries portray their actions and must work to ensure that their actions are consistent with their own campaign messages. In an environment where nonstate actors can more effectively use pitch, land forces must be more effectively engaged in the battle of narratives.

The same phenomenon is true concerning the power of "code." Code consists of norms and moral obligations, which promote legitimacy. These can be powerful motivators. "Using the logic of appropriateness, actors behave based on their identity and what is appropriate behavior given that identity."[14] The increasing ability (enabled by globalization) of nonstate actors to employ the power of code can mitigate the state's advantages in muscle power. It is much easier to control the actions of humans if they are bound by a sense of duty or obligation. Globalization provides nonstate actors with the mechanisms to promulgate their own norms or codes of behavior to create a similar sense of obligation. ISIS has exploited the use of code, or the sense of obligation among the *umma* (the global community of Muslims), to summon supporters to jihad. The power of code also gives nonstate actors the ability to undermine the authority of states by subverting the rule of law. Landpower has to be cognizant of the power of code and be sensitive to local contexts and cultures in which it is used. It must promote the legitimacy of the host government being supported. If the people believe in the legitimacy and moral authority of the state, they are more likely to support it.

The final type of power discussed by Naím is the power of "reward." Reward refers to the use of incentives or punishments to achieve a desired outcome. Unlike code, reward power is based on the logic of consequences. Accordingly, rational actors often respond to incentives and punishments in making decisions. Military forces have always relied on rewards and punishments to achieve local effects. In COIN, rewards are an essential part of the hearts and minds approach, as well as the cost-benefit theory.[15] At the strategic level, states have often used payments to support larger political and diplomatic initiatives. As with muscle power, the advantage in the employment of reward power used to reside with the state. States provided security, social services, and other public goods to their citizens and enacted punishments for infractions of laws. However, the global interconnectedness that has increased worldwide prosperity has also increased the reward power of criminal networks and violent nonstate actors. For example, the profits from opium trade at one point represented up to 15 percent of Afghanistan's Gross Domestic Product (GDP).[16] Because of their illicit revenue streams, nonstate actors sometimes have greater reward power than do the states in which they operate.

Naím's four categories of power illuminate the diffusion of power to nonstate actors. Hybrid warfare is just one example where this diffusion of power has influenced landpower. *Army Doctrine Reference Publication 3-0* defines hybrid warfare as conflict involving traditional landpower against "the diverse and dynamic combination of regular forces, irregular forces, terrorist forces, or criminal elements unified to achieve mutually benefitting threat effects."[17] The increased complexity of the current strategic environment requires reconsideration of landpower and the hybrid threats impeding the pursuit of US strategic objectives. It further demands a reexamination of the power environment, which Naím has argued three revolutions have influenced.

Naím asserts that three revolutions have removed previous barriers to power and diminished the capability of the state. The first, the "more revolution," has resulted in a proliferation of consumer goods, an increase in crop yields, a rise in education levels, and an expansion of economic and political opportunities. Nothing indicates the more revolution better than population growth. The world population in the 1800s was around 1 billion, while by 1950 the population was about 2.5 billion. In 2017, the world had about 7.4 billion people.[18] As Naím points out, the more revolution challenges notions of traditional governance: "The task of governing, organizing, mobilizing, influencing, persuading, disciplining, or repressing a large number of people . . . requires different methods."[19] The more revolution has also increased the amount of global trade, making it easier for illicit trade to hide within the ever-increasing global flow of goods and services. All of these developments have increased the complexity of using landpower to control people, resources, and land.

Not only are there more people today, but those people are more mobile and thus harder to control or protect.[20] The "mobility revolution" has swayed almost every aspect of human life. According to General Martin Dempsey, the former chairman of the Joint Chiefs of Staff, "people, products, and information are flowing across borders at unprecedented speed and volume, acting as catalysts for economic development while also increasing societal tensions, competition for resources, and political instability."[21] One example of this increased mobility concerns finance. Money used to be physically transported across national borders; with sufficient resources and capabilities, states could easily intercept illicit flows. Today, money moves digitally, almost instantaneously, around the globe. The amount of money that moves across the globe daily exceeded $4 trillion in 2010, making it difficult for states to control.[22] Another example of the "mobility revolution" is the global flow of refugees and migrants. In 2015 there were more than 60 million displaced people globally.[23] When paired with natural disasters, or pandemics such as Ebola, this mobility can significantly disrupt governmental power and capacity. It is also easier for nefarious actors to exploit the "more" and "mobility" revolutions to maintain freedom of action. These mobility trends require landpower to become even more agile and flexible.

The final revolution is the "mentality revolution." People are now more aware of conditions in other parts of the globe. They often see events as soon as they occur. This revolution has also raised the expectations of people, leading to demands increasing much more quickly than states can react to meet them. The mentality revolution has changed expectations, which can breed discontent, and actors such as terrorists and criminal organizations can capitalize on this discontent.[24] With the proliferation of information and inexpensive global connections enabled by the mobility revolution, it is also much easier to spread ideology contesting state power, or to challenge the legitimacy claims of sovereign states and international organizations. The mentality revolution, perhaps even more than the others, determines how effective states are in maintaining control over their citizens. As with the other two revolutions, the mentality revolution also challenges the effectiveness of landpower. Destructive capability alone may not be enough to accomplish desired outcomes. All of these revolutions have empowered deviant actors to challenge traditional state power, including landpower.

Landpower and Insurgents, Terrorists, and Violent Extremist Organizations

Insurgencies are perhaps the most dangerous nonstate actors because they seek to overthrow legitimate state authorities. Some, such as the Fuerzas Armadas Revolucionarias de Colombia (FARC), have been able to successfully challenge traditional state power for extended periods of time. The FARC began as a rural, communist revolutionary force in the 1960s and morphed into one of the wealthiest guerrilla movements in the world.[25] In remote areas of Colombia, the FARC often provided public goods like security and social services to local populations: "For the peasants, the presence of the FARC guaranteed that the cattlemen would not be able to expel them from those lands that they had painstakingly maintained in the preceding years."[26] The FARC also created relationships with drug cartels to transport cocaine in order to finance its insurgency. Globalization allowed organizations such as FARC to use global markets to launder money. The FARC would use profits from the drug trade to purchase legitimate goods overseas and then sell them domestically.[27]

In many ways, combating insurgencies is a more traditional use of land-power. Campaigns relying on COIN utilize landpower (muscle power) to secure land, to protect resources (for example, oil fields) and people, and to target insurgent forces and their bases.[28] State forces often have an advantage in muscle power over insurgent forces, but must be careful not to inflict civilian casualties. Landpower is also essential in building governmental capacity through education, training and equipping governmental agencies, and convincing civilians to resist insurgents. During COIN, landpower must be used in a manner that enhances the legitimacy of the host government (code power). Landpower must also use the power of pitch and reward to win over supporters in an insurgency.[29] The power of pitch underpins the hearts and minds and cost-benefit theories of COIN. Colombia's battle against the FARC demonstrates the potential impact of COIN: "As a result of direct US military assistance to Colombia, the capacities of the Colombian military significantly increased and the Colombian state was able to substantially weaken the FARC's operational capacity and territorial control.[30] However, brute force alone has not proven effective in the modern era and sometimes has had negative, unintended consequences. For example, aggressive poppy eradication efforts in Afghanistan actually increased the legitimacy of the Taliban while reducing the authority of the Afghan government. The Taliban responded by "offering to protect villagers against government attempts to eradicate the illegal poppy fields and seize opium stocks."[31]

Globalization has also contributed to the threat of terrorism. Al Qa'ida and ISIS have used the Internet and social media to create global networks and affiliates and to inspire individuals to act on their behalf. Globalization sometimes creates instability that weakens the nation-state. Terrorists tend to establish operations where governments are weakest, such as in failed or failing states. They normally target noncombatants, who are more difficult to protect than are government institutions and forces. Global interconnectedness has facilitated the ability of geographically dispersed terrorist groups to cooperate. For example, connections exist between Boko Haram in Nigeria, Al Qa'ida in the Islamic Maghreb in Mali, and Al-Shabaab in Somalia. Many of these linkages later transferred to ISIS.[32] Terror groups also use the Internet to perpetrate criminal activity to support their other activities.[33] They use cybercrime, such as bank fraud, and then launder, disseminate, and manage the money to fund operations. They also use legitimate organizations, including businesses and charities, to fund their activities.[34]

COIN often employs landpower to garner intelligence, to deny sanctuaries, and to target key terrorist leaders. While COIN is sometimes a law enforcement issue, more kinetic forms of landpower can also play a constructive role. Landpower can support law enforcement, such as hardening defenses in the event of an attack and freeing up law enforcement to conduct the investigative tasks for which they are better suited. France used up to ten thousand troops to provide security around tourist areas in the aftermath of the 2015 terrorist attack.[35] There are often legal constraints on the use of military forces domestically, such as *posse comitatus*.[36] Landpower can also be used to provide additional capacity to other, non-law enforcement-related government institutions, facilitating planning and interagency cooperation in countering terrorist threats and ensuring that the command and control elements are organized and trained to synchronize and coordinate effects across multiple domains, such as land, air, and space.

Landpower also plays a vital role in addressing the threat from other violent nonstate actors, such as ISIS. An offshoot of Al Qa'ida in Iraq, ISIS later expanded to Syria and other countries.[37] In addition to promoting a terrorist message, ISIS seeks to create a caliphate, a state-like entity relying on the code power embodied in Islamic law. Within the territory it controls, ISIS also has sought to provide public goods to the population. As the territory ISIS controls has shrunk, the group has morphed into something more nebulous. Its pitch has changed from encouraging the faithful to come to the caliphate to fight the crusaders. ISIS now encourages followers to attack the West abroad with available tools.

Landpower has played an important role in combating the territorial expansion of ISIS. Turkish use of landpower along its border with Syria has helped restrict illicit ISIS trade. This along with the use of airpower to target oil fields and ISIS-controlled banks has been very effective in denying ISIS needed resources. SOF have also been used to support Iraqi and Kurdish forces battling ISIS.

Landpower and Transnational Criminal Networks

Terrorist organizations like ISIS and transnational criminal networks (TCNs) sometimes work together and use the same methods, but often in pursuit of different objectives.[38] TCNs are primarily concerned with profits, or reward power; they use the other elements of power to support their business objectives. Criminal syndicates have a great deal of economic power; some scholars estimate that they account for 15–20 percent of global GDP.[39] Drug trafficking networks are a major subset of this group. The United Nations and the International Monetary Fund estimated that the profits of illegal drug trade equaled about $600 billion, or the combined "Gross Domestic Product (GDP) of New Zealand, Ireland, and Portugal."[40]

The link between TCNs and the three revolutions remains clear. As a RAND study on countering TCNs indicates, "over time, the illicit economy grows and nonstate actors provide an increasing range of social goods and fill the security and political vacuum that emerges from the gradual erosion of state power, legitimacy, and capacity."[41] In addition to enabling these revolutions, deviant globalization has also increased the muscle power of TCNs. TCNs have greater access to weapons, communications, and surveillance technology to resist government forces' coercive efforts. TCNs have leveraged social media and the Internet to promote norms and values that coincide with their interests. One example is found in the *narco-cultura*. In his 2012 book, Paul Kan, an expert on criminal drug organizations, discussed the impact of the drug culture on the acceptability of drug trafficking and other criminal activities in Mexico.[42] These TCNs use the power of pitch to spread their countercultural values and to intimidate law enforcement, journalists, and other societal actors that seek to reduce their activities. The dark net, and encrypted sites such as Silk Road, have opened pathways to illicit trade using crypto-currencies such as bitcoin to make their transactions.[43] TCNs use these profits to incentivize the public, public officials, and institutions to tolerate and even participate in their illicit activities.

As with terrorism, combating TCNs has normally been the purview of law enforcement agencies and thus has not often garnered the attention of the military. Traditional concerns over proper civil-military relations have often hampered military involvement in countering criminal activity. However, US law allows "military support for law enforcement activities when the military proves a direct connection between counterterrorism efforts and counternarcotic operations."[44] In these circumstances, the capabilities provided by landpower are essential in supporting civilian operations targeting TCNs. The

Army continues to explore its role in countering criminal and terrorist activities in Latin America.[45] Most of these roles include support to law enforcement agencies.

The employment of landpower can provide key organizational, training, firepower, and logistical resources to support law enforcement operations. The RAND study provided detailed recommendations for using landpower to counter TCNs.[46] These included developing interagency and multinational strategies, increasing participation of land forces in joint interagency task forces, leveraging regionally aligned forces (especially the Reserve Component), and partnering with gendarmerie forces.[47] Some argue that any efforts to suppress illicit economies will be ineffective without first establishing security.[48] The resources, skills, and organizations that come with landpower can augment the limited capabilities of host nation agencies in a sustainable and credible manner. For example, there is an important role for SOF in combating TCNs. According to Kan, "a global SOF network can be particularly valuable in tackling the expansive challenges of the international drug trade. SOF personnel are accustomed to operating in complex political, social and economic environments where the drug-security nexus exists."[49] Ground forces can provide intelligence preparation of the battlefield, reconnaissance, and threat analysis to support law enforcement efforts. Landpower has unique ground and air reconnaissance and conventional signals, cyber, and radar capabilities that can be used in support of law enforcement and border control agencies. It can also provide the data collection and analysis to help map and track changes in complex TCN networks.[50]

The mobility revolution, which has empowered TCNs, has also constrained traditional states: "States are disadvantaged by their very nature, requiring complicated interagency coordination within countries, and even worse, across borders just to keep track of the movements and doings of highly autonomous businessmen who hop constantly across frontiers."[51] Landpower can help states mitigate these constraints by supporting border control operations used to disrupt TCN supply networks.

One example of the potential pitfalls of using landpower to combat illicit activity comes from Mexico. Since 2006, the Mexican Army has played a major role in Mexico's war against drug cartels. This effort, however, has not been paired with an equally capable law enforcement effort. As a result, while over 160,000 people were murdered in Mexico between 2007 and 2014, only 2 percent of all violent crimes were prosecuted.[52] This effort also demonstrated landpower drawbacks, by implementing it in a role for which it was ill prepared, or where a complementary civilian capability was lacking.[53]

Potential corruption of the military is another risk of using military forces to combat criminal activities.[54] In spite of these challenges, landpower can play a productive role in promoting the rule of law.

Landpower and the Rule of Law

The rule of law is perhaps the most fundamental aspect of governance in that it provides legitimacy to state actors. The rule of law is also the institution most at jeopardy due to deviant globalization. The United States Institute of Peace defines the rule of law as a "principle of governance in which all persons and institutions, public and private, including the state itself, are accountable to laws that are publicly announced, equally enforced and independently adjudicated, and consistent with international human rights norms and standards."[55] Without the rule of law, states lack the legitimacy necessary to provide secure and stable governance. Using Naím's typology of power, the rule of law relates to the power of code (it promotes the authority of the government) and the power of reward (it legitimizes the ability to punish offenders). Insurgents, terrorists, violent extremist organizations, and transnational criminal networks exploit gaps in the rule of law to promote their interests. By pursuing illicit activities, these nonstate actors undermine the rule of law. For example, criminal organizations often "control political parties, own significant media operations, or are the major philanthropists behind nongovernmental organizations."[56] In West Africa, weak military and law enforcement institutions "left West African political systems and 'rule of law' arrangements highly susceptible to penetration by the drug trade and other dangerous criminal flows."[57] This political, informational, and economic power allows these organizations to avoid accountability to the law and even to enact laws that benefit their private interests. As TCNs infiltrate (and in some cases coopt) governmental institutions, they threaten the very foundations of modern society, which are based on an adherence to the rule of law.[58]

Rule of Law in Security Sector Assistance

While the DoS is the lead agency in security sector assistance, the DoD, and thus landpower, has played a supporting role in this area. These efforts help allies and partners build and strengthen the rule of law.[59] For example, USSOUTHCOM developed a legal engagement strategy in 1998 for Latin America that "sought to promote the concept of professional law based militaries that operate in accordance with the rule of law . . . and are subordinate to and controlled by democratically elected civilian governments."[60] Landpower has also provided support to build partner capacity in establishing and maintaining the rule of law in countries of the former Soviet Union through the State Partnership Program.[61] Within partner countries, military commanders work with the country team to coordinate support to rule of law efforts. These efforts, though vital in maintaining stability, are often overshadowed by other activities during stability operations.

Rule of Law in Stability Operations

As with security assistance, promotion of the rule of law during reconstruction and stability operations requires a "whole of government" approach. Early on in operations, landpower may play a primary role in establishing the rule of law. For example, the Coalition Provisional Authority's "responsibilities included establishing the rule of law to replace Saddam Hussein's rule by decree."[62] The Coalition Provisional Authority worked with the Interim Iraq Government to establish the rule of law while in transition to an elected government. Once an elected government is in place, landpower can then supplement the capacity of the civilian government and reinforce other governmental agencies. Establishing the rule of law is so critical that it is listed as a key objective in the US Army's counterinsurgency manual.[63] Provincial Reconstruction Teams were used in Iraq and Afghanistan, among other things, to promote the rule of law, even after indigenous governments were in place.

Landpower also brings unique capabilities to rule of law efforts during stability operations, projecting power and maneuver capability in support of stability operations. It can also provide the firepower for rule of law activities in high-intensity operations. However, the use of force may be counterproductive, stifling the ability of local security to "self-organize, adapt, and ultimately transform in response to problems."[64] Landpower can also provide intelligence, training, and logistical support to law enforcement, thus enhancing efforts to establish the rule of law. Landpower has been used to build partner rule of law capacity in places as diverse as Afghanistan, Iraq, Pakistan, and Columbia.

Strategic Landpower and Deviant Globalization

Strategic Landpower requires linking landpower with appropriate political objectives, effective ways of pursuing those objectives, and the means or resources required to carry them out. When dealing with nonstate actors empowered by deviant globalization, strategic landpower must be ready to create the conditions for peace and security, as well as to support allies and host nations in developing capabilities to do so. In these operations, landpower will be essential in achieving strategic goals. *Joint Publication 3-07: Stability*, outlines some of these goals, such as "denying sanctuary to terrorists, insurgents, criminals, or other hostile transnational elements; countering terrorism; countering the proliferation of weapons of mass destruction; sharing intelligence; providing or protecting access to global commons; supporting a regional security framework; or deterring state aggression."[65]

The first imperative in successfully employing strategic landpower is clearly defining the strategic outcomes. As the Army and Marine Corps have become increasingly involved in stability operations and cooperative security efforts, the traditional application of landpower has become more complex.[66] The second requirement for successful application of strategic landpower is developing and educating strategic leaders. Institutions like the US Army War College seek to educate senior officers on the employment of strategic landpower in a joint, interagency, intergovernmental, and multinational environment (JIIM). As a 2016 article in *Defense and Security Analysis* argues, "strategic landpower creates linkages across the JIIM environment to combat . . . illicit commerce."[67] Finally, the effectiveness of strategic landpower relies on the development of a strong doctrinal foundation for addressing TCNs and terrorist networks. The utility of strategic landpower also depends on appropriate legal authorities to support (and at times constrain) the employment of landpower to achieve overarching political objectives. When used in conjunction with other instruments of national power, landpower can be effective in combating deviant actors and their networks.

The DoD must continue to examine the appropriate roles and functions of landpower in addressing threats from nonstate actors, such as terrorists and TCNs. It must balance the need for landpower in conventional defense, crisis management, and cooperative security operations. That analysis will be based on the grand strategy the United States employs to pursue its national interests, as indicated in this volume. If landpower is increasingly required to address threats from nonstate actors, this will require appropriate doctrine, organization, training, materials, leadership, education, personnel, and facilities.[68] It will also require appropriate legal authorities, as found in the National Defense Authorization Act of 2015.[69]

Deviant globalization and the empowerment of nonstate actors have increased the challenges in the application of landpower. Since the terrorist attacks on 9/11, landpower has been employed to address a much broader range of traditional and nontraditional threats. While the United States has a strong record of accomplishment in successfully employing landpower at the tactical and operational levels, its ability to achieve desired political outcomes with the application of landpower is less stellar. By examining the diffusion of power and its impact on nonstate actors, senior military leaders will be better equipped to employ landpower in pursuit of US interests. Leaders seeking to employ strategic landpower have to improve linking tactical and operational success to strategic victory.[70]

Notes

1. Steven Pinker, *The Better Angels of Our Nature: Why Violence Has Declined* (New York: Penguin, 2012).

2. Michael Mandelbaum, *The Road to Global Prosperity* (New York: Simon and Schuster, 2014).

3. See Nils Gilman, Jesse Goldhammer, and Steven Weber, eds., *Deviant Globalization: Black Market Economy in the 21st Century* (New York: Continuum, 2011), and Michael Miklaucic and Jacqueline Brewer, eds., *Convergence: Illicit Networks and National Security in the Age of Globalization* (Washington, DC: NDU Press, 2013).

4. Mikkel Vedby Rasmussen, "A Parallel Globalization of Terror: 9-11, Security and Globaliztion," *Cooperation and Conflict* 37, no. 3 (2002): 325–326.

5. Joel R. Hillison and Avram Isaacson, "Deviant Globalization: The Application of Strategic Landpower," *Defense and Security Analysis* 32, no. 4 (2016): 282.

6. Ibid.

7. Department of the Army, *Operations, Army Doctrine Reference Publication 3-0* (Washington, DC: Headquarters, Department of the Army, 11 November 2016), 1–9.

8. Lieutenant Colonel Scott Stephenson, "The Revolution in Military Affairs," *Military Review* 90, no. 3 (May–June 2010): 38–46.

9. Michael O'Hanlon, *The Future of Land Warfare* (Washington, DC: Brookings Institution Press, 31 August 2015).

10. Moisés Naím, *The End of Power* (New York: Basic Books, 2013), 115.

11. Ibid., 23.

12. Ibid., 24.

13. "Terrorism Online: Fighting the Cyber-Jihadists," *The Economist*, 10 June 2017, 59.

14. Hillison and Isaacson, "Deviant Globalization," 281. For more information, see James March and Johan Olsen, "The Institutional Dynamics of International Political Orders," *International Organization*, 52, no. 4 (1998): 943–969.

15. James D. Fearon, "Economic Development, Insurgency, and Civil War," in *Institutions and Economic Performance*, ed. Elhanan Helpman (Cambridge, Massachusetts: Harvard Univ. Press, 2008), 292–298.

16. Gretchen Peters, "Traffickers and Truckers: Illicit Afghan and Pakistani Power Structures with a Shadowy but Influential Role," in *Impunity: Countering*

Illicit Power in War and Transition, ed. Michelle Hughes and Michael Miklaucic (Carlisle, Pa.: US Army War College Press, 2016), 20.

17. Department of the Army, *Operations, Army Doctrine Reference Publication 3-0* (Washington, DC: Headquarters, Department of the Army, 11 November 2016), 1–3.

18. The US Census Bureau, "World Population," https://www.census.gov/population/international/data/worldpop/table_population.php (accessed 29 June 2017).

19. Naím, *The End of Power,* 58.

20. Ibid., 62.

21. General Martin Dempsey, *The National Military Strategy of the United States of America 2015* (Washington, DC: US DoD, 2015), 1.

22. Naím, *The End of Power,* 62.

23. Phillip Connor and Jens Manuel Krogstad, "Key Facts about the World's Refugees," Pew Research Center, 5 October 2016, http://www.pewresearch.org/facttank/2016/10/05/key-facts-about-the-worlds-refugees/ (accessed 12 June 2017)

24. Naím, *The End of Power,* 64.

25. "Who Are the FARC?" BBC, 24 November 2016, http://www.bbc.com/news/world-latin-america-36605769.

26. Alain Labrousse, "The FARC and the Taliban's Connection to Drugs," *Journal of Drug Issues* 35, no. 1 (winter 2005): 172.

27. Jennifer S. Holmes and Sheila Amin Gutiérrez de Piñeres, "The Illegal Drug Industry, Violence, and the Colombian Economy: A Department Level Analysis," *Bulletin of Latin American Research* 25, no. 1 (2006): 108.

28. Gregory Roberts later addresses the role of landpower in denying sanctuaries.

29. Hillison and Isaacson, "Deviant Globalization," 285.

30. Vanda Felbab-Brown, "Organized Crime, Illicit Economies, Civil Violence and International Order: More Complex Than You Think," *Daedaluas, the Journal of the American Academy of Arts and Sciences* 146, no. 4 (fall 2017): 104.

31. Ibid., 98.

32. Herman J. Cohen, "Al Qaeda in Africa: The Creeping Menace to Sub-Sahara's 500 Million Muslims," *American Foreign Policy Interests* 35, no. 2 (2013): 63–69.

33. Denise N. Baken and Ioannis Mantzikos, "The Cyber Terrorism Shadow Networks in Africa: AQIM and Boko Haram," *African Renaissance* 9, no.1 (2012): 27–45.

34. Jill Rowland, Mason Rice, and Sujeet Shenoi, "Whither Cyberpower," *International Journal of Critical Infrastructure Protection* 7, no. 2 (June 2014), http://dx.doi.org/10.1016/j.ijcip.2014.04.001.

35. Angelique Chrisafis, "Thousands of Troops on Paris Streets, but Are They France's New Maginot Line?" *Guardian,* 15 April 2016.

36. Gene Healy, "What of 'Posse Comitatus'?" CATO Institute, 7 October 2005, https://www.cato.org/publications/commentary/what-posse-comitatus.

37. Jason Hanna, "Here's How ISIS Was Really Founded," CNN, 13 August 2016, https://www.cnn.com/2016/08/12/middleeast/here-is-how-isis-began/index.html.

38. Louise I. Shelley and John T. Picarelli, "Methods Not Motives: Implications of the Convergence of International Organized Crime and Terrorism," *Police Practice and Research*, 30, no. 4 (2002): 306.

39. Tim Hall, "Geographies of the Illicit: Globalization and Organized Crime," *Progress in Human Geography* 37, no. 3 (June 2013): 387.

40. Paul R. Kan, "Forces of Habit: Global SOF's Role in Countering Illicit Drug Trafficking," *Journal of Strategic Security* 7, no. 2 (2014): 21.

41. Angel Rabasa, Christopher Schnaubelt, et al., *Counternetwork: Countering the Expansion of Transnational Criminal Networks* (Santa Monica, Calif.: RAND Corporation, 2017), xiv.

42. Kan, *Cartels at War* (Washington, DC: Potomac Books, 2012), 32.

43. Andy Greenberg, "The Silk Road's Dar-Web Dream Is Dead," *Wired*, 14 January 2016, https://www.wired.com/2016/01/the-silk-roads-dark-web -dream-is-dead/.

44. Kan, "Forces of Habit," 25.

45. Colonel Todd E. Key, ed., "Key Strategic Issue List: Academic Year 2018" (Carlisle, Pa.: US Army War College Press, 7 August 2017), 19.

46. Rabasa, Schnaubelt, et al., *Counternetwork*.

47. Ibid., xx—xxii.

48. Felbab-Brown, "Organized Crime, Illicit Economies, Civil Violence and International Order," 107.

49. Ibid., 22.

50. Philippe Leroux-Martin and Vivienne O'Connor, "Systems Thinking for Peacebuilding and Rule of Law," in *PeaceWorks*, no. 133 (Washington, DC: United States Institute of Peace, 2017), 20.

51. Moisés Naím, *Illicit: How Smugglers, Traffickers, and Copycats Are Hijacking the Global Economy* (New York: Doubleday, 2005), 62.

52. Felbab-Brown, "Organized Crime, Illicit Economies, Civil Violence and International Order," 100.

53. Christopher Woody, "After a Decade Fighting the Cartels, Mexico May Be Looking for a Way to Get Its Military off the Front Line," *Business Insider*, 13 February 2017, http://www.businessinsider.com/mexican-military-role-in-fighting-drug -war-and-cartels-2017-2.

54. Kan, *Cartels at War* (Washington, DC: Potomac Books, 2012), 138.

55. "What Is the Rule of Law?" United Nations, https://www.un.org/ruleoflaw/ what-is-the-rule-of-law/ (accessed 12 October 2018).

56. Naím, *Illicit*, 8.

57. Felbab-Brown, "Organized Crime, Illicit Economies, Civil Violence and International Order," 107.

58. Naím, *Illicit*, 8.

59. DoD Directive 5132.03, "DOD Policy and Responsibilities Relating to Security Cooperation" (Washington, DC: DoD, 29 December 2016).

60. The Judge Advocate General's Legal Center and School, *Rule of Law Hand-*

book: A Practitioner's Guide for Judge Advocates (Charlottesville, Va.: US Army Center for Law and Military Operations, 2015), 15.

61. Ibid., 67.

62. Robert M. Perito, "Special Report 104: Establishing the Rule of Law in Iraq" (Washington, DC: United States Institute of Peace, April 2003), 1.

63. Department of the Army, *Field Manual 3-24, Insurgencies and Countering Insurgencies* (Washington, DC: Headquarters Department of the Army, May 2014), 3–13.

64. Leroux-Martin and O'Connor, "Systems Thinking for Peacebuilding and Rule of Law," 20.

65. US Joint Chiefs of Staff, *Joint Publication 3-07: Stability* (Washington, DC: US Joint Chiefs of Staff, 3 August 2016), IV-32.

66. Richard Lacquement examines the Army's role on stability operations in a later chapter.

67. Hillison and Isaacson, "Deviant Globalization," 288.

68. Rabasa, Schnaubelt, et al., *Counternetwork,* xvi—xvii.

69. Ibid.

70. Sean Kimmons, "Army Strategizing for Holistic Change, Not Just New Tech," US Training and Doctrine Command, 31 March 2017, https://www.army.mil/article/185089/army_strategizing_for_holistic_change_not_just_new_tech.

4

Civil-Military Relations Post-9/11

Donald S. Travis

A generation shaped by Vietnam must remember the lessons of Vietnam. When America uses force in the world, the cause must be just, the goal must be clear, and the victory must be overwhelming.
—George W. Bush, 3 August 2000

Since 9/11, the United States carries on more than a few limited wars against a variety of enemies lacking in sophisticated conventional weapons, such as combat aircraft, strategic bombers, ballistic missiles, and naval vessels. These enemies wage irregular (guerrilla/asymmetric) warfare in desert, mountainous, urban, jungle, and cyber terrain.[1] The segments of the US military mostly responsible for opposing them are what General Peter Schoomaker refers to as the "twenty-first-century strategic triad," composed of the Army, Marine Corps, and special operations forces (SOF).[2] This "landpower triad" sustains a larger number of casualties and sacrifices compared to other armed services. It also confronts significant civil-military challenges resulting from frequent turnover of political and military leadership, an inattentive populace, and a corpulent and well-entrenched defense bureaucracy; all together, these three components of the state's civil-military nexus are responsible for geopolitical uncertainty and obscured war objectives.[3] America's pluralistic defense bureaucracy combined with the prerogatives of Congress accommodate differing and countervailing approaches to diplomacy and war, while the landpower triad endures sustained and extra-legal operations against assorted enemies in Afghanistan, Iraq, Syria, Yemen, Somalia, Libya, and other regions across Africa, Latin America, and Asia.[4]

The post-9/11 civil-military challenges and their implications for landpower will be examined through the Clausewitzian framework known as the "paradoxical trinity."[5] It is the conceptual lens used to examine interactions between the people, the military establishment, and the civilian government to reassess three interrelated lessons drawn from the Vietnam War: the legality of war, the use of advanced weapons and their associated strategies, and the persistent debates over how best to employ military power focused on conventional versus unconventional forces' roles, missions, and tactics. Such lessons will help identify and highlight potential implications for the future of landpower and civil-military relations, understanding that the responsibility to develop war policies and objectives rests with a government that is responsive and sensitive to the people. The military carries out the operations to achieve those objectives; the development of policy and strategy is a shared task among all parts of society, whereas its implementation is chiefly (but not exclusively) the military's responsibility.[6]

The Clausewitzian Trinity

Carl von Clausewitz recognized that war is "an instrument of policy" that "must vary with the nature of their motives and of the situations which give rise to them." Any theory of war is based on "the most far-reaching act of judgement that the statesman and commander have to make, [which] is to establish . . . the kind of war on which they are embarking." Equally important are consequences, which Clausewitz examined and assessed through a "paradoxical trinity" composed of the people, a military, and their government.[7] Clausewitz explained the significance of this "trinity":

> These three tendencies are like three different codes of law, deep-rooted in their subject and yet variable in their relationship to one another. . . . A theory that ignores any one of them or seeks to fix an arbitrary relationship between them would conflict with reality. . . . Our task therefore is to develop a theory that maintains a balance between these three tendencies, like an object suspended between three magnets.[8]

Clausewitz's model reveals both simplicity and complexity, depending on the nation-state examined and the kinds of wars waged. Figure 4.1 illustrates the US political and security system formatted on the trinity.

Clausewitz's metaphor of suspending an object between magnets represents a political equilibrium—or balance of power—between the three dynamic social forces of a nation-state that influence civil-military relations: the people (the passions), the military (probability and courage), and the government (political aims). Stability supports political, economic, and social predictability to mitigate conflict within a society. The "National Security

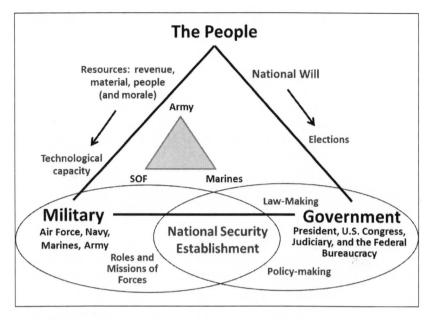

Figure 4.1. The Clausewitzian Trinity and the Landpower Strategic Triad for the Limited Wars of the Twenty-First Century.

Establishment" (or "Military-Industrial Complex") reflected at the bottom center of figure 4.1 is recognized as a true phenomenon as well as a "trope."[9]

Applying the Clausewitzian trinity to the United States demands recognition of four interrelated conditions.[10] First, the American people remain a potent and ever-present political force as voters, taxpayers, and soldiers. The most significant power is the transfer of sovereignty (the ballot) to elected representatives working in Washington, DC. Other powers include "national will" to support war policies and sustain armed struggles, material and bureaucratic labor, and that most essential resource required to conduct war: motivated and disciplined soldiers, sailors, marines, and airmen.[11] Second, the US governing system is disposed to stasis; law-making, law-interpreting, and executive powers along with a pluralistic character of federal and state bureaucracies enable debates and policy struggles. This allows entrenched and questionable military policies to survive in the face of determined opposition. A third condition is the growth of the national defense establishment since the Second World War that has expanded in technological power and political influence since 9/11.[12] Finally, and reflected at the center-lower-left of figure 4.1, is the recognition that the multiple and limited wars require disproportionate effort from the "landpower strategic triad."[13]

The Enduring Lessons of Vietnam

Paul Yingling's assertion that the generals in Iraq repeated the blunders of Vietnam was recognized as a bellwether of sentiments among junior officers.[14] Barbara Tuchman identified three lessons from the Vietnam War that still inform post-9/11 war policies and can be used to test Yingling's assertion. The first is that the legality of the war was always in question. The Gulf of Tonkin Resolution of August 7, 1964, gave LBJ "a blank check" to escalate the war: "Johnson thought he could pursue the war without the nation noticing. He did not ask Congress for a Declaration because he was advised or worried that he might not get it, nor did he ask for a renewed vote on the Tonkin Gulf Resolution for fear of being embarrassed."[15] General William Westmoreland lamented that LBJ's mishandling of Congress and the public became "a leaden liability."[16]

A second lesson was the misuse of advanced weapons and the related strategy of dissuasion: "how to escalate the war until the North Vietnamese were ready to quit."[17] Dissuasion policies demand the use of lethal force applied to an extent that it will force the enemy to back away from seeking to achieve their war aims and instead will work out a peace settlement.[18] It is backed by a hollow faith that technologically superior firepower (such as bombing campaigns) will force enemies to "relent" and seek resolution. In 1966, the JASON study debunked the idea that airpower could achieve "unacceptable punishment" on the North. Using British, German, and Japanese case studies as supporting evidence, the study concluded that "direct frontal attack on a society tended to strengthen the fabric, increase popular determination and stimulate protective devices and capacity for repair." By 1967 the use of heavy firepower by the United States and its allies had had questionable impact on the enemy's will or ability to fight.[19]

A third lesson from Tuchman was the apparent inability of the US military to successfully wage a limited war against an enemy employing guerrilla war tactics and strategies. Americans understood how to conduct guerrilla warfare but were unwilling to sacrifice for Vietnam.[20] The "short-term one-year tours of duty, intended to avoid discontent, prevented adaptation to irregular jungle warfare, thereby increasing casualties. . . . Adaptation never matched circumstances. American fighting tactics were designed in terms of large troop formations . . . once in motion the American military machine could not readjust."[21] This lesson is manifested in debates across the American military between "conventional" versus "unconventional" devotees arguing over the appropriate ways to train and employ land forces.[22] These three lessons—war authorization, misapplication of weapons, and the proper employment of forces—can be used to examine Yingling's assertion and post-9/11 American civil-military relations using Clausewitz's paradoxical trinity.

The Clausewitzian Trinity: The Government and the Military

President George W. Bush promised to reduce the burdensome number of operations placed on the military.[23] In the summer of 2001 a "new Bush doctrine" advocated "freedom of action" to pursue "unilateralism."[24] US forces were expected to fight and win wars while other countries performed peacekeeping and nation-building.[25] Secretary of Defense Donald Rumsfeld, who set the tone for civil-military relations, was determined to upgrade military capabilities to meet anticipated threats. Believing the military was resistant to reform, he worked to "show the generals and admirals who was boss. . . . He was rude, abrasive, and relied heavily on a small group of advisors," showing little respect for the "top brass."[26] His support for "transformation" was as ambitious as it was costly. Military forces were expected to operate anywhere in the world within twenty-four hours and resolve conflicts "within 30 days."[27] The 2001 Quadrennial Defense Review (QDR), conducted prior to 9/11, supported the transformation of military forces to dominate every conceivable adversary.[28]

The 9/11 attacks provided the pretext to test transformation.[29] SOF with their indigenous partners (militias) toppled the Taliban regime in Afghanistan with the help of combat airpower, showing that such wars could be won rapidly, decisively, and cheaply against rudimentary armies of failing states.[30] Such success challenged the value of conventional armor and infantry formations, leading to conflict between the Army and the DoD over preparations to invade Iraq. Rumsfeld's Pentagon was ready to demonstrate a second time how fewer troops and high-tech weapons would achieve rapid and decisive military outcomes.[31] CSA General Eric Shinseki's notable testimony to Congress that "several hundred thousand" soldiers might be needed to secure Iraq initiated a civil-military calamity. Rumsfeld's response to Shinseki was public and immediate: "The idea that it would take several hundred thousand US forces I think is far off the mark."[32] Soon after, and fourteen months before Shinseki's term was scheduled to end, Rumsfeld undermined the authority of the Army's top leader by signaling his intention to appoint General John

"Jack" Keane as Shinseki's successor, thereby devaluing the Army's standing as it prepared to invade Iraq. This turned Shinseki into a "lame duck" and branded him as uncooperative and unprepared.[33]

After Keane's retirement, he testified before the House Armed Services Committee regarding Army transformation and the situation in Iraq. First, he described how the active Army relied on the Reserve Component due to an over-dependence on military police, civil affairs, intelligence, and other specialties needed for larger deployments such as Afghanistan and Iraq. Second, regarding the perceived war against radical Islam and the operations across the Middle East, he asserted that "we have done a horrible job in explaining what this war is about and defining it properly to the American people." He emphasized that waging war requires more than killing; it necessitates additional skills and broadened operational approaches to defeat the attackers responsible for 9/11. Third, Keane described the lack of planning that led to inadequate preparations for postwar Iraq. US forces were unprepared because senior war planners under Rumsfeld's supervision were "seduced by the Iraqi exiles" into believing that the aftermath of the invasion would yield conditions favorable for postwar tasks: "We toppled the regime in April. We had lawlessness and looting in May. We had targeted violence against us in June. It doubled in July, it doubled in August. . . . And obviously . . . we did not see it coming, and we were not properly prepared and organized to deal with it."[34] Yet, postwar stabilization planning for Iraq had been accomplished at USCENTCOM. They "conceptualized and inventoried" post-hostilities actions and tasks, with the intent of "putting Iraq back together again," but in November 2001 significant elements of such planning were transferred to the Pentagon.[35]

As the wars continued through 2005, the Army and Marine Corps toiled through the occupation of Iraq, witnessing the disintegration of Iraqi civil society, with marginal troop reinforcements and little guidance other than pre-9/11 flawed assumptions and broken strategies. Through 2006, insurgents waged guerrilla war by capturing and using coalition resources and killing off the civilian professionals supporting the newly installed Iraqi government.[36]

The 2006 QDR affirmed the importance of land forces, but it did so in veiled language. It referred to "future warriors" expected to "be as proficient in irregular operations, including counterinsurgency and stabilization operations, as they are . . . in high-intensity combat." All services were expected to participate in "long-duration" irregular campaigns. The marines and SOF would increase their numbers and grow their capacity to conduct unconventional warfare. The Air Force pledged "to increase joint air-ground integration" to support ground forces in conventional and irregular operations. Finally, the maritime force would improve its SOF "to penetrate denied areas to locate high-value individuals, designate targets for precision strike, or conduct direct action missions."[37] As the Air Force and Navy joined the Army and Marine Corps to fight unconventional wars, civilian government agencies, private corporations, and contracting firms joined in to form a "holistic" effort to confront "Traditional, Irregular, Catastrophic, and Disruptive" threats.[38] The QDR also made numerous references to a "Long War" where conflict was going to be waged anywhere using every kind of tactic and strategy.[39] The demise of rapid and decisive war theories signaled the end of Rumsfeld's tenure.

The Clausewitzian Trinity: The People and the Military

From the people's perspective, all wars should be legal and fought with a degree of transparency and accountability.[40] Achieving these goals serves to protect soldiers ethically and legally when in harm's way. By the fall of 2006, with Afghanistan perceived as dormant and other numerous military operations being conducted with little notice, the American people understood how badly the Iraq War was going.[41] This translated into the November 2006 midterm congressional election results showing that the American people were ready for change: the Democratic Party took power in both houses of Congress and numerous governorships.[42] The Bush administration was going into its final two years confronting civil war and insurgency that was getting worse, with no end in sight.[43] As battles raged across Iraq between Arab Sunni insurgents and Shiite-backed government forces, Bush decided to increase military involvement by sending an additional 21,500 ground troops, in opposition to the advice of many top military leaders. Bush argued that past efforts to stabilize Iraq failed because "there were not enough Iraqi and American troops to secure neighborhoods that had been cleared of terrorists and insurgents."[44] Several members of the Joint Chiefs of Staff, along with the former commander of USCENTCOM, General John Abizaid, opposed increasing the number of troops. Reminiscent of Vietnam, a divided Pentagon grudgingly went along with Bush's "Surge" plans, as they were promised that the escalation would be backed by renewed political and economic efforts.[45]

The Iraq Surge in 2007 vindicated Shinseki's earlier estimates, as the United States was mired in a trap similar to that of 1967.[46] Lethal air strikes sought to acquire discrete targets and avoid collateral damage while providing close air support to US and Iraqi ground forces in mostly urbanized terrain. On the ground in the dust, sweat, and blood, Army, Marine Corps, and SOF personnel endured the brunt of a complex war as they were stretched to their limits of availability, with no end in sight and little hope of departure from the all-volunteer military system.[47]

Determining whether the 2007 Surge was successful depends on the species of military authority giving the assessment. Since the 1950s, the US military has been divided between conventional versus unconventional advocates. Internecine debates over "correct" military doctrine are centered between "conventional" versus "unconventional" roles, missions, tactics, and strategies.[48] Such debates cut across services, units, and individual leaders, with second- and third-order consequences. Such contentious views might find their way into the extended families of fallen soldiers, and then across local communities, where parents and grandparents blame incompetent strategies for "unnecessary" combat deaths and injuries. Both views were described by Morris Janowitz, with his paradigm of two opposing bureaucratic forces called "absolutists" and "pragmatists."[49] These two opposing "world views" struggle to identify "the proper balance of forces" and "relative weight" of resources to assign to either "massive versus graduated deterrence." The two perspectives dominate twenty-first-century US politico-military strategy and policy development.

Pragmatists realize that "the military establishment had become a multipurpose organization in which 'ancillary' functions—military government, military assistance programs, political propaganda, and police functions—assumed great importance."[50] By contrast, absolutists consider limited wars as temporary aberrations, only to be fought as an intermediate step toward achieving total victory against near-peer rivals in the imminent "big war." The absolutist and "massive deterrence" school pursues more lethal technologies and "final victory." Pragmatists avoid impulsive (reflex) reactions to violence, preferring persistent diplomacy, limited force, and the subtle employment of human skill sets to prevent or settle conflicts.[51]

Conventionalists argue that the 2007 Iraq Surge was unnecessary because US forces were already tackling the problems across Iraq long before General Petraeus and his "COIN-dinistas" arrived.[52] They consider COIN doctrine and operations to be flawed for three key reasons. First, they are "anti-Clausewitzian," meaning that COIN "denies the interactive nature of conflict as manifest in the will, chance, and anger of conflicting parties as in the duel."[53] Second, soldiers provided with military training based on proper "organizational and methodological" frameworks develop competencies to adapt to any form of warfare. Adding *Field Manual 3-24: Counterinsurgency* to their training is wasted effort because soldiers provided with the fundamentals of discipline and training can adapt and fight against any adversary. To them: "War is war! . . . that is prosecuted on several levels depending on the enemy, the geography, and the politics of the situation."[54] Third, COIN is invested with bogus moral righteousness: "the ostensible moral objective of protecting innocent civilians and making their lives better." Instead, more firepower applied against the enemy will hasten the reduction of violence.[55] Thus, conventional forces can wage COIN better than so-called "special forces" because "professional soldiers" are better trained and disciplined. Hence, the 2007 Surge with the arrival of twenty-one thousand additional soldiers under alleged improved COIN doctrine and "exceptional" leadership was a "myth" and superfluous.[56]

Paul Yingling's assertion that the generals in Iraq waged unconventional wars with conventional tactics and strategies implies that senior military leaders had trouble adapting to enemies that deviated from conventional state-versus-state warfare.[57] US forces on the ground proved that the clear-hold-build strategy could be made to work if given the right leadership and assets, supporting the argument that the Surge was "a case study of counterinsurgency warfare planned and executed brilliantly."[58] The temporary success of the Surge was too little and too late, as it was followed by the 2008 election results that translated into a textbook case on how "operational success could not be translated into strategic success."[59]

Proponents of alternatives to conventionalist dogma reject the belief that increasing violence is the sole answer to defeating guerrilla insurgencies; such an enemy "cannot be bombed into submission."[60] Four crucial elements of the unconventional COIN approach are: first, to have American advisors partner with local forces to defeat common enemies; second, assist the partner government to resolve political strife and corruption, and improve its ability to effectively manage its own affairs; third, provide time and have patience to allow the partner government to become established; and finally, protect populations caught in the middle of the struggle while practicing respect and empathy for the societies and cultures that are bearing the brunt of their bloody conflicts.[61]

Woefully, the debate between conventionalists and "COIN-dinistas" might be a manifestation of a debilitating trend that befalls many large institutions waging limited and bureaucratic wars: careerism; who gets deployed to a combat zone, the credit for success, and then promotion? Under such struggles for limited resources and billets, the people and their government must be watchful that one side does not get "set up to fail" by the other.[62]

Appraising the People's Will: Election Trends and Legal Wars

To help avoid "self-delusion" and "conceptual flaws," Lieutenant General H.
R. McMaster recommended "thorough study of contemporary conflict in
historical perspective . . . to correct flawed thinking about the character of
conflict, help define future challenges to international security, and build
relevant military and civilian governmental capabilities to meet those challenges."[63] Studying will assist understanding of civil-military relations concerning the people's preferences involving the post-9/11 wars. Voting trends,
and legal challenges to foreign policy actions and activities demonstrate the
effectiveness of the relationship.

Election results of 2006, 2008, 2012, and 2016 served as bellwethers for
the people's feelings. After the failures in Iraq and the 2006 election contributed to the demise of Rumsfeld and the decision to prosecute the Iraq Surge
in 2007, Barack Obama was elected in 2008 with the mandate to restrain
military operations around the world and remove US forces from Afghanistan and Iraq. The premise that the government sets the war aims and the
military will carry them out continued to function: military forces followed
orders to carry out the painful process of partially dismantling the post-9/11
wars. As US forces departed Iraq, and then finished "retrograde" operations
with the intention of ending US combat operations by the end of 2014 in
Afghanistan,[64] a new phase began for post-9/11 wars.

Like Obama, Donald Trump was elected as an "anti-establishment" candidate. He gave strong indications of his intention to get out of "unnecessary" wars, including Afghanistan: "In 2012, he said the war was 'wasting
our money' . . . and called it 'a total disaster' . . . in 2013 he said 'we should
leave immediately.' President Donald Trump continued his criticism of the
war during the year and a half he campaigned for the White House."[65] By the
spring of 2016 Trump was the only candidate from all parties taking such a
negative view of the Afghan war, which did not harm him, especially among
rural voters—the same constituency that joins the all-volunteer military.[66] In
Trump's first speech before Congress, he "lamented that for the cost of the
Iraq and Afghanistan wars, 'we could have rebuilt our country—twice.'"[67] It
would be a worthy civil-military research effort to explore any associations
between former/current military personnel, who sacrificed the most in the
post-9/11 wars, and the voters that rebelled against the "Beltway establishment" to vote for Obama in 2008 and Trump in 2016.

When the American people oppose a war, they seem to direct their frus-
trations toward the government instead of the soldiers.[68] But respect and trust
for the military is not unconditional. For the Vietnam War, the "stalemate

strategy" that the United States adopted was ineffective: "Stalemate strategies that don't show rapid progress will soon eat away at public and domestic political support."[69] The dissuasion strategy currently being prosecuted by the US commander in Afghanistan is based on the belief that military pressure will enable the United States to attain a "political agreement" by compelling the Taliban to accept a compromise.[70] For Vietnam, the Johnson administration might have thought that public support was unconditional until millions of Americans took to the streets in mass protests across the United States and around the world beginning in 1967.[71] Antiwar protests since 9/11 remain muted for reasons that may not be fully understood.[72] Maybe it is because there is no draft and war casualties are so few within an all-volunteer military comprising less than 1 percent of the populace.[73]

Authorization for War

The importance of the citizen's role (passion) in the nation's security should not be underestimated. Military power depends on soldiers drawn from a willing and supportive people. Serving in harm's way for the country might not be honorable when more is asked of a few as little is asked of the majority.[74] The will to fight in wars, and its relationship to achieving proper war authorization from the people, is among the oldest lessons of civilizations. It accounts for the unprecedented military potency of the Mongol armies and the accomplishments of Genghis Khan; he went to great lengths to achieve buy-in and unwavering support from his people prior to waging military campaigns.[75] There is growing concern that no authorization is given for new incursions into Syria, Libya, Somalia, Niger, and other locations.[76] The approval given from the Obama and Trump administrations to expand post-9/11 military actions is based on the 2001 Authorization for the Use of Military Force that was initially intended for operations against Al Qa'ida.[77] Its viability to justify operations against a plethora of enemies is doubted.[78] The Taliban of 2020 may not be the same Taliban from 2001, just as the Al Qa'ida of 2020 may not be the same entity from 2001.[79]

 The legal status of the post-9/11 wars impacts the landpower triad more than it does the air and maritime services because field soldiers are physically committed over longer tours of duty in routine and intimate surroundings alongside their foreign partners to advise and assist ground forces and enable civil authorities, while often confronting hostile fire and face-to-face combat. In this way, operational transparency and accountability with the American people impacts soldier honor and integrity. Serving in a war that may not be considered legal or morally acceptable by a segment of the home population exposes military leaders and soldiers to legal and moral hazards. For example, reporting 11,000 soldiers in Afghanistan when only 8,400 were authorized or 500 soldiers in Syria when there were actually 2,000—while few in Congress were aware of US military involvement in Niger—are unsettling indicators of institutionalized ethical lapses.[80]

President Obama attempted to reconcile military actions with the law by developing a "Presidential Policy Guidance" in 2013 to provide a "set of rules" to "apply restraints on the use of lethal force outside areas of active hostilities." But the guidance was focused on specific circumstances for Yemen. With growing concern over the legality of the post-9/11 wars, the military must provide information to link the 9/11 attackers and enemies operating in Somalia, Yemen, Syria, Niger, Iraq, and elsewhere. The people, and their soldiers, must know who they are fighting and for what purpose.[81]

Americans appear to respect their military and admire its sacrifices, but it is not certain whether the citizenry would accept responsibility for any negative or catastrophic consequences resulting from the post-9/11 wars. Andrew Bacevich asserts that there is a "decoupling of the people from war waged in their name," as Cheyney Ryan and James Fallows describe a "chickenhawk nation" where "the vast majority of Americans are fond of war but have little interest in its sacrifices." Waging war is fine "as long as someone else is going."[82] With less than 1 percent of the citizenry serving in the military, there is concern about what the people perceive and deem important; do we understand the difference between popular fantasy and geopolitical reality?[83] Further, the prospect of "a widening and worrisome divide between the American public and its military" will remain if the people lack a realistic perspective of the limits of military power and the risks of waging limited wars.[84] Citizen misunderstanding may be leading to government mismanagement of military policies.

Tentative Conclusions

The Clausewitzian trinity helps to analyze the post-9/11 dystopian civil-military landscape. The people, with their government and military, share responsibility for the post-9/11 wars as they strive to maintain a balance of power and achieve agreement on war policies to maximize the state's diplomatic and military power "like an object suspended between three magnets."[85]

If operations against nonstate actors, insurgents, and terrorists continue for the foreseeable future, it is necessary for the trinity to reconcile several ambiguities.[86] First, debates between conventional versus unconventional warfare advocates require attention. Richard Kohn justifies this need:

"Very few of these threats can be countered by the high-tempo, high-technology conventional military power that has become the specialty—almost the monopoly—of the United States, shaped and sized to fight conventional wars against other nation-states."[87] If this is the "Age of the Commando" with "Top Secret missions, mythical warriors and a state of perpetual warfare," should conventional forces continue to dominate as unconventional wars multiply and persist?[88] The next QDR can learn from Rumsfeld's example. His Pentagon advanced a stunted military transformation during three years of irregular conflict. Soldiers received less than satisfactory assistance from a defense establishment beholden to special interests and a bureaucracy in stasis, enabling military conventionalists to dominate: "The top civilian and military leadership of each of the services must undertake a systematic effort to eradicate careerism, anti-intellectualism, and politicization of their officer corps—in other words, to change the organizational culture."[89] This requires an *intellectual* and *collegial* approach to military strategy, planning, and policy development.

Second, it is questionable that an all-volunteer system can provide enough ground forces to fight the post-9/11 wars while providing a strategic deterrent. As the military struggles to recruit, a lack of "passion" for the wars from the people persists.[90] Congress must decide what is required over the next generation to prevail in long wars. The quantity and quality of manpower required to sustain them may call into question the viability of the all-volunteer military.

Third, for the post-9/11 wars, when does "victory" lose its meaning? Strategists must work to adapt "military means to achieve desired political ends."[91] For the on-going and evolving limited wars, military planning requires some understanding of political calculations to identify achievable objectives.[92] To avoid miscalculations that result in credibility gaps, the responsibility to challenge civilian assumptions, when supporting foreign armies fighting insurgents, should rest with the leaders of the landpower triad.[93]

The United States is undecided about what to do with the post-9/11 wars. Dissuasion and stasis will not last forever in Afghanistan, Yemen, Somalia, Syria, and elsewhere. America's trinity will neither decide to pull out nor commit enough resources to pursue decisive outcomes.[94] Such inertia results from a combination of cultural awkwardness between the military and civilian spheres, ambivalence over legal authorities, difficulty determining the nature of the enemy, and military leadership in need of improved intellectual range.[95] As a pluralistic political system operates alongside an entrenched and vast military establishment, war powers threaten to emerge as a serious issue.[96] Until now, "the serial disappointments of Iraq and Afghanistan—the two longest wars in US history—had surprisingly little effect on the army's overall standing in the eyes of the American people and American elites . . . yet after more than a decade of continuous combat, what exactly did this army exist to do, either in its own eyes or in the nation's?"[97]

Notes

Epigraph: ABC News, "Transcript of George W. Bush's Acceptance Speech," Republican National Convention in Philadelphia, 3 August 2000, retrieved from: http://abcnews.go.com/Politics/story?id=123214&page=1.

1. For a discussion of the semantics of irregular warfare, see Huba Wass de Czege, "A Reflection on the Illogic of New Military Concepts," *Army Magazine,* May 2008, 19–23.

2. Referring to the triad, see Megan Scully, "U.S. Army Chief Seeks New 'Triad,'" *Defense News,* 13 December 2004, 1, 6; and Thomas P. M. Barnett, "The Monks of War," *Esquire,* March 2006, http://www.esquire.com/news-politics/a2290/iraq-war-petraeus-mattis-wallace/. For a description of the land force triad concept, see DoD, *Quadrennial Defense Review Report,* 6 February 2006, 5, 42–45.

3. See Beth Bailey and Richard H. Immerman, eds., *Understanding the U.S. Wars in Iraq and Afghanistan* (New York: New York Univ. Press, 2015), especially Stephen Biddle and Peter D. Feaver, "Assessing Strategic Choices in the War on Terror," 103–104; Lisa Mundey, "The Combatant Experiences," 175–178; Robert K. Brigham, "The Lessons and Legacies of the War in Iraq," 286–304; and Aaron B. O'Connell, "The Lessons and Legacies of the War in Afghanistan," 308–325.

4. Ben Hubbard and Michael R. Gordon, "U.S. War Footprint Grows, with No Endgame in Sight," *New York Times,* 30 March 2017, A1, A6; Editorial Board, "America's Forever Wars," *New York Times,* 22 October 2017, https://www.nytimes.com/2017/10/22/opinion/americas-forever-wars.html.

5. Carl von Clausewitz, *On War,* ed. and trans. Michael Howard and Peter Paret (Princeton: Princeton Univ. Press, 1989), 89.

6. B. H. Liddell Hart, *Strategy,* 2nd rev. ed. (New York: Meridian Books, 1991), 319–330.

7. Clausewitz, *On War,* 88–89.

8. Ibid., 89.

9. Alex Roland, "The Military-Industrial Complex: Lobby and Trope," in *The Long War: A New History of U.S. National Security Policy since World War II,* ed. Andrew J. Bacevich (New York: Columbia Univ. Press, 2007), 335–370.

10. Three books give a representation of the US political system for the Clausewitzian trinity: C. Wright Mills, *The Power Elite* (New York: Oxford Univ. Press, 1956), Samuel P. Huntington, *The Common Defense* (New York: Columbia Univ. Press, 1961), and Edward N. Luttwak, *The Pentagon and the Art of War* (New York: Simon and Schuster, 1985).

11. Luttwak, *The Pentagon and the Art of War*, 144–145.

12. See Mills, *The Power Elite*, and Roland, "The Military-Industrial Complex."

13. The three legs of the triad are complementary in their operational roles, missions, and functions. See DoD, *Quadrennial Defense Review Report* (2006), 42; and John C. Knie, "Special Forces Skills: Are They Special Enough?" (Carlisle Barracks, Pa.: US Army War College, April 2002); and Patricia M. Shields, "An American Perspective on 21st Century Expeditionary Mindset and Core Values: A Review of the Literature," in *Core Values and the Expeditionary Mindset: Armed Forces in Metamorphosis*, ed. Henrik Fürst and Gerhard Kummel (Baden-Baden, Germany: Nomos), 17–34.

14. Paul Yingling, "A Failure in Generalship," *Armed Forces Journal* (1 May 2007): 16–23, 46. Also see Thomas E. Ricks, "Army Officer Accuses Generals of 'Intellectual and Moral Failures,'" *Washington Post*, 27 April 2010.

15. Barbara W. Tuchman, *The March of Folly* (New York: Ballantine Books, 1984), 314–315, 326. Also H. R. McMaster, *Dereliction of Duty: Lyndon Johnson, Robert McNamara, the Joint Chiefs of Staff, and the Lies that Led to Vietnam* (New York: HarperCollins, 1997), 311–314, 325–332.

16. William C. Westmoreland, *A Soldier Reports* (New York: Doubleday, 1976), 412.

17. Tuchman, *The March of Folly*, 320.

18. Donald S. Travis, "US Progress Reports for the Vietnam War: A Study of the Hamlet Evaluation System and the Enemy Order of Battle" (Master's thesis, University of Louisville, 1990), 16–17, 78–79, http://www.dtic.mil/docs/citations/ADA226232.

19. Tuchman, *The March of Folly*, 319–321, 336–338, 346–347. Also see Robert K. Brigham, *Iraq, Vietnam, and the Limits of American Power* (New York: Public Affairs, 2006), 42–43.

20. Westmoreland, *A Soldier Reports*, 414. Westmoreland explained that the US Army anticipated guerrilla war.

21. Tuchman, *The March of Folly*, 332–333. Also see Luttwak, *The Pentagon and the Art of War*, 40–43.

22. Five books published since 2011 provide arguments on both sides of the debate: Max Boot, *The Road Not Taken: Edward Landsdale and the American Tragedy in Vietnam* (New York: Liveright, 2018); Gian Gentle, *Wrong Turn: America's Deadly Embrace of Counterinsurgency* (New York: New Press, 2013); Andrew Mackay and Steve Tatham, *Behavioural Conflict: Why Understanding People and Their Motivations Will Prove Decisive in Future Conflict* (Essex: Military Studies Press, 2011); Peter R. Mansoor, *Surge: My Journey with General David Petraeus and the Remaking of the Iraq War* (New Haven, Conn.: Yale Univ. Press, 2013); and Douglas Porch, *Counterinsurgency: Exposing the Myths of the New Way of War* (Cambridge: Cambridge Univ. Press, 2013).

23. Conrad C. Crane, "Military Strategy in Afghanistan and Iraq," in Bailey and Immerman, eds., *Understanding the U.S. Wars in Iraq and Afghanistan*, 125.

24. Charles Krauthammer, "The New Bush Doctrine," *Cincinnati Enquirer,* 10 June 2001, F2, http://www.chron.com/opinion/editorials/article/Krauthammer-The-Bush-doctrine-new-2055304.php.

25. Charles Krauthammer, "We Don't Peacekeep," *Washington Post,* 18 December 2001, https://www.washingtonpost.com/archive/opinions/2001/12/18/we-dont-peacekeep/45dd2154-c2ac-474a-a9ca-03499d0a0c0e/?utm_term=.5102576805c7.

26. Dale R. Herspring, *Rumsfeld's Wars* (Lawrence: Univ. Press of Kansas, 2008), xv–xvi, 6–7.

27. George H. Quester, "The Politics Of Conventional Warfare in an Unconventional Age," in Bacevich, ed., *The Long War,* 126–132; Andrew Bacevich, *Breach of Trust* (New York: Holt, 2013), 91–95; Roberto Suro, "Quick Strike Forces Urged for Military," *Washington Post,* 13 June 2001, A1, A18.

28. DoD, *Quadrennial Defense Review Report,* 30 September 2001.

29. James Kurth, "Variations on the American Way of War," in Bacevich, ed., *The Long War,* 85–91. Also see Herspring, *Rumsfeld's Wars,* 22–44; and Bacevich, *Breach of Trust,* 91–99.

30. This is called "catastrophic success." See Steve Coll, *Directorate S: The CIA and America's Secret Wars in Afghanistan and Pakistan* (New York: Penguin, 2018), 100–112.

31. Herspring, *Rumsfeld's Wars,* xiii–xv.

32. Eric Schmitt, "Threats and Responses: Military Spending; Pentagon Contradicts General on Iraq Occupation Force's Size," *New York Times,* 28 February 2003.

33. Herspring, *Rumsfeld's Wars,* 46. Also see Bradley Graham, *By His Own Rules: The Ambitions, Successes, and Failures of Donald Rumsfeld* (New York: Public Affairs, 2009), 383–386, 412.

34. Hearing before the Committee on Armed Services, House of Representatives (H.A.S.C. No. 108–38) (Washington, DC: Government Printing Office, 2005), 15 July 2004, 30, 36, 40–41. Also see Lisa Burgess, "General: U.S. Didn't Plan for Iraqi Insurgency," *Stars and Stripes,* 16 July 2004, 3, and Graham, *By His Own Rules,* 382–385.

35. Colonel Stephen D. Kidder (Ret.) to author via e-mail, 6 July 2017.

36. Insurgents and criminals murdered thousands of skilled and educated Iraqi citizens in Iraq between 2003 and 2006. A sample of news reports by John Ward Anderson of the *Washington Post* helps to illustrate: "They Tell Me They've Assassinated My Brother," 31 October 2005; "Dozens Die in Violence in Iraq," 3 November 2005; "Iraqi Checkpoints Still a Target," 5 November 2005; "Troops Fend off Attacks in West," 8 November 2005.

37. DoD, *Quadrennial Defense Review Report* (2006), 42–51. For an analysis of the QDR, see Jason Sherman, "U.S. Revises Threat Scenarios," *Defense News,* 22 November 2004, 1, 8.

38. Sherman, "U.S. Revises Threat Scenarios."

39. DoD, *Quadrennial Defense Review Report* (2006), 22–24.

40. On transparency in military operations, see Mansoor, *Surge,* 117–119.

41. Regarding the severe conditions in Iraq, see note 36 above. Also see David S. Cloud and Thom Shanker, "Despite Politics, Logistics Pinning down U.S. in Iraq," *New York Times,* 14 May 2006, 10; and Ann Scott Tyson, "Pentagon Issues Dire Look at End of '06 in Iraq," *Washington Post,* 15 March 2007, A15. For a concise history of the war in Afghanistan, see Helene Cooper, "Attacks Belie U.S. Optimism in Afghan War," *New York Times,* 30 January 2018, A1, A6.

42. Dan Balz, "Democrats Take House," *Washington Post,* 8 November 2006. Also see Graham, *By His Own Rules,* 2–9, 650–656.

43. Brigham, "The Lessons and Legacies of the War in Iraq," 291–304; Mansoor, *Surge,* 5–33, 47.

44. Thom Shanker, "New Strategy Vindicates Ex-Army Chief Shinseki," *New York Times,* 12 January 2007. Also see Michael Abramowitz and Robin Wright, "Bush to Add 20,000 Troops in an Effort to Stabilize Iraq," *Washington Post,* 11 January 2007, A1, A11.

45. Michael Abramowitz, Robin Wright, and Thomas E. Ricks, "With Iraq Speech, Bush to Pull Away From His Generals," *Washington Post,* 10 January 2007, A1, A10. Also see Sudarsan Raghavan and Joshua Partlow, "U.S. Airstrikes Back Troops in Baghdad Clash," *Washington Post,* 10 January 2007, A1, A10.

46. Graham, *By His Own Rules,* 650–656. Also see Shanker, "New Strategy Vindicates Ex-Army Chief Shinseki."

47. Stop-loss policies added an Orwellian flavor to the all-volunteer military. Numerous news reports published in 2007–2008 make reference to the multiple tours of soldiers. Rumsfeld even considered filling Iraq ministry support positions with military retirees and reservists due to the lack of support from the other US government departments. See Graham, *By His Own Rules,* 651–652.

48. Bacevich calls the two factions "Crusaders and Conservatives." See also Andrew Bacevich, "The Petraeus Doctrine," *The Atlantic,* October 2008, 17–20, 18.

49. Morris Janowitz, *The Professional Soldier* (New York: Free Press, 1971), xxxvii–xlvi.

50. Ibid., 258–279, 303–321.

51. Ibid., 304–311. Mackay and Tatham take the pragmatist approach in their book *Behavioural Conflict.*

52. Porch, *Counterinsurgency,* 202. Also see Gentile, *Wrong Turn,* 105–110.

53. Porch, *Counterinsurgency,* 303.

54. Ibid., 289–317.

55. Gentile, *Wrong Turn,* 140–141.

56. Ibid., 6, 28–33, 87–92, 141. Also see Porch, *Counterinsurgency,* 289, 300–303.

57. Yingling, "A Failure in Generalship." Also see Antulio Joseph Echevarria, *Toward an American Way of War* (Carlisle Barracks, Pa.: US Army War College Strategic Studies Institute, 2004), 12–18.

58. Thomas Donnelly and Frederick W. Kagan, "The Proud, the Few," *New York Post,* 25 May 2008. Also see Mackay and Tatham, *Behavioural Conflict,* 52, 102.

59. Charlotte F. Blatt, "Operational Success, Strategic Failure: Assessing the 2007 Iraq Troop Surge," *Parameters* 47, no. 1 (spring 2017): 55

60. Boot, *The Road Not Taken*, 526–527, 601. Also see Mackay and Tatham, *Behavioural Conflict*, 25, 135, 143–144.

61. See Patricia M. Shields and Joseph L. Soeters, "Peaceweaving: Jane Addams, Positive Peace, and Public Administration," *American Review of Public Administration* 47, no. 3 (April 2017): 323–339. Also see Boot, *The Road Not Taken*, xxxix, 252, 526–530, 599–605; Mackay and Tatham, *Behavioural Conflict*; and Mansoor, *Surge*, 108–116.

62. Thomas Gibbons-Neff, "Training Quick and Staffing Unfinished, Army Units Brace for Surging Taliban," *New York Times*, 27 January 2018, A6.

63. McMaster, "On War: Lessons to Be Learned," *Survival* 50, no. 1 (February–March 2008): 19–20, 25–28.

64. Coll, *Directorate S*, 668–669.

65. Philip Rucker and Robert Costa, "Troop Increase Planned in Afghan War," *Washington Post*, 22 August 2017, A1, A11. Also see Mark Landler and Michael R. Gordon, "President Cedes Afghan Strategy to the Pentagon," *New York Times*, 19 June 2017, A10. "Mr. Trump in 2013 favored a full withdrawal from Afghanistan, calling the war a waste of money." See *New York Times* staff editorial, "Afghanistan Is Now Mr. Trump's War," 10 March 2017, A28.

66. See Dale Balz, "Support for Trump Heavy, Not Uniform," *Washington Post*, 19 June 2017, A1, A7. The areas of the country that voted for Trump are the same that yield the greater proportion of recruits for the all-volunteer military. One key factor is "urbanicity": 76 percent of the citizens who served in the military after 9/11 were from suburban or rural areas, while 24 percent were from urban ones. See Amy Lutz, "Who Joins the Military: A Look at Race, Class, and Immigration Status," *Journal of Political and Military Sociology* 36, no. 2 (winter 2008): 177–178. Also see Tim Kane, *Who Bears the Burden, Demographic Characteristics of U.S. Military Recruits Before and After 9/11* (Washington, DC: Heritage Foundation Center for Data Analysis, 7 November 2005), 2, 3, 12. Trump won the rural vote over Hillary Clinton 62–34 percent, and he also won the suburban vote 50–45 percent. Also see Skye Gould and Rebecca Harrington, "7 Charts Show Who Propelled Trump to Victory," *Business Insider*, 10 November 2016.

67. Steve Chapman, "Trump Should End the US War in Afghanistan," *Chicago Tribune*, 2 March 2017.

68. David Farber asserts that it is "simply not true . . . that protesters often spat on returning soldiers or called them baby killers" during the Vietnam War. See David Farber, "Fighting (Against) the Wars in Iraq and Afghanistan," in Bailey and Immerman, eds., *Understanding the U.S. Wars in Iraq and Afghanistan*, 194, 204–211.

69. David Elliot, "What Trump Needs to Learn From Vietnam," *New York Times*, 17 September 2017, 5.

70. Missy Ryan and Greg Jaffe, "U.S. Poised to Ramp up Taliban Fight," *Wash-*

ington Post, 9 May 2017, A1, A10. Also see Thomas Gibbons-Neff, Pamela Constable, and Sayed Salahuddin, "Mattis Visits a Shaken Afghanistan," *Washington Post,* 15 April 2017, A1, A9.

71. See Tuchman, *The March of Folly,* 311–356. Also see Travis, "US Progress Reports for the Vietnam War," 25–27.

72. According to Farber, antiwar protests were muted because of the initial successes in Iraq in 2003 and the respect given to the all-volunteer military force. This might have carried into 2004–2008, but these factors are no longer as relevant. See Farber, "Fighting (Against) the Wars in Iraq and Afghanistan," 204–205.

73. Bacevich is cited in Editorial Board, "America's Forever Wars," *New York Times,* 22 October 2017, https://www.nytimes.com/2017/10/22/opinion/americas-forever-wars.html.

74. Bacevich, *Breach of Trust,* 10–14, 120–123, 193–196.

75. See Jack Weatherford, *Genghis Khan and the Making of the Modern World* (New York: Three Rivers Press, 2004).

76. See Rukmini Callimachi, Helene Cooper, Eric Schmitt, Alan Blinder, and Thomas Gibbons-Neff, "A Risky Patrol, A Desert Ambush and New Anguish Over 'an Endless War,'" *New York Times,* 18 February 2018, 1, 8. Also see Charlie Savage, "Lawmakers to Revisit 9/11 Law Authorizing Ever-Expanding War," *New York Times,* 29 October 2017, 19; Charlie Savage, Eric Schmitt, and Mark Mazzetti, "Obama Expanding War with Al Qaeda to Include Somalia," *New York Times,* 28 November 2016, A8; *Washington Post* editorial, "An Overdue Debate," *Washington Post,* 14 September 2017, A16; Bruce Ackerman, "Trump, Congress and Syria," *New York Times,* 8 April 2017, A23; Stephen Vladeck, "Take Guantanamo Off the Table," *New York Times,* 2 November 2017, A23.

77. 107th Congress, Public Law 107-40, "To authorize the use of United States Armed Forces against those responsible for the recent attacks launched against the United States," 18 September 2001, https://www.congress.gov/107/plaws/publ40/PLAW-107publ40.pdf

78. See Editorial Board, "America's Forever Wars," *New York Times,* 22 October 2017, https://www.nytimes.com/2017/10/22/opinion/americas-forever-wars.html. Also see Cory A. Booker and Oona A. Hathaway, "A Syria Plan That Breaks the Law," *New York Times,* 24 January 2018, A23; and Savage, "Lawmakers to Revisit 9/11 Law Authorizing Ever-Expanding War."

79. Mackay and Tatham, *Behavioural Conflict,* 9, 25, 102, 158. Also see Savage, "Lawmakers to Revisit 9/11 Law Authorizing Ever-Expanding War."

80. Regarding the issue of transparency in Niger, Afghanistan, and Syria, see the following: Callimachi, Cooper, et al., "A Risky Patrol, a Desert Ambush and New Anguish Over 'an Endless War'"; Thomas Gibbons-Neff, "U.S. Military to Conceal Afghan War Statistics," *New York Times,* 31 October 2017, A8; Helene Cooper, "Pentagon, Seeking Transparency, Says 11,000 U.S. Troops Are in Afghanistan," *New York Times,* 31 August 2017, A8; Gardiner Harris, "Tillerson Says U.S. Troops Will Remain in Syria Beyond the Battle with ISIS," *New York Times,* 18 January 2018, A8;

Editorial Staff, "Syria Is Now Mr. Trump's War," *New York Times*, 20 January 2018, A22; Michael R. Gorgon, "More U.S. Troops May Be Needed Against ISIS in Syria, Central Command Says," *New York Times*, 23 February 2017, A6.

81. Hubbard and Gordon, "U.S. War Footprint Grows, with No Endgame in Sight," A1, A6; Charlie Savage et al., "Obama Expanding War with Al Qaeda to Include Somalia," *New York Times*, 28 November 2016, A8; Charlie Savage, "Lawsuit Seeks Rationale for Syria Strike," *New York Times*, 9 May 2017, A15; Staff Editorial, "Congress's Duty in the War with ISIS," *New York Times*, 26 March 2017, 8.

82. Bacevich, *Breach of Trust*, 32. Also see Cheyney Ryan, *The Chickenhawk Syndrome* (Lanham, Md.: Rowman and Littlefield, 2009), ix, x. Also see James Fallows, "The Tragedy of the American Military," *The Atlantic*, January/February 2015, 72–80, 83–90, 76.

83. See Sam Lebovic, "Limited War in the Age of Total Media," and Andrew C. McKevitt, "Watching War Made Us Immune," in Bailey and Immerman, eds., *Understanding the U.S. Wars in Iraq and Afghanistan*, 220–237; 238–258. Also see Karl W. Eikenberry and David M. Kennedy, "Americans and Their Military, Drifting Apart," *New York Times*, 26 May 2013.

84. See Thom Shanker, "At West Point, a Focus on Trust," *New York Times*, 22 May 2011, 18. Admiral Mike Mullen warned: "A people uninformed about what they are asking the military to endure is a people inevitably unable to fully grasp the scope of responsibilities our Constitution levies upon them."

85. Clausewitz, *On War*, 89. For perspective on the interplay of elements of the trinity, see pages 75–88.

86. Brian Castner, "Still Fighting, and Dying, in the Forever War," *New York Times*, 12 March 2017, SR 3.

87. Richard Kohn, "Tarnished Brass: Is the U.S. Military Profession in Decline?" *World Affairs Journal* (spring 2009): 73–83.

88. Matt Gallagher, "Welcome to the Age of the Commando," *New York Times*, 31 January 2016, Sunday Review, 6–7. Also see Dan Lamothe, "Conventional Troops' Role Changing in Afghanistan," *Washington Post*, 6 July 2017, A7. Michael E. O'Hanlon advocates for little change in how the US land forces should operate: "The Army of the future should not be radically different from the Army of today." See Michael E. O'Hanlon, *The Future of Land Warfare* (Washington, DC: Brookings Institution Press, 2015), 167–172. Also see John R. Deni, "Land Power Is Still Necessary," *National Interest*, 4 June 2013; and Michael Allen Hunzeker and Alexander Lanoszka, "Landpower and American Credibility," *Parameters* 45, no. 4 (winter 2015–2016): 17–26.

89. Kohn, "Tarnished Brass." Professional military officers are expected to possess "intellectualized skill, mastery of which requires intense study." Samuel P. Huntington, *The Soldier and the State* (Cambridge, Mass.: Belknap Press of Harvard Univ. Press, 1957), 15. For a discussion on intellectual broadening, see Jason W. Warren, "The Centurion Mindset and the Army's Strategic Leader Paradigm," *Parameters* 45, no. 3 (autumn 2015): 27–38.

90. "The greatest error the statesman can make is to commit his nation to a great conflict without mobilizing popular passions to a level commensurate with the stakes of the conflict." Yingling, "A Failure in Generalship," 17.

91. Janowitz, *The Professional Soldier,* 264–265.

92. William E. Rapp, "Ensuring Effective Military Voice, *Parameters* 46, no. 4 (winter 2016–2017): 13–25.

93. See C. Dale Walton, "The War without a Strategy: Presidents, the Pentagon, and Problems in Civil-Military Relations since the 9/11 Attacks," in Stephen J. Cimbala, *Civil-Military Relations in Perspective: Strategy, Structure, and Policy* (New York: Routledge, 2016), 107–109; and Bacevich, *Breach of Trust,* 51, 58, 110–112. Also see Coll, *Directorate S.*

94. Landler and Gordon, "President Cedes Afghan Strategy to the Pentagon," A1, A10. Also see Pamela Constable and Sayed Salahuddin, "Setbacks Cloud Afghan Strategy," *Washington Post,* 19 June 2017, A1, A14.

95. Warren, "The Centurion Mindset and the Army's Strategic Leader Paradigm," 27–38. Also see Chalmers Johnson, *Nemesis* (New York: Holt, 2007), 19–22.

96. Aside from the numerous references cited above, see *New York Times* editorial, "The Groundhog Day War," *New York Times,* 29 May 2017, A20.

97. Bacevich, *Breach of Trust,* 110; Also see Bacevich, "The Never-Ending War," *New York Times Book Review,* 18 February 2018, 9.

PART II

The Projection of US Landpower

5

The Tortured Path to Strategic Failure
US Landpower in Iraq, 2003–2011

Frank Sobchak

During the post-9/11 conflicts, policymakers shouldered the US military with considerable responsibilities, many of which military theorists believe fall outside the conventional understanding of warfare. In broad terms, the uniformed services have had to fight traditional armies, tamp down civil wars and ethnic conflicts, battle insurgents, construct the infrastructure and institutions of a modern nation state, organize and secure elections, and advise heads of state in democratic governance—among a myriad of other responsibilities. "Nation-building," a term actively resisted for the greater part of the 1990s and the early phases of the Afghanistan and Iraq wars, became a critical component of national strategy and was seen as a way to inoculate failed or failing states from becoming terrorist sanctuaries. As the vast majority of these duties fell primarily on the backs of soldiers and marines, these wars have been primarily landpower conflicts.

The Iraq War has been fully representative of these trends. What started with a lightning invasion that decapitated the regime of Saddam Hussein quickly devolved into a "long, hard slog" of an occupation and insurgency, only to morph again into a brutal civil war.[1] After a strategic rebalancing of ways and means by a series of operations often referred to as the Surge, American forces arrested Iraq's nihilistic descent and the country stabilized by the end of 2008. With Iraqi and American populations having lost patience with the mission, the United States withdrew its military forces in 2011, setting the stage for the embers of chaos to ignite again. Ultimately, after spending in the realm of $2 trillion, losing 4,500 American lives, and causing between 200,000 and 1 million Iraqi deaths, the war appears to have resulted in a strategic failure for the United States, at least when reviewing the postwar geopolitical situation at the time of this chapter's publication.[2]

Some have argued that the US mission in Iraq was doomed from the start, positing that nation-building expeditions and interventions in civil wars are strategic folly. Such arguments of inevitability are simplistic and do not fairly explain the relative tranquility that had been established by the summer of 2008—nor do they examine the decisions that were made in the post-Surge period that contributed to Iraq's unravelling. Such a conclusion was not foretold, and the Iraq War ended in defeat due to a series of bad decisions, some consequential, some bordering on catastrophic.

That is not to say that it was wise to invade Iraq in the first place. It was not, and the decision to go to war will likely be deemed by historians to be one of the worst foreign policy decisions in the history of the Republic. But, beginning after the George W. Bush administration's decision to go to war, if different decisions had been made the United States could have achieved its strategic objective of a stable Iraq with a representative government able to maintain domestic order and deny Iraq as a safe haven for terrorists.[3] It would not have been easy, and it would have required a commitment far beyond what the United States ultimately made, but it was possible. It is worth noting that even with numerous and sizeable mistakes, the US military—in this case mainly the Army and Marine Corps—nearly was successful. The Iraq War, which was recognized by both Al Qa'ida and the United States as the central theater in a conflict that spanned the globe, reflected the post-9/11 state of American landpower in many ways, and its failure overshadowed other operational and tactical successes.

Some of the consequential decisions that ultimately led to failure are well known, such as the decision to begin the war with an inadequate postwar plan and the irrational decisions made in the immediate aftermath of the fall of the regime. Other decisions are less well known, but contributed just as equally or more to the eventual failure—the decision to pursue a transition strategy for two years, which put increased responsibility on Iraqis when they were least able to accept it; the decision not to intervene in the 2010 parliamentary election when Prime Minister Nuri al Maliki subverted the democratic process; and the tortured decision to withdraw fully all military forces at the end of 2011. Finally, the absence of a definitive policy on how to address external malignant actors, specifically Iran and Syria, also played a considerable role.

Initial Planning and Reactions to Regime Collapse

A series of decisions for the invasion of Iraq and its aftermath greatly complicated US efforts to achieve its national objectives and set the stage for future problems. After considerable deliberations between USCENTCOM, the Office of the Secretary of Defense (OSD), and the White House, the final proposal called for a relatively light ground force component for the invasion, a near simultaneous air and ground attack, and few forces or detailed planning dedicated to the post-regime Iraq. This war plan that the invasion force executed in March 2003 focused on defeating Iraq's Republican Guard, putting military pressure on Baghdad until the regime collapsed from within, and transitioning the administration of the country quickly to an interim authority.[4]

Decision-makers believed the United States would not require a large number of forces because of the seemingly successful precedent set in Afghanistan, where a small contingent of SOF and airpower had decapitated the Taliban regime quickly. This assumption also flowed from a belief held by many civilian leaders that a Revolution in Military Affairs (RMA) centered on information and technology had upended the normal calculus involved in land conflicts. The smaller force package would also allow for the operation to be launched more quickly, thereby minimizing the possibility that Iraq could use chemical weapons on coalition forces as they staged and massed for the invasion.[5] At the same time, planners assumed that the bulk of the Iraqi army would not fight and could be recalled to active service after the regime fell. The result of these assumptions was a small post-invasion force.[6] Some architects of the war, particularly those in OSD, believed US forces would be welcomed as liberators and would not need to conduct large-scale security operations. This tacked conveniently with the Army's institutional bias toward conventional combat operations and its distaste for stability and support operations, further helping to minimize the size of invasion and occupation forces.

The consequences of these assumptions were considerable. When military leaders determined on 9 April 2003 that organized resistance in Baghdad had disappeared along with Saddam Hussein and his regime, the war, in fact, was far from over. Much of the country remained unsecured—including Anbar and Iraq's northern provinces—and some parts of the country had not seen any coalition forces at all. Furthermore, since the regime had collapsed far more rapidly than any of the military plans had envisioned, many organizations and units designated to manage the transition between major combat operations and its aftermath had not arrived in theater.[7] Secretary of Defense Donald Rumsfeld's decision to not deploy the entire 1st Cavalry Division and quickly redeploy Marine Corps elements greatly exacerbated the challenge of insufficient forces.[8]

Rumsfeld also created an ad hoc headquarters (Combined Joint Task Force-7 [CJTF-7]) to head the Iraq theater and selected the Army's newest three-star general, Lieutenant General Ricardo Sanchez, as its commander.

The decision to build a new headquarters, rather than use a standing organization such as the experienced Coalition Forces Land Component Command (CLFCC), appears to have been made at least in part due to a personality conflict.[9] As the new organization was stood up from scratch, it suffered greatly from personnel shortages and staff capability mismatches, further hobbling coalition efforts to gain control of a deteriorating situation. Such an environment provided the space for insurgent networks to incubate. The general lack of security also resulted in porous borders, allowing Sunni extremists to flood into Anbar and Ninewa in search of jihad, and facilitated Iranian efforts to assist Shi'a militants opposing coalition forces.

The assumptions had political implications as well. The coalition had intended a surgical regime change, which quickly deteriorated into the general collapse of the Iraqi state, creating a power vacuum and a breakdown of law and order. In the absence of any authority that could govern or maintain order, Iraqis looted the public infrastructure and carried out reprisal attacks as ethno-sectarian factions jockeyed for power. The coalition did not have enough ground forces to effectively intervene in this chaos and made matters worse by reacting slowly to events with what it did have available. Although the coalition military eventually regained some measure of control in many urban areas, the damage was done. Iraqis, who had expected the United States quickly to reestablish order and improve standards of life, became disillusioned as the essentials of their state evaporated and social order began to disintegrate.[10]

Consequences of Early Coalition Decisions

A second set of contributing factors to the US strategic failure is generally well known. In the immediate aftermath of the collapse of Saddam's regime, the weakness of coalition transition plans became apparent as the impromptu Coalition Provisional Authority (CPA) made a series of catastrophic missteps. With little coordination, CPA Administrator L. Paul Bremer issued a pair of orders that would haunt ground forces for the remainder of the war.

These orders, de-Ba'athification of the Iraqi civil service and disbanding of the Iraqi army, severely hobbled coalition stabilization and reconstruction efforts because they removed the Iraqi civil servants and military personnel that coalition military leaders had hoped would keep the decrepit Iraqi state functioning. The decisions also unemployed overnight a large number of Iraqis, especially many Sunnis with military skills and training. No element of society was spared, and up to forty thousand schoolteachers and administrators were dismissed, effectively crippling the Iraqi education system as well. Unable to support their families and alienated by the punitive decisions, many Iraqis were drawn to the insurgency.[11] Even worse, coalition leaders intensified the backlash to the orders by seating a new Shi'a-majority Iraqi Governing Council comprised largely of expatriates, many of whom went to work with sectarian cudgels.

One other early decision had long-term consequences. In the fall of 2003, US strategic leaders committed fully to transfer sovereignty to the Iraqis in June 2004—an action that was originally intended to occur years later.[12] Lieutenant General Sanchez opposed the decision and strongly recommended that more time should be allotted in order to prepare the shattered Iraqi state to take control of its own destiny. But given Iraqi and international opposition to the US occupation, strategic leaders set a time line that would take Iraq from independence from the Ba'ath regime to an approved constitution in roughly thirty months. By comparison, the fledgling United States—a nation with a tradition of democracy and a robust civil society—spent twelve years navigating a similar path.

This decision had two major consequences. First, once sovereignty was returned to Iraqis, the United States—especially its ground forces—lost a large degree of control over the construction of that state's institutions. Coalition commanders were unable to select or replace Iraqi military commanders easily, oversight of reconstruction funds became difficult, and preventing corruption and graft in contracts became nearly impossible.[13] Second, the decision to transfer sovereignty early created an abridged electoral path. Consistent with US military doctrine, political and military leaders believed that elections would have a stabilizing influence in Iraq, imbuing legitimacy on the host-nation government that would take the wind out of the insurgency's sails.[14] However, as other post-9/11 wars have shown, elections are not always stabilizing events. In fact, the Iraqi elections of 2005 exacerbated the ethnosectarian conflict and contributed to the sectarian civil war that followed. The haste with which the United States carried out that process heightened the stakes of each event by providing insufficient time for reconciliation.

Casey in Command and the Transition Strategy

This series of bad decisions put Iraq on a downward spiral that culminated in April 2004, when nationwide Sunni and Shi'a uprisings surprised coalition military forces. Insurgents took control of Fallujah, temporarily cut coalition supply lines, and nearly overran a handful of isolated units. While the coalition quickly recovered tactically, the shock and intensity of the attacks had strategic consequences with the Americans, many of whom had assumed the war was nearly over and that the invasion's mission had been accomplished. Nearly simultaneously, the Abu Ghraib detention scandal broke in the international media, creating an information nightmare and an additional narrative to inspire jihadists to fight in Iraq.

Analyzing this tumultuous period, senior leaders in the Bush administration realized they had under-resourced the Iraq mission and that new leadership would be required. General George Casey replaced Sanchez, and his understaffed and improvised headquarters was disbanded and replaced by two more robust ones: one focused on the theater-strategic level and a second formed around a standing corps headquarters that focused on the operational level. Casey ushered in a new strategy: after clearing insurgent sanctuaries that threatened the pending elections, the COIN campaign would be progressively transitioned to the Iraqi government and security forces.[15]

The new strategy had several key components. While coalition forces held insurgents at bay, Military Transition Teams (MiTTs), would directly advise and assist the Iraqi police and army, preparing them to take responsibility for security matters. As Iraqi security forces became more numerous and capable, the coalition would downsize its military presence, which in turn would trigger the transfer of bases and territory to the Iraqis. Each transfer was meant to be conditions-based, but a decrease in presence was also meant to serve as a forcing function to ensure that Iraqis did not become too dependent on coalition forces. To underscore this change in strategy, General Casey emphasized to his commanders that their mission was "to help the Iraqis win, not to win it for the Iraqis."[16] In Casey's view, US leaders constantly had to guard against their units' tendency to fix problems that a host nation should correct itself. Solutions stemming from overzealous American military assistance would dissipate as soon as coalition forces departed. Warning against the dangers of creating Iraqi dependency on coalition military might, Casey noted that "the longer the coalition leads the fight, the more dependent the ISF becomes."[17]

The transition strategy was also meant to be a salve against the perceived danger of "antibodies" building up against a foreign military presence, an idea espoused by USCENTCOM commander General John Abizaid. This theory held that Iraq, like most of the Middle East, was highly xenophobic due to deep physical and psychological scars from colonialism, occupation, and western hegemony. Therefore, US forces in Iraq, no matter how benevolent, were equivalent to an infection that quickly would create "antibodies" among the Iraqi population that would seek to eliminate the foreign presence.[18] To minimize the number of antibodies created, the strategy held that the American footprint and presence should be reduced as quickly as possible to remove a principal force fueling the insurgency. To speed the goal of closing military bases, a detailed system was created, nicknamed "Iraqi BRAC" after the stateside US base realignment and closure commission, and across 2005 coalition forces closed thirty-one bases.[19] Coalition commanders called for a further decrease in coalition bases from 110 to 54 the next year.[20]

Troop reductions, which were driven by assessments of how the Iraqi army was performing, paralleled cuts in bases but occurred more slowly. In December 2005, General Casey made the first such reduction when he opted to decline two brigades scheduled to deploy in 2006. Although the decision reduced the number of brigades in Iraq to thirteen, Casey believed that he could cut even further, ultimately reaching only ten brigades by the end of the year.[21] His decision was grounded on the philosophical underpinnings of the transition strategy: fear of Iraqi dependency and the prevention of "antibodies." It was also based on faulty assessments that the successfully held Iraqi elections were stabilizing factors and that the Iraqi security forces had progressed significantly in capability. All of these beliefs would be proven to be false and Casey's decision to reduce forces would throw Iraq into dire crisis.

As US military leaders implemented the transition strategy, the ground in Iraq decisively shifted under them. Following the second battle of Fallujah in November 2004, Abu Musab Zarqawi rose to preeminence in the Sunni insurgency. Zarqawi and his Al Qa'ida in Iraq (AQI) aimed to provoke a civil war by carrying out a relentless terror campaign against the Iraqi Shi'a community.[22] Iraq's Shi'a population responded by turning to its own ruthless militias to protect its communities and strike back against Iraqi Sunnis, further escalating the sectarian conflict. After the seating of the government of Prime Minister Ibrahim al-Ja'afari in the spring of 2005, many of the Iraqi governance and security institutions the coalition was helping to build came under the control of sectarian Shi'a parties, which used those institutions for their own ends. As death squads from rival sects preyed upon civilians from the opposing confessional, Iraq slipped closer to full-blown civil war.

The simmering civil war exploded into the open with the February 2006 Samarra Mosque bombing, leaving a surge of violence in its wake. Coalition commanders conducted three sequential operations in Baghdad to try to quell the violence, but were unsuccessful. Elements of the Iraqi government became more deeply immersed in the civil war, and evidence of government complicity in the unlawful detention, torture, and killing of Sunni civilians became clearer. Yet, despite the mounting evidence showing that continuing the transition strategy was perilous, coalition commanders did not alter course from the premise that responsibility must be shifted to the Iraqis as quickly as possible.[23]

By the summer of 2006 the transition strategy had failed. As coalition forces withdrew from Iraqi population zones, they left a security vacuum that the warring parties' militants filled, to the detriment of the population. Consolidating on larger bases, units began to lose awareness of the security situation in the streets and neighborhoods of their areas of operations, undermining their ability to conduct counterinsurgency operations. This loss of situational awareness masked the growing danger of sectarian violence, a danger that coalition leaders compounded by deciding to reduce the number of brigades in Iraq during 2006. Accelerating the transition of security responsibility to Iraqi forces that themselves were complicit in sectarian violence only served as an accelerant to the civil war, as many Iraqis lost faith in their government and grudgingly decided to rely on sectarian militias for their security. Government functions collapsed as ministries became combatants themselves and ministerial officials lived and worked under siege. Provincial and local governments in large swaths of the country fell out of contact with the central government in Baghdad.[24]

The result of the transition strategy was that during its implementation the war in Iraq evolved from a relatively loose insurgency against the US-led coalition into a horrific ethno-sectarian civil war that tore at the fabric of Iraqi society and threatened Iraq's very existence as a unitary state. By the time coalition leaders realized in mid-2006 that the character of the conflict had changed, it was too late—the coalition did not have enough forces to suppress the escalating violence. Worse yet, two and a half more years of precious time had been spent without achieving comparable returns in progress.

The Surge

By the summer of 2006, the consequences of the transition strategy had become clear and President George W. Bush quietly instructed the National Security Council to begin looking for alternatives. After reviewing the options, Bush settled on a surge of additional military power in order to fix the ends and means imbalance, and he chose General David Petraeus to lead the effort.

Iraq's new commanders implemented a totally different strategy from Casey's transition plan, emphasizing that coalition forces focus on protecting the population rather than pushing Iraqis to take the lead. Protecting the population meant a reversal of Iraqi BRAC, and dozens of bases, often down to company and platoon size, were added in urban areas. Ultimately the new policy would result in a total of 495 US bases and installations spread across Iraq.[25] With the additional Surge forces bringing the number of brigades in

Iraq to twenty, the new outposts could be persistent and did not have to recede after coalition forces cleared an area of insurgents.[26] Rather than rely on compromised or ineffective Iraqi forces, the new strategy put American and coalition troops into the forefront to tamp down the drivers of sectarian conflict, another reversal of the transition strategy's central premises. Most of these measures reflected a renewed institutional support for COIN practices across the Army, as evinced by the December 2006 issuance of *Field Manual 3-24*.

At the same time, an organic phenomenon served to magnify the effects of the new strategy. By the summer of 2007, many Sunnis realized that they were fighting a multi-front war against AQI, the coalition, Shi'a militias, and government forces. Faced with the prospects of catastrophic defeat and tiring of the abuses and extremism of AQI, many Sunnis chose to join forces with the coalition. This movement, named the Awakening, earned the unequivocal support of senior coalition leaders, who realized the advantages of the potential alignment and pushed their subordinates to help provide organization and support.[27] Taking advantage of the timely opportunity was not a uniformly popular decision. For some of their subordinates, providing support—even paying the irregular forces—was extremely difficult, knowing that most of the Awakening leaders were former insurgents who had blood on their hands. But supporting the Awakening provided even more manpower to coalition commanders, and it offered the hope of political reconciliation.[28] In sum, these changes reflected an entirely new strategy. Ends and means had been realigned by the addition of forces, while the emphasis on COIN measures and reversal of transition strategy policies amounted to revolutionary changes in ways.

The long-term impact of these changes was striking. Although casualties initially increased as coalition forces fought to regain terrain that had been ceded to insurgents and militias, by the fall of 2008 the security situation had changed so drastically that it was almost unrecognizable when compared to early 2007. US casualties had fallen so low that noncombat-related deaths began to approach the number of combat casualties, and in September and November 2008 they exceeded the amount killed in action.[29] The number of security incidents, always a difficult metric to judge at a micro scale, but useful at a macro scale to note trends, similarly plummeted to the lowest levels of the war.[30] Weekly averages dropped below two hundred incidents, and individual days began to pass without any civilian casualties, indicators that had not occurred since before the 2003 invasion.[31] In many places across Iraq, life began to return to normal as the clouds of civil war receded.

Yet the successes of the Surge would not be capitalized upon, as the effort had come too late. Having spent four years searching for an effective strategy and the correct balance of ends and means, the Washington and Baghdad "clocks" that General Petraeus had worried about had expired. The patience of the American and Iraqi publics had ended and American commitment and interest would wane precipitously after 2008.[32]

The 2010 Parliamentary Election

The US decision to stand aside while Prime Minister Nuri al Maliki subverted the democratic process and manipulated the 2010 parliamentary election results reflected this loss of interest and commitment. Ultimately, more than any other decision, it would prove to be catastrophic and unrecoverable. It put the United States on a path to strategic failure as it set the stage for a complete withdrawal and provided the spark that would reignite the Iraqi civil war.

In Iraq's March 2010 parliamentary election, Ayad Allawi, a secular Shi'a politician leading a mixed (but majority Sunni) party, had finished first in the voting.[33] Without a majority of votes, Allawi and his party had to assemble a coalition in order to form a new government, but his victory meant Allawi was to be given the first chance to form a new government. Maliki and his allies, however, had other plans. First, Maliki secured a ruling from Iraq's constitutional court that whatever parties could form the largest post-electoral bloc would win the right to form a government, regardless of the election results. The decision was legally questionable and, given the chief justice's personal and political connections to Maliki, many Sunnis and coalition officials saw the ruling as overt sectarianism and illegitimate. Maliki took the matter further by publicly denouncing Iraq's electoral commission and signaling his intention not to recognize Allawi's victory. Maliki sent threatening messages to several commission members and attempted to obtain arrest warrants against them, leading General Raymond Odierno, the theater commander, to consider providing security for the electoral commission's headquarters.[34] Maliki also used Iraq's de-Ba'athification committee to disqualify scores of candidates from Allawi's party, thereby hurting Allawi's chances of gaining a parliamentary majority.[35] General Odierno was so concerned with the direction Maliki seemed to be following that he consistently recommended that action should be taken and warned Washington that Maliki might stage "a rolling coup d'état of the Iraqi state."[36] Odierno was not alone in his warnings, as Maliki had long shown a disquieting trend toward sectarianism and authoritarianism.[37]

Yet in the midst of Maliki's election chicanery, the United States chose to do nothing. Contrary to Odierno's view, many senior Obama administration officials believed Maliki's return to the premiership was the best outcome for US interests. As a majority Shi'a country, the prevailing wisdom held that Iraq should be governed by a Shi'a majority coalition, and Maliki as the strongest of the Shi'a leaders was thought be the most reliable US partner. Others believed it was inappropriate for the United States to meddle too deeply in internal Iraqi affairs. Iraq was a sovereign nation, and trying to affect an outcome was something that could only be done at great peril.[38] Without US support, Allawi was unable to assemble a majority coalition and Maliki instead retained the premiership. It would be a most consequential decision, with its effects playing out across the months before and after the US withdrawal.

The Withdrawal and Aftermath

One of the first repercussions of the decision to stay with Maliki was that US negotiations for a residual force became significantly more difficult. Senior military leaders had long considered the retention of a sizable residual force essential to future success in Iraq, with General Odierno estimating that at least twenty-five thousand personnel would be required, and General Lloyd Austin estimating that an absolute minimum presence would be at least a full division.[39] Seeing a continued American presence as a potential brake on his efforts to consolidate power, Maliki was extremely reluctant to support requests of immunity for military personnel—a red line for US negotiators. A lackluster effort to obtain agreements on the size of a residual force also contributed to the US inability to maintain personnel in Iraq after 2011. The Obama administration, having won office at least in part on a platform of withdrawing troops from Iraq, vetoed the large numbers proposed by its military commanders. Compromise proposals resulted in troop numbers that were too small for Iraqi leaders, who considered the American options too politically costly for little perceived benefit. When the negotiations ultimately failed, US military planners faced a scenario that went unanticipated: the withdrawal of all forces.

What followed withdrawal was a dizzying series of purges and consolidation of political power. On the same December 2011 day that the United States furled the colors to its nearly nine-year mission, Prime Minister Maliki moved against a series of prominent Sunni politicians, calling for the impeachment of his Sunni deputy prime minister, while simultaneously sending government forces to arrest his Sunni vice president and ordering the arrest of the Sunni governor of Diyala Province. Across the next two years,

Maliki continued to consolidate power by replacing members of the Iraqi judiciary, government auditors, and inspectors general. The head of Iraq's independent election commission, who had resisted Maliki's 2010 electoral machinations, was arrested as well.[40] Maliki reneged on his promises to bring Sunni Awakening members into the security forces, instead using Shi'a units to harass and intimidate those who had arguably been most responsible for bringing Iraq's sectarianism under control.[41]

Iraq's security forces suffered as well when Maliki personally appointed a series of senior officers—without the required parliamentary approval—who had little qualifications other than sectarian and personal loyalty to Maliki. Across the span of two years, nearly every division commander and above was replaced, usually with inexperienced Shi'a officers swapping into veteran wartime commanders' positions.[42] Without a residual military presence, the United States was unable to challenge the trend, and the Iraqi military's logistics and training fell into disarray. Tactical level corruption, usually involving "ghost soldiers," who existed only to pad commanders' wallets, crept back into the army's ranks, with some Iraqi leaders estimating the actual effective strength of units to be no more than 40 percent.[43]

Maliki finally went too far in late 2012, when he demanded the arrest of Finance Minister Rafe Issawi, the most senior Sunni politician in his cabinet.[44] On top of Maliki's other sectarian and authoritarian moves, Issawi's attempted arrest was the last straw for Iraq's Sunni population, and large protest camps sprang up in major Sunni cities across the country. AQI, rejuvenated in the ungoverned spaces created by the Syrian civil war and rebranded as ISIS, exploited Maliki's sectarian moves. It successfully launched sophisticated information operation campaigns that stoked fears among Iraq's Sunnis and carried out terrorist attacks against Shi'a targets that caused government and Shi'a militia reprisals against Sunni civilians, recreating the cycles of violence that had thrown Iraq into civil war in 2006.

When Maliki ordered government troops to surround the protesters in Sunni cities across Anbar, it was only a matter of time before violent confrontations would occur. Government troops fired on protesters in Fallujah and Hawijah in early 2013, and open rebellion broke out throughout the Sunni heartland. Faced with few options, broad swaths of the Sunni population—including many former members of the Awakening who had been persecuted by Maliki's government—joined ISIS. By early 2014, Fallujah was back in insurgent hands, and five months later Mosul fell. Eroded by Maliki's politicized decisions and enfeebled by the lack of American advisors, the four Iraqi army divisions in Ninewa and Salahadin Provinces collapsed. In the ensuing chaos, ISIS fighters advanced all the way to the outskirts of Baghdad and to the hinterland of Erbil. With no aircraft and only 157 American military personnel remaining in Iraq, the United States was powerless to arrest the extremist advance.[45] By the end of the summer of 2014, US forces had begun to return to Iraq. The war that had begun in 2003 was far from over.

External Actors

While a series of concrete decisions helped lead the United States down the path to failure, its inability to establish an effective policy to counter the malignant influences of external actors played a part as well. From an early stage in the war, Iran and Syria performed a highly destabilizing role in Iraq. Both regimes sought to bog down the American-led coalition in Iraq in order to gain advantage in the regional political struggle and discourage the United States from seeking regime change in their countries. They also manipulated Iraqi politics to prevent the emergence of a new US-allied Iraqi government. Syria and Iran gave sanctuary and strategic assistance to the Sunni and Shi'a insurgencies, respectively, and contributed materially to the killing and wounding of tens of thousands of Iraqis and hundreds if not thousands of coalition troops. At the high point of Syrian intervention, conservative coalition estimates gauged that more than 150 foreign fighters slipped across the Syrian-Iraqi border every month, often with the assistance of the Assad regime and sometimes after attending training camps on Syrian soil.[46] These foreign fighters provided the vast majority of drivers for suicide car bombs, which produced the largest number of civilian casualties and helped spin Iraq into civil war. During the summer of 2005, over 130 suicide car bomb attacks hit Shi'a civilian targets in Baghdad each month, a trend that accelerated as the civil war intensified, eventually peaking at 175 car bomb attacks during the month of March 2007.[47]

US military and civilian leaders recognized the problem early in the war, but they struggled to formulate an effective strategy for ending or even neutralizing it. Theater commanders presented options to the national command authority as early as the summer of 2005 for Syria and the fall of 2006 for Iran, but US strategic leaders refrained from taking direct measures.[48] Instead, they left the matter to the theater commander, who could only operate against Syrian and Iranian operatives and proxies inside Iraq itself—with very rare exceptions.[49] As a result, the Syrian and Iranian regimes became more and more emboldened in their destabilizing activities. In particular, the Iranian regime produced sophisticated lethal technology for their Iraqi proxies to use against US troops, such as explosively formed penetrators and improvised rocket-assisted munitions. These weapons killed and wounded scores of Americans, but the United States responded to them only at the tactical and operational levels, not the strategic level of war.

By imposing artificial geographic boundaries and not employing all the elements of national power against de facto combatants in a regional conflict, the United States limited the war in a way that made it difficult to achieve strategic end states. Crafting a policy that addressed this issue undoubtedly would have been extremely difficult—the issue of insurgent sanctuaries itself has been an issue that has vexed the United States since the end of World War II. But the absence of a strategic-level decision to address the matter was a major contributing factor to the ultimate US failure to achieve its objectives.

Conclusions

The beginning of the Iraq War, with its tactically successful "shock and awe" campaign that decapitated the Saddam regime within weeks, appeared to validate that a landpower revolution had occurred. On the heels of the apparently successful defeat of the Taliban by a small contingent of SOF and airpower, landpower theorists pontificated that technological changes had altered warfare forever. Those conclusions were misleading, and by the time US forces withdrew from Iraq, many longstanding, traditional lessons on the use of landpower had been revalidated instead.

Primarily, the Iraq conflict reiterated the importance of correctly aligning ends, ways, and means. When any of these elements were misaligned, as they had been from the post-invasion period until the Surge brigades arrived, achieving an operational or strategic goal was nearly impossible. For the first four years of the war there simply were not enough forces in the theater to achieve the desired end state. As a result, the campaign to stabilize Iraq most likely required far more time than it otherwise would have needed—time that ultimately was politically unavailable. Tragically, across the four-year span when the United States relearned this lesson, the Iraqi and American populations' support for the war dropped precipitously.

The war also reinforced a key component of the Weinberger-Powell Doctrine: that political and military leaders should have the support of the American people and their elected representatives before committing forces.[50] While this is a good metric to consider when deciding on the initial use of force, it also is a critical element to assess as the conflict is ongoing. This concept of the importance of maintaining public and congressional support—essentially General Petraeus's concerns with the Washington and Baghdad clocks—is influenced by many factors. The greater the perception of danger to the homeland, the longer support is likely to last; the higher the rate of US casualties, the faster support is likely to dissipate. And similarly, the less ethical the conduct of operations is perceived to be (such as the Abu Ghraib detainee scandal), the faster support declines. In Iraq, after four years of violent conflict—roughly the same length as the US Civil War or the American involvement in World War II—much of the public support had dissipated, thereby undermining support for a long-term commitment. If those first four years had produced the level of progress that the Surge had, with its more balanced ends and means and more effective ways, support for an extended commitment at lower levels of violence likely would not have precipitated an early withdrawal.[51]

Finally, the war also provided a reminder that despite the enticing promise of the impact of information and technology, in land conflicts, numbers of troops still matter. Technological advancements only go so far in enabling a reduction in military end strengths and forces on the ground. Stability and COIN are by their very nature political-military endeavors in which every operation has political implications. This is why establishing relationships with local leaders and understanding sociocultural dynamics is critical to landpower success. These activities require human interaction, and large amounts of it across an entire country, more than the application of technology. Technology has long been seen as a panacea for the costs of a large standing army, but time and again it has proven to be more of a placebo.

The compounding effects of these mistakes are likely to produce a second "Vietnam syndrome" for another generation. Civilian leadership will likely curtail American involvement in foreign commitments—whether military, diplomatic, or economic—as the country's predilection toward isolationism returns. The political intelligentsia, including think tanks and defense and diplomatic veterans, are likely to be discredited for a generation as the country experiments with ideas from "enlightened amateurs" and others outside the traditional foreign policy realm. Barring an existential crisis, American political leaders will apply the minimum amount of commitment to military and diplomatic problems under the assumption that the voting public will not support sustained commitments.

With small numbers of American and allied troops now deployed to Syria as well as back in Iraq again after less than a three-year hiatus, understanding the 2003–2011 successes and failures has become more important. The critical decisions that led the United States to an eventual path of failure must be evaluated in depth. Failure was not inevitable, and the bravery and initiative of many marines, soldiers, and their leaders nearly was enough to achieve victory. Let us hope American military and political leaders have learned enough to perform better next time, and thus to make certain the sacrifices of 2003–2011 are not in vain.

Notes

1. The quote is from Secretary of Defense Donald Rumsfeld in Brian Knowlton and *International Herald Tribune*, "With a Smile and a Joke, Rumsfeld Defends Memo," *New York Times*, 23 October 2003, http://www.nytimes.com/2003/10/23/international/middleeast/with-a-smile-and-a-joke-rumsfeld-defends-iraq-memo.html (accessed 31 May 2017).

2. Daniel Trotta, "Iraq War Costs U.S. More than $2 Trillion: Study," Reuters, 14 March 2013, http://www.reuters.com/article/us-iraq-war-anniversary-idUS-BRE92D0PG20130314 (accessed 31 May 2017). Iraqi civilian casualties are difficult to estimate, but the 200,000 figure comes from the Iraq Body Count Project (https://www.iraqbodycount.org/); the 1 million estimate comes from Physicians for Social Responsibility, "Body Count: Casualty Figures after 10 Years of the 'War on Terror,'" March 2015, http://www.psr.org/assets/pdfs/body-count.pdf (accessed on 13 July 2017).

3. The complete objective, from the National Strategy for Victory in Iraq, was "Iraq at peace with its neighbors and an ally in the War on Terror, with a representative government that respects the human rights of all Iraqis, security forces sufficient to maintain domestic order and to deny Iraq as a safe haven for terrorists, and effective national, regional, and provincial institutions capable of meeting the needs of the Iraqi people and creating conditions for rule of law and prosperity." National Security Council, *National Strategy for Victory in Iraq*, November 2005, 1–3.

4. Michael R. Gordon and Bernard E. Trainor, *Cobra II: The Inside Story of the Invasion and Occupation of Iraq* (New York: Pantheon, 2006), 80–98.

5. Ibid., 53–54, 66–67.

6. Interviews, Major Jeanne Godfroy-Hull, CSA OIF Study Group, with Colonel John Agoglia (Ret.), 7 November 2013, 14 March and 16 April 2014, with Major Thomas Fisher (Ret.), 6 April 2014.

7. The 4th Infantry Division, 1st Armored Division, 3rd Armored Cavalry Regiment, and their supporting forces were still flowing into the theater at the time the regime fell.

8. Interview, Major Jeanne Godfroy and Major Wilson Blythe, CSA OIF Study Group, with General William S. Wallace (Ret.), 17 June 2014; interview, Major Jeanne Godfroy, CSA OIF Study Group, with Lieutenant General David McKiernan (Ret.), 24 November 2014. During this last interview, McKiernan provided a PowerPoint slide from the fall of 2003 differentiating between units that were expected to participate in the entire operation from Phase I to Phase IV, and units that actually came into the theater.

9. David Cloud and Greg Jaffe, *The Fourth Star: Four Generals and the Epic Struggle for the Future of the United States Army* (New York: Crown, 2009), 164–165; interview, Major Jeanne Godfroy, CSA OIF Study Group, with General David McKiernan (Ret.), Commanding General (CG), Coalition Forces Land Component

Command (CFLCC), 24 November 2014; interview, Lieutenant Colonel Joel Rayburn, Colonel Frank Sobchak, and Lieutenant Colonel James Powell, all CSA OIF Study Group, with Colonel Kevin Benson (Ret.), CFLCC Campaign Planner, 24 September 2013; interview, Lieutenant Colonel Joel Rayburn, Colonel Frank Sobchak, and Lieutenant Colonel James Powell, Major Jeanne Godfroy-Hull, Lieutenant Colonel Matthew Zais, and Lieutenant Colonel Matthew Hardman, all CSA OIF Study Group, with Colonel Marty Stanton (Ret.), Chief of Reconciliation, CJTF-7, 17 March 2014.

10. Sterling Jensen, "Iraqi Narratives of the Anbar Awakening" (Ph.D. diss., King's College, London, 2014); conference call interview, Major Jeanne Godfroy and Major Steven Gribschaw, CSA OIF Study Group, with James Sullivan, 27 October 2014. Sullivan was one of two lead analysts in CJTF-7's Intelligence "Red Cell" in the summer of 2003. This opinion was also posited by senior resistance leaders, such as Mullah Nadhim Jabouri: interview, William Knarr, Lieutenant Colonel David Graves, and Mary Hawkins, Institute for Defense Analyses, with Mullah Nadhim al-Jabouri, 12 and 14 February 2011.

11. James P. Pfiffner, "US Blunders in Iraq: DeBaathification and Disbanding the Army," *Intelligence and National Security* 25, no. 1 (February 2010): 76–85.

12. Interview, Major Jeanne Godfroy-Hull and Colonel Frank Sobchak, CSA OIF Study Group, with Lieutenant General Ricardo Sanchez (Ret.), CG, CJTF-7, 28 May 2014.

13. Even before the actual transfer of sovereignty, Iraqi leaders were demanding that the change should give them "absolute control of the administration of Iraq's armed forces and security apparatus, absolute control of the management of Iraq's national and natural resources, and full and complete management of Iraq's development and aid budget." Memo, Office of the MNF-I Political Adviser for Lieutenant General Ricardo Sanchez, 22 May 2004, sub: IGC and Sovereignty.

14. American doctrine going back at least as far as the Marine Corps *Small Wars Manual* considered the holding of elections to be a sign of progress in COIN.

15. MNF-I, Campaign Action Plan for 2005-Transition to Self Reliance, 22 April 2005. Casey initially ordered a strategy that focused equally on conducting full-spectrum COIN and on training and equipping the Iraqi security forces, but less than a year later he implemented the transition strategy, which would guide coalition efforts for nearly two years.

16. Research paper for *Strategic Reflections,* Sandy Cochran and Captain Kelly Howard, Multi-National Force-Iraq (MNF-I) Chronology Reference, 12 November 2008, 93.

17. Ibid.

18. Gordon and Trainor, *Cobra II,* 163; Bing West, *No True Glory: A Frontline Account of the Battle for Fallujah* (New York: Bantam Dell, 2005), 185.

19. Briefing, MNF-I SPA (Strategy Plans and Assessments) Office, "Iraqi Theater Basing Process," 6 September 2004; MNF-I, Contingency Plan (CONPLAN),

Transition to Iraqi Security Self-Reliance and Coalition Transformation, 25 April 2005; PowerPoint Briefing, MNC-I, Bases Closed Since TOA—10 February 2005, 26 September 2005.

20. MNC-I Operations Order (OPORD) 06-01, 21 April 2006, 20–21; MNC-I OPORD 06-03, 5 November 2006, 24.

21. PowerPoint Briefing, MNF-I to Secretary of Defense, Force Structure Assessment, 21 June 2006; Michael Gordon, "US General in Iraq Outlines Troop Cuts," *New York Times*, 24 June 2006.

22. Letter, terrorist Abu Musab al-Zarqawi to Al Qa'ida senior leader, either Osama bin Laden or Ayman al-Zawahiri, February 2004, Coalition Provisional Authority (CPA) English translation, obtained by the US government in Iraq, US DoS Archive; interview, Colonel Frank Sobchak, CSA OIF Study Group, with Dan Darling, Marine Corps Intelligence Activity Intelligence Officer, 18 March 2014.

23. An April 2006 update to the campaign plan noted, "We will succeed by increasingly putting Iraqis in charge across all lines of operations, moving to a supporting role, reducing our visibility and level of involvement, and by pressing them to address and resolve Iraqi problems with Iraqi resources." Paper, MNF-I Joint Campaign Plan, 28 April 2006.

24. Interview, CW2 Andrew Wickland, CSA OIF Study Group, with Major General Rick Waddell, 13 November 2014; interview, Colonel Joel Rayburn and Colonel James Powell, CSA OIF Study Group, with Major General Rick Waddell, 30 June 2014.

25. USF-I, Quarterly History, 1 January–31 March 2010.

26. The Surge also added two Marine Corps rifle battalions and a Marine Expeditionary Unit (MEU) to further balance means and ends, as well as critical enablers, such as rotary wing aviation, intelligence, and military police. An additional division headquarters rounded out the troop increase and greatly improved span of control issues.

27. Letter, MNC-I Commander to troops, 24 June 2007, sub: Reconciliation guidance; MNF-I, Secretary of Defense Weekly Update, 17–23 June 2007; MNC-I, Fragmentary Order (FRAGO) 007, 4 June 2007; Peter R. Mansoor, *Surge: My Journey with General David Petraeus and the Remaking of the Iraq War* (New Haven, Conn.: Yale Univ. Press, 2013), 134.

28. Many commanders at all levels felt that the irregular forces developed by the Awakening increased coalition combat power. In 2006 and 2007 in Ramadi, coalition forces convinced Awakening leaders to provide Sunni men directly into the ISF. As a result, the BCT commander, Colonel Sean MacFarland, commented, "We have more friendly forces than we almost know what to do with." (Timothy S. McWilliams and Kurtis P. Wheeler, eds., *Al-Anbar Awakening, American Perspectives*, vol. 1 (Quantico, Va.: Marine Corps Univ. Press, 2009), 179. Although the exact size of the movement is difficult to estimate, by 2008 the Iraqi government had plans to pay nearly 54,000 members ("Baghdad to Pay Sunni Groups," *Al Jazeera*, 3 October 2008, http://www.aljazeera.com/news/middleeast/2008/10200810151630737451.

html). In terms of reconciliation, General Petraeus and Odeirno directly linked the Awakening to a broader Iraqi reconciliation (letter, MNC-I Commander to troops, 24 June 2007, sub: Reconciliation guidance; MNF-I, Secretary of Defense Weekly Update, 17–23 June 2007).

29. MNF-I, Secretary of Defense Weekly Update, 29 September–5 October 2008; and 24–30 November 2008.

30. The number of security incidents occurring was a challenging issue for coalition officials throughout the war. Among the many problems of measuring this statistic were matters of accuracy, scale, and situational awareness. Iraqi officials often contributed to the measurement, but at the height of the civil war attacks on Shi'a were exaggerated, while attacks on Sunnis were downplayed and underreported. The issue of scale made comparing different types of attacks troubling: should a mortar attack that did not cause any casualties be counted the same as a car bomb that killed hundreds? Finally, situational awareness challenges also complicated obtaining accurate statistics, for if coalition or Iraqi forces were not present to observe an incident it often was not included in the measurement.

31. Security incidents in this case were based on coalition and host nation reports and were defined as attacks against infrastructure and government organizations; found and cleared bombs (IEDs and mines); detonated bombs; sniper, ambush, grenade, and other small arms attacks; and mortar, rocket, and surface to air attacks. MNF-I, Secretary of Defense Weekly Update, 15–21 September 2008, 27 October–2 November 2008, 24–30 November 2008; and 29 December 2008–4 January 2009.

32. Thomas E. Ricks, "A Military Tactician's Political Strategy," *Washington Post,* 9 February 2009, https://www.pressreader.com/usa/the-washington-post/20090209/281487862243707 (accessed on 9 June 2017); Austin Bay, "Petraeus' Pivotal Report," *Washington Times,* 31 August 2007, http://www.washingtontimes.com/news/2007/aug/31/petraeus-pivotal-report/ (accessed on 25 May 2017).

33. Allawi led the Iraqiya party, while Maliki led the State of Law party. Iraqis voted for political parties and coalitions on election day, but it was understood that voting for a party meant voting for the leader of that party as prime minister. Leila Fadel and Karen DeYoung, "Ayad Allawi's Block Wins Most Seats in Iraqi Parliamentary Elections," *Washington Post,* 27 March 2010, http://www.washingtonpost.com/wp-dyn/content/article/2010/03/26/AR2010032602196.html (accessed 9 June 2015).

34. USF-I Quarterly History, 1 January–31 March 2010.

35. Ian Black, "Iraq Election Chaos as 52 Candidates Are Disqualified," *Guardian,* 26 April 2010. The committee Maliki used was a byproduct of Bremer's de-Ba'athification order.

36. Ambassador Christopher R. Hill, *Outpost: Life on the Frontlines of American Diplomacy: A Memoir* (New York: Simon and Schuster, 2014), 371.

37. In July 2008, Maliki had used Iraqi troops against the Diyala provincial government, including the governor, in a politicized effort to intimidate local Sunnis. It

was the first of many instances in which he used troops for intimidation, resulting in his commandos earning the moniker "Fedayeen Maliki," in a comparison to Saddam's paramilitary organization that he used to threaten and arrest opponents. As early as 2009, Maliki delayed the integration of Awakening members into the Iraqi Security Forces and began arresting key leaders of the group on trumped-up charges.

38. Interview, Lynne Chandler Garcia, Contemporary Operations Study Team, with Ambassador Gary Grappo, Minister Counselor for Political Affairs, 30 July 2012, US Embassy, Iraq; Hill, *Outpost,* 384.

39. Interview, Colonel Matthew D. Morton, CSA OIF Study Group, with Colonel Matthew Q. Dawson, 8 October 2014; interview, Colonel Joel Rayburn and Colonel Frank Sobchak, CSA OIF Study Group, with General Lloyd Austin (Ret.), USF-I CG, 4 October 2106; Colonel Thomas Goss, notebook entries for 26 July 2010, 12 August 2010, 20 August 2010, 21 August 2010, and 22 August 2010. It is worth noting that when General Austin identified that he wanted a division to lead the residual force, he was basing his measurement in pre-modular metrics.

40. Ben Van Heuvelen, "Iraqi Leaders Criticize Nouri al-Maliki after Arrest of Top Elections Official," *Washington Post,* 17 April 2012.

41. Maliki also reneged on the power sharing agreement he made in Erbil in 2010, which specified an expanded presidency council of himself, Jalal Talabani, Masood Barzani, and Iraq's two vice presidents to decide major policy questions. In addition, Ayad Allawi's Iraqiyah was promised the right to select a defense minister (with the provision that the choice would be a nonpolitician, as would the new interior minister and Iraqi National Intelligence Service director). Maliki refused to appoint an interior minister and personally retained the ministry portfolio until he was removed from office in 2014. He also blocked Iraqiyah's nominations for defense minister, instead appointing one of his supporters.

42. Marisa Sullivan, "Maliki's Authoritarian Regime," *Middle East Security Report 10,* April 2013, Institute for the Study of War, 16–19.

43. Interview, Colonel Joel Rayburn, CSA OIF Study Group, with Major General Aziz Swaidy (Republic of Iraq, Ret.), 11 May 2016.

44. Michael Gordon, "Tensions Rise in Baghdad with Raid on Official," *New York Times,* 20 December 2012.

45. Interview, Colonel Joel Rayburn and Colonel Matthew Morton, CSA OIF Study Group, with Lieutenant General Robert Caslen, 18 December 2014, West Point, New York.

46. Operation Order (OPORD), MNC-I, app. 1 to an. B to Operation Sayaid: Intelligence Estimate, 1 July 2005; Multi-National Force–West, chapter 5, in *Sunni Insurgency Study,* 13 June 2007.

47. Paper, Sandy Cochran and Captain Kelly Howard, MNF-I Chronology Reference, 12 November 2008 (2005 data); General David H. Petraeus, "Report to Congress on the Situation in Iraq," 10–11 September 2007, http://burgess.house.gov/uploadedfiles/petraeus%20testimony.pdf (2007 data) (accessed 10 February 2016).

48. Interview, Colonel Frank Sobchak and Major Jeanne Godfroy-Hull, CSA OIF Study Group, with General Richard Myers (Ret.), 8 December 2014; interview, Colonel Joel Rayburn and Colonel Frank Sobchak, CSA OIF Study Group, with Stephen Hadley, 30 March 2015.

49. Some scholars have assessed that the refusal to take strategic action and instead returning the problem of sanctuaries to the operational level was an attempt to avoid blame on the part of political leaders. The majority of the senior leaders (political and military) that we interviewed indicated they did not possess the political capital to expand the war. When the Surge was announced, it was (and still is) divisive enough that Congress almost voted against its execution. The thought of expanding the GWOT to another country (or two) was just unfathomable politically, and it is likely that members of the Bush administration felt they could not pull it off. There was also the "Cambodian incursion" historical example, where trying to resolve the sanctuary issue via military force created shockwaves of such magnitude that political support evaporated nearly immediately.

50. Prepared remarks of Secretary of Defense Caspar Weinberger, "The Uses of Military Power," Washington, DC, 28 November 1984, http://www.pbs.org/wgbh/pages/frontline/shows/military/force/weinberger.html (accessed on 1 June 2017); Walter LaFeber, "The Rise and Fall of Colin Powell and the Powell Doctrine," *Political Science Quarterly* 124, no. 1 (March 2009): 71–93.

51. Some theorists argue that the perception of progress and success is most important, while others have argued that although progress and success are important, the perception of failure and number of casualties are far more significant factors in determining popular support. The Iraq War appears to have validated the pessimists in this case, as popular support was essentially unrecoverable in 2008 despite the evidence of the progress and success of the Surge.

6

Denying Sanctuary

A Strategic Analysis of
Operation Enduring Freedom

Gregory Roberts

It is often argued that the United States lost sight of its goals in Afghanistan over the course of Operation Enduring Freedom (OEF).[1] George W. Bush reportedly made this observation in a National Security Council meeting near the end of his second term.[2] The same belief underpinned the Obama administration's first review of US strategy in Afghanistan.[3] Yet the historical record shows that the United States retained the same goal throughout OEF: to eliminate a terrorist safe haven and prevent its reemergence. The Bush administration launched the Global War on Terrorism (GWOT) toward this end shortly after 9/11, and made Al Qa'ida's sanctuary in Afghanistan the war's first target.[4] Although the Obama administration rejected many of the GWOT's policies, it retained the goal of denying Al Qa'ida sanctuary in Afghanistan and the surrounding region.[5] This remained the US objective for its employment of landpower through the conclusion of OEF at the end of 2014, when the United States officially terminated its combat mission—without having achieved victory.

If the United States never lost sight of *why* it was in Afghanistan, however, it did not always have a clear idea of *how* to achieve its desired end state. The evolving use of American landpower over the course of OEF is perhaps the best evidence of this lack of strategic clarity. After ousting the Taliban regime at the start of OEF, the Bush administration maintained a light military footprint focused on counterterrorism, relying heavily on coalition partners to stabilize and rebuild Afghanistan. Gradually the administration came to embrace, if not "nation-building," a state-building approach that witnessed expanded US and allied stability operations. The Bush administration then sought to hand responsibility for the mission over to NATO, only to discover that coalition landpower was insufficient to quell the growing insurgency. The Obama administration responded by adopting a resource-intensive counterinsurgency (COIN) approach combined with an accelerated effort at security force assistance. This integrated civil-military campaign aimed to roll back the insurgency and simultaneously build the capacity of the Afghan National Security Forces (ANSF), such that the ANSF could manage the insurgency and allow US forces to draw down within a fixed period of time. All of these operational approaches aimed to prevent the return of Al Qa'ida, but none managed to achieve decisively that political aim.

This chapter contends that the United States' inability to conclude the war in Afghanistan has been a direct consequence of its political aim. Policymakers intended OEF to achieve a state of perpetual prevention. To avert further attacks on the homeland, the United States sought not only to eliminate terrorist sanctuaries, but also to deny terrorists the possibility of sanctuary in the future.[6] Attaining this goal required an open-ended commitment of American landpower, until such time as a new Afghan political order could prevent terrorist safe havens from reemerging. Yet, as this brief history of OEF shows, US policymakers repeatedly planned for the termination of the military campaign rather than the achievement of its political objective. In part, this was because they underestimated the time and resources it would take to establish an Afghan state fully capable of policing its own territory. Indeed, the achievement of that end state was inherently difficult to measure and define, making it nearly impossible for commanders to develop clear termination criteria for the military campaign. At the same time, policymakers repeatedly sought to conclude OEF because they did not find it politically acceptable to make the lengthy and costly commitment that its political goal demanded.[7] Consequently, the United States conducted OEF in the absence of a strategy for achieving its ambitious end state.[8]

A War on Terrorist Safe Havens

Although OEF later became synonymous with the war in Afghanistan, it originally referred to the GWOT. The United States' political goal in Afghanistan arose from the policy framework of the GWOT—or more precisely, from the Bush administration's assumptions about the terrorist threat in the aftermath of 9/11. For administration officials, 9/11 showed that international terrorism threatened nothing less than "the American way of life."[9] The Bush administration also believed that this threat stemmed not from the perpetrators of 9/11 or any one terrorist group, but from a global network of terrorists and their state (and nonstate) sponsors.[10] To eliminate the threat of terrorism, the US response to 9/11 would have to address the sources of terrorist support globally, not just Al Qa'ida's sanctuary in Afghanistan.

This expansive definition of the enemy had two consequences for the strategic planning of OEF. First, it led policymakers to plan OEF as a multitheater campaign from the start. OEF would be a "different type of war," bringing "multiple instruments" of national power to bear on "multiple fronts" for an "extended duration."[11] Second, policymakers' conception of the threat led them to focus the campaign on so-called rogue and failed states—and the "ungoverned" spaces within their borders—as much as terrorist groups themselves.[12] OEF would seek to create "an international political environment hostile to terrorism," in part by convincing or compelling states to cut ties and eliminate terrorist activity within their borders.[13] On the evening of 9/11, the president therefore declared a sweeping new foreign policy, which came to be known as the Bush Doctrine: the United States would no longer distinguish between terrorists and states who harbored them.[14] In effect, OEF threatened regime change for any government that failed to cut ties with terrorist groups.[15]

The Bush administration quickly applied its new doctrine to South Asia in the form of a black-and-white ultimatum: You're either with us or against us. The opposite responses of Taliban leader Mullah Omar and Pakistan's President Pervez Musharraf decided the battle lines for the remainder of OEF. For his part, Mullah Omar refused to cooperate with the demand to expel Osama bin Laden, which made the Taliban an enemy on par with Al Qa'ida.[16] The opening campaign of OEF would therefore seek to topple the Taliban regime and eliminate its leadership along with Al Qa'ida's personnel and sanctuary.[17] Musharraf, on the other hand, responded to the US ultimatum within two days of 9/11 by declaring Pakistan's unstinting support for the United States. Although Pakistan had helped foster the Taliban regime into power and viewed the regime as a strategic asset, Musharraf agreed (among other conditions) to "break diplomatic relations with the Taliban government, end support for the Taliban and assist [the United States] . . . to destroy Usama bin-Ladin and his Al Qaida network."[18] It would later become evident that the Taliban enjoyed sanctuary in Pakistan, but by then the United States could not easily address the threat without jeopardizing its own lines of communication or Islamabad's cooperation in other areas of strategic interest.[19] Thus, by making an enemy of the Taliban regime and ally of Pakistan, the Bush Doctrine unwittingly drew a boundary for the use of US landpower for the duration of OEF, and made regime change in Afghanistan a strategic objective separate and apart from the core goal of eliminating terrorist sanctuaries in South Asia.

Despite the overtly political goals of the GWOT, the Bush administration proceeded to launch OEF without a clear strategy for Afghanistan. At the White House's urging, military leaders rapidly developed a plan to oust the Taliban through a hybrid approach that combined unconventional and conventional warfare. CIA operatives and special operations forces (SOF) would spearhead the invasion and partner with anti-Taliban forces supported by US airpower; a conventional ground force would follow, if necessary, after winter.[20] It was not clear, however, what would come after decisive operations against the Taliban. Granted, the Bush administration recognized that a new government would be necessary to prevent the return of Al Qa'ida to Afghanistan. Within days of 9/11, the DoS fixed on the goal of bringing together "non-Taliban Afghans . . . to form [a] broad-based coalition government with broad appeal across geographic and ethnic lines."[21] However, the administration also made clear that the UN and coalition partners should lead the efforts to form a new government and consolidate post-Taliban governance.[22] American landpower would play only a supporting role in stabilizing the new government, as indicated by the campaign's "Phase Four" objective: "Establish capability of coalition partners to prevent the reemergence of terrorism and provide support for humanitarian assistance efforts."[23] In effect, this meant that the United States had no strategy of its own for achieving its political goal. USCENTCOM Commander General Tommy Franks would have to depend on coalition partners—not American landpower—to achieve the campaign's political end state.

The Bush administration's lack of strategic planning can be attributed in part to the political pressure it faced. Congressional leaders, the media, and the American public all clamored for a rapid response to the shocking attacks.[24] Secretary of Defense Donald Rumsfeld added to this pressure. He believed a rapid response was essential to mitigate the risk of a follow-on attack, to warn terrorist sponsors around the globe, and to garner more actionable intelligence for future operations.[25] Franks, for his part, chafed under Rumsfeld's relentless demands and on one occasion in early October even offered to resign. Yet this seems to have owed more to his discomfort with Rumsfeld's management style than to any misgivings about the course of US strategy.[26]

More important, however, was the administration's views on the appropriate use of American landpower. Bush and Rumsfeld shared an aversion to "nation-building," a term they used to refer to the complex contingency operations of the Clinton era. They believed such missions created economic dependencies and tied up US troops indefinitely, as in peacekeeping in the Balkans.[27] Afghanistan was an especially poor candidate for nation-building since, in Rumsfeld's words, it was "anti-foreigner."[28] Many in Bush's cabinet also recalled the Soviet experience in Afghanistan, which illustrated the "potentially catastrophic consequences" of a long-term military occupation.[29] Furthermore, the administration sought to "transform" the US military into a lighter, more lethal, and more responsive force, in keeping with the Revolution in Military Affairs (RMA) concept of the 1990s. 9/11 made the need for defense transformation seem all the more urgent, and a full-scale invasion by conventional ground forces would have run counter to Rumsfeld's initiative.[30] Finally, administration officials did not want US forces to lead Afghanistan's reconstruction because they would soon be needed in other theaters of the GWOT, as a Pentagon memo from October 2001 expressly stated.[31] For all these reasons, the Bush administration had no intention of leading Afghanistan's post-Taliban reconstruction as OEF got underway.[32]

OEF's unexpectedly swift success against the Taliban regime seemed to validate the administration's approach. American airpower and SOF combined with Afghan opposition groups to topple the Taliban in a matter of weeks, an apparent proof of concept for a transformed US military. Simultaneously, a UN-led diplomatic effort established an interim government under Hamid Karzai, along with a political process to adopt a new constitution and elect a representative government within the next few years.[33] However, Afghanistan was still full of "ungoverned" spaces after the Taliban's ouster, and the Karzai administration was many years away from being able to govern. Thus, OEF's opening successes merely obscured the chasm between the US operational approach and the campaign's end state.

From Counterterrorism to Nation-Building

Consistent with its views on nation-building, the Bush administration limited US landpower to a "light footprint" focused on counterterrorism after removing the Taliban.[34] Rumsfeld suggested that the military mission would be accomplished once the United States had killed or captured the rest of Al Qa'ida's personnel.[35] At the same time, Franks struggled to articulate the termination criteria that would mark OEF's successful conclusion.[36] Yet by December 2001, Franks had already turned his attention—at the president's orders—to planning for the invasion of Iraq, the next theater of the GWOT.[37] Around the same time, Pentagon budget planners estimated that US military involvement in Afghanistan would not last beyond two years.[38]

The light footprint approach undermined OEF's goal of preventing the reemergence of a safe haven in two ways. First, the United States did not have enough landpower to secure Afghan territory or complete its kill-or-capture mission. The US-led coalition routed Al Qa'ida from its last strongholds in Tora Bora and the Shah-i-Kot Valley, but with barely five thousand American troops in country in early 2002, it could not prevent the enemy from escaping across the border or melting into the population. By the spring of 2002, the US military had few identifiable targets in Afghan territory but a clear sense that the mission remained unaccomplished. USCENTCOM ordered Lieutenant General Dan McNeill to establish a new corps-level headquarters at Bagram Airfield, but with strict orders from Pentagon leaders not to "do anything that looks like permanence," in the vein of Kosovo's Camp Bondsteel.[39] McNeill's forces continued the hunt for Al Qa'ida and the Taliban, largely through cordon-and-search operations near the Afghanistan-Pakistan border.[40] Although these operations maintained pressure on the enemy, they did little to create lasting security.

Second, the United States' reluctance to project landpower for the stabilization mission hampered the efforts of coalition partners and stunted the growth of the new Afghan government. The United Kingdom and then Turkey agreed to lead a UN-authorized peacekeeping mission in Kabul, the International Security Assistance Force (ISAF). But the Pentagon refused to contribute US troops to ISAF or even to provide allied logistical support beyond Kabul, effectively quashing proposals by the DoS and allies to expand the peacekeeping force to other cities.[41] The United States agreed to serve as one of five "lead nations" in reforming Afghanistan's security sector, but this stove-piped approach proved woefully inadequate to the task of building Afghanistan's army, police, and judiciary after decades of conflict.[42] Afghanistan was left with virtually no legitimate security institutions outside of Kabul, and governance in many provinces fell to "warlords" and local powerbrokers.[43] With few security forces he could call his own, Karzai worked to secure his own political survival through informal arrangements that, as would later become evident, institutionalized corruption.[44] Yet the Pentagon actively encouraged these developments, unmoved by the CIA's assessment that factionalism could easily plunge Afghanistan back into past internecine conflicts.[45]

Over the course of 2002, the Bush administration grew impatient with the progress of the reconstruction mission.[46] Recognizing Afghanistan's continuing instability, the administration came around to a "nation-building"— or at least "state-building"—approach of the sort it had initially rejected.[47] In July 2003, the Office of the Secretary of Defense (OSD) issued new guidance that reflected this major policy shift. OEF's core goal remained the same, as the US-led coalition worked "to help the Afghans create a stable government and society that will prevent Afghanistan from serving as a base for terrorists." But the campaign now sought to establish an Afghan government that was: "[1] Moderate and democratic . . . ; [2] Representative of all responsible elements in Afghan society and formed through the political participation of the Afghan people; [3] Capable of effectively controlling and governing its territory; [4] Capable of implementing policies to stimulate economic development; and [5] Willing to contribute to a continuing partnership with the Coalition in the global war against terrorism." OSD's guidance even committed the coalition to "defending the central government" against collapse or overthrow, as the success of OEF became inextricably linked with the success of the Karzai administration.[48] For the remainder of the Bush presidency, OEF's desired end state would remain "a moderate, stable and representative Afghanistan capable of controlling and governing its territory."[49] NATO shared this vision as it assumed leadership of ISAF in August 2003 and developed plans to expand its peacekeeping force.[50]

The administration operationalized its new policy through a political-military action plan called Accelerating Success, which the National Security Council endorsed in June 2003.[51] The plan sought to lay the groundwork for national elections by making Afghan institutions more inclusive, weakening warlords, and countering the growing insurgency in the south and east.[52] The plan called for training more Afghan soldiers and police and building more infrastructure—namely roads, schools, and health clinics—to boost economic development. Accelerating Success also came with increased resources, since it aimed (as its name implied) to invest more up front so as to reduce costs over the long term.[53] The administration therefore tripled the budgets of State and USAID for Afghanistan in FY 2004, and nearly doubled the number of US troops to help secure the 2004 presidential elections.[54] NATO also poured in more resources and helped establish Provincial Reconstruction Teams—the first of which had been established in Gardez in February 2003—in more provinces.[55] American landpower would be employed to bolster political stability, not merely to hunt terrorists.[56]

Accelerating Success worked largely as intended, securing the presidential election and boosting the reconstruction mission. A January 2005 White House review pointed to the waning of warlords' influence, the number of police and soldiers trained, and the miles of road built as evidence of the "transformative changes" taking place in Afghanistan.[57] However, the Bush administration's belief that Afghanistan was "in relatively good shape" was colored by the increasingly dire situation in Iraq, where it had nearly 150,000 troops deployed. As the new "central front" of the GWOT demanded more of its attention and resources, the administration sought to shift more of the burden in Afghanistan to NATO. It welcomed the alliance's plans to take command of the US-led coalition in 2006, when ISAF would finish its expansion to the south and east.[58] But much to the consternation of its allies, the Pentagon also planned to begin drawing down forces. Rumors of this first surfaced in September 2005, and three months later Rumsfeld gave them credence, ordering a reduction in force from nineteen thousand to sixteen thousand troops the following spring.[59] The Bush administration also cut assistance spending for Afghanistan in FY 2006 as it prioritized emergency funding for Iraq and the aftermath of Hurricane Katrina.[60]

The administration's pivot to Iraq and handoff to NATO proved to be major setbacks for OEF. Whatever Accelerating Success had accomplished, US and coalition landpower had not broken the Taliban's will to fight nor enabled the government in Kabul to extend its writ fully into the provinces. Indeed, the security situation had gradually deteriorated since 2002, as the Taliban took advantage of sanctuaries in Pakistan and the vacuum of governance in the south and east to rebuild its forces and regain influence in "friendly" districts.[61] After three years of creeping violence, the insurgency erupted in the spring of 2006 with its first major offensive, aimed in large part at countering ISAF's expansion into the Taliban heartland. For its part, NATO had been expecting to conduct peacekeeping operations, and member states were not prepared for combat against a well-armed insurgency.[62] By August 2006, the security situation had deteriorated to such a degree that Ambassador Ronald Neumann cabled Washington with the message: "We're not losing, but we're not winning either."[63] Over the next two years, the United States responded to the mounting violence by taking command of ISAF from NATO and sending what troops it could. The new secretary of defense, Robert Gates, found he could not fully resource the Afghan theater in the middle of the Iraq Surge.[64] When the Bush administration left office in January 2009, the war in Afghanistan was at best a strategic stalemate.[65]

From COIN to Security Force Assistance

As a candidate, Barack Obama had pledged to end the war in Iraq and "finish the fight against al-Qaeda and the Taliban," which he described as the "war that has to be won."[66] Thus, one of his administration's top priorities on entering office was to review US strategy in Afghanistan.[67] In March 2009 the president presented the conclusions of that review as a new strategy for Afghanistan and Pakistan. The "Af-Pak" strategy, as it was known, did not substantively change the core goal of denying terrorists safe haven, but it extended that goal to Pakistan.[68] Thus, for the remainder of the Obama presidency the United States would seek "to disrupt, dismantle and defeat al-Qaeda in Pakistan and Afghanistan, and to prevent their return to either country in the future."

With regard to Afghanistan, the Af-Pak strategy also limited US objectives. It tempered American expectations for the Afghan government. Instead of "a moderate, stable and representative Afghanistan capable of controlling and governing its territory," the United States now sought "a more capable, accountable, and effective government" that could "eventually function, especially regarding internal security, with limited international support."[69] That is, instead of transforming Afghanistan into a liberal democracy, the Obama administration would only try to create an effective counterterrorism partner. Thus, the Af-Pak strategy shifted the US landpower approach from "nation-building" to its lesser cousin, "capacity building." The United States also no longer sought to defeat the Taliban, but to reverse the insurgency's momentum while enabling ANSF to assume the security mission. Thus, the Obama administration tacitly acknowledged that it did not have to defeat the Taliban—as the Bush Doctrine had assumed—to achieve its core goal of denying Al Qa'ida sanctuary. In pursuit of these more modest objectives, the administration prescribed "an integrated civilian-military counterinsurgency strategy," bolstered by "a substantial increase" in the number of civilians on the ground and an increase in civilian assistance.[70] Obama also responded to ISAF commander General David McKiernan's pending manpower request by sending an additional twenty-one thousand troops to the theater.[71] At the time of this announcement, the administration planned to reassess its Af-Pak strategy one year later.[72]

Just a few months after the strategy rollout, however, a new ISAF commander, General Stanley McChrystal, warned the White House that "mission failure" was likely without a further troop increase.[73] In September 2009—against a backdrop of perceived pressure from military leaders for a "fully resourced counterinsurgency" campaign—the Obama administration began a second strategic review. Though its outcome was hardly a foregone conclusion, this second review eventually led the White House to double down on its Af-Pak strategy. More explicitly than its predecessor, the revised strategy acknowledged the "profound problems of legitimacy and effectiveness with the Karzai government," as relations between the two administrations had soured further.[74] But the strategic concept remained "to degrade the Taliban insurgency while building sufficient Afghan capacity to secure and govern their country." Obama supported this strategy by authorizing an additional "surge" of 30,000 troops—less than the 40,000 McChrystal had requested, but enough to bring US troop levels close to 100,000 within the next year. Crucially, this surge also came with a timetable, as it aimed to create "conditions for the United States to begin reducing its forces by July 2011."[75]

In effect, the new strategy set an expiration date for a surge in US land-power. Obama was keenly aware of the opportunity costs of sustaining a resource-intensive war effort while the country was still recovering from the financial crisis of 2008. But he also intended the timetable—which he announced publicly along with the troop increase—to compel the Afghans to take responsibility for their own security, rather than count on a blank check from the United States.[76] In November 2010, NATO's Lisbon Summit established a related timetable, whereby member states agreed with the Afghan government to phase out combat operations by the end of 2014 as the ANSF transitioned to lead responsibility for security.[77]

The Obama administration's time-bound strategy succeeded in rolling back the insurgency in key areas, accelerating the growth of the ANSF, and—after a brief surge—reducing coalition troop levels. The transition to Afghan security responsibility officially began in March 2011, and US surge recovery began on schedule three months later.[78] The ANSF reached its target strength of 352,000 in September 2012—two months ahead of schedule—and in June 2013 the ANSF assumed the lead for combat operations.[79] As planned at Lisbon, the US combat mission formally concluded at the end of 2014. Obama marked the occasion by declaring that Afghanistan was "not going to be a source of terrorist attacks again."[80] At the time, the administration planned to keep 9,800 troops in theater to support the counterterrorism and train, advise, and assist missions, before drawing down to a "normal embassy presence" of roughly 1,000 troops by the end of 2016.[81] This timetable would have fulfilled Obama's 2012 campaign pledge to "end the war in Afghanistan."[82]

In reality, however, the timetables for the surge and security transition effectively disconnected the campaign's termination criteria from its political objective. Rather than measure the Afghan government's ability to lead COIN and counterterrorism operations, the Obama administration measured progress by the number of American "boots on the ground" and the number of ANSF personnel trained. Skeptical of what its own strategy could accomplish in Afghanistan, the White House unofficially lowered the bar for success to "Afghan Good Enough," the politically incorrect term for the minimum results necessary to justify a US withdrawal.[83] The administration's operational approach also rested on two questionable assumptions: first, that a COIN campaign could succeed without an adequate host nation partner against an enemy that enjoyed cross-border sanctuary; and second, that self-sustaining security institutions could be built within a government that continued to suffer from a lack of capacity and transparency.[84]

The disconnect between the Obama administration's time-bound use of landpower and the campaign's desired end state became clear in the two years following the conclusion of OEF. Taking advantage of the absence of coalition landpower and the ANSF's enduring institutional weaknesses, the Taliban soon seized control of more territory than at any time since 2001.[85] Al Qa'ida also found space to operate in Afghanistan once again, establishing a large training camp in southern Kandahar that went undetected until October 2015.[86] To its credit, the administration adopted a more conditions-based approach in its final two years, ultimately deciding to keep 8,400 troops in country when it left office in January 2017.[87] In announcing his decision, Obama reasoned that he could "not allow Afghanistan to be used as a safe haven for terrorists to attack our nation again."[88] The comment revealed the sobering truth that OEF had concluded without attaining its strategic goal.

The Elusiveness of Victory in Afghanistan

OEF failed to conclusively project American landpower. It eliminated the bases and safe havens that Al Qa'ida enjoyed at the time of 9/11 and helped to establish a new Afghan government as a partner in the War on Terror. Yet OEF did not achieve its goal of preventing the reemergence of terrorist safe havens. The Afghan government remains far from capable of providing for its own security and does not control a large percentage of its territory.[89] Without sustained US counterterrorism pressure, it seems likely that Al Qa'ida and other extremists like ISIS would enjoy sanctuary in Afghanistan once again.

To some extent, the absence of a clear victory in OEF was a logical outcome of the war aim. OEF sought neither a limited military objective nor the defeat of a conventional enemy, but the management of an enduring threat. Thus, in a sense, policymakers framed the war in Afghanistan not as a traditional armed conflict so much as an open-ended police action conducted through military means.[90] Preventing the reemergence of a terrorist threat requires constant vigilance and, in the absence of a capable host government, sustained US engagement.

At the same time, policymakers undermined the campaign by failing to appreciate—or perhaps failing to accept—the resource implications of their political goals. The Bush administration underestimated the costs of building a fully sovereign Afghan state and overestimated the ability of the Afghans and other allies to take on that burden themselves. The Bush and Obama administrations both overestimated what could be achieved within the time horizons they were willing to allow for military intervention. Indeed, policymakers seemed to let their political sense of what costs were acceptable color their assessment of what goals were feasible. Instead of setting limited objectives that operations could actually achieve—or committing the time and resources necessary to achieve ambitious goals—policymakers repeatedly sought to extricate US forces from Afghanistan in order to pursue other priorities, such as the war in Iraq or "nation building here at home."[91]

It is beyond the scope of this essay to assess whether the opportunity costs of an open-ended engagement in Afghanistan are worth the gains to US national security or whether it was ever necessary to remake the Afghan state to prevent another 9/11. But OEF reminds us that policy goals exercise a certain tyranny over military campaigns. Simply put, an open-ended goal necessitates an open-ended commitment. If the pursuit of that goal is truly vital to the national interest, then political leaders must accept the cost and work to maintain the American public's support for the cause. If the cost is out of proportion to the benefit of national security, however, then policymakers must set more limited objectives that can be attained within acceptable means. In OEF, the United States chose instead to pursue a virtually limitless strategic goal through the limited use of landpower. The result was not a strategic failure so much as the absence of effective strategy—a campaign whose termination criteria satisfied competing political priorities but not the desired end state.

Notes

1. See Aaron B. O'Connell, "The Lessons and Legacies of the War in Afghanistan," in *Understanding the U.S. Wars in Iraq and Afghanistan,* ed. Beth L. Bailey and Richard H. Immerman (New York: New York Univ. Press, 2015), 308–312.

2. Michael G. Waltz, *Warrior Diplomat: A Green Beret's Battles from Washington to Afghanistan* (Washington, DC: Potomac Books, 2014), 217–218.

3. Michael Crowley, "Hawk Down," *New Republic,* 24 September 2009, https:// newrepublic.com/article/69645/hawk-down; Jonathan Alter, *The Promise: President Obama, Year One* (New York: Simon and Schuster, 2010), 132–133; Bob Woodward, *Obama's Wars* (New York: Simon and Schuster, 2010), 72.

4. DoS, "Secretary's PC Package," 13 September 2001, National Security Archive, http://nsarchive.gwu.edu/NSAEBB/NSAEBB358a/doc04.pdf; Donald Rumsfeld, "Strategic Guidance for the Campaign Against Terrorism," memo, 3 October 2001, National Security Archive, http://nsarchive.gwu.edu/NSAEBB/NSAEBB358a/doc15.pdf.

5. Barack Obama, "A New Strategy for Afghanistan and Pakistan," 27 March 2009, https://obamawhitehouse.archives.gov/blog/2009/03/27/a-new-strategy-afghanistan-and-pakistan; "White Paper of the Interagency Policy Group's Report on U.S. Policy toward Afghanistan and Pakistan," 27 March 2009, https://foreign-

policy.com/2009/03/27/white-house-white-paper-on-u-s-policy-to-afghanistan-and-pakistan/; Woodward, *Obama's Wars,* 385.

6. Douglas J. Feith, *War and Decision: Inside the Pentagon at the Dawn of the War on Terrorism* (New York: Harper, 2008), 50.

7. For the political commitments inherent in war, see Nadia Schadlow, *War and the Art of Governance: Consolidating Combat Success into Political Victory* (Washington, DC: Georgetown Univ. Press, 2017).

8. Hew Strachan has argued that the GWOT was "astrategic"; see Hew Strachan, *The Direction of War: Contemporary Strategy in Historical Perspective* (New York: Cambridge Univ. Press, 2013), 11.

9. Feith, *War and Decision,* 10, 50–51, 56, 68–71; National Commission on Terrorist Attacks upon the United States, *The 9/11 Commission Report* (Washington, DC: Government Printing Office, 2004), 11, https://9-11commission.gov/report/911Report.pdf; George W. Bush, "Address to a Joint Session of Congress and the American People," speech, 20 September 2001, https://georgewbush-whitehouse.archives.gov/news/releases/2001/09/20010920-8.html.

10. Paul D. Wolfowitz, "DoD News Briefing," 13 September 2001, http://archive.defense.gov/Transcripts/Transcript.aspx?TranscriptID=1622.

11. For OEF as a "different type of war," see George W. Bush, "Remarks by President Bush and President Megawati of Indonesia," 19 September 2001, https://georgewbush-whitehouse.archives.gov/news/releases/2001/09/20010919-1.html. Rumsfeld summarized the strategic concept as: "multiple agencies, multiple fronts, multiple instruments, multiple methods, and extended duration"; see "Strategic Guidance for the Campaign Against Terrorism." Bush also told the American public on multiple occasions to expect a long fight; see "Address to the Joint Session of the 107th Congress."

12. The Bush administration understood Al Qa'ida's safe haven in Afghanistan to be a physical, ungoverned space within a failed state. "The National Security Strategy of the United States of America," September 2002, https://www.state.gov/documents/organization/63562.pdf; "Intelligence Reform and Terrorism Prevention Act of 2004," Pub. L. No. 108-458 (2004), https://www.gpo.gov/fdsys/pkg/PLAW-108publ458/pdf/PLAW-108publ458.pdf; Robert D. Lamb, "Ungoverned Areas and Threats from Safe Havens: Final Report of the Ungoverned Areas Project" (Washington, DC: Office of the Under Secretary of Defense for Policy, 2008), http://www.dtic.mil/get-tr-doc/pdf?AD=ADA479805. For critiques of the concept of "ungoverned" space, see Michael A. Innes, ed., *Denial of Sanctuary: Understanding Terrorist Safe Havens* (Westport, Conn: Praeger Security International, 2007); Anne L. Clunan and Harold A. Trinkunas, eds., *Ungoverned Spaces: Alternatives to State Authority in an Era of Softened Sovereignty* (Stanford, Calif.: Stanford Security Studies, 2010); Stewart Patrick, *Weak Links: Fragile States, Global Threats, and International Security* (New York: Oxford Univ. Press, 2011).

13. Donald Rumsfeld to George W. Bush, "Strategic Thoughts," memo, 30 September 2001, National Security Archive, http://nsarchive.gwu.edu/NSAEBB/

NSAEBB358a/doc13.pdf; Rumsfeld, "Strategic Guidance for the Campaign Against Terrorism."

14. George W. Bush, "Address to the Nation on the September 11 Attacks," 11 September 2001, https://georgewbush-whitehouse.archives.gov/infocus/bushrecord/documents/Selected_Speeches_George_W_Bush.pdf. In his 20 September 2001 address to the joint session of Congress, the president restated the policy: "Every nation, in every region, now has a decision to make. Either you are with us, or you are with the terrorists. From this day forward, any nation that continues to harbor or support terrorism will be regarded by the United States as a hostile regime." For the president's own definition of the Bush Doctrine, see George W. Bush, *Decision Points* (New York: Crown Publishers, 2010), 396–397.

15. Rumsfeld to Bush, "Strategic Thoughts."

16. For the American demands to the Taliban, see DoS, "Gameplan for Pol-mil Strategy for Pakistan and Afghanistan," 14 September 2001, National Security Archive, http://nsarchive.gwu.edu/NSAEBB/NSAEBB358a/doc06.pdf. For an account of Mullah Omar's deliberations, see Alex Strick van Linschoten and Felix Kuehn, *An Enemy We Created: The Myth of the Taliban-Al Qaeda Merger in Afghanistan* (New York: Oxford Univ. Press, 2012), 223–226. See also Richard Armitage, "Deputy Secretary Armitage-Mamoud Phone Call," cable, 18 September 2001, National Security Archive, http://nsarchive.gwu.edu/NSAEBB/NSAEBB358a/doc09.pdf; Wendy Chamberlin, "Mahmud Plans 2nd Mission to Afghanistan," cable, 24 September 2001, National Security Archive, http://nsarchive.gwu.edu/NSAEBB/NSAEBB358a/doc11.pdf; Wendy Chamberlin, "Mahmud on Failed Trip to Kandahar," cable, 29 September 2001, National Security Archive, http://nsarchive.gwu.edu/NSAEBB/NSAEBB358a/doc12.pdf.

17. Office of the Secretary of Defense, "U.S. Strategy in Afghanistan," 16 October 2001, National Security Archive, http://nsarchive.gwu.edu/NSAEBB/NSAEBB358a/doc18.pdf.

18. For Pakistan's relationship with the Taliban before 9/11, see Peter Tomsen, *The Wars of Afghanistan: Messianic Terrorism, Tribal Conflicts, and the Failures of Great Powers* (New York: PublicAffairs, 2011); Steve Coll, *Ghost Wars: The Secret History of the CIA, Afghanistan, and Bin Laden, from the Soviet Invasion to September 10, 2001* (London: Penguin, 2004). For the US ultimatum to Pakistan, see Richard Armitage, "Deputy Secretary Armitage's Meeting with Pakistan Intel Chief Mahmud: You're Either with Us or You're Not," cable, 13 September 2001, National Security Archive, http://nsarchive.gwu.edu/NSAEBB/NSAEBB358a/doc03-1.pdf; Wendy Chamberlin, "Musharraf: 'We Are With You in Your Action Plan in Afghanistan,'" cable, 13 September 2001, National Security Archive, http://nsarchive.gwu.edu/NSAEBB/NSAEBB358a/doc02.pdf; Richard Armitage, "Deputy Secretary Armitage's Meeting with General Mahmud: Actions and Support Expected of Pakistan in Fight Against Terrorism," cable, 13 September 2001, National Security Archive, http://nsarchive.gwu.edu/NSAEBB/NSAEBB358a/doc05.pdf; Wendy Chamberlin, "Musharraf Accepts the Seven Points," cable, 14 September 2001, National Security

Archive, http://nsarchive.gwu.edu/NSAEBB/NSAEBB358a/doc08.pdf.

19. Steve Coll details this story in *Directorate S: The CIA and America's Secret Wars in Afghanistan and Pakistan* (New York: Penguin Books, 2018).

20. For the development of this hybrid approach, see Henry H. Shelton, *Without Hesitation: The Odyssey of an American Warrior*, 1st ed (New York: St. Martin's Press, 2010), 441–444; Feith, *War and Decision*, 16–17; Richard B. Myers, *Eyes on the Horizon: Serving on the Frontlines of National Security* (New York: Threshold, 2009), 167. For the pre-9/11 roots of the unconventional warfare plan, see National Commission on Terrorist Attacks upon the United States, "The 9/11 Commission Report," 205–206.

21. DoS, "Gameplan for Polmil Strategy for Pakistan and Afghanistan"; James Dobbins, *After the Taliban: Nation-Building in Afghanistan* (Washington, DC: Potomac Books, 2008), 83–84.

22. "It would be a useful function for the United Nations to take over the so-called 'nation-building'—I would call it the stabilization of a future government—after our military mission is complete." George W. Bush, "Prime Time News Conference," 11 October 2001, https://georgewbush-whitehouse.archives.gov/news/releases/2001/10/20011011-7.html; Donald Rumsfeld, "DoD News Briefing," 9 October 2001, http://archive.defense.gov/Transcripts/Transcript.aspx?TranscriptID =2034.

23. Tommy Franks, *American Soldier* (New York: Regan Books, 2004), 420.

24. In a 20 September memo, Rumsfeld acknowledged the "requirement to initiate military strikes within a very short time" as a key constraint on CENTCOM's planning; see Feith, *War and Decision*, 63. Condoleezza Rice admitted that "in the aftermath of 9/11, we were essentially just reacting. It took some time before we could stop, catch our breath, and make a critical reappraisal." See David J. Rothkopf, *National Insecurity: American Leadership in an Age of Fear* (New York: PublicAffairs, 2014), 13.

25. Rumsfeld to Bush, "Strategic Thoughts"; Peter W. Rodman to Donald Rumsfeld, "Why Time Is of the Essence in the Afghan Campaign," memorandum, 12 October 2001, Rumsfeld Papers, http://library.rumsfeld.com/doclib/sp/283/2001-10-12%20from%20Peter%20Rodman%20re%20Why%20Time%20is%20°f%20 the%20Essence%20in%20the%20Afghan%20Campaign.pdf; Office of the Secretary of Defense, "U.S. Strategy in Afghanistan"; Feith, *War and Decision*, 62–66.

26. For Franks's offer to resign, see Franks, *American Soldier*, 300. For his relationship with Rumsfeld, see Bradley Graham, *By His Own Rules: The Ambitions, Successes, and Ultimate Failures of Donald Rumsfeld* (New York: PublicAffairs, 2009), 517–518.

27. Donald Rumsfeld, "Beyond Nation Building," 14 February 2003, http://www.au.af.mil/au/awc/awcgate/dod/sp20030214-secdef0024.htm. For Rumsfeld's push to extricate US forces from the Bosnia peacekeeping mission, see Dobbins, *After the Taliban*, 14–15.

28. Donald Rumsfeld to George W. Bush, "Decisions," memorandum, 19 Janu-

ary 2002, Rumsfeld Papers, http://library.rumsfeld.com/doclib/sp/743/2002-01-19 To President George W Bush re Decisions- Memo Attachment.Bush re Decisions-Memo Attachment 01-19-2002. According to Richard Haass, the "consensus was that little could be accomplished in Afghanistan given its history, culture, and composition." See Richard Haass, "Time to Draw Down in Afghanistan," *Newsweek*, 18 July 2010, http://www.newsweek.com/haass-time-draw-down-afghanistan-74467.

29. Paul D. Wolfowitz to Donald Rumsfeld, "Using Special Forces on 'Our Side' of the Line," memorandum, 23 September 2001, http://library.rumsfeld.com/doclib/sp/267/2001-09-23 from Wolfowitz re Using Special Forces on Our Side of the Line.pdf.

30. Keith L. Shimko, *The Iraq Wars and America's Military Revolution* (New York: Cambridge Univ. Press, 2010), 131–134; Frederick W. Kagan, *Finding the Target: The Transformation of American Military Policy*, 1st ed. (New York: Encounter Books, 2006), 265–286. On the RMA and Rumsfeld's desire to validate the concept, see also the essays by Lukas Milevski, Peter Mansoor, and Donald Travis in this volume.

31. "The U.S. should not commit to any post-Taliban military involvement, since the U.S. will be heavily engaged in the anti-terrorism effort worldwide." Office of the Secretary of Defense, "U.S. Strategy in Afghanistan."

32. For a broader historical perspective, see Schadlow, *War and the Art of Governance.*

33. Stephen Biddle, "Afghanistan and the Future of Warfare: Implications for Army and Defense Policy" (Carlisle, Pa.: Strategic Studies Institute, US Army War College, November 2002), 1–2, http://ssi.armywarcollege.edu/pdffiles/pub109.pdf.

34. In early 2002, US commanders understood there to be an unofficial force cap of roughly seven thousand troops; Brian F. Neumann, Lisa M. Mundey, and Jon Mikolashek, *The U.S. Army in Afghanistan: Operation Enduring Freedom, March 2002–April 2005* (Washington, DC: US Army Center of Military History, 2013), 11, http://www.history.army.mil/html/books/070/70-122-1/CMH_Pub_70-122-1.pdf. Troop levels would not exceed 10,500 over the course of that year. Amy Belasco, "The Cost of Iraq, Afghanistan, and Other Global War on Terror Operations since 9/11," Congressional Research Service, 8 December 2014, 81, https://fas.org/sgp/crs/natsec/RL33110.pdf.

35. Donald Rumsfeld, "Interview with Lally Weymouth, Washington Post and Newsweek," 18 December 2001, http://archive.defense.gov/Transcripts/Transcript.aspx?TranscriptID=2660.

36. George W. Bush and Tommy Franks, "PBS NewsHour Interview," 28 December 2001, https://georgewbush-whitehouse.archives.gov/news/releases/2001/12/20011228-1.html; Tommy Franks, "PBS NewsHour Interview," 8 January 2002, http://www.pbs.org/newshour/bb/terrorism-jan-june02-franks_1-8/.

37. Bob Woodward, *Plan of Attack* (New York: Simon and Schuster, 2004), 1–8.

38. Dov S. Zakheim, *A Vulcan's Tale: How the Bush Administration Mismanaged the Reconstruction of Afghanistan* (Washington, DC: Brookings Institution Press,

2011), 145.

39. Donald P. Wright et al., *A Different Kind of War: The United States Army in Operation Enduring Freedom (OEF), October 2001–September 2005* (Fort Leavenworth, Kans.: Combat Studies Institute Press, 2010), 190.

40. Neumann, Mundey, and Mikolashek, *The U.S. Army in Afghanistan: Operation Enduring Freedom, March 2002–April 2005*, 13–21.

41. For the policy debate on the expansion of ISAF, see Dobbins, *After the Taliban*, 130–131, "Views on Security in Afghanistan: Selected Quotes and Statements by U.S. and International Leaders," Peace Operations Factsheet (Stimson Center, June 2002), https://www.files.ethz.ch/isn/31674/ViewsonAfghanistan.pdf. For the impact of US policy on ISAF contributors, see Elizabeth Neuffer, "US, Britain Asking Turkey to Oversee Security in Afghanistan," *Boston Globe*, 14 March 2002, https://www.globalpolicy.org/component/content/article/178/33087.html.

42. The five "lead nations" were: the United States (army), Germany (police), Italy (judiciary), Great Britain (counternarcotics), and Japan (disarmament, demobilization, and reintegration). For an assessment, see Seth G. Jones, *In the Graveyard of Empires: America's War in Afghanistan* (New York: Norton, 2010), 239–243.

43. On warlordism in Afghanistan, see Dipali Mukhopadhyay, *Warlords, Strongman Governors, and the State in Afghanistan* (Cambridge: Cambridge Univ. Press, 2014); Antonio Giustozzi, *Empires of Mud: War and Warlords in Afghanistan* (New York: Columbia Univ. Press, 2009).

44. Joshua Partlow, *A Kingdom of Their Own: The Family Karzai and the Afghan Disaster* (New York: Knopf, 2016); Sarah Chayes, *The Punishment of Virtue: Inside Afghanistan After the Taliban* (New York: Penguin Press, 2006).

45. Rumsfeld "was convinced Karzai needed to learn to govern the Chicago way . . . using maneuver, guile, money, patronage, and services" to keep fractious leaders under his authority. Donald Rumsfeld, *Known and Unknown: A Memoir* (New York: Sentinel, 2011), 407. Rumsfeld therefore refused to give Karzai US military backing against armed challengers. Feith, *War and Decision*, 140–143, 145–146. More generally, Rumsfeld preferred for US Special Forces to use their influence to keep the peace among warlords. Dobbins, *After the Taliban*, 131. In a May 2002 memo, OSD assessed that order was "good" in provinces where dominant warlords existed. See Feith, *War and Decision*, appendix 2. For the CIA assessment, see Michael R. Gordon, "A Nation Challenged: Policy Divisions; C.I.A. Sees Threat Afghan Factions May Bring Chaos," *New York Times*, 21 February 2002, http://www.nytimes.com/2002/02/21/world/nation-challenged-policy-divisions-cia-sees-threat-afghan-factions-may-bring.html.

46. Rumsfeld believed the critical problem in Afghanistan was not security, but "the slow progress that is being made on the civil side"; Donald Rumsfeld to George W. Bush, "Afghanistan," memorandum, 20 August 2002, Rumsfeld Papers, http://library.rumsfeld.com/doclib/sp/439/To President George W. Bush et al. re Afghanistan 08-20-2002.pdf.

47. James Dao, "Threats and Responses: Afghanistan; Wolfowitz, in Kabul,

Calls for Rebuilding," *New York Times,* 16 January 2003, https://www.nytimes.com/2003/01/16/world/threats-and-responses-afghanistan-wolfowitz-in-kabul-calls-for-rebuilding.html.

48. Office of the Secretary of Defense, "Principles for Afghanistan—Policy Guidelines," 7 July 2003, Rumsfeld Papers, http://library.rumsfeld.com/doclib/sp/438/2003-07-07 re Principles for Afghanistan-Policy Guidelines.pdf.

49. Robert Kemp, *Counterinsurgency in Eastern Afghanistan 2004–2008: A Civilian Perspective* (Washington, DC: New Academia Publishing, 2014); DoD, "Progress Toward Security and Stability in Afghanistan," Section 1230 Report, January 2009, https://www.defense.gov/Portals/1/Documents/pubs/OCTOBER_1230_FINAL.pdf.

50. NATO-ISAF defined the political end state as "A self-sustaining, moderate and democratic Afghan government able to exercise its sovereign authority, independently, throughout Afghanistan." See ISAF, "SACEUR OPLAN 10302 (REVISE 1)," December 2005, http://www.ft.dk/samling/20051/UM-del/Bilag/44/242709.pdf.

51. Zalmay Khalilzad, *The Envoy: From Kabul to the White House, My Journey Through a Turbulent World* (New York: St. Martin's Press, 2016), chapter 17.

52. For this early COIN campaign, see David W. Barno, "Fighting 'The Other War': Counterinsurgency Strategy in Afghanistan, 2003–2005," *Military Review* 87, no. 5 (September–October 2007): 32–44.

53. Zalmay Khalilzad, "Hearing on Nomination of Zalmay Khalilzad to Be Ambassador to Afghanistan," Senate Committee on Foreign Relations (29 October 2003). OSD aimed for key reconstruction objectives to be completed by the end of 2007. Office of the Secretary of Defense, "Principles for Afghanistan—Policy Guidelines."

54. Belasco, "Cost of Iraq, Afghanistan."

55. On the genesis of the Provincial Reconstruction Team concept, see Jack Fairweather, *The Good War: Why We Couldn't Win the War or the Peace in Afghanistan* (New York: Basic Books, 2014), chapter 11.

56. For the importance of the "political" side of political-military affairs in this period, see David W. Barno, "Economy of Force: Building a Headquarters for Afghanistan, 2003–2005," in *Essential to Success: Historical Case Studies in the Art of Command at Echelons above Brigade,* ed. Kelvin Dale Crow and Joe R. Bailey (Fort Leavenworth, Kans.: Army Univ. Press, 2017), 237–248.

57. Condoleezza Rice, "'Accelerating Success in Afghanistan' in 2004: An Assessment," memorandum, 18 January 2005, Rumsfeld Papers, http://library.rumsfeld.com/doclib/sp/440/From the White House re Accelerating Success in Afghanistan in 2004 an Assessment 01-18-2005.pdf.

58. Quote taken from Condoleezza Rice, *No Higher Honor: A Memoir of My Years in Washington* (New York: Crown Publishers, 2011), 345. For NATO's takeover of the Afghan mission, see Graham, *By His Own Rules,* 644–645.

59. Eric Schmitt and David S. Cloud, "U.S. May Start Pulling Out of Afghan-

istan Next Spring," *New York Times,* 14 September 2005, https://www.nytimes.com/2005/09/14/washington/world/us-may-start-pulling-out-of-afghanistan-next-spring.html; Eric Schmitt, "U.S. to Cut Force in Afghanistan," *New York Times,* 20 December 2005, https://www.nytimes.com/2005/12/20/world/asia/us-to-cut-force-in-afghanistan.html.

60. Ronald E. Neumann, *The Other War: Winning and Losing in Afghanistan* (Washington, DC: Potomac Books, 2009), 39–50.

61. DoS, "Counterterrorism Activities (Neo-Taliban)," 9 December 2005, National Security Archive, http://nsarchive.gwu.edu/NSAEBB/NSAEBB325/doc14.pdf; Ronald E. Neumann, "Policy on Track, but Violence Will Rise," cable, 21 February 2006, National Security Archive, http://nsarchive.gwu.edu/NSAEBB/NSAEBB325/doc15.pdf; Marin Strmecki, "Afghanistan at a Crossroads: Challenges, Opportunities, and a Way Ahead," presentation, 17 August 2006, Rumsfeld Papers, http://library.rumsfeld.com/doclib/sp/456/2006-08-17%20from%20Marin%20Strmecki%20re%20Afghanistan%20at%20a%20Crossroads%20Briefing.pdf.

62. Sten Rynning, *NATO in Afghanistan: The Liberal Disconnect* (Stanford, Calif.: Stanford Univ. Press, 2012).

63. Ronald E. Neumann, "Afghanistan: Where We Stand and What We Need," cable, 29 August 2006, National Security Archive, http://nsarchive.gwu.edu/NSAEBB/NSAEBB358a/doc26.pdf.

64. Robert M. Gates, *Duty: Memoirs of a Secretary at War* (New York: Knopf, 2014), 200–202.

65. Gates, 210; Ann Scott Tyson, "NATO's Not Winning in Afghanistan, Report Says," *Washington Post,* 31 January 2008, http://www.washingtonpost.com/wp-dyn/content/article/2008/01/30/AR2008013004314.html.

66. Barack Obama, "Address Accepting the Presidential Nomination at the Democratic National Convention in Denver: 'The American Promise,'" Denver, Colorado, 28 August 2008, http://www.presidency.ucsb.edu/ws/index.php?pid=78284; Barack Obama, "The War We Need to Win," speech, Washington, DC, 1 August 2007, http://www.presidency.ucsb.edu/ws/?pid=77040.

67. The Bush White House had undertaken its own strategic review in the fall of 2008, but it left the decision-making to the next administration. Gates, *Duty,* 222; Woodward, *Obama's Wars,* 43–44; Bush, *Decision Points,* 218.

68. For the reasons behind this policy change, see Carlotta Gall, *The Wrong Enemy: America in Afghanistan, 2001–2014* (Boston: Houghton Mifflin Harcourt, 2014).

69. Obama, "A New Strategy for Afghanistan and Pakistan."

70. At the administration's request, Congress increased the civilian assistance budget for Afghanistan by more than 50 percent for FY 2010; Belasco, "Cost of Iraq, Afghanistan."

71. Obama, "A New Strategy for Afghanistan and Pakistan."

72. Woodward, *Obama's Wars,* 123.

73. Bob Woodward, "McChrystal: More Forces or 'Mission Failure,'" *Wash-*

ington Post, 21 September 2009, http://www.washingtonpost.com/wp-dyn/content/article/2009/09/20/AR2009092002920.html.

74. For the deterioration of US-Karzai relations, see Partlow, *A Kingdom of Their Own*; Kai Eide, *Power Struggle over Afghanistan: An Inside Look at What Went Wrong, and What We Can Do to Repair the Damage* (New York: Skyhorse, 2012).

75. Woodward, *Obama's Wars,* 385.

76. Barack Obama, "Remarks by the President in Address to the Nation on the Way Forward in Afghanistan and Pakistan," 1 December 2009, https://obamawhitehouse.archives.gov/the-press-office/remarks-president-address-nation-way-forward-afghanistan-and-pakistan.

77. NATO, "Lisbon Summit Declaration," 20 November 2010, http://www.nato.int/cps/en/natohq/official_texts_68828.htm.

78. NATO, "Inteqal: Transition to Afghan Lead," NATO, http://www.nato.int/cps/en/natohq/topics_87183.htm (accessed 21 June 2017); Barack Obama, "Remarks by the President on the Way Forward in Afghanistan," 22 June 2011, https://obamawhitehouse.archives.gov/the-press-office/2011/06/22/remarks-president-way-forward-afghanistan.

79. Kenneth Katzman, "Afghanistan: Post-Taliban Governance, Security, and U.S. Policy," Congressional Research Service, 4 January 2013, 32, http://www.au.af.mil/au/awc/awcgate/crs/r130588.pdf.

80. Tanya Somanader, "On Christmas Day, President Obama Thanks Troops in Hawaii for Their Extraordinary Service," *White House Blog* (blog), 27 December 2014, https://obamawhitehouse.archives.gov/blog/2014/12/27/christmas-day-president-obama-thanks-troops-hawaii-their-extraordinary-service.

81. Barack Obama, "Statement by the President on Afghanistan," 27 May 2014, https://obamawhitehouse.archives.gov/the-press-office/2014/05/27/statement-president-afghanistan; Dan Lamothe, "Meet Operation Freedom's Sentinel, the Pentagon's New Mission in Afghanistan," *Washington Post,* 29 December 2014, https://www.washingtonpost.com/news/checkpoint/wp/2014/12/29/meet-operation-freedoms-sentinel-the-pentagons-new-mission-in-afghanistan/.

82. Barack Obama, "Address to the Nation from Afghanistan," 1 May 2012, https://obamawhitehouse.archives.gov/the-press-office/2012/05/01/remarks-president-obama-address-nation-afghanistan.

83. For "Afghan Good Enough," see David E. Sanger, *Confront and Conceal: Obama's Secret Wars and Surprising Use of American Power* (New York: Crown Publishers, 2012), 49–51.

84. Colin Jackson, "Government in a Box? Counter-Insurgency, State Building and the Technocratic Conceit," in *The New Counter-Insurgency Era in Critical Perspective,* ed. Celeste Ward Gventer, David Martin Jones, and M.L.R. Smith (Basingstoke: Palgrave Macmillan, 2014), 82–110; Karl W. Eikenberry, "The Limits of Counterinsurgency Doctrine in Afghanistan," *Foreign Affairs,* 1 September 2013, https://www.foreignaffairs.com/articles/afghanistan/2013-08-12/limits-counterinsurgency-doctrine-afghanistan; Eric Schmitt, "U.S. Envoy's Cables Show Deep Con-

cerns on Afghan Strategy," *New York Times,* 25 January 2010, http://www.nytimes.com/2010/01/26/world/asia/26strategy.html.

85. Jonathan Schroden et al., "Independent Assessment of the Afghan National Security Forces," CNA, 2014, https://www.cna.org/CNA_files/PDF/DRM-2014-U-006815-Final.pdf; M. Chris Mason, *The Strategic Lessons Unlearned from Vietnam, Iraq, and Afghanistan: Why the Afghan National Security Forces Will Not Hold, and the Implications for the U.S. Army in Afghanistan* (Carlisle, Pa.: Strategic Studies Institute and US Army War College Press, 2015), http://ssi.armywarcollege.edu/pdffiles/PUB1269.pdf; T. X. Hammes, "Raising and Mentoring Security Forces in Afghanistan and Iraq," in *Lessons Encountered: Learning from the Long War,* ed. Richard D. Hooker Jr. and Joseph J. Collins (Washington, DC: National Defense Univ. Press, 2015), 277–344, http://ndupress.ndu.edu/Portals/68/Documents/Books/lessons-encountered/lessons-encountered.pdf.

86. Thomas Joscelyn and Bill Roggio, "US Military Strikes Large Al Qaeda Training Camps in Southern Afghanistan," *Long War Journal* (blog), http://www.longwarjournal.org/archives/2015/10/us-military-strikes-large-al-qaeda-training-camps-in-southern-afghanistan.php (accessed 21 June 2017).

87. Mark Landler, "The Afghan War and the Evolution of Obama," *New York Times,* 1 January 2017, https://www.nytimes.com/2017/01/01/world/asia/obama-afghanistan-war.html.

88. Barack Obama, "Statement by the President on Afghanistan," 15 October 2015, https://obamawhitehouse.archives.gov/the-press-office/2015/10/15/statement-president-afghanistan.

89. Bill Roggio, "Afghan Taliban Lists 'Percent of Country under the Control of Mujahideen,'" *FDD's Long War Journal* (blog), 28 March 2017, http://www.longwarjournal.org/archives/2017/03/afghan-taliban-lists-percent-of-country-under-the-control-of-mujahideen.php.

90. Scott Sigmund Gartner and Leo Blanken, "Beyond Victory and Defeat," in *Afghan Endgames: Strategy and Policy Choices for America's Longest War,* ed. Hy S. Rothstein and John Arquilla (Washington, DC: Georgetown Univ. Press, 2012), 128.

91. For the quotation, see Obama, "Remarks by the President on the Way Forward in Afghanistan."

7

Reading Manila, Thinking Wiesbaden

Current Parallels to Pre-World War II Army Unpreparedness

James DiCrocco

On 7 May 1942 an exhausted but defiant General Jonathan Wainwright, commander of the US forces in the Philippines, broadcast a surrender announcement to the world from the studios of radio station KZRH in Manila, ending a six-month struggle against a Japanese invasion that began on 8 December 1941. Seventy-five years later, a similarly small (given the threat) contingent in US Army Europe (USAREUR), of about thirty thousand, prepares with its allies of NATO for a possible defense of Europe against Russia. This scenario seemed incomprehensible even a few short years ago.

The differences between the two situations are many. USAREUR is composed of many troops hardened by many years of constant combat deployments. It is equipped with some of the most advanced military equipment. Morale among the force is high, and it undergoes scheduled tough training at all levels of war. The command is well integrated with the allied armies of NATO, many of which have trained and operated with each other for decades, and supply lines, while vulnerable, are well protected. On the other hand, the US and Philippine Army forces who surrendered to the Japanese in 1942 were composed of officers and troops who had not fought since World War I, or who had no combat experience at all. Their equipment was a mixture of mostly obsolescent equipment with a modicum of untested gear. Morale was generally high before the surrender, as the troops had become hardened, but despair occasioned by the fading promises of relief was also not uncommon. Desertions had been high, especially in the first few weeks when untried Philippine and American troops faced the experienced Japanese military. Training had been limited mostly to the unit level for most of the troops prior to the war, if they had any at all. The American and Philippine armies had not been integrated, nor had they operated together in any meaningful way. With the destruction of the American Pacific fleet at Pearl Harbor in

December 1941, the Japanese severed the American-Philippine army's supply lines. It was soon isolated on Bataan with dwindling provisions. These are just a few of the dissimilarities between the two situations.

Nonetheless, there are some broad observations from the fall of the Philippines that may be pertinent to USAREUR as it increases its readiness in the face of another revanchist great power (Russia) following an extended period of American defense budget tightening and reduced forces in Europe. From the mid-1930s through 1941, the US Army Forces in the Far East (USAFFE) and its immediate antecedent commands in the Philippines prepared for a possible conflict with Japan in a similarly resource-constrained era. USAREUR in the current period has a number of challenges similar to those that confronted USAFFE. Similar initiatives undertaken by US commanders in the Philippines some seventy-five years prior will help frame a brief review and comparison of three of the pillars of what USAREUR refers to as "Strong Europe."[1] USAREUR embraces five pillars in its "Strong Europe" concept of supporting US Army priorities in the European region. These are the empowerment of junior leaders, Reserve Component integration, a focus on allies and partners, regionally allocated forces, and maintaining a dynamic presence.[2] This parallel allows for insight into the problems and opportunities concerning the projection of landpower in a theater considered to be of secondary importance.

One of these pillars stresses the integration of Reserve Component soldiers into USAREUR. Much like Europe in the twenty-first century, the Philippine-based American army commanders prior to the start of World War II relied heavily on the incorporation of Reserve Component soldiers to augment their forces.[3] Today there are Army National Guard and US Army Reserve troops supporting the training of both US and regional forces in at least twenty-two European countries through the National Guard state partnership program. There also is reserve unit overseas deployment training and various theater-dedicated Army Reserve units. Likewise, from the late 1930s through 1941, first through the activities of General Douglas MacArthur's military advisory mission to the Philippine Commonwealth, US Army officers assisted in the development, training, and support of the new Philippine Army, which itself consisted overwhelmingly of reserve soldiers. In 1941, the US Army deployed to the Philippines a cadre of over four hundred Reserve officers to expand and intensify this training of the Philippine Army. MacArthur also requested Army National Guard units to augment his forces, including armor and coastal and field artillery. These units mobilized in the United States and were then subsequently dispatched to aid defensive preparations of the Philippines.[4]

USAREUR strives to increase interoperability with its allies and partners in the region as the "normal way to cooperate in Europe" to strengthen NATO's collective defense. Cuts in NATO defense budgets and the resulting drastic reduction in the alliance's land forces since the Cold War have necessitated cooperation. Part of this includes the shared use of both scarce enablers (for example, heavy equipment transporters and engineer bridging assets) and other resources, some of which may only be readily available from one NATO ally. Similarly, US commanders had to recognize the strengths, weaknesses, and capabilities of their Filipino partners in the newly created Philippine Army. The vast majority of the ground forces available to US commanders at that time would not be American. Over 80 percent of the soldiers available to General MacArthur and his commanders were Filipino. Even within the US Army's Philippine Division, the largest American unit, the vast majority of the soldiers were Filipinos recruited into US-officered Philippine Scout regiments. Two of the three infantry regiments in the division were Philippine Scout regiments, and most of the combat support and combat service support elements were as well.[5]

A third USAREUR pillar relates to "dynamic presence" or active engagement, but it comprises only about 30,000 US soldiers. Due to its small size, USAREUR's forces must be agile and adaptable to both geopolitical circumstances and the dictates of geography. Remaining in Europe is only 11 percent of the two-corps force of approximately 277,000 soldiers stationed in Europe in the early 1960s at the height of the Cold War Berlin Crisis.[6] These troops were located primarily in western Germany and northern Italy, in accordance with specific NATO defense plans. Similarly, on 30 November 1941, only a week before the American entry into World War II, there were about 31,000 US Army troops in the Philippines. About 12,000 of these soldiers were locally recruited Philippine Scouts.[7]

In another rough parallel, USAREUR forces currently are concentrated primarily in Germany and Italy, much as they were thirty years ago. However, unlike the Cold War years, USAREUR has extended geographical responsibilities that stretch its units' areas of operation into many other countries in Central and Eastern Europe over a very broad footprint. This leads to what the command refers to as a "dynamic presence" with its NATO host nations.[8] While the US Army in the late 1930s Philippines concentrated in major posts like Fort Stotsenburg and Clark Army Airfield on the main island of Luzon and on the fortress-like Corregidor Island located at the entrance to Manila Bay, it had responsibilities far beyond the Manila-Luzon area. US troops had divisional training missions on numerous other islands in the archipelago. These missions extended as far south as the island of Mindanao, over six hundred miles from Manila.

A closer examination of the situation facing the US Army in the Philippines immediately prior to and during the first American land campaign in World War II may illuminate and contextualize some of the challenges confronting USAREUR today. In the fall of 1935, former CSA Major General Douglas MacArthur arrived in the Philippines to assume the title of military advisor to the commonwealth government. He was conferred the rank of field marshal, a new Philippine position specially created for him with the endorsement of the US government. Manuel Quezon, the president of the United States' new Commonwealth of the Philippines,[9] charged MacArthur and his small handpicked staff, including Lieutenant Colonel Dwight D. Eisenhower, with developing a national defense apparatus in anticipation of Philippine independence in ten years.[10]

The new Philippine National Assembly ratified the Philippine National Defense Act in December 1935 with input from MacArthur and his staff. The act provided an outline for the development of a new, indigenous Philippine national defense force. It appropriated $8 million for the establishment of a new Philippine Army. The act envisioned a very small regular Philippine Army of only about 10,000 men supplemented by a larger trained reserve force of up to 400,000 troops. The Philippine Commonwealth's defense establishment would grow this reserve force over the next ten years through the raising and training of 40,000 conscripts for five and a half months annually. These troops would return to their homes following the training period and the Philippine government would only mobilize them again in response to a major crisis. The act also established a Philippine Military Academy modeled on West Point; reserve officer training; 120 army training camps for about 200 troops each; the formation of other military schools in the Philippines; and the procurement of initial supplies and equipment.

During the late 1930s and into 1941, MacArthur and his staff began to develop a military establishment from scratch despite encountering numerous fiscal and political constraints imposed first by the United States, then the Philippine Commonwealth, and finally by both governments. Akin to USAREUR's depleted situation over the past twenty-five years since the end of the Cold War, only rarely would MacArthur and Quezon be able to gain precedence from Washington for the funding of defense requests, no matter the perceived urgency of the requirements in the Philippines.[11]

There was a mixed reaction to the Philippine Defense Plan among US senior officers. In addition, American media criticized MacArthur for making an "unauthorized move to militarize the Filipino people."[12] Likewise, some politicians in Washington became concerned that the development of the Philippine armed forces and any increase in US forces in the Philippines might antagonize Japan.[13] There soon was criticism of the revenue allocations for Philippine defense from some of the Filipinos themselves. A number of Philippine politicians made charges that there was excessive militarization and that funding was being diverted from civilian education. There was also contention that it was a ploy to keep a US presence on the islands after the scheduled independence date.[14]

Despite the controversy, training camps were established in early 1937 and the first twenty thousand Philippine Army conscripts began reporting for duty. The training staffs soon encountered many issues with the education levels of their new conscripts. Troops in the same units frequently spoke several different languages, and few of the conscripts' newly commissioned Philippine Army officers had any previous military experience, leading to even more disarray. MacArthur's appeals for supplies and equipment at his staff's formulated minimum planning levels went unheeded. The new army lacked equipment of every type, partly due to an inadequate budget for such an ambitious enterprise.[15] As an example, by July 1937 the funding for the entire fiscal year already had run out, and the new Philippine military had to borrow from its next year's budget. From the time the mission began in 1935, neither MacArthur nor his assistants believed that the Philippine Department considered the development of the Philippine Army as its major priority, despite the US War Department's direction to that effect. Philippine Departmental support consisted almost exclusively of the release of a few dozen officers and noncommissioned officers to train the new army.[16]

As of January 1938, all of MacArthur's requests for equipment, ammunition, other materiel, and US Army personnel support were routed through the US Army's commanding general of the Philippine Department and then on to the War Department. Meanwhile in 1938, President Quezon grew more distant from MacArthur. He and some of his defense advisors, worried about an aggressive Japan and a lack of US response, shifted toward an attempt at accommodation with Japan. As a result, their support for MacArthur's activities and the military's growth declined compared to the previous several years. At this point in 1938, MacArthur had to receive approval from both Quezon and the Philippine secretary of defense in order to purchase ammunition, induct conscripts, and build new military facilities.

The Philippine military's share of the commonwealth's annual budget declined by 21 percent in the last years of the 1930s. During the same period, the Philippine National Assembly cancelled a plan to accelerate the army's development.[17] The number of registered conscripts fell by 65,000 over the course of the four years prior to 1941 due to "indifference on the part of" provincial officials.[18] For multiple additional reasons, many registered conscripts simply never showed up to their mobilization stations.[19] The Philippine Army never reached its stated goal of 40,000 trainees per year prior to the general mobilization in 1941. The 1940 reserve force consisted on paper of almost 6,500 officers and 120,000 enlisted men in ten reserve infantry divisions (one located in each Philippine military district), but only 857 officers and 24,174 soldiers had received practical training in the field, mostly in 1939.[20] However, the troops' lack of both training and equipment called into question their utility if mobilized for any real contingency. Furthermore, continued shortages resulted in little weapons training for mobilized reserve conscripts.

Meanwhile, the Philippine Regular Army stood at only 468 officers and 3,697 enlisted men. The Philippine 1st Infantry Division consisted of only 286 men in one regiment. Most of the division's remaining regular soldiers were scattered among the many training camps, providing instruction to conscripted reserve soldiers. Much like its reserve brethren, the Philippine regular soldiers suffered from low morale due to low pay, poor rations, and low educational levels. The number of officers produced by the three reserve officer schools, the Philippine Reserve Officers Training Corps, and the Philippine Military Academy in its first graduating classes all fell well short of the Philippine Army's needs. About 20 percent of its enlisted trainees were illiterate, while only about the same percentage had finished the first year of high school. In addition, there were occasional "trainee strikes and demonstrations against officers." Lieutenant Colonel F. G. Oboza, the Philippine adjutant general, lamented in 1940 that "the individual trainee has not learned his basic duties as a Soldier . . . [as] the training method prescribed has not been followed."[21]

MacArthur's relations with the Philippine Department improved in May 1940 when Major General George Grunert took departmental command. He and MacArthur worked together to increase the defense of the Philippines. In September 1940, Grunert told the new CSA, General George Marshall, of a sense of defeatism pervading the Philippines. He attributed this to the US government's "lack of an announced policy backed by visual evidence of defense means and measures" in support of the commonwealth.[22]

Partially as a result of this perceived continued lack of support, Quezon and the Philippine National Assembly again reduced military budgets during 1940–1941. The 1941 budget called for the training of reservists to be cut by 50 percent and for half of the Philippine Army's training camps to be closed, along with two of the three officer schools. Quezon now required MacArthur to communicate with him only through his presidential secretary, Jorge Vargas. When told by Vargas that President Quezon was too busy to meet with him, MacArthur replied, "Jorge, someday your boss is going to want to see me more than I want to see him."[23]

Nonetheless, MacArthur realized that no matter what the Philippine government did, the adequate defense of the Philippines would fall not on the defense establishment he was helping to build, but on any American reinforcements in the form of both personnel and materiel. To this end, with the deterioration of the security situation in the Far East and as a result of aggressive Japanese acts toward China and Indochina, Washington was now slowly moving toward action. During the summer of 1940, Grunert said that there was enough ammunition for "only about three or four days of fire per weapon" for American-led troops in the Philippines.[24] Following the latest request by Grunert to the War Department for more defense supplies and equipment, he received the following reply: "A sufficient number will be available in 1942 to meet the approved requirements of all overseas departments."[25] Washington still had little to spare for Philippine defense, as American mobilization was only just beginning.

The state of affairs in the Far East continued to deteriorate in the spring and summer of 1941. On 22 July, the Japanese occupied air and naval bases in Vichy French Indochina. Following a recommendation by Secretary of War Henry Stimson to respond to the Japanese threat to the rest of Southeast Asia, on 26 July President Franklin Roosevelt authorized the creation of a new American command charged with defense of the Philippines—USAFFE. The War Department called MacArthur back to active duty from retirement. It placed him in command of the new organization and designated him a temporary US Army lieutenant general on 27 July. MacArthur's new command absorbed the Philippine Department, and Grunert soon returned stateside. In addition to the department's largest American unit, the Philippine Division, the new command encompassed the Philippine Army now being mobilized and inducted into active US service by President Roosevelt's invocation of a provision of the Tydings-McDuffie Act of 1935.[26]

MacArthur's first task was to organize his headquarters. He retained the chief of staff and deputy chief of staff from his military mission for USAFFE and filled many other key staff positions with former acquaintances and officers from the military mission and the Philippine Department. He also appointed his subordinate unit commanders.[27] The headquarters now set a "grueling pace."[28]

The staff immediately requested large quantities of equipment from the War Department: helmets, boots, field gear, the latest Army rifle (the M-1 Garand), machine guns, mortars, antitank guns, antiaircraft guns, medical equipment, vehicles, and artillery pieces. While CSA General Marshall gave the supplying, equipping, and reinforcing of the Philippines the Army's top priority during the summer and fall of 1941, the materiel was not received in the quantities needed, nor was its transportation timely enough. Most of the materiel would not be available for shipment until sometime in December or even later in 1942.[29]

In June 1941, a War Department memorandum remarked that the Philippine Army "is of doubtful combat efficiency, lacking competent leadership above the company grades, important items of equipment requisite to a balanced force, and adequate supplies for extended campaign."[30] On 15 August, MacArthur chaired a conference to plan the mobilization training of the Philippine Army, set to commence in two weeks, on 1 September. As facilities had previously been required for the training of only up to 20,000 soldiers at a time, construction would have to be rushed to accommodate all mobilized Philippine Army soldiers, numbering up to 100,000. USAFFE structured the ten Philippine Army reserve divisions along organizational lines equivalent to US divisions, with three infantry regiments in each division. However, while authorizations for US divisions totaled 15,000 men, the Philippine divisions only totaled 8,000 men, with 1,850 soldiers authorized for each infantry regiment. These divisions would be mobilized in stages running through the end of November 1941, at the rate of about one regiment per division per month. Forty US officers and twenty US or Philippine Scout noncommissioned officers would be allocated to each division as training instructors. MacArthur estimated that American units would be ready by the end of April 1942 and that the Philippine Army could fight the Japanese by the end of July.[31]

In general, the growth of the Philippine Air Corps and MacArthur's Army Air Corps formation was even slower than the development of the Philippine Army. The goal established in 1935 for the Philippine Air Corps was a force consisting of 250 aircraft by 1946. Yet, the first squadron of twenty-one planes was not organized until 1939. Even at the end of 1940, the air corps stood at merely forty obsolescent planes with only four hundred pilots and ground crew at five airfields. Finally, in June 1941, the War Department allocated 130 modern P-40 fighters and 272 of the latest bombers to outfit the newly formed Far East Air Forces (FEAF), a subordinate USAFFE organization, under the command of Major General Lewis Brereton. In November, the US Army's air staff decided to send the bulk of America's most modern B-17 and B-24 heavy bombers to equip FEAF. By early December 1941, Brereton's airmen in FEAF had 74 bombers, 175 pursuit planes, and 58 other aircraft on hand—more bombers and fighters than in the Army's Hawaiian Department. Even with these aircraft, FEAF suffered from an inadequate dispersion of the aircraft on-hand due to a lack of sufficient high-quality airfields. Additional airfields were being planned. There also were just two newly delivered radar sets by early December, and they were only in the early stages of operation. In addition, only two facets of the inadequate air defense protection were available for USAFFE despite the rush to upgrade. The embryonic Philippine Navy fared the worst of all. By the start of the war, it was almost nonexistent, consisting of only two motor torpedo boats of British design.[32]

On 21 November, Marshall authorized USAFFE to plan to defend the entire Philippine Islands archipelago and not to restrict itself to defense of the entrances to Manila and Subic Bays, as was previously established in War Plan Rainbow 5, the latest war plan published by the War Department in October 1941.[33] As late as 27 November, MacArthur was still convinced that the Japanese would not attack the Philippines until the spring of 1942 and that USAFFE would have a force trained, equipped, and ready to defend the commonwealth by that time.[34] Nonetheless, and despite the concerted efforts of Marshall, MacArthur, and countless others—American and Filipino—USAFFE was not ready when the Japanese struck the Philippines on 8 December 1941, several months ahead of MacArthur's expectation. Despite shortages of personnel, lack of training, and the want of equipment and supplies of all kinds, the Filipino and American defenders desperately and heroically held out for five of the six months originally called for under variations of the US war plans.

While there are many causes for losing the Philippines at the beginning of World War II, one important aspect worthy of emphasis was the unpreparedness of USAFFE forces confronting the Japanese. Discussion of other reasons for the defeat is beyond the scope of this chapter, but they included an overreliance on airpower in the command's planning assumptions; a lack of concentrated prewar joint cooperation in theater between the Army and the Navy; an inadequate prioritization by the US War Department and the Philippine Department for MacArthur's mission from 1935 until 1941; the lack US War Department funding toward the structure of the Philippine Army from 1935; and MacArthur's overconfidence in 1941, leading to untimely changes to plans.

USAREUR's five pillars for a Strong Europe bear many similarities with the initiatives MacArthur intended to implement with enough time and resources. In 2015, Lieutenant General Ben Hodges, a recent USAREUR commander, noted that in his opinion "the Russians are mobilizing right now for a war that they think is going to happen in five or six years"—or about the same amount of time MacArthur's military mission unknowingly had to prepare for its war.[35]

Over the past decade, the United States has neglected its European-based force partially due to the operational demands of their almost continuous rotational deployments to Iraq and Afghanistan since 2003. In 2005, decisions were initiated that ultimately led to the departure of the 1st Armored Division from USAREUR to Fort Bliss, Texas, which was completed in 2011.[36] That same year, the post of USAREUR commander, which had once been the most prestigious army-level command in the US Army, was reduced from a four-star rank to that of three-star for the first time since the Korean War era.[37] This drawdown continued the following year.

At the beginning of 2012, USAREUR still had a four-brigade permanently positioned force led by a corps. The corps headquarters, V Corps, with two heavy mechanized brigades, the 170th and 172nd, along with a motorized brigade, 2nd Cavalry, was in Germany, and an airborne brigade, the 173rd, was split between Italy and Germany. On 26 January 2012, then CSA General Raymond Odierno released the decision that the two brigades would be deactivated and withdrawn.[38] The 170th cased its colors in the fall of 2012, and the 172nd did likewise in 2013. This left the United States' forward-deployed army in Europe with no permanently stationed armored force in theater.[39] At that point, the US Marine Corps had a larger American armored force in the European theater than did the US Army.[40] In 2014, the Army reintroduced a small number of tanks, twenty-nine, for rotational training purposes, but they were unassigned to a permanently stationed unit.[41] In yet another important cut to USAREUR, V Corps inactivated on 12 June 2013 after ninety-five years of service, leaving the command with no operational headquarters in theater.[42] The following year, Russia annexed the Crimea from Ukraine.[43] During 2017 and 2018, additional US armor was reintroduced into the theater via brigade rotations from the United States. However, the overall number of armored vehicles was still much lower than that present even less than a decade earlier.

As USAREUR continues to rebuild its capabilities, it would be useful to reflect on a prophetic quote given by General MacArthur to an American journalist shortly before the beginning of World War II: "The history of failure in war can almost be summed up in two words: Too Late. Too late in comprehending the deadly purpose of a potential enemy; too late in realizing the mortal danger; too late in preparedness; too late in uniting all possible forces for resistance; too late in standing with one's friends."[44] The United States should heed this warning from the past and ensure that both its army and those of its allies in Europe do not meet a fate similar to that which befell the soldiers, sailors, and marines who bravely fought and sacrificed alongside their valiant Filipino comrades in arms during the fall of the Philippines.

Notes

1. See USAREUR's website for more information on the five pillars: http:// www.eur.army.mil/pillars/.

2. Empowering junior leaders and regionally allocated forces are not specifically addressed here.

3. Reservists comprised the vast majority of the Philippine Army. In addition, many US officers and enlisted men were from the Army Reserve. There also were several federalized US Army National Guard units present in the Philippines by the fall of 1941.

4. Louis Morton, *The Fall of the Philippines* (Washington, DC: Office of the Chief of Military History, Department of the Army, 1953), 32–37.

5. Morton, *The Fall of the Philippines*, 21.

6. Craig A. Daniel and Robin T. Dothager, "Resetting the Theater to Equip Rotational Forces in Europe," *Army Sustainment Magazine* 48, no. 3 (May–June 2016), 38.

7. Morton, *The Fall of the Philippines*, 49.

8. USAREUR's website: http://www.eur.army.mil/pillars/.

9. The Philippine Commonwealth was formed on 23 March 1935 following passage of the Tydings-McDuffie Act, or Philippine Independence Act, on 24 March 1934. Morton, *The Fall of the Philippines*, 4–5. The Philippine government made MacArthur a field marshal in the nascent Philippine Army on 24 August 1936. D. Clayton James, *The Years of MacArthur*, vol. 1, *1880–1941* (Boston: Houghton Mifflin, 1970), 505.

10. Morton, *The Fall of the Philippines*, 9.

11. James, *The Years of MacArthur*, 1:510–551; Morton, *The Fall of the Philippines*, 9–13.

12. James, *The Years of MacArthur*, 1:506.

13. R. M. Connaughton, *MacArthur and Defeat in the Philippines* (Woodstock, N.Y.: Overlook Press, 2001), 69.

14. James, *The Years of MacArthur*, 1:520.

15. Morton, *The Fall of the Philippines*, 28.

16. James, *The Years of MacArthur*, 1:514–515.

17. Ricardo Trota Jose, *The Philippine Army: 1935–1942* (Manila, Philippines: Ateneo de Manila Univ. Press, 1998), 126.

18. James, *The Years of MacArthur*, 1:527.

19. Jose, *The Philippine Army*, 126.

20. Ibid., 170.

21. James, *The Years of MacArthur*, 1:529.

22. Ibid., 1:549.

23. Ibid., 1:538.

24. Ibid., 1:580.

25. Ibid., 1:581.

26. Morton, *The Fall of the Philippines*, 18.

27. Ibid., 19.

28. James, *The Years of MacArthur*, 1:596.

29. Morton, *The Fall of the Philippines*, 32–37.

30. James, *The Years of MacArthur*, 1:581.

31. Ibid., 1:596–599.

32. Morton, *The Fall of the Philippines*, 13, 37–45.

33. Ibid., 64–71.

34. Connaughton, *MacArthur and Defeat in the Philippines*, 150.

35. Sohrab Ahmari, "The View from NATO's Russian Front," *Wall Street Journal*, 6 February 2015.

36. Mark Patton, "Old Ironsides Bids Farewell to Germany," *Stars and Stripes*, 13 May 2011, https://www.stripes.com/news/old-ironsides-bids-farewell-to-germany-1.143477.

37. Nancy Montgomery, "Hertling Takes the Helm at U.S. Army Europe," *Stars and Stripes*, 25 March 2011, https://www.stripes.com/news/europe/hertling-takes-the-helm-at-u-s-army-europe-1.138887.

38. Steven Beardsley and Jennifer H. Svan, "DOD Plan Indicates 172nd and 170th Infantry Brigades to Be Eliminated," *Stars and Stripes*, 26 January 2012.

39. John Vandiver, "US Army's Last Tanks Depart from Germany," *Stars and Stripes*, 4 April 2013, https://www.stripes.com/news/us-army-s-last-tanks-depart-from-germany-1.214977.

40. The US Marine Corps had about a company of tanks in a depot in Norway during this time.

41. Michael S. Darnell, "American Tanks Return to Europe after Brief Leave," *Stars and Stripes*, 31 January 2014, https://www.stripes.com/news/american-tanks-return-to-europe-after-brief-leave-1.264910.

42. Matt Millham, "V Corps Cases Its Colors in 'Bittersweet' Ceremony," *Stars and Stripes*, 12 June 2013, https://www.stripes.com/news/v-corps-cases-its-colors-in-bittersweet-ceremony-in-wiesbaden-1.225552.

43. Mark MacKinnon, "Putin Moves to Annex Crimea as U.S. Denounces 'Land Grab,'" *Globe and Mail*, 18 March 2014, https://www.theglobeandmail.com/news/world/defiant-putin-approves-crimea-bid-to-join-russia/article17538515/.

44. James, *The Years of MacArthur*, 1:552.

8

Mountain Storm

Counterinsurgency and the Air-Ground Task Force as a Microcosm of Marine Landpower Projection

Paul Westermeyer and Mark Balboni

The Global War on Terrorism has not led to fundamental changes in the US Marine Corps, as it has in the US Army. With only minor changes to force structure, specifically the creation of the Marine Corps Forces Special Operations Command (MARSOC) in 2006, the Marine Corps has remained an expeditionary organization based on its traditional use of Marine Air-Ground Task Forces (MAGTFs), which are capable of projecting landpower from the maritime domain.[1] The Marine Corps has been able to quickly deploy forces where needed from amphibious warfare ships. With their light footprint, marine units are well suited to conduct counterinsurgency operations (COIN) that require forces to remain agile and lethal as they pursue an elusive enemy across challenging terrain.

The 22nd Marine Expeditionary Unit (MEU) (Special Operations Capable [SOC]) was the MAGTF employed in Operation Mountain Storm. MEUs are the smallest and most commonly deployed of the three standard MAGTFs in the Marine Corps. For decades, the Corps has continually maintained at least two MEUs forward deployed (most often in the Mediterranean and the Pacific) aboard US Navy amphibious ready groups. Each MEU is capable of responding on short notice to various international crises, whether humanitarian or military. Like all MAGTFs, it is comprised of a command element, a ground combat element, an air combat element, and a logistics element. Unlike comparable Army combined arms forces, it fully integrates organic fixed wing air support. MEUs are flexible formations, capable of task organizing for the addition of subordinate units.

On 25 November 2001, as part of Operation Enduring Freedom (OEF), the 15th MEU began occupying Forward Operating Base Rhino, previously seized and abandoned by US Army Rangers, several miles southwest of the key Afghan city of Kandahar. Personnel of the 15th MEU deployed from the USS *Bataan* and *Peleliu* of Task Force 58 and flew 371.5 nautical miles inland aboard CH-53s. After expanding FOB Rhino and consolidating forces, the 15th MEU (working in conjunction with the 26th MEU as the 1st Marine Expeditionary Brigade under Brigadier General James Mattis) secured the vital Kandahar Airfield until relieved by elements of the US Army in mid-January.[2]

For Operation Iraqi Freedom in March 2003, the I Marine Expeditionary Force (I MEF) invaded Iraq as part of the Coalition Forces Land Component Command under Lieutenant General David McKiernan (US Army). Led by Lieutenant General James T. Conway, I MEF included the 1st Marine Division (Major General James Mattis), 2nd Marine Expeditionary Brigade (Brigadier General Richard Natonski), the British 1st Armoured Division (Major General Robin Brims), and over 2,700 US Army personnel providing capabilities not resident in Marine Corps formations. The marines to the east of the US Army V Corps fought on a parallel approach as a conventional land force on their way through the Rumaila oil fields, Al Kut, and Nasiriyah while securing key areas of Iraq on their way to Baghdad; their British contingent secured the port of Umm Qasr and Basra.[3]

After mostly withdrawing from Iraq in 2003, the Marines returned to establish Multi-National Force-West (MNF-W) in March 2004 to provide command and control of the coalition's effort primarily in the volatile Anbar Province of western Iraq. Marine and Army elements engaged in vicious combat as coalition forces fought to clear the Sunni Muslim-majority province, attempting to break the back of the insurgency. By partnering with local tribes, US forces were able to engage the population and, through the local citizenry, deny Al Qa'ida safe havens in an area that had previously been deemed of ancillary importance. This tribal engagement allowed for Iraqi forces to take the lead in securing cities and towns throughout the province. Marine tactics evolved while conducting large clearing operations (heavily supported by Army forces) aimed at pacification in Iraqi cities.

In late 2004, these tactics would culminate with the massive Battle of Fallujah during Operation Phantom Fury.[4] In the largest urban battle for the Marine Corps since the battle for Hue City during the Vietnam War, six Marine battalions, three Army battalions, three Iraqi battalions, and a British infantry battalion cordoned and cleared Fallujah from 7 November 2004 through 24 December 2004.[5] With significant US casualties, the battle ultimately drove a reevaluation of US tactics, as Iraqi forces were eventually trained to take the lead in providing security.[6]

22nd MEU (SOC) in Operation Mountain Storm

While still engaged in Iraq, the Marines projected landpower during Operation Mountain Storm as CENTCOM's strategic reserve for OEF. In February 2004, the 22nd MEU (SOC) boarded the amphibious warfare ships of Expeditionary Strike Group 2 and proceeded across the Atlantic toward Southwest Asia via the Mediterranean. Expeditionary Strike Group 2 was built around amphibious assault ship USS *Wasp* (LHD 1), amphibious transport dock USS *Shreveport* (LPD 12), and dock landing ship USS *Whidbey Island* (LSD 41). The 22nd MEU (SOC) provided the landing force and airpower for the amphibious task force, and the cruisers USS *Yorktown* (CG 48) and USS *Leyte Gulf* (CG 55), the destroyer USS *McFaul* (DDG 74), and the attack submarine USS *Connecticut* (SSN 22) provided the naval punch.[7]

These forces represented the Marine Corps' commitment to its "Expeditionary Maneuver Warfare" concept, which emphasized "strategically agile and tactically flexible [MAGTFs] with the operational reach to project power directly against critical points in the littorals and beyond."[8] Although the Marine Corps had an extensive history with COIN, the doctrinal focus remained on the ideas of maneuver warfare, which utilized "high-tempo operations and surprise with a bias for action to achieve operational advantage—physical, temporal, and conditional—over an enemy. The aim is to defeat the enemy by shattering his cohesion and to prevail by rapidly responding to events, if not anticipating them before they occur."[9] In 2004, in both Iraq and Afghanistan, the challenge was to adapt this maneuver warfare mind-set to a COIN environment.[10]

In 2004, Afghanistan was struggling to establish its first legitimate government after decades of conflict. In December 2001, the Bonn Agreement set the plan for a new government. This UN agreement called for an interim government to be developed and led by Hamid Karzai and an emergency Loya Jirga, a traditional Afghani council. These would organize the transitional authority and a subsequent Loya Jirga to develop a constitution. It also called for the creation of the International Security Assistance Force (ISAF) to support and aid the nascent Afghan national government. The Loya Jirga had written and approved a new constitution in 2003, and Afghanistan's first direct national elections ever were scheduled for July 2004. The Taliban announced it would disrupt the election and undermine the legitimacy of the nascent Afghan government.[11]

Security concerns delayed the elections until October due to the Taliban's resurgence in the southern provinces as well as the difficulty of registering voters, especially women, who were generally not allowed to the leave the house. Furthermore, many women were intentionally left uneducated and had little desire to vote. By June 2004, women made up only 23 percent of registered voters in the south (up from 13 percent at the beginning of the year).[12] The Taliban used guerrilla warfare to prevent Afghans from registering and argued that it was an American-imposed process. The Taliban also targeted clerics, particularly those who disagreed with their movement, and according to the deputy leader of the Kandahar Clerics' Council, "it was because of their support for the government."[13] This highlighted the lack of security in rural areas "where many Taliban leaders have sought shelter and have been able to operate with relative freedom in order to coordinate the insurgency."[14]

The nascent Afghanistan armed forces, along with US forces and ISAF, opposed the Taliban's efforts. ISAF was established in 2001 by UN Security Council Resolution 1386 in accord with the Bonn Agreement, which included a resolution that Afghans were responsible for security, but acknowledged that it would take time for Afghanistan to develop its own security forces and thus the international community would assist in the interim. Despite its genesis, ISAF was not a UN force, but rather "a coalition of the willing deployed under the authority of the UN Security Council."[15]

In May 2003, NATO took control of the ISAF mission at Canada's behest. Canada had considered taking the lead, but it lacked the resources to do so. The first NATO troops were sent to Kabul on 5 July 2003, taking command of ISAF on 11 August 2003. This was NATO's first ever mission outside Europe, providing ISAF with stability, as it no longer had to deal with rotational command of the force.[16]

In 2004, Lieutenant General David W. Barno, US Army, commanded Combined Forces Command-Afghanistan, or all American military forces in Afghanistan. Under Barno, American military operations in Afghanistan were divided between operating forces under Combined Joint Task Force-180 (CJTF-180) and training forces under the Office of Military Cooperation-Afghanistan.[17] General Barno shifted the focus of the American military effort in Afghanistan from the destruction of enemy forces to COIN, focusing on the Afghan people. The Taliban's challenge to the 2004 elections was a direct threat to this population-focused strategy, and CJTF-180 planned Operation Mountain Storm in order to provide the security environment the elections required.[18]

Central Command ordered the 22nd MEU to serve as the main effort of Operation Mountain Storm in order to preempt the spring Taliban offensive and stabilize Afghanistan enough to allow the national elections to occur.

The operation called for marines to cross Afghanistan to the airfield at Kandahar, and then proceed to Uruzgan Province, where they would create an environment that would allow for unmolested voter registration followed by the elections.[19]

Uruzgan Province, one of Afghanistan's central provinces, is extremely rural and mountainous and consists of a predominantly Pushtan population. The capital, Tarin Kowt, is a small city of fewer than twenty thousand people. Mullah Omar fought the Soviets from this province during the Soviet occupation, and the mujahideen of Uruzgan were among the first to join the Taliban when he founded it in the 1990s. The province is underdeveloped and rugged, accessible from Kandahar by only two mountain passes. In 2004, under the Afghan Transitional Administration, Uruzgan's governor was Jan Mohammad Kahn. He was unpopular with much of the province and created "an atmosphere of mistrust not conducive to the establishment of local governance structures that could have served as a platform to elicit mutual trust between the government . . . and the different communities."[20] Uruzgan was long considered a Taliban stronghold, its geography and culture suiting it well to the methods of guerrilla warfare and insurgency.[21]

Commanded by Colonel Kenneth F. McKenzie Jr., the 22nd MEU's major subordinate commands were Battalion Landing Team, 1st Battalion, 6th Marines, commanded by Lieutenant Colonel Asad A. Khan, Marine Medium Helicopter Squadron 266 (Reinforced), commanded by Lieutenant Colonel Joel R. Powers, and MEU Service Support Group 22, commanded by Lieutenant Colonel Benjamin R. Braden.[22]

Colonel McKenzie's staff thoroughly coordinated and planned the operation with CJTF-180; they were prepared to conduct "combat operations to defeat anti-Coalition militants (ACMs), secure major population areas, and support civil military operations (CMO) in [Area of Operations] AO Linebacker (Uruzgan) to create a secure and stable environment in order to facilitate United Nations Assistance Mission in Afghanistan (UNAMA)-sponsored voter registration and elections." Early in the planning stages for Operation Mountain Storm, CJTF-180 made two decisions that Colonel McKenzie later identified as critical to mission success. The MEU was assigned its own AO for Uruzgan Province, which gave Colonel McKenzie freedom of movement. Second, the force was employed as a fully functioning MAGTF rather than being cannibalized and split up among other American and allied forces in Afghanistan.

Colonel McKenzie's staff created a four-phase plan for Operation Mountain Storm. In Phase I, they would shape the battlefield, opening contact with civilians in the region, reconnoitering, and choosing the site required for the forward operating base. In Phase II, the "bowl" around Tarin Kowt would be secured and the forward operating base established. In Phase III, the MEU would secure southern Uruzgan and conduct voter registration. In Phase IV, the final phase, operations would target Taliban sanctuaries in northern Uruzgan, securing the province and enabling a successful election.

In late March, after the 420-mile transit by air across Pakistan to Kandahar from the amphibious warships of Expeditionary Strike Group 2, the 22nd MEU began Phase I of Operation Mountain Storm, shaping and preparing the battlefield. Five long-range patrols were conducted into the province, with the marines surveying the ground, selecting a site for the required forward operating base, and liaising with US Army Special Forces teams in the area. Colonel McKenzie spent two days coordinating with Governor Jan Mohammad Khan in Tarin Kowt. A Marine Corps liaison officer from Colonel McKenzie's staff was attached to the governor's staff, providing secure communications with the Afghan civilian authority. The marines saw first contact with the enemy when an IED struck one of the patrols moving through the mountain pass, destroying a vehicle and seriously wounding a marine. Remarkably, this was the only effective IED attack on the 22nd MEU during this deployment.[23]

Knowing that subsequent operations would involve searching Afghan females and that this could breed resentment among the local population if male marines conducted these searches against Afghan custom, Colonel McKenzie ordered the formation of female search teams to deploy with the infantry. Initially, three female sailors and nine female marines were selected and divided into two teams of six. Each team was attached to an infantry company through the later phases of Operation Mountain Storm. The teams searched Afghan civilians throughout the operation, and though under fire several times they suffered no casualties.[24]

On 25 April, McKenzie's command began Phase II of the operation. Three rifle companies of 1st Battalion, 6th Marines, conducted air assaults into Taliban-controlled areas of the province, capturing caches of weapons and pushing the Taliban onto the defensive as six large convoys carried the equipment and supplies of Lieutenant Colonel Braden's logistics units to the dirt airfield just outside Tarin Kowt that was chosen for Forward Operating Base Ripley.[25] Ripley featured a six thousand-foot runway, a complete helicopter fueling and rearming point, and thirteen helicopter landing pads.

Phase III of Operation Mountain Storm began on 11 May, after Forward Operating Base Ripley was fully functional. The marines began to work with Governor Khan's provincial government and the United Nations voter registration teams to register voters and protect voting sites in the province. Prior to the arrival of the marines, it was considered unsafe for these teams to operate in Uruzgan, even though civil affairs projects were identified to establish the new Afghanistan government as a superior option to the Taliban. During this phase, combat was light, as the Taliban generally chose to retire rather than engage the marines. Company-size patrols failed to bring the enemy to battle as they swept through the southern part of the province. The marines determined that the Taliban's centers of resistance were in the highlands surrounding Tarin Kowt, especially Dey Chopan to the east and Cehar Cineh to the west.[26]

Operation Asbury Park, launched on 1 June, opened Phase IV of the 22nd MEU's plan to secure Uruzgan Province. Operating a large patrol commanded by Lieutenant Colonel Khan, mounted entirely in HMMWVs and locally purchased vehicles, and reinforced with Afghanistan militia led by Governor Khan, the marines scoured the Dey Chopan highlands. The marines of 1st Battalion, 6th Marines, fought eight engagements, employing all of their weapons and calling in numerous air strikes from the plethora of available air support, killing scores of Taliban while suffering only fourteen wounded in return.[27]

The success of Operation Asbury Park convinced CJTF-76 to extend 22nd MEU's tour in Afghanistan and reinforce their success by placing the 2nd Battalion,[28] 5th Infantry, of the Army's 25th Infantry Division (Light) under Colonel McKenzie's tactical control. With two infantry battalions available, Operations Thunder Bolt and Asbury Park II were planned to strike the Cehar Cineh and Dey Chopan highlands respectively. Both operations uncovered numerous caches of weapons, but the Taliban's strategy returned to avoidance and disengagement, retiring from Uruzgan Province altogether, or fading back into the civilian population. In July, with Uruzgan Province seemingly pacified, the 22nd MEU exfiltrated back through Pakistan by air to the waiting ships of Expeditionary Strike Group 2.[29]

Aftermath of Mountain Storm

The deployment of the marines to Uruzgan greatly aided the United Nations' voter registration drive and reduced Taliban attacks in the province to nearly zero in the short term. Locals were cooperating with troops, and even leading them to IEDs and weapons caches. The Taliban gradually became more assertive in the province, and an American soldier and an Afghan soldier were killed there later in 2005.[30]

The NATO-led ISAF gradually took over control of security in much of Afghanistan, and in 2006 the Dutch forces of the ISAF became the lead force in Uruzgan Province. The Dutch pressured President Karzai to remove Governor Kahn in 2006 due to his ties to the drug trade. He became an advisor to President Karzai and continued to build his influence until his assassination in 2011.[31] In 2006, it was estimated that 98 percent of insurgents in Uruzgan were originally from the province, suggesting that there was significant Taliban influence and disapproval of the government and that the Taliban were still effectively recruiting. The Dutch approach was to establish contact with the civilian population and focus on supporting the local government rather than conducting combat patrols aimed at killing insurgents. The Dutch left the province in 2010 because of internal national politics.[32] In July 2012, the Afghan National Army and Afghan National Police began to take over security for the province and coalition forces began to pull out after a Karzai announcement in April that Afghan forces were ready to assume security duties there.[33]

The 22nd MEU's operations in Uruzgan Province highlight the strategic and operational flexibility of the MAGTF, even in a COIN environment, but also demonstrate the limitations of the concept. Colonel McKenzie's 2,400 sailors and marines secured the province and dramatically, albeit temporarily, reduced Taliban attacks. The initial effort was not reinforced when the MAGTF withdrew, and the Taliban was able to continue to influence, recruit, and maneuver in the province, erasing many of the MEU's hard-earned successes.

In order to maintain strategic flexibility, Marine Corps involvement in both Afghanistan and Iraq was often limited following initial successes. This allowed Marine Corps units to return to their tasks of conducting crisis response, power projection from the sea, and littoral maneuver.[34] In order to provide forces to support maritime commitments, Marine battalions and smaller tactical units typically deployed for six- to seven-months to ensure they would remain on cycle to support their next deployment aboard ship. Higher headquarters elements, such as regimental headquarters, could be extended out for a year in order to provide continuous command and control without degrading future operations.

Return to Afghanistan

In many ways, the 22nd MEU's deployment served as a preview of the Marine Corps' far larger scale contributions to OEF during the "surge" of 2008 to 2014. As progress occurred in Iraq, the situation in Afghanistan became more volatile. In the spring of 2008, the 24th MEU deployed in support of British forces in Helmand Province. Despite operating in the province for only

130 days, the 24th MEU was able to temporarily pacify the Garmsir City District of Helmand Province before turning control of the district back over to British forces.[35] The marines' control of targeted areas during surge periods would often revert back to the Taliban after the marines departed. These short-term gains had negligible long-term effects, as the Taliban learned to wait it out until the marines left. On 23 January 2010 in Iraq, II Marine Expeditionary Force transitioned Multi-National Force-West (MNF-W) to Army control. The success of the marines of MNF-W in Anbar transformed the province from one of the most violent to an example of how Iraqis could take over security throughout the country. As with ISIS's eventual reoccupation of Anbar, the Taliban having recovered from their losses earlier in the war had regained momentum and were gaining control of the key areas in southern Afghanistan.

As part of the US surge, a major Marine Corps command headquarters returned to Afghanistan. On 3 July 2010, Regional Command Southwest (RC [SW]) was established by I MEF (Forward) as a division-size unit. RC (SW) consisted of the Helmand and Nimroz Provinces that had previously been part of the British-Dutch Regional Command South (RC [S]). RC (SW) would become important in the fight for Afghanistan. As Marine Corps elements engaged a determined enemy, the Afghan Army established the new 215th Corps to partner with the marines and local Afghan police.[36] The marines would be involved in some of the heaviest fighting of the war as battles raged for control of the Sangin District.[37] Marines remained in force in Afghanistan until 2014, when OEF transitioned to the Resolute Support mission. A small Marine Task Force would later return to Helmand Province in late 2017, as they supported US Army efforts to bolster Afghan security forces in the region.[38]

Conclusion

During operations in the CENTCOM area of responsibility since 9/11, the Marine Corps has preferred the deployment of entire MAGTFs as discrete independent commands capable of controlling specific geographic regions rather than deploying haphazardly across Iraq or Afghanistan, and focused on one province (Anbar and Uruzgan in 2004, Helmand in 2009). In all cases, this permitted the Marines to retain greater operational control over their attached air assets, a degree of doctrinal independence, and the traditional Marine Corps public relations advocacy. Every Marine deployment began with an aggressive offensive intended to assert Marine control over the province prior to handing the province back to Iraqi or Afghan security forces. The results were always similar. The relatively successful Marine Corps deployments were not always followed up successfully by allied forces, and the gains achieved were often lost to the insurgents' sweeping counterattacks.

Notes

1. https://www.socom.mil/ussocom-enterprise/components/marine-corps-forces-special-operations-command; Dr. Frank L. Kalesnik, "MARSOC in Afghanistan, 2010–14," in *U.S. Marines in Afghanistan, 2010–2014: Anthology and Annotated Bibliography,* ed. Paul Westermeyer (Quantico, Va.: US Marine Corps History Division, 2017), 169–180; Lieutenant Colonel John P. Piedmont, *Det One: U.S. Marine Corps, U.S. Special Operations Command Detachment, 2003–2006* (Quantico, Va.: US Marine Corps History Division, 2010).

2. Jay M. Holtermann, "The 15th Marine Expeditionary Unit's Seizure of Camp Rhino," https://www.mca-marines.org/gazette/2002/06/th-15th-marine-expeditionary-units-seizure-camp-rhino; Colonel Nathan S. Lowrey, *U.S. Marines in Afghanistan, 2001–2002: From the Sea* (Quantico, Va.: US Marine Corps History Division, 2011) (hereafter Lowrey, *From the Sea*), and Charles H. Briscoe et al., *Weapon of Choice: US Army Special Operations Forces in Afghanistan* (Fort Leavenworth, Kans.: Combat Studies Institute Press, 2003), 109–113, 204, and 208. See also Leigh Neville, *Special Forces in the War on Terror* (Oxford, UK: Osprey Publishing, 2015), 43.

3. Gregory Fontenot, E. J. Degen, and David Tohn, *On Point: US Army in Operation Iraqi Freedom* (Fort Leavenworth, Kans.: Combat Studies Institute Press, 2004), 52, 64, 141–144, and 246. For the Marine Corps and Operation Iraqi Freedom in 2004, see Lieutenant Colonel Kenneth W. Estes, *U.S. Marines in Iraq, 2004–2005: Into the Fray* (Quantico, Va.: US Marine Corps History Division, 2011).

4. CWO4 Timothy S. McWilliams with Dr. Nicholas J. Schlosser, *U.S. Marines in Battle: Fallujah, November–December 2004* (Quantico, Va.: US Marine Corps History Division, 2014); and Dan Lamothe, "Remembering the Iraq War's Bloodiest Battle, 10 Years Later," https://www.washingtonpost.com/news/checkpoint/wp/2014/11/04/remembering-the-iraq-wars-bloodiest-battle-10-years-later/.

5. "ScanEagle Proves Worth in Fallujah Fight" (press release), US DoD, 11 January 2005, archived from the original on 14 April 2012, retrieved 22 March 2018.

6. For more on the Marine Corps in Iraq, see Dr. Nicholas J. Schlosser, *U.S. Marines in Iraq, 2004–2008: Anthology and Annotated Bibliography* (Quantico, Va.: US Marine Corps History Division, 2010).

7. Lowrey, *From the Sea,* 299–300; David W. Kummer, "Rebuilding a Nation, 2003–7," in *U.S. Marines in Afghanistan, 2001–2009: Anthology and Annotated Bibliography,* ed. David W. Kummer (Quantico, Va.: US Marine Corps History Division, 2014), 56–57; Gunnery Sergeant Keith A. Milks, "22nd MEU (SOC) Sets Sail for European and Central Command Theaters," *Marine Corps News,* 21 February 2004; 22nd Marine Expeditionary Unit Command Chronology February–September 2004 (Quantico, Va.: Grey Research Center, n.d.), hereafter 22nd MEU ComdC.

8. US Marine Corps, *Concepts and Programs 2003* (Washington, DC: HQMC, 2003), 23.

9. Ibid., 4.

10. Ibid., 23. For more on the Marine Corps and COIN, see Dr. Nicholas J. Schlosser, *U.S. Marines and Irregular Warfare Training and Education: 2000–2010* (Quantico, Va.: US Marine Corps History Division, 2015).

11. UN Security Council, "Agreement on Provisional Arrangements in Afghanistan Pending the Re-Establishment of Permanent Government Institutions," 5 December 2001; Rasul Bux Rais, *Recovering the Frontier State: War, Ethnicity, and State in Afghanistan* (Karachi: Oxford Univ. Press, 2008), 126.

12. Carlotta Gall, "Out of Sight, Afghans Register Women to Vote," *New York Times*, 26 June 2004, A5.

13. Carlotta Gall, "Taliban Are Killing Clerics Who Dispute Holy War Call," *New York Times*, 4 August 2003, A3

14. Rais, *Recovering the Frontier State*, 130; David Rohde, "14 Afghans Are Killed Registering to Vote" *New York Times*, 28 June 2004.

15. Quote from "ISAF Mandate," www.nato.int/isaf/topics/mandate/index.html, 29 April 2009; otherwise see UN Security Council, "Agreement on Provisional Arrangements in Afghanistan Pending the Re-Establishment of Permanent Government Institutions, Annex I" (2001); Amin Saikal, "Afghanistan's Transition: ISAF's Sabilisation [*sic*] Role," *Third World Quarterly* 27, no. 3 (2006): 527; "Reinforcements Needed: NATO and Afghanistan," *The Economist* (Asia edition) (17 June 2004): 41–42.

16. "ISAF: The Origins," www.nato.int/cps/in/natohq/topics_69366.htm, 1 September 2015, "ISAF Chronology," www.isaf.nato.int/chronology.html, 7 July 2017; Amin Saikal, "Afghanistan's Transition: ISAF's Sabilisation [*sic*] Role" *Third World Quarterly* 27, no. 3 (2006): 528.

17. CJTF-180 was built around the headquarters of the 10th Mountain Division at the beginning of 2004.

18. Lowrey, *From the Sea*, 288, 298; Lieutenant General David W. Barno, "Fighting the 'Other War': Counterinsurgency Strategy in Afghanistan, 2003–5," in *U.S. Marines in Afghanistan, 2001–2009: Anthology and Annotated Bibliography*, ed. David W. Kummer (Quantico, Va.: US Marine Corps History Division, 2014), 59–75; Donald P. Wright et al., *A Different Kind of War: The United States Army in Operation Enduring Freedom (OEF), October 2001–September 2005* (Fort Leavenworth, Kans.: Combat Studies Institute Press, 2010), 237–253.

19. Colonel Kenneth F. McKenzie, Major Roberta L. Shea, and Major Christopher Phelps, "Marines Deliver in Mountain Storm," in *U.S. Marines in Afghanistan, 2001–2009: Anthology and Annotated Bibliography*, ed. David W. Kummer (Quantico, Va.: US Marine Corps History Division, 2014), 127–133, hereafter McKenzie, "Marines Deliver"; 22nd MEU ComdC.

20. Sebastiaan Rietjens, "Between Expectations and Reality: The Dutch Engagement in Uruzgan," in *Statebuilding in Afghanistan: Multinational Contribu-*

tions to Reconstruction, ed. Nik Hynek and Péter Marton (New York: Routledge, 2001), 65–66.

21. McKenzie, "Marines Deliver"; Rais, *Recovering the Frontier State*; Larry P. Goodson, "Afghanistan in 2004," *Asian Survey* 45, no. 1 (January–February 2005); Rietjens, "Between Expectations and Reality," 65–66.

22. David W. Kummer, "Appendix A: Command and Staff List," in *U.S. Marines in Afghanistan, 2001–2009: Anthology and Annotated Bibliography,* ed. David W. Kummer (Quantico, Va.: US Marine Corps History Division, 2014), 350–351; 22nd MEU ComdC.

23. McKenzie, "Marines Deliver"; 22nd MEU ComdC.

24. Colonel Nathan S. Lowrey, "On The Front Lines in Afghanistan: Female Searchers during Operation Mountain Storm," *Fortitudine* 37, no. 4 (2013): 6–18.

25. The forward operating base was named after Colonel John W. Ripley, USMC, who earned the Navy Cross at the bridge of Dong Ha during the Vietnam War.

26. McKenzie, "Marines Deliver"; 22nd MEU ComdC.

27. Ibid.; Erin F. Bergmeister and Dr. Nathan S. Lowrey, "Task Force Genghis and Operation Asbury Park," *Fortitudine* 35, no. 2 (2010): 4–9; Elizabeth J. Bubb and Dr. Nathan S. Lowrey, "Battlefield Valor in Khabargho, Afghanistan," *Fortitudine* 35, no. 2 (2010): 9–12; 22nd MEU ComdC.

28. CJTF-180 changed in mid-April 2004 to the 25th Infantry Division (Light), resulting in a designator change to CJTF-76.

29. McKenzie, "Marines Deliver"; 22nd MEU ComdC.

30. "Afghan Citizens Lead Coalition Troops to Explosive Devices," US Fed News Service, 1 March 2005; "Heavy Fighting in Afghanistan Kills US, Afghan Soldiers," US Fed News Service, 25 July 2005.

31. Dexter Filkings, "With US Aid, Warlord Builds Afghan Empire," *New York Times,* 5 June 2010.

32. Antonio Giustozzi, *Koran, Kalashnikov and Laptop: The Neo-Taliban Insurgency in Afghanistan 2002–2007* (Oxford: Oxford Univ. Press, 2009), 43.

33. Specialist Nevada Jack Smith, "Afghan National Army Takes Charge in Providing Security," www.army.mil/article/83286/, 10 July 2012; Ayaz Ahmed Khan, "Afghanistan after NATO Withdrawl," *Defense Journal* 15, no. 9 (April 2012): 13–16.

34. MCPD 1: Marine Operations, http://www.marines.mil/Portals/59/Publications/MCDP%201-0%20Marine%20Corps%20Operations.pdf.

35. "British Troops Help US Marines Tackle the Taliban in Garmsir-UK MoD 7 May 08," http://www.militaryforums.co.uk/forums/viewtopic.php?t=17862.

36. Regional Command Southwest Press Room, https://regionalcommand-southwest.wordpress.com/about/.

37. Tony Perry, "Camp Pendleton Remembers, Mourns 17 Marines Killed in Afghanistan," *Los Angeles Times,* 5 November 2011, http://articles.latimes.com/2011/nov/05/local/la-me-marines-memorial-20111105.

38. Shawshank Bengali, "The Marines Returned to Helmand Province. Is Their Mission a Blueprint for Trump's Afghanistan Strategy?" *Los Angeles Times,* 10 November 2017, http://www.latimes.com/world/middleeast/la-fg-afghanistan-marines-helmand-2017-htmlstory.html.

PART III

Other Purveyors of Landpower

9

Not Only Above, But Among

American Airpower and Leadership into the Twenty-First Century

William Waddell

> Pour faire de grandes choses . . . il ne faut pas être au-dessus des hommes, il faut être avec eux. [To do great things, you don't need to be above men; you must be with them.]
> —Montesquieu, *Sur l'homme*

In 1985, Major Karl Eschmann, a maintenance officer for the F-4E Phantom formerly deployed to Southeast Asia, produced a report entitled "The Role of Tactical Air Support: Linebacker II." The report is highly critical of Strategic Air Command's (SAC) management of Linebacker II and its emphasis on textbook, technocratic management techniques for the bombing of North Vietnam. While recapitulating the plan for Day 2 of the bombing campaign, Eschmann relates that the SAC Wing Commander in 1972 was incensed that certain B-52 pilots on the Day 1 missions had engaged in "evasive maneuvers" in order to escape incoming surface-to-air missiles (SAMs). This commander threatened his own pilots with court-martial if any "aircraft commander . . . knowingly disrupted his cell's integrity to evade SAMs," thus violating SACs narrow and unwavering commitment to specific technical and tactical procedures. In his own copy of this report, the late Joe Guilmartin—historian, aviator, multiple Silver Star recipient from the war in question, and airpower enthusiast/aficionado in his own right—made the following marginal comment: "If that motherfucker was not flying the missions himself, *he* should have been court-martialed for physical and/or moral cowardice."[1]

What struck Joe Guilmartin, clearly, was the apparent disconnect between SAC's overwhelming preference for a certain tactical/technical scheme and the perhaps hasty judgment that the commander in question would intentionally put his men in jeopardy specifically because of that scheme. It might have cooled Joe Guilmartin's professional ire to know that the wing commander did in fact lead the next day's mission in the lead bomber.[2] But this is the expectation of leadership. There must be a close correlation between word and deed.

This tension is related to leadership and heroism, and it lives in our collective consciousness. Speech is conditioned by the speaker. In the Archaic period there was a division between *logos* and *mythos*. Logos was the word by itself, separate from the speaker. It was rational and of this world. It was only perhaps true. *Mythos,* before it became *myth* as we now know it—a story— was the word of the poet, ideally the hero-poet. It had divine origin and was sanctified in action. *Mythos* was word and speaker together. As Robert Fowler tells it, "the warrior's ideal is to be the doer of deeds and the speaker of *mythoi*"; it is "significant speech; it is speech with accoutrements."[3] *Mythos* was the pronouncement of heroes, things that could not be ignored. *Logos* held no such sense of the word as coupled with the bearing and accomplishments of the man who uttered it. It was instead an "account" or "theory" about the rationality in the world, but it held no sense of awe.[4]

There is a paradoxical relationship in the US Air Force (USAF) between the need for technical experts capable of fielding and maintaining sophisticated equipment, and the moral leadership necessary to face the risk of death in pursuit of mission—in other words, the grim reality that one must "live in fame or go down in flame." The tension is inescapable. It cannot be wished away, and for the majority of the USAF's short history it has been a tension grasped and maintained by the pilot/commander who fulfills at once the need for technical skill and heroic leadership. The tension is only reconciled in the person of the pilot/commander who understands his technology and accepts the moral challenge of taking that technology to war. Proponents of "airpower" have traditionally favored the technical over the heroic qualities of the USAF, believing that, as a rhetorical device, the uniqueness of air technology and its subsequent use as "airpower" would help justify it first as an independent service, and subsequently ensure its leadership in a world of joint operations.

The tension has become unbalanced of late. American airpower has no current opponents who can routinely expose the pilot/commander to a realistic threat of death. The number of US fixed-wing airframes shot down since 1999 can be counted on one hand. Whereas for a brief time the US victories in 1991 and 2003 seemed to lay out a bright future of uncontested superiority for the USAF vis-à-vis its sister services (in many ways, rival services), operations since 2003 have been marked by long, slow-grinding irregular warfare fought in cities, villages, and on mountainsides. Airpower has had a crucial role to play in these engagements, but the USAF would be hard-pressed to say it has been a leading role. With the retreat of the state as the sole arbiter of armed conflict, the Air Force's ability to target the state's highly articulated limbs has declined in equal proportion. While the other services have perhaps taken US "air superiority" for granted, the USAF's attempts to reorient the notion of airpower to cover these developments have not been convincing.[5] Its emphasis on speed and hi-tech approaches to age-old problems of civil disorder, insurrection, and poor governance strike casual observers as terribly discordant with current realities. In terms of command opportunities at the highest level, the USAF has not fared well. USCENTCOM, the central focus for US war fighting for sixteen years, has never been led by an Air Force general.

The nettlesome post-2001 world has occasioned some manner of an identity crisis for the USAF; or more accurately, it has spawned a new permutation of a habitual crisis of identity for the service. Faced with this impasse, the organization has a number of options. In the first place, it can accept that it plays second fiddle to the Army and the Marines, drop its narrative that it is the quintessentially "strategic" branch of the military, and seek to provide the best, most technologically robust *donum superadditum* to the ministrations of national power provided under almost exclusive Army or Marine leadership. This would involve essentially adopting or melding into the landpower perspective.

The second option is for the USAF to maintain its rhetorical position that airpower is "fundamentally different from other forms of power," that it is unique, peculiarly strategic, and capable of addressing strategic issues directly and with greater efficiency than the other services.[6] This is more or less the status quo, with other services suspicious that the USAF offers its supporting functions only begrudgingly while it dreams of "peer competitors" against whom it can wield its decisive impact. This perspective necessarily causes the USAF to highlight the growing challenge of sophisticated state powers like Russia and China while downplaying the ongoing struggles against insurgents, radicals, and revolutionaries.

Neither of these options is acceptable, though the reasons differ. On the one hand, the USAF is organizationally unwilling to melt into the other services, suborning its direction and prerogatives entirely to the landpower components. Nor should it. Airpower is distinguishable from—but not separate from—the other varieties of power, and maintaining this perspective may serve as a useful correction to strategic myopia. On the other hand, the service cannot simply ignore the current wars against subnational (or supranational) actors because they are organizationally inconvenient. Policy will continue to demand that the USAF devote significant resources to the fight at hand.

Soon after assuming his post as Chief of Staff Air Force (CSAF), General David Goldfein issued three short position papers detailing his "big rocks" for his time as head of the nation's air service. One of these, "Strengthening Joint Leaders and Teams," makes an interesting point, and sets a significant challenge before the USAF. In the paper Goldfein calls for greater appreciation of and experience with joint operations, specifically the Joint Task Force (JTF).[7] He expresses a desire for the service to place greater value on "joint" experience—time spent in commands made up of blended service personnel. He specifically states that airmen cannot limit themselves to their knowledge of "Airpower"; they also have to become "knowledgeable in how to optimize every component as part of a Joint Task Force."

This emphasis on "jointness" is a problem for airpower as generally understood. Advocates for airpower have consistently argued for its specificity, uniqueness, and for a particular state of mind—"airmindedness"—that makes airpower a brand of arcane knowledge different from (read superior to) traditional notions of power, land, sea, or otherwise. USAF doctrine states baldly that the "flexibility and utility of airpower is best fully exploited by an air-minded Airman."[8] The implication is that airpower is special, and best wielded by its own devotees. Airpower theorists argue that it is "inherently . . . strategic" and "primarily . . . offensive."[9] At least rhetorically, airpower thinkers have been rather comfortable arguing for airpower as *wholly other,* not truly in communion with standard military power, and by implication disconnected from the "joint fight." In some sense, therefore, the USAF's lack of joint credibility is a result of its own rhetorical position. General Goldfein's hope for a more joint-minded Air Force requires a less exclusive notion of airpower.

The major source for the argument that airpower is a thing apart has come by way of technology. Colonel Phillip Meilinger, formerly the don of the USAF's School for Advanced Airpower Studies, argued that "technology and air power are integrally and synergistically related."[10] Technology for the other services is important, but not so intimately linked as it is with the USAF. None of its "domains" are accessible except through technology. The Navy can at least go swimming. One cannot get to the sky, to space, or to the cyber realm without some technological extension to the human form.

That close connection with technology is what has given the USAF its distinctiveness. At base, the argument since Billy Mitchell has been that the technology of flight is so different and marks so dramatic a change in human affairs (particularly warfare) that a brand new kind of man was needed to manage, train, and implement the power that resulted from the opening of these new technological horizons. Mitchell was adamant that world history had already passed through the "continental era" (read age of army or land-power), as well as the "era of the great navigators," and that human history had turned to an "aeronautical era" and henceforth "the destinies of all people will be controlled through the air."[11] Airpower was the way, the theory, by which the airplane and those who fly would come to dominate those "destinies." At the outset, of course, airpower was really just code for "strategic bombing."[12] Not decisive in its own right, airpower did perform sufficiently well to yield organizational independence for the USAF in 1947.[13]

Since that time airpower theory in the United States has undergone various intellectual twists and turns. At one level the nuclear mission was largely subsumed into deterrence theory, which became something other than, though related to, airpower theory. The same was true of game theory and strategic signaling. These were the work of civilian academics, not of the air service itself.[14] Practitioners of "tactical" airpower have always been a strong force within the service, but they seldom made theoretical contributions, and the main thrust of airpower theory has almost considered them a threat to airpower's main concern. For example, Claire Chennault, one of the few advocates for pursuit aviation at the Air Corps Tactical School in the interwar years (despite its name, the school was the chief repository for thinking about *strategic* bombing), was an organizational pariah, shunned by his fellow officers until his retirement.[15]

At the conventional *qua* strategic level, thought moved in other directions. Some of the salient moments here did not occur until much later in the life of airpower as theory, notably the work of the Johns: Boyd and Warden.[16] In the main, these theories retread much of what had been covered by the strategic bombing theorists—Giulio Douhet, Mitchell, or proponents of the Air Corps Tactical School. The interest, objectives, and assumptions remained largely the same; the targeting was different. John Warden, often credited as the architect behind the 1991 air campaign against Iraq, argued that states—really any "enemy"—can be thought of as a system that can be targeted strategically at its centers of gravity,[17] the loss of which will result in system paralysis and the long-sought-for "morale" collapse à la strategic airpower's earliest advocates. This notion of airpower was welded to the great strides made in information and precision-guided munitions technology. As Warden argued, "technology has made possible the near simultaneous attack on every strategic- and operational-level vulnerability."[18]

The victory of 1991 and the collapse of the Soviet threat presented equal parts consternation and opportunity. While some wondered what the loss of a peer rival meant for American military power—the USAF's near perpetual talk about "transformation" was soon to take root—others rhapsodized about the coming age of American power and the central role airpower would play. The CSAF raised considerable controversy by his laser focus on the air arm's contribution to victory, seemingly at the expense of the other services. He called the Gulf War an "American success story . . . largely a story about airpower."[19] So long tied at the hip to the land component in preparation for the potential face off with the Russian Bear, airpower theorists were now free to speculate on how a thoroughly air-oriented US defense policy might function, despite the considerable budget cuts facing the DoD following the Gulf War.[20] In reality this helped; what better argument for an agile, lethal, and most of all cost-efficient USAF as the primary agent of American influence on the globe?

For a time, the service's gnawing fear that it would be reabsorbed back into the Army abated. Airpower was ascendant, though still somewhat ill-defined. What stood in strategic bombing's place was a kind of aestheticization of speed, a combination of high-tempo information operations coupled with nearly instantaneous precision strikes. Technology had liberated man (well, the airman) from the tyranny of time. Less precise conceptions of airpower focusing on the USAF's attributes and capabilities replaced the historically dubious but abstractly appealing logic of strategic bombing. The service's "core competencies" appeared in 1995. From 1996 onward the list expanded: *Air and Space Superiority, Global Attack, Rapid Global Mobility, Precision Engagement, Information Superiority,* and *Agile Combat Support.* Explicitly, the "core competencies" were drafted and propounded as those things meant to "[distinguish] the Air Force from the other services."[21]

Airpower—despite any reservations raised about the efficacy of the 1991 air campaign—gained considerable prestige. Airpower analysts considered the air arm freed from its dubious record in Vietnam and now, finally, fulfilling what the earlier theorists had prophesied. The brief (though longer than expected) air war over Kosovo against Slobodan Milosevic went further to bolster these beliefs. In seventy-eight days sans any kind of appreciable ground effort, airpower alone had won.[22] Airpower as a collection of evolving models seemed validated. Each one back to strategic bombing assumes that an opponent can be modeled, and that the model, provided it focuses on the correct things, will expose vulnerable weak points that can be identified and targeted, leading to paralysis and collapse.[23] Airpower was the answer; it was an answer now looking for a question.

The period of the 1990s and into the early 2000s represented in some ways the triumph of the USAF's perspective. It was time, as RAND researcher Benjamin Lambeth maintained, to reevaluate the supporting/supported command dynamic within the DoD. At last and undeniably airpower could "in some circumstances achieve strategic effects directly."[24] Airpower became the apotheosis of a techno-strategic rationale based on the rapid acquisition of information, its distillation to intelligence to be fed into a targeting system, the effects of which could be observed, measured, and then fed back into that information system for the next targeting permutation, if that were even necessary. Of course, ideally the model deduced beforehand would be sufficiently clear and clean to affect a prompt, near frictionless paralysis on the part of the enemy.

So was born "effects-based operations" (EBO). It originated in the USAF as an emendation of the work of John Warden by then Colonel David Deptula, who played an important role in 1991. By 1995 he released *Firing for Effect: Change in the Nature of Warfare.* In this brief work he argued that the genius of the Gulf War was not that "a lot of targets could be destroyed, but that vital enemy systems could be brought under effective control."[25] This kind of "parallel war," as he initially termed it, had achieved a terminal velocity of sorts because of the USAF's increased capacity for information tied to precision targeting.

As with previous iterations of airpower theory, EBO promised quick, decisive (and cheap) war, bypassing the slow, grinding, attritional struggles of yesteryear; this was the same raft of promises strategic bombing advocates had made a generation before. But what if the enemy could not be modeled? As General Paul Van Riper pointed out some years later: "The method has little utility against dynamic systems such as economies and social groups whose elements are only loosely coupled and with relationships that are frequently unclear."[26] The idea of bombing to achieve an "effect" rather than bombing just to blow something up is not at all ridiculous. The problem emerged when thinkers/planners once again believed they could accurately predict effects in most circumstances, could tie those effects together fairly neatly, and even more dangerously could extrapolate those effects far into the future.

Nevertheless, effects-based operations spread like wildfire throughout the DoD. The USAF ultimately enshrined EBO in its *Air Force Basic Doctrine 3—Command,* and there it remains as "Effects-Based Approach to Operations," putatively shorn of EBO's more baleful elements.[27] But EBO found advocates and acolytes in every service. The Army's artilleryman, for instance, became an "effects coordinator." Most dramatically, the US Joint Forces Command, responsible for cross-service doctrine, began pumping out "effects-based" planning instructions. By 2000 it was producing a heady brew of acronyms like PMESII (political, military, economic, social, infrastructure, information) to account for the vital components of potential adversaries and ONA (Operational Net Assessment) as the way in which these things could be related to one another and subsequently targeted to achieve the desired "effect."[28] Read as charitably as possible, the initial impulse for EBO was greater creativity in the application of military force. Its metamorphosis into doctrine perversely made creativity a matter of heavily routinized military cant.

In 1997, a former Navy man and thinker with the Center for Naval Analyses turned National Defense University student, Harlan Ullman, devised a new concept called "Rapid Dominance," clearly drawing on the same 1991 experiences that gave rise to EBO. It later became colloquially known by its tag line of "shock and awe." Ullman's contribution was to argue forcefully that this way—really the USAF way expanded—should be pressed into service across the DoD toward the ultimate aim of building a single, undifferentiated "Rapid Dominance Force."[29] Though Ullman and coauthor James Wade were careful to say that they did not see "technology as a 'silver-bullet,'" it was clear that technology was driving thinking, not the other way around.

The victory of the airpower perspective was quite nearly complete, but a cohort of opponents did an admirable job making their concerns known. Army officer and Princeton graduate Antulio Echevarria, a near constant fly in the ointment for techno-strategic salesmen, pointed out a considerable number of problems with Rapid Decisive Operations (RDO), the doctrinal flag under which Ullman's theory marched. Echevarria prophesied darkly that RDO rested on a series of highly dubious assumptions, and that at best it was *only* applicable to a very narrow band of "high-end, smaller scale contingencies," situations in which the United States was "already superior."[30]

Iraq in 2003 was at first blush just such a situation. It was a conventional semipower (not too powerful), with high-tech weapon systems (not too high-tech) backed by a fairly intricate and articulated communications and economic infrastructure. The answer found its question—again. So confident were the new converts to these ideas that the foremost among them, Secretary of Defense Donald Rumsfeld, continued to push "transformation" even as the war in Iraq was teeing off. In his "Planning Guidance" delivered in April 2003—remember, the war had commenced in late March—Rumsfeld argued for a radically new force that was "fundamentally joint, network-centric" and "capable of rapid decision superiority and massed effects across the battlespace."[31] While Rumsfeld presented the transformation as critical and specific to the changed strategic context following the 9/11 attacks, in reality his model was firmly rooted in 1990s-era thinking and extrapolations from the airpower dogmas reified in the first Gulf War.

The war to topple Saddam Hussein proceeded as advertised, at least initially. Few doubted that the leaner US-led coalition could overrun Iraqi opposition, but even so the speed with which Saddam's regime collapsed was remarkable. Baghdad was in American hands in a mere twenty-one days. Some of that speed was doubtless due to the poor placement of Saddam's forces—his greater fear leading up to the invasion seemed to be internal unrest—but no one could argue that American combat effectiveness was not light-years ahead of the slipshod Iraqi resistance.[32] While the air campaign tried to avoid striking infrastructure targets, Iraqi combat forces, headquarters, and communication systems were fair game, and they were devastated. Ironically, despite Warden's hope that strategists could "rid [themselves] of the idea that the central feature of war is the clash of military forces," the most reliable "effects" still seemed to come through the blowing up of military hardware and the killing of troops.[33] Though the USAF might have bemoaned that it had not been allowed to strike everything and fully drink in the implications of Warden and Deptula's hoped-for "parallel attack," the service did succeed in crippling Iraqi ground forces, the foundation upon which Saddam's power rested. The success was also much more efficient than Desert Storm. The US coalition in 2003 at the outset of the campaign deployed less than half the number of combat aircraft as had been on hand in 1991 (1,800 in 1991 compared to 790 in 2003). An even greater prevalence of guided munitions made up the difference.[34]

Airpower was delivered with speed, predictability, and to greater effect than even hoped. Writing in the *Air and Space Power Journal* in the summer of 2003, editor Colonel Anthony Cain extolled the "transformational capability" of air and space power, such that the United States could and did achieve "*predictive battlespace awareness.*" The outcome was never in doubt. For Colonel Cain, "the stunning effectiveness that characterizes combat operations will carry over into war-winning, post-hostilities operations."[35]

The predictions were wide of the mark. Swift victory over the Saddam regime gave way to a protracted insurgency against a US occupation that gradually took on the character of a holy war against a perceived crusader state. Crushing Saddam's army and government had cost 122 American and 33 British lives. By February 2005, 1,500 Americans had been killed, with almost 100 British deaths tacking alongside.[36] The war was spiraling out of control. Low-tech (almost no tech) insurgents gave the high-tech Americans fits. It was an "effect" for which no one had really planned.

The insurgency that developed in Iraq after 2003 conjured up painful memories for the Air Force, memories the service had been quite content in suppressing. It was not that airpower had played no role in US operations against insurgent movements—far from it—it was rather, as James

Corum noted, that "counterinsurgency and counterterrorism campaigns are, by their nature, joint operations, and airpower has generally been employed as a support arm."[37] And there was the rub. Airpower as a theoretical body had existed from the beginning as a way to support the independence of the USAF by claiming the air arm's unique ability to bypass attritional conflict. Vietnam had exposed the so-called "limits of air power" to achieve this aim, and the service had good reason for not wanting to relive those days.[38] The war that developed in Iraq and the one still boiling in Afghanistan would not be fought without the USAF—certainly not—but they *could not* be fought according to airpower predilections for tempo and technology.

Airpower—not the USAF—entered an exilic period. While airmen as individuals and as organizations fought on and contributed vital functions to the prosecution of the war, airpower as a theoretical body receded from view. The service as a whole—an organization birthed by the idea of airpower—lapsed again into identity crisis. Airpower was about rapidity, reach, information, precision, and transcendence. The wars in Iraq and Afghanistan seemed much more about patience, proximity, uncertainty, mass, and immanence.

The low point came in 2008. In April, Secretary of Defense Robert Gates appeared at Maxwell Air Force Base to chide the service for its apparent disinterest in the wars in Iraq and Afghanistan. Specifically, he tasked the USAF to send more assets, particularly surveillance drones, into the theaters.[39] In June he dismissed the CSAF, General Michael Moseley, and the secretary of the Air Force, Michael Wynne. The reason was ostensibly that Moseley and Wynne had presided over two serious breaches of policy with regard to the handling of nuclear weapons, but there was also significant suspicion that Moseley went before the executioner's axe for his too "strong advocacy of airpower" and ipso facto lukewarm support for the war on the ground.[40] Replacing Moseley, Gates appointed General Norman Schwartz, a special operator and C-130 transport aircraft pilot. Schwartz was the first USAF headman to have no bomber or fighter experience. Gates's message was clear.[41]

Airpower, and the USAF, have been struggling to regain lost ground ever since. General Goldfein was doubtless correct when he took the reins in 2016: "the reality is you can't find a mission that [the] Joint Force performs where an Airman is not engaged and essential for success."[42] Airmen have been consistently and critically engaged, but not in charge. The USAF has been relegated to a technical support branch.

An overly technological view of airpower and its capabilities has led the air service to this leadership desert. On the one hand, the USAF's immense technological superiority has rendered its enemies in the air almost entirely impotent. Now few dare to enter the skies; it seems more are willing to try their luck in the ether of space or cyberspace. But as "war is the realm of danger," so is courage the "first requirement" of command.[43] Largely unchallenged in his chosen sphere, the airman has not had much scope to demonstrate this quality. In fact, the current CSAF is one of a small handful of active duty USAF pilots to have been shot down by ground fire.[44] No US pilot has been downed in aerial combat since the Vietnam War.[45] Floating far above the "realm of danger," the technical element of airpower has eclipsed the moral.

Carl Builder once described the USAF as a cult that "has long worshipped at the altar of technology."[46] It is a strange image, for the Western tradition has assumed an abiding tension between technology and the divine. The ancient Greeks—Plato in particular—contrasted our temporal, fleshy existence with a divine origin. Our minds have given us a certain artifice over nature (*technē*), but that skill is pushing against our desire to return to the ethereal, to the supersensible. These qualities were best accessed through poetry, a thing accomplished more through intuition than logic and the mechanical arts.[47] Poetry was a gift from the gods, not an aspect of *technē*. In Plato's dialogue with Ion, the rhapsode, he informs his interlocutor that one can have skill *or* be divine; one cannot do both.[48] Flight for man in the ancient world was a part of the imagination, it was a divine attribute somehow lost (or forgotten) when men left the divine and became material. The soul's principal job, therefore, is to remember this divine feat, as Plato's interpreter Angus Nicholls says, "[to regrow] its wings and [return] to its former divine status."[49]

Technology carries with it the fear of dehumanization. Man is not comfortable being absorbed into the machine, losing all sense of self. By the early twentieth century those fears were more powerful than ever. Technology had led to industrialization, industrialization to mass production, mass production to mass war.[50] Here the plane and pilot provided a crucial bridge. Flight in the 1920s represented the sharpest of cutting edges technologically, and furthermore gave wing to an "individualism [which] could persist in the wake of mass war and in the midst of mass culture."[51] As Michael Sherry points out, men like Charles Lindbergh and Billy Mitchell seemed perfect specimens who "embodied at once the promise of the machine age and the virtues of frontier individualism."[52] The hero and the technician could be one and the same.

Cutting to the core, Mitchell argued for the hero-pilot not just for his technical mastery, or for a specific method of bombing, but because of the pilot's close communion with danger and death. Combat deaths in World War I for the aerial class were significant. This was Mitchell's primary argument for a separate air service—those who die in such numbers should be commanded by those who are familiar with the danger.[53] That existence continued into the Second World War. Army Air Force (AAF) officers in World War II died at twice the rate of their ground-bound brethren, a fact USAF officers like to reiterate even today.[54] The Air Service was *the* sacrificial service. The problem is that this rhetorical well is not being refilled. *Mythos* passes to *logos*.

Perhaps what is necessary is for Billy Mitchell's notion of airpower in terms of men and leadership to be rescued from his notion of airpower *qua* techno-strategic rationale. The second aspect of his vision has dominated airpower thinking—implicitly or explicitly—for too long. Airpower can be both foil and friend to landpower, for both depend on the agency of men. Airpower in its narrower sense, however, is limiting. For example, the unalloyed faith the AAF placed in strategic bombing blinded it to other possibilities. In the late 1930s through the early 1940s, the Air Corps actively fought against Army efforts to grant the AAC control over airborne forces, presumably because it would distract the air service from its main concern—strategic bombing.[55]

In this case, as in others, a narrow techno-strategic view of airpower limited the incipient USAF from pursuing a more expansive view of what is possible from aloft, and might possibly have kept some greater balance between the moral and the technical within the service. With drones killing and surveilling around the globe, it is even more critical that the USAF keep the machine from devouring the man. Martin van Creveld has argued that with the decline in conventional war and the passing away of the "fighter jock," the "age of airpower" is at an end.[56] It does not need to be, but the USAF must return to the fight with the "bold spirits" Mitchell lauded nearly a hundred years ago. Billy Mitchell famously defined airpower as the "ability to do something in the air."[57] Perhaps airpower needs to be recast as the ability to *anything* from the air, whatever is necessary.[58] Airpower is just as much—even more—a description of the airman as it is doctrine.

In Book V of Homer's *Iliad* the Achaeans are found hard-pressed. Ares, the god of war, has entered the lists on the Trojan side. Though they hold on, they are unwilling to face the mad deity who rages before the hosts of Troy. Pallas Athena, goddess of wisdom and war, sees their plight, particularly that of Diomedes, chief of the Greek heroes, save Achilles. Moved to help him, Athena dons her armor: "buckled her breastplate geared for wrenching war / and over her shoulders slung her shield, all tassels / flaring terror—Panic mounted high in a crown around it."[59] She mounts her "flaming chariot" in the heavens and hurtles to the battlefield. She takes the place of Diomedes's companion in his own chariot, joining the Achaeans' champion in the fray. She spurs them forward, riding at Diomedes's side. The chariot's reins are in her hands. Ares hurls his spear at Diomedes, but the goddess turns the shaft aside. Then Diomedes, war cry in his throat, strikes at Ares. The goddess pushes the spear point home. Wounded, Ares shrieks and flees. The Trojans shudder at his departure.[60] What was most important about the gods of the Greek pantheon was not that they could fly, or that they viewed the world from afar, high atop Mount Olympus, it was that they sometimes came down and fought alongside men.

Notes

1. Karl J. Eschmann, "The Role of Tactical Air Support: Linebacker II" (Maxwell AFB: Air Command and Staff College, 1985), 65 (emphasis in original) (author's personal collection). Eschmann turned this work into a book entitled *Linebacker: The Untold Story of the Air Raids over North Vietnam* (New York: Ivy Books, 1989).

2. Eschmann, "The Role of Tactical Air Support," 66–72. Day 2's attack went off with very little damage to the attacking bomber waves. The apparent success, however, caused SAC to use the same attack plan on Day 3. That time the attacking waves lost four B-52Gs and two B-52Ds.

3. Robert Fowler, "Mythos and Logos," *Journal of Hellenic Studies* 131 (2011): 53.

4. Ibid., 56.

5. Alan Vick, *Proclaiming Airpower* (Santa Monica, Calif.: RAND Corporation, 2015), xv.

6. *AFDD 1, Air Force Basic Doctrine*, 27 February 2015, 28.

7. General David Goldfein, "CSAF Focus Area: Strengthening Joint Leaders and Teams," October 2016, http://www.af.mil/Portals/1/documents/csaf/letters/16%2010%2013%20Focus%20Area%20II.pdf?ver=2016-10-13-105649-460&timestamp=1476371621707.

8. *AFDD 1, Air Force Basic Doctrine*, 27 February 2015, 33.

9. Phillip Meilinger, *10 Propositions Regarding Air Power* (Maxwell AFB: Air Force History and Museums Program, 1995), 1–2.

10. Ibid., 2.

11. William Mitchell, *Winged Defense: The Development and Possibilities of Modern Air Power* (Mineola, N.Y.: Dover Publications, 2006), 3.

12. Phillip Meilinger, *The Paths of Heaven: The Evolution of Airpower Theory* (Maxwell AFB: Air Univ. Press, 2014), xxviii. Phillip Meilinger makes this point explicitly.

13. Robert Ehlers, *Targeting the Third Reich: Air Intelligence and the Allied Bombing Campaigns* (Lawrence: Univ. of Kansas Press, 2009). Ehlers's book is an excellent example of how important strategic bombing was in World War II, but how its efficacy proceeded along a different path than the theorists had imagined.

14. Beatrice Heuser, *The Evolution of Strategy: Thinking War from Antiquity to the Present* (Cambridge: Cambridge Univ. Press, 2010), 345–346.

15. Stephen Budiansky, *Air Power—From Kitty Hawk to Gulf War II: A History of the People, Ideas and Machines That Transformed War in the Century of Flight* (New York: Viking Books, 2003), 186.

16. See David S. Fadok, "John Boyd and John Warden: Airpower's Quest for Strategic Paralysis," in Meilinger, *The Paths of Heaven: The Evolution of Airpower Theory*, 357–398.

17. It is important to note that the USAF notion of "center of gravity" as a weak point is not really in keeping with Clausewitz's original concept. However, the Army and the Marine Corps concepts are not entirely in keeping either. See Antulio Echevarria, "Clausewitz's Center of Gravity: It's Not What We Thought," *Naval War College Review* (winter 2003).

18. John Warden, "The Enemy as a System," *Air and Space Power Journal* (1995): 55.

19. Merrill McPeak, "DOD News Briefing, 15 March 1991," *Selected Works 1990–1994* (Maxwell AFB: Air Univ. Press, 1995), 15.

20. Merrill McPeak, *Selected Works 1990–1994* (Maxwell AFB: Air Univ. Press, 1995), 13. In remarks to the Air Force Association in January 1991, General McPeak argued that the USAF was more able at that point to explore its strategic role, and could put some distance between itself and the Army's doctrine of AirLand battle, which McPeak pointed out was "not a strategy" in his mind.

21. Chris J. Krisinger, "Who We Are and What We Do: The Evolution of the Air Force's Core Competencies," *Air and Space Power Journal* (fall 2003): 16–17.

22. Daniel L. Byman and Matthew C. Waxman, "Kosovo and the Great Air Power Debate," *International Security*, no. 4 (spring 2000): 5.

23. Carl von Clausewitz, *On War*, trans. Michael Eliot Howard and Peter Paret, rev. ed. (Princeton, N.J.: Princeton Univ. Press, 1984), 139–140. This was Clausewitz's objection to the model builders of his day. The "very nature of interaction [in war] is bound to make it unpredictable." It is therefore "simply not possible to construct a model for the art of war." This is obviously a chief insight made new for a generation of strategic thinkers by Alan Beyerchen in his seminal article on Clausewitz and nonlinearity. Alan Beyerchen, "Clausewitz, Nonlinearity, and the Unpredictability of War," *International Security* 17, no. 3 (1992/93): 59–90.

24. Benjamin S. Lambeth, *The Transformation of American Air Power* (Ithaca, N.Y.: Cornell Univ. Press, 2000), ix.

25. David A. Deptula, *Firing for Effect: Change in the Nature of Warfare*, Defense and Airpower Series (Arlington, Va.: Aerospace Education Foundation, 1995), 6.

26. Paul K. Van Riper, "EBO: There Was No Baby in the Bathwater," *Joint Forces Quarterly*, no. 52 (2009): 83.

27. *AFDD 3, Air Force Basic Doctrine*, 22 November 2016, 18.

28. Van Riper, *EBO*, 83.

29. Harlan K. Ullman and James P. Wade, *Rapid Dominance—A Force for All Seasons* (London: Royal United Services Institute for Defence Studies, 1998), vii.

30. Antonio J. Echevarria II, *Rapid Decisive Operations: An Assumptions-Based Critique* (Carlisle, Pa.: Strategic Studies Institute, 2001), v.

31. DoD, *Transformation Planning Guidance,* April 2003, http://oai.dtic.mil/oai/oai?verb=getRecord&metadataPrefix=html&identifier=ADA459607.

32. Walter Perry et al., eds., *Operation Iraqi Freedom: Decisive War, Elusive Peace* (Santa Monica, Calif.: RAND Corporation, 2015), xxiv.

33. John Warden, "The Enemy as a System," *Air and Space Power Journal* (1995): 55.

34. Perry et al., eds., *Operation Iraqi Freedom,* 151–155.

35. Anthony C. Cain, "The Transformation of Air and Space Power in Operation Iraqi Freedom," *Air and Space Power Journal* 17, no. 2 (2003): 6–7.

36. John Keegan, *The Iraq War* (New York: Vintage Canada, 2005), 204, 224. It is also important to note that most of the casualties in the initial invasion were accidental, not combat related.

37. James Corum and Wray Johnson, *Airpower in Small Wars: Fighting Insurgents and Terrorists* (Lawrence: Univ. of Kansas Press, 2003), xii.

38. See Mark Clodfelter, *The Limits of Air Power* (New York: Free Press, 1989).

39. Associated Press, 21 April 2008.

40. John T. Correll, "The Assault on EBO: The Cardinal Sin of Effects-Based Operations Was That It Threatened the Traditional Way of War," *Air Force Magazine* (January 2013), 54.

41. Andrew Gray, "Gates Picks New Leaders for U.S. Air Force," Reuters (9 June 2008), http://in.reuters.com/article/idINIndia-33982520080609.

42. David Goldfein, "The Future of American Air Power," remarks at American Enterprise Institute, Washington, DC, 18 January 2017.

43. Clausewitz, *On War,* 101, book 1, chapter 3.

44. Goldfein was downed in his F-16 in 1999 over Serbia as part of Operation Allied Force. Dan Lamothe, "Fighter Pilot Once Shot Down Over Serbia, Tapped to Head Air Force," *Stars and Stripes,* 26 April 2016.

45. Daniel Haulman, "No Contest: Aerial Combat in the 1990s," in *Society for Military History* (Calgary, 2001), 9.

46. Carl H. Builder, *The Icarus Syndrome: The Role of Air Power Theory in the Evolution and Fate of the U.S. Air Force* (New Brunswick, N.J.: Transaction Publishers, 1994), 155.

47. Angus Nicholls, *Gothe's Concept of the Daemonic: After the Ancients* (Rochester, N.Y.: Camden House, 2006), 34–54.

48. Nicholls, *Gothe's Concept of the Daemonic,* 56.

49. Ibid., 41.

50. Michael S. Sherry, *The Rise of American Air Power: The Creation of Armageddon* (New Haven, Conn.: Yale Univ. Press, 1987), 39.

51. Ibid., 22.

52. Ibid., 40.

53. Mitchell, *Winged Defense,* 220.

54. Michael Worden, *Rise of the Fighter Generals: The Problem of Air Force Leadership, 1945–1982* (Maxwell AFB: Air Univ. Press, 1998), 8.

55. Sean Klimek, "Strategic Bombardment as an Obstacle to Strategic Airpower: Why the Early American Airborne Was Shortchanged" (Ph.D. diss, Florida State University, 2015). This unpublished dissertation explores the logic behind the Air Corps' lack of interest in airborne operations.

56. Martin van Creveld, *The Age of Airpower* (New York: Public Affairs, 2011), 439–440.

57. Mitchell, *Winged Defense*, xii.

58. The recent flexibility the Air Force has shown in the acquisition process for the OA-X light observation/attack aircraft shows that this kind of adaptability in its conception of airpower is possible. See Frank Blazich, "When the Piper Cub Roamed the Battlefield," *War on the Rocks*, https://warontherocks.com/2017/12/when-the-piper-cub-roamed-the-battlefield/, for a discussion of the parallels with observation aircraft acquisition and utilization in World War II.

59. Homer, *The Iliad*, trans. Robert Fagles (New York: Viking, 1990), 188.

60. Ibid., 192.

10

The Damaged Alliance

The Intelligence Community, the Military, and the Sociopolitical System that Influences Them

Edward A. Gutiérrez

Please the customer. It is a Beltway maxim that most accept, some discuss, and few challenge. When the Intelligence Community (IC) and military officers discuss the topic, they refer to pleasing the customer (policymaker) as politicization.[1] This word evokes a shudder within the IC and military—it is Beltway taboo. There is meager scholarship on the topic, and with few exceptions those that acknowledge politicization do not believe it is a detriment to Washington's sociopolitical landscape.[2] They are wrong. This chapter addresses the issue of Beltway politicization within the executive branch, the IC, and the military. Politicization is toxic, and the way forward must originate from the top down, with policymakers that desire and accept honesty, not evidence that solidifies their biases, goals, or preconceived notions. In addition, the second step, which can only occur with the first, is terminating the careerism and corporate atmospheres found within the IC and military.[3] Although this chapter concerns the IC and military, it focuses on the Central Intelligence Agency (CIA) and the US Army—the two principal arms within their respective spheres.

Middle East instability, Russian operations in the Black Sea region, and especially the Afghanistan and Iraq wars serve as solemn reminders that land-power remains vital. The post-9/11 geopolitical situation continues to grow in complexity with erratic sectarian violence and ceaselessly hostile nonstate actors. As Eliot A. Cohen asserts, "The United States will need more and better military power in the future."[4] America must preserve hard power. Furthermore, the military and the IC must maintain adaptability and transparent coordination—ready for whatever scenario or enemies arise. It is in peacetime, not during a conflict, that strong relationships and understanding are forged. Whether the mission requires an assault from special operations forces, an air strike from a remotely piloted aircraft, or conventional landpower to support an ally or crush a foe, America must use hard power and intelligence with justice and reason. Therefore, the IC, the military, and above all, policymakers (for example, the secretary of state) require humility. When reflecting on lessons learned in Afghanistan and Iraq, Lieutenant General Daniel P. Bolger (Ret.) asserts, "Our generals did not stumble due to a lack of intellect. Rather, we faltered due to a distinct lack of humility."⁵ The virtue of humility originates from the top down. It begins with the president himself and trickles throughout his administration and policymakers, into Congress, and into the managers and officers of the IC and military. This long-lost vital virtue would enable the IC and the military to present their data without fear of reprisals from policymakers. This change requires a major cultural transformation of Beltway identity.

Although most careerists acknowledge politicization, according to them it is not a serious issue; it is part of the job. Therefore, they have accepted the system's flaws. Akin to an unhappy marriage, one spouse submits because it is easier than rattling the cage. They have accepted their fate. There are a few career insiders, however, with the courage to point out the dent in the system's armor and demand that changes must occur, such as career intelligence officer Paul R. Pillar. He argues:

> Once intelligence estimation becomes in large part a contest—as it often has been—between intelligence officers and policymakers, with the latter having strong preferences about the issue at hand, the former have to pick and choose which contest they will try hard to win. Or, rather, they have to choose not to make a contest of some issues at all as long as there is some path of lesser resistance available, as there almost always is, that at least minimally satisfies the policymakers and at the same time presents a plausible and defensible judgment. The intelligence community has only a limited supply of fuel to burn in bureaucratic battles. The other corollary is that the IC's reputation from previous successes and failures affects the amount of fuel it has to fight those battles. Recent, salient failures diminish the community's inclination and ability to resist politicizing pressures. An ironic consequence is that failure (or, more precisely, the perception of and response to failure) increases the chance of still more failure.⁶

The fuel Pillar mentions is almost dried up. The IC has little left in the tank after the Iraq War fiasco because intelligence officers are afraid to be wrong—they are afraid to lose face. Concerning politicization and the Iraq War, Pillar adds:

> There still is no official acknowledgement in the United States that it occurred on the issue of Iraq. One reason for this lack is intelligence officers' reluctance to admit they were bent by the policy wind. Even those who have felt pressure and may speak of it to ombudsmen and others find it hard to say they succumbed to it. Moreover, many of the ways of succumbing to it . . . are sufficiently indirect and subtle that it is easy for the officer to convince himself as well as others that he did not bend at all.[7]

It is difficult to accept your imperfections when gazing into the mirror, and far easier to deflect the blame onto external forces outside your control, or better yet, to just ignore them. It is within our nature to accept the reality the system provides, especially when one reaches GS-15 or the rank of colonel; the desire to "check the boxes" and advance one's career eclipses concerns of "truth to power."

Lieutenant General Michael T. Flynn (Ret.) recognizes this exact issue. He contends, "Nowadays we call this 'politicization of intelligence,' but its older name is 'don't deliver bad news to your leaders.' You don't want to be that messenger. And so you keep quiet. This is what appears to be going on in our intelligence system regarding our fight against Radical Islamists—and it all starts at the very top of our government. The president sets the tone and the priorities. This doesn't surprise me. The policymakers in the administrations of both George W. Bush and Barack Obama did not want bad news either."[8] Flynn is right. It starts at "the very top." The incongruity of Flynn's words (here and below) considering his resignation as President Donald J. Trump's national security adviser for misleading and lying present the sobering reality of Beltway politicization: even senior leaders that profess a stand against it commit the act themselves.[9]

The Trinity

Both Plato's city-soul analogy/tripartite psychology and Carl von Clausewitz's paradoxical trinity clarify the politicization milieu that infects Washington, DC.[10] The three peoples of Plato's tripartite and Clausewitz's trinity are represented by the desire that drives citizens, the talent of the general and

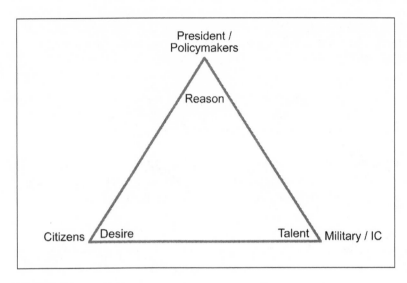

Figure 10.1.
The Platonic-Clausewitzian Trinity.

his army (including the IC), and the reason of the political leader, the latter being the only one who can harness the talent of the commander and assuage the passion of the people, as seen in figure 10.1. As Plato and Clausewitz proved, the issue is one of understanding, because conflicting attributes motivate each side: reason (rationality), talent (spirit), and desire (appetite). These are conflicting motivations. Thus, a complex triangular and dysfunctional relationship clouds understanding of the other.

Historian Hew Strachan emphasizes, "The people are as central to war as are the government and army."[11] Moreover, in a democracy (especially modern America), the people are the most central element of the Platonic-Clausewitzian trinity because the president and policymakers desire the people's approval, or at the very least their consent. Here lies the core of the problem. The president craves society's consent—this becomes more important during elections, or when key pieces of legislation need passing. This desire for approval infects the senior policymaker, who craves the president's consent because if the policymaker loses it, the job is lost as well. This in turn forces senior IC and military leadership to kowtow to the policymaker. As former White House staffer and policymaker William Inboden concludes, "At the end of the day the NSA and other three-letter agencies are merely serving the mandate of senior policymakers."[12] The president and policymakers misdirect the talent of the military and the IC, and a sycophantic culture driven by careerism rather than independent, honest thought thrives. The cure for this malady is thus: the president must foster an environment of humility and virtue. Otherwise, the now hollow adage of the IC, "speak truth to power," remains worthless. As Pillar and Flynn note above, policymakers rarely want to hear bad news or facts not supporting their bottom line. Robert Jervis states that politicization "can take many forms," including which conclusions to reach, demotion of analysts who provide "wrong" answers, promotion for those who provide answers approved by policymakers, and bias by personnel who feel their careers threatened.[13] All these issues can—and many times do—put immense strain on professional integrity.

Almost seventy years ago, Sherman Kent, the godfather of CIA education, believed that the IC and policymakers should maintain a delicate balance between being too close and too far apart. The danger of being too close equates a loss of objectivity and "integrity of judgment." If the relationship between the two groups strays too great a distance apart, the IC loses its ability to offer appropriate guidance to its consumers. Kent stresses, "intelligence is not knowledge for knowledge's sake alone, but . . . knowledge for the practical matter of taking action."[14] Many times the IC cannot escape from "swinging into line behind the policy of the employing unit." Furthermore, if drawn into the center of policymaking, intelligence may be "the unabashed apologist for a given policy rather than its impartial and objective analyst."[15] Kent's statements, written decades ago, are more urgent to heed now than ever. In recent years, blame for erroneous intelligence has fallen on the IC and not the policymakers. It is the IC (and the military) that absorb the criticism.

A byproduct of Washington's politicization atmosphere is the corporate mind-set, which solidified itself well before 9/11. In 1992, the Director of Central Intelligence (DCI) at the CIA, Robert M. Gates, told his officers, "We do produce a corporate product. . . . Analysts must understand and practice the corporate concept. They must discard the academic mindset that says their work is their own, and they must take into account the views of others during the coordination process." Yet he adds, "We must protect ourselves from groupthink, an institutional mind-set, or personal bias. . . . Greater intellectual honesty on everyone's part can make the process less bureaucratic, less hierarchical, and less of a win-lose situation." Gates then stresses that "to ensure that our consumers get the benefit of differing analytic perspectives and to demonstrate the directorate's openness to new ideas and thoughtful alternative viewpoints, I have asked the DDI to restate his support for the inclusion of well-reasoned, relevant and factually supported alternative views in mainline products, and to appoint a committee to develop practical means to accomplish this goal."[16] There lies the conundrum. How can a corporate product exist without groupthink and with alternative viewpoints? It cannot. Gates's idealism is a chimera. Sherman Kent acknowledged this issue in 1949.[17] Nothing has changed.

The "coordination process" referenced by Gates has grown into a bloated, inefficient system. The old saying that "too many cooks in the kitchen spoil the broth" best illustrates the process within the IC. Former daily intelligence briefer Derek Grossman declares, "The onerous coordination and review process has too often resulted in watered-down and less impactful analysis. Unlike in the academic community where a diversity of views based on the same evidence is encouraged, the intelligence community actively admonishes against it in favor of a review process meant to build a consensus, even if one does not exist."[18] Indeed, the CIA (and most of the IC) abandoned the academic mind-set per Gates's direction.

The 9/11 Commission, however, points out that this was a severe error in CIA strategy beginning with the end of the Cold War. The report states, "A university culture with its versions of books and articles was giving way to the culture of the newsroom. During the 1990s, the rise of round-the-clock news shows and the Internet reinforced pressure on analysts to pass along fresh reports to policymakers at an ever-faster pace, trying to add context or supplement what their customers were receiving from the media . . . the dispersal of effort on too many priorities, the declining attention to the craft of strategic analysis and security rules that prevented adequate sharing of information."[19] Over a decade later, it seems no one has taken these truths to heart. CIA analysts are constantly haunted by the fear that their work will become stale, "overcome by events," and be a lackluster intelligence product that policymakers saw on CNN several nights ago. As Richard K. Betts stresses, "Policymakers . . . are more interested in papers that are turned out fast, that offer quick responses to help them put out fires . . . immediate problems drive out distant ones."[20]

The Cold War

The last point referenced by the 9/11 Commission above, the "sharing of information," remains vital, especially between the CIA and the Army. The uneasy relationship between the two began with the former's inception from the 1947 National Security Act. The CIA received its own personnel, budget, and mandate to gather and produce independent intelligence, which curtailed the role of the Army's director of intelligence in influencing national intelligence decisions. In addition, the CIA now oversaw a great deal of economic and political intelligence that was within the Army's former sphere.[21]

CIA-Army tension and politicization reached its Cold War apex during the Vietnam War. While there were several issues between the CIA and the Army, the most infamous incident occurred from the fallout of the 1968 Tet Offensive over the Order of Battle (OB) of enemy troop strength. CIA analyst Sam Adams was at the center of the OB controversy. Late in 1965, Adams began studying the troop strength of the Viet Cong and the North Vietnamese Army. He worked alone and received little support or encouragement on his OB assignment. He concluded that total enemy strength was close to 600,000 and should include irregulars (guerrillas), rather than the 280,000 figure cited by General William Westmoreland's Military Assistance Command, Vietnam (MACV).[22] When reflecting on his tenure as MACV commander, Westmoreland discounted Adams's claims that MACV ignored his estimates and underrated enemy strength. Westmoreland stated, "The problem might have been handled by other than a unified command had each of the intelligence agencies been assigned as a 'lead agency' on some particular aspect of intelligence." For Westmoreland, too many agencies contested with each other and "when something is everybody's business, it is nobody's business."[23]

The OB was significant to Westmoreland if it illustrated that progress was being made in his quest to reach his "cross-over" point, which indicated the enemy could not replace its troops lost to attrition. The estimates of OB were the responsibility of MACV J-2 (joint staff intelligence), and they kept these estimates low in order to demonstrate American success, per the order of Westmoreland.[24] Veteran senior CIA officer Harold P. Ford explains, "In 1967–1968 . . . available evidence convinced virtually all CIA officers that the enemy had additional tens of thousands of irregular troops that were militarily significant, but which MACV would not count."[25] MACV would not change its troop strength estimates despite new recommendations, and the CIA ultimately gave in to Westmoreland and MACV's demands. DCI Richard Helms accepted this and acknowledged in his memoir a "significant political problem . . . in view of the continuing increase in U.S. personnel and armaments in South Vietnam, any admission that the Viet Cong were actually gaining strength would obviously have stirred public reaction on the home front."[26]

Westmoreland and his staff felt obliged to show progress. They would not admit enemy strength was greater than their own estimates. Returning from his visit to the troops at Cam Ranh Bay in South Vietnam, President Lyndon

B. Johnson, at a meeting with General Earle Wheeler, noted, "I like West-moreland . . . Westmoreland has played on the team to help me."[27] The Army trained MACV's advisers to give positive reports. A negative report from an advising officer jeopardized that officer's career opportunities—thus, the ten-dency to "tell their superiors what they wanted to hear" flourished.[28]

Adams's superiors blocked his every attempt to bring his findings to the attention of the White House. Adams obtained a meeting with CIA Execu-tive Director-Comptroller Lawrence K. White. During the meeting, accord-ing to Adams, White declared, "I would like you to know that if you take your complaints independently to the White House . . . your usefulness to the agency will thereafter be nil. Let me repeat that: Nil."[29] Undeterred, Adams then met with DCI Helms on 8 November 1968, when Helms told Adams: "You don't know what it's like in this town . . . I could have told the White House there were a million more Vietcong out there, and it wouldn't have made the slightest difference in our policy." Adams retorted, "Our job is to send up the right numbers and let them worry." Helms then conceded and said he would arrange for Adams to meet key White House staffers. The meeting never occurred.

On 19 November 1968, Deputy Director of Intelligence Edward W. Proctor told Adams that he was the problem, not the CIA.[30] Helms agreed. In his memoir, Helms dismissed Adams as an egotist, obsessed with his own data.[31] Michael T. Flynn argues, "Adams relentlessly exposed the nonsense for the better part of ten years, all to no avail. CIA and the military had their numbers—numbers that showed we were winning the war—and would not change them."[32] Helms had committed his support to President Johnson, who needed positive reports regarding American progress in the war.[33] When Richard M. Nixon took office, Helms admitted to differences of opinion with his new president but stated that on one issue they agreed: "The DCI must refrain from taking sides in policy debates. CIA's most important responsibil-ity is to present the President with the best possible data on which decisions can be made. The unvarnished intelligence and the National Estimates of its importance must be presented accurately, no matter whether the material supports the incumbent administration's policy or not."[34]

In addition to the OB controversy, another example of CIA intelligence designed to placate to the White House involved the influx of enemy supplies, especially the disputed distribution of supplies to the enemy through the port of Sihanoukville, Cambodia. Career CIA officer James Graham refused to believe that large amounts of military supplies came through this location. The truth proved to be the opposite. MACV J-2's Lieutenant General Phil-lip B. Davidson later remembered Graham told him, "Sometimes you've got to find what you've got to find."[35] Graham's cynical comment encapsulates Cold War politicization and became more relevant three decades later during another war.

Post-9/11 Augmentation

Politicization did not dwindle with the end of the Cold War. Even though documents remain classified, and with additional hindsight more information will reveal greater understanding of the Iraq War, over a decade later, policymakers, the IC, and the military blame each other for the 2003 invasion. In a now infamous moment, Secretary of State Colin Powell appeared before the UN Security Council in February 2003 to justify America's invasion of Iraq. He stated that "solid intelligence" pointed to the existence of weapons of mass destruction (WMD) in Iraq. Several months earlier, the CIA's October 2002 National Intelligence Estimate had confirmed the continuation of Iraq's WMD program and stated that Iraq could construct a nuclear weapon in about a year with a sufficient amount of fissile material.

America and its allies found no evidence for such a program in Iraq after the invasion, even after CIA Director George J. Tenet labeled Iraq's WMD program "a slam dunk case."[36] This notorious phrase uttered by Tenet, assuring President George W. Bush that WMD existed, tarnishes Tenet's place in intelligence history. Despite reports to the contrary, Tenet held on to the belief that Iraq's WMD program existed. The CIA's own main investigator in charge of the search for Iraqi WMD, David Kay, left the CIA in 2004 and affirmed that such weapons did not exist. Kay believed Tenet was "personally invested" in promoting the presence of such weapons.[37] James Bamford relates, "Ultimately Tenet lost sight of his role. Instead of the country's apolitical eyes and ears around the world, a spymaster charged with telling the President the bad as well as the good, he simply became the President's cheerleader, shouting slam dunk when he should have been asking for a time-out."[38] Former CIA Deputy Director Michael Morell disagrees. He argues, "When we wrote pieces for the president, the analysts wrote with authority on the issue. This is why I personally never found fault with George Tenet's alleged 'slam dunk' comment. The way the analysts talked and wrote about their judgements would have led anyone to think it was a slam dunk—that is, that Saddam definitely had active WMD programs."[39]

Robert Jervis determines that due to persuasion by certain individuals, the IC took information that they believed to be plausible while failing to employ better methods of analysis. Direct evidence took a backseat to what was believable in the case of Iraq's developing WMD. As Jervis states,

"Although decision makers call for better intelligence, under many circumstances they do not want it."[40] The Iraq WMD issue represents the Platonic-Clausewitzian trinity's apex: no one accepts blame (particularly those at the top). Moreover, no one understands each other, and most important, the president and policymakers blame commanders, who in turn blame those underneath them, all the while the citizens claim innocence—although they vote their leaders into office and demand illogical solutions to war and diplomacy. Hence, the triangular relationship of misunderstanding solidifies further.

Policymakers labeled Iraq's nonexistent WMD a drastic intelligence failure, but they deserve the greater blame. Less than a year after the war began, articles appeared concerning President George W. Bush and his administration. Walter Pincus and Dana Priest state, "In its fall 2002 campaign to win congressional support for a war against Iraq, President Bush and his top advisers ignored many of the caveats and qualifiers included in the classified report on Saddam Hussein's weapons that CIA Director George J. Tenet defended."[41] In a scenario akin to Sam Adams's plight, senior CIA analyst Ben Bonk said that he was prevented from providing intelligence to President Bush concerning Iraq. He lamented, "Maybe if they hadn't deceived me, I could have done something. . . . Maybe I could have stopped the Iraq War."[42] Undeterred by any doubters, the Bush administration moved ahead with plans for war. Joshua Rovner stresses the role politicization played in decisions made regarding Iraq: "Policymakers pressured intelligence to join the policy consensus after making public commitments in the face of domestic opposition using intelligence to oversell the need for military action."[43]

The politicization that infected the WMD/Iraq War debacle spawned stifling fallout. Fearing a repeat of the Iraq episode, the IC added layers of additional review and guidelines to their analytic product. The cogs slowed to a crawl. Analysts feared that events would overcome the product as team chiefs and those above imposed intricate changes to products. As former CIA Deputy Director for Intelligence Jami Miscik notes, "Having learned from the mistakes made about Iraq, the intelligence community now carefully conveys the level of confidence it places on the judgments it makes."[44] Examining the "level of confidence" in the latest *Analytic Standards,* issued by the Office of the Director of National Intelligence, provides ample evidence of the desire to systematize and formulate intelligence.[45] The only problem: intelligence is not a science, it is an art. This is why former DCI Allen W. Dulles titled his 1963 opus *The Craft of Intelligence.* Dulles concluded this book by writing: "The last thing we can afford to do today is to put our intelligence in chains."[46] A craft cannot be conquered by formulas, it can only be honed with continued training and practice.

After President Bush left office, his successor, President Barack H. Obama, concluded the war, but it did not end with his 2011 drawdown, and resurged in a new fight against ISIS in 2014. In the second year of the conflict against ISIS, fifty Defense Intelligence Agency analysts asserted that senior USCENTCOM officers altered their intelligence reporting on ISIS.[47] Almost two years later, it appeared USCENTCOM began to apply changes to curb further incidents of politicization.[48] It is yet to be seen if this incident will aid in correcting the politicization paradigm.

In Afghanistan, the war has continued since 2001. Nine years into the war, with no signs of the Taliban insurgency abating, Michael T. Flynn, Matt Pottinger, and Paul D. Batchelor recommended "sweeping changes to the way the intelligence community thinks about itself—from a focus on the enemy to a focus on the people of Afghanistan . . . the United States has focused the overwhelming majority of collection efforts and analytical brainpower on insurgent groups, our intelligence apparatus still finds itself unable to answer fundamental questions about the environment in which we operate and the people we are trying to protect and persuade."[49] They later concluded, "The intelligence community—the brains behind the bullish might of military forces—seems much too mesmerized by the red of the Taliban's cape. If this does not change, success in Afghanistan will depend on the dubious premise that a bull will not tire as quickly as a Russian bear."[50] The Soviet general staff agreed. Years prior to the Flynn, Pottinger, and Batchelor report, the Soviet generals prophesized, "It is easy to dismiss the Soviet failure in Afghanistan, but it is not wise. Armies seldom get to chose [sic] the wars in which they fight and this type of difficult war is as likely to future conflict as a war involving high-technology systems in which the sides seldom get close enough to see each other. Russia continues to fight guerrilla wars. Other nations may also have to."[51] Scores of retired military commanders and IC officers echo the Soviet prophecy of learning from history, but few listen.

Adaptation and Virtue

On his first day in office on 21 January 2017, for his initial stop, President Donald J. Trump visited CIA headquarters and stated, "I want to say that there is nobody that feels stronger about the intelligence community and the CIA than Donald Trump. There's nobody." A few minutes later Trump concluded by saying: "I love honesty. I like honest reporting . . . I love you, I respect you. There's nobody I respect more. You're going to do a fantastic job. And we're going to start winning again, and you're going to be leading the charge. So thank you all very much. Thank you—you're beautiful."[52] Exactly seven months later, President Trump presented his new strategy for Afghanistan. Trump professed, "My original instinct was to pull out—and, historically, I like following my instincts. But all my life I've heard that decisions are much different when you sit behind the desk in the Oval Office; in other words, when you're President of the United States. So I studied Afghanistan in great detail and from every conceivable angle. After many meetings, over many months, we held our final meeting last Friday at Camp David, with my Cabinet and generals, to complete our strategy."[53]

The president must remember his words from these two days. He must continue listening to his analysts and officers who tell the truth rather than promote the party line. Trump must maintain an environment where the IC adage "truth to power" exists. He must foster an atmosphere that fuels unbiased opinion rather than a "pleasing the customer" mentality. The system must change. For this to happen, it must emanate from the top down. It begins with the president, trickling down to the policymakers, and then to the senior leaders of the CIA and the Army (and to the rest of the IC and military). The president and his advisers must establish close communication with intelligence chiefs and give sober attention to analysis without merely seeking confirmation of their own agendas; as Richard K. Betts notes, "The typical problem in whirlwind policymaking at the top of government is less often the misuse of intelligence than the failure to use it."[54]

Politicization aside, regardless of whether Army commanders believe that the age of landpower is at an end, the last two decades illustrate that it is critical for the Army to be adaptable and prepared to respond to whatever the future might bring. Only with great hubris do analysts and commanders assume that they know what eventual missions and conflicts will be asked of the IC and the Army. It would have been difficult on 10 September 2001 for the CIA and the Army to fathom what policymakers would require of them in the years to come. New vehicles, new languages, new terrain, new enemy . . . the list goes on. How then does the CIA and the Army prepare for the future?

The answer lies in adaptation. The seventeenth-century expert swordsman Musashi Miyamoto professed, "You must have a position, without a position. Where you hold your sword depends on your relationship to the opponent, it depends on the place, and must conform to the situation; whenever you hold it, the idea is to hold it so that it will be easy to kill the opponent. Therefore, the principle is to have a guard position without a position."[55] He concludes almost every paragraph within his treatise by comparing the lone warrior to the general because the principles run parallel. Whether you are in a duel or waging a war between armies, the lesson remains static. To succeed in battle, you must adapt. And to adapt, you must study, reflect, and practice—you must prepare. It is essential that we remember Musashi's maxim of adaptation and not having a position, thus remaining unbiased. The military and intelligence communities must continue to hone the craft of intelligence and war—because like any craft, without practice it rusts and atrophies. The CIA and Army cannot know what current or future geopolitical scenarios they will face, requiring the study and preparation for diverse, even unthinkable scenarios.

As Roman strategist Vegetius famously remarked, "He who desires peace, let him prepare for war. He who wants victory, let him train soldiers diligently."[56] Roman philosopher Younger Seneca agreed. Writing in the first century, Seneca concluded, "It is in times of security that the spirit should be preparing itself to deal with difficult times; while fortune is bestowing favours on it then is the time for it to be strengthened against her rebuffs. In the midst of peace the soldier carries out manoeuvres, throws up earthworks against a non-existent enemy and tires himself out with unnecessary toil in order to be equal to it when it is necessary. If you want a man to keep his head when the crisis comes you must give him some training before it comes."[57]

Most important to this "training," however, is not advanced technology, military preparation, adaptation, or classes in writing intelligence briefs, it is combating what James J. Wirtz dubs "intelligence-to-please syndrome."[58] Politicization is an ethical problem—it is one of virtue. Thus, Seneca's most vital lesson is this: "Virtue only comes to a character which has been thoroughly schooled and trained and brought to a pitch of perfection by unremitting practice. We are born for it, but not with it. And even in the best of people, until you cultivate it there is only the material for virtue, not virtue itself."[59] We are not preprogrammed to be virtuous. Leading an ethical life, especially in the Beltway, becomes unnecessary when leaders such as presidents and chief advisers preach virtue but do not practice it. Sherman Kent determined, "Intelligence work is in essence nothing more than the search for the single best answer."[60] Most will not submit the ethical "best answer" if they know their superiors will not listen—or worse.

Notes

1. The US Intelligence Community consists of seventeen branches, led by the Office of the Director of National Intelligence. The other sixteen members are the Central Intelligence Agency, Defense Intelligence Agency, Federal Bureau of Investigation, National Geospatial-Intelligence Agency, National Reconnaissance Office, National Security Agency, Department of Energy, Department of Homeland Security, Department of State, Department of the Treasury, Drug Enforcement Administration, US Air Force, US Army, US Coast Guard, US Marine Corps, and US

Navy. The US Intelligence Community webpage contains specific information on each member's role within the IC. See https://www.intelligencecareers.gov/icmembers.html.

2. Three of the standard texts on intelligence studies that address politicization are Mark M. Lowenthal, *Intelligence: From Secrets to Policy*, 7th ed. (Thousand Oaks, Calif.: CQ Press, 2017), Roger Z. George and James B. Bruce, eds., *Analyzing Intelligence: National Security Practitioners' Perspectives*, 2nd ed. (Washington, DC: Georgetown Univ. Press, 2014), and Loch K. Johnson and James J. Wirtz, eds., *Intelligence: The Secret World of Spies: An Anthology*, 4th ed. (Oxford: Oxford Univ. Press, 2014). The three essential books, however, that reveal the true severity of the issue are: Joshua Rovner, *Fixing the Facts: National Security and the Politics of Intelligence* (Ithaca, N.Y.: Cornell Univ. Press, 2011), Robert Jervis, *Why Intelligence Fails: Lessons from the Iranian Revolution and the Iraq War* (Ithaca, N.Y.: Cornell Univ. Press, 2010), and Richard K. Betts, *Enemies of Intelligence: Knowledge and Power in American National Security* (New York: Columbia Univ. Press, 2007).

3. This volume's editor calls for similar change within the US Army culture, which also dissuades independent, noncareerist thought. See Jason W. Warren, "The Centurion Mindset and the Army's Strategic Leader Paradigm," *Parameters* 45, no. 3 (autumn 2015): 27–38. James Risen also discusses this careerism and describes the culture of both the US Army and the CIA as "dominated by career professionals," and that "both institutions abhor sudden change and tend to force policy toward the middle." Risen adds that when participating in meetings with President George W. Bush and Secretary of Defense Donald Rumsfeld, American commanders kept silent on areas of concern that they frequently complained about among themselves. James Risen, *State of War: The Secret History of the CIA and the Bush Administration* (New York: Free Press, 2007), 4.

4. Eliot A. Cohen, *The Big Stick: The Limits of Soft Power and the Necessity of Military Force* (New York: Basic Books, 2016), xii.

5. Daniel P. Bolger, *Why We Lost: A General's Inside Account of the Iraq and Afghanistan Wars* (Boston: HMH, 2014), 431. This is not a new lesson, with an example being from the Byzantine emperor Maurice (who reigned from AD 582 to 602), who states in the introduction to his military treatise that a commander must maintain his humility. Maurice, *Maurice's Strategikon: Handbook of Byzantine Military Strategy*, trans. George T. Dennis (Philadelphia: Univ. of Pennsylvania Press, 1984), 9.

6. Paul R. Pillar, *Intelligence and U.S. Foreign Policy: Iraq, 9/11, and Misguided Reform* (New York: Columbia Univ. Press, 2011), 124.

7. Ibid., 151.

8. Michael T. Flynn, *The Field of Fight: How We Can Win the Global War against Radical Islam and Its Allies* (New York: St. Martin's Press, 2016), 35.

9. Peter Nicholas and Byron Tau, "On a Big Day, Flynn Grabs the Spotlight," *Wall Street Journal*, 1 December 2017, https://www.wsj.com/articles/on-a-big-day-flynn-grabs-the-spotlight-1512174716?mod=searchresults&page=1&pos=8; Byron

Tau, "Pentagon Opens Probe into Michael Flynn's Foreign Payments," *Wall Street Journal,* 27 April 2017, https://www.wsj.com/articles/pentagon-opens-probe-into-michael-flynns-foreign-payments-1493303790?mod=searchresults&page=2& pos=20; Maggie Haberman, Matthew Rosenberg, Matt Apuzzo, and Glenn Thrush, "Michael Flynn Resigns as National Security Adviser," *New York Times,* 13 February 2017, https://www.nytimes.com/2017/02/13/us/politics/donald-trump-national-security-adviser-michael-flynn.html.

10. Regardless of whether the reader subscribes to the blueprint theory of Plato's republic and his interpretation of the city-soul analogy/tripartite psychology, the applicable key aspects are the three types of people within the city: the gold-reasoned guardians, the silver-spirited warriors, and the bronze-craving citizens—a superb mirror to Clausewitz's paradoxical trinity. See books II, IV, and IX in Plato, *The Republic of Plato,* trans. Allan Bloom (New York: Basic Books, 2016), and Carl von Clausewitz, *On War,* trans. and ed. Michael Howard and Peter Paret (Princeton, N.J.: Princeton Univ. Press, 1984), 89. Donald S. Travis's chapter in this volume makes excellent use of the Clausewitzian paradoxical trinity.

11. Hew Strachan, *Clausewitz's On War: A Biography* (New York: Grove Press, 2007), 194, see also 2–3. For a study of Clausewitz's modern military application, see Antulio J. Echevarria II, *Clausewitz and Contemporary War* (Oxford: Oxford Univ. Press, 2007), especially pages 69–74 for a taut discussion of the trinity. For further detail on the trinity's society element, see chapter 6 in Thomas Waldman, *War, Clausewitz and the Trinity* (New York: Routledge, 2016).

12. William Inboden, "The Seven Impossible Demands Policymakers Place on Intelligence," *Foreign Policy,* 18 February 2014, http://foreignpolicy.com/2014/02/18/the-seven-impossible-demands-policymakers-place-on-intelligence/.

13. Jervis, *Why Intelligence Fails,* 172.

14. Sherman Kent, *Strategic Intelligence for American World Policy* (Princeton, N.J.: Princeton Univ. Press, 1966), 180.

15. Ibid., 200.

16. Robert M. Gates, "A Message to Analysts: Guarding Against Politicization," 16 March 1992 (CIA Library), 9-11, https://www.cia.gov/library/center-for-the-study-of-intelligence/kent-csi/volume-36-number-1/pdf/v36i1a01p.pdf.

17. See Kent, *Strategic Intelligence for American World Policy,* notably chapter 11.

18. Derek Grossman, "Giving Intelligence Analysts Their Voices Back: The Case for Analyst Perspectives," *War on the Rocks,* 20 October 2016, https://warontherocks.com/2016/10/giving-intelligence-analysts-their-voices-back-the-case-for-analyst-perspectives/.

19. 9/11 Commission, *The 9/11 Commission Report: Final Report of the National Commission on Terrorist Attacks upon the United States* (New York: Norton, 2004), 91.

20. Betts, *Enemies of Intelligence,* 70.

21. John Patrick Finnegan, *Military Intelligence* (Washington, DC: Center of Military History, 1998), 105.

22. For detailed troop numbers and a reassessment of Adams, see James J.

Wirtz, "Intelligence to Please? The Order of Battle Controversy during the Vietnam War," *Political Science Quarterly* 106, no. 2 (summer 1991): 239–263, especially table 1 on page 244.

23. William C. Westmoreland, *A Soldier Reports* (New York: Da Capo Press, 1989), 416.

24. Lewis Sorley, *Westmoreland: The General Who Lost Vietnam* (Boston: HMH, 2011), 159–162. For a reevaluation of Westmoreland, see Gregory A. Daddis, *Westmoreland's War: Reassessing American Strategy in Vietnam* (Oxford: Oxford Univ. Press, 2014).

25. Sorley, *Westmoreland,* 164.

26. Richard Helms, *A Look Over My Shoulder: A Life in the Central Intelligence Agency* (New York: Random House, 2003), 325–326.

27. Lewis Sorley, *A Better War: The Unexamined Victories and Final Tragedy of America's Last Years in Vietnam* (Orlando, Fla.: Harcourt, 1999), 159.

28. Andrew F. Krepinevich Jr., *The Army and Vietnam* (Baltimore, Md.: Johns Hopkins Univ. Press, 1986), 80.

29. Sam Adams, *War of Numbers: An Intelligence Memoir* (South Royalton, Vt.: Steerforth Press, 1994), 165.

30. Ibid., 168–170. For further details on the Adams and Helms encounter, see C. Michael Hiam, *Who the Hell Are We Fighting?: The Story of Sam Adams and the Vietnam Intelligence Wars* (Hanover, N.H.: Steerforth Press, 2006), 148–155.

31. Helms, *A Look Over My Shoulder,* 326–328.

32. Flynn, *Field of Fight,* 34–35.

33. Rhodri Jeffreys-Jones, *The CIA and American Democracy,* 3rd ed. (New Haven, Conn.: Yale Univ. Press, 2003), 168–169.

34. Helms, *A Look Over My Shoulder,* 382.

35. Sorley, *A Better War,* 102, see also footnote 6 on 419.

36. Bob Woodward, *Plan of Attack: The Definitive Account of the Decision to Invade Iraq* (New York: Simon and Schuster, 2004), 249.

37. Risen, *State of War,* 122–123. See also George Tenet, *At the Center of the Storm: My Years at the CIA* (New York: HarperCollins, 2007), chapters 16–24, and *The Commission on the Intelligence Capabilities of the United States Regarding Weapons of Mass Destruction,* https://www.gpo.gov/fdsys/pkg/GPO-WMD/pdf/GPO-WMD.pdf.

38. James Bamford, *A Pretext for War: 9/11, Iraq, and the Abuse of America's Intelligence Agencies* (New York: Anchor Books, 2005), 385.

39. Michael Morell, *The Great War of Our Time: The CIA's Fight against Terrorism from Al Qa'ida to ISIS* (New York: Twelve, 2015), 103.

40. Jervis, *Why Intelligence Fails,* 154–155.

41. Walter Pincus and Dana Priest, "Bush, Aides Ignored CIA Caveats on Iraq: Clear-Cut Assertions Were Made before Arms Assessment Was Completed," *Washington Post,* 7 February 2004, A17, http://www.washingtonpost.com/wp-dyn/articles/A20194-2004Feb6.html. See also David Barstow, "The Nuclear Card: The

Aluminum Tube Story—A Special Report: How White House Embraced Suspect Iraq Arms Intelligence," *New York Times,* 3 October 2004, http://www.nytimes.com/2004/10/03/washington/us/the-nuclear-card-the-aluminum-tube-story-a-special-report-how.html. For a detailed report on the earlier search for WMD by the UN Special Commission (UNSCOM), see Charles Duelfer, *Hide and Seek: The Search for Truth in Iraq* (New York: Public Affairs, 2009).

42. Kurt Eichenwald, "Dick Cheney's Biggest Lie," *Newsweek,* 19 May 2015, http://www.newsweek.com/2015/05/29/dick-cheneys-biggest-lie-333097.html. For additional details see Kurt Eichenwald, *500 Days: Secrets and Lies in the Terror Wars* (New York: Touchstone, 2012).

43. Rovner, *Fixing the Facts,* 181.

44. Jami Miscik, "Intelligence and the Presidency: How to Get It Right," *Foreign Affairs* 96, no. 3 (May/June 2017): 61.

45. See the chart on page 3 of the "Intelligence Community Directive 203: Analytic Standards," 2 January 2015, https://www.dni.gov/files/documents/ICD/ICD%20203%20Analytic%20Standards.pdf.

46. Allen W. Dulles, *The Craft of Intelligence: America's Legendary Spy Master on the Fundamentals of Intelligence Gathering for a Free World* (Guilford, Conn.: Lyons Press, 2006), 265.

47. Mark Mazzetti and Matt Apuzzo, "Inquiry Weighs Whether ISIS Analysis Was Distorted," *New York Times* 25 August 2015, https://www.nytimes.com/2015/08/26/world/middleeast/pentagon-investigates-allegations-of-skewed-intelligence-reports-on-isis.html; Nancy A. Youssef and Shane Harris, "'Cancer Within': Exclusive: 50 Spies Say ISIS Intelligence Was Cooked," *Daily Beast,* 9 September 2015, http://www.thedailybeast.com/exclusive-50-spies-say-isis-intelligence-was-cooked. For a pithy overview, see Robert Tomes, "On The Politicization of Intelligence," *War on the Rocks,* 29 September 2015, https://warontherocks.com/2015/09/on-the-politicization-of-intelligence/.

48. John Grady, "CENTCOM Already Implementing Recommendations to Improve Intelligence Efforts," *USNI News,* 1 March 2017, https://news.usni.org/2017/03/01/centcom-already-implementing-recommendations-to-improve-intelligence-efforts. See also Inspector General, *Unclassified Report of Investigation on Allegations Relating to USCENTCOM Intelligence Products,* 31 January 2017, http://www.dodig.mil/pubs/documents/DODIG-2017-049.pdf?source=GovDelivery.

49. Michael T. Flynn, Matt Pottinger, and Paul D. Batchelor, "Fixing Intel: A Blueprint for Making Intelligence Relevant in Afghanistan" (Washington, DC: Center for a New American Security, 2010), 4, http://online.wsj.com/public/resources/documents/AfghanistanMGFlynn_Jan2010.pdf.

50. Flynn, Pottinger, and Batchelor, "Fixing Intel," 24.

51. The Russian General Staff, *The Soviet-Afghan War: How a Superpower Fought and Lost,* trans. and ed. Lester W. Grau and Michael A. Gress (Lawrence: Univ. Press of Kansas, 2002), 314.

52. "President Trump Remarks at the Central Intelligence Agency," *C-SPAN,*

21 January 2017, https://www.c-span.org/video/?422418-1/president-trump-tells-cia -get-rid-isis.

53. "Presidential Address on U.S. Policy in Afghanistan," *C-SPAN*, 21 August 2017, https://www.c-span.org/video/?432890-1/president-trump-addresses -nation-us-policy-afghanistan-south-asia.

54. Betts, *Enemies of Intelligence*, 138, see also 135–141.

55. Musashi Miyamoto, *The Book of Five Rings*, trans. Thomas Cleary (Boston: Shambhala, 2010), 44–45.

56. Vegetius, *Epitome of Military Science*, 2nd ed., trans. N. P. Milner (Liverpool: Liverpool Univ. Press, 1997), 67.

57. Seneca, *Letters from a Stoic*, trans. Robin Campbell (London: Penguin Books, 2004), 67.

58. James J. Wirtz, *The Tet Offensive: Intelligence Failure in War* (Ithaca, N.Y.: Cornell Univ. Press, 1991), 8, 273–274; Wirtz, "Intelligence to Please?," 263.

59. Seneca, *Letters from a Stoic*, 176–177.

60. Kent, *Strategic Intelligence for American World Policy*, vii.

11

US Policy and East Asian Allied Projection of Landpower

Eric Setzekorn

Since 9/11, the US Army has struggled to balance immediate national security requirements in the Middle East with long-term national interests in other parts of the world. In the past fifteen years US Army forces in East Asia often focused on antiterrorist activities and frequently deployed outside the region to Iraq or Afghanistan. In this vacuum, America's Asian partners, South Korea and Taiwan, took positive steps to redesign their force structure and conduct extensive force modernization in order to deter North Korea and China.

Equipment modernization has been a clear success, but both Taiwan and South Korea are beginning to encounter severe problems with force generation planning and manpower due to a demographic cliff. Political pressure and social disdain for mandatory service has increased significantly in the past decade, leading both nations to seek a volunteer military. The stunted development of army reserve structures complicated this shift, as an augmentation of a smaller force in a large conflict will be necessary. The US Army can and must provide assistance in adapting personnel policies and reserve force structure in South Korea and Taiwan.

Fortunately, the US Army has a long history of successful engagement in East Asia. Speaking in 2013, Secretary of the Army John M. McHugh remarked that "the Army has for decades upon decades been a major presence in the Pacific. The last twelve years have caused us to focus in two theaters of conflict, but as those have begun to wind down in the last year, it allows us to get back to the things we've been doing very, very well for a very long time."[1] The US Army established cooperation with South Korea and Taiwan in the 1950s, when it was responsible for training and equipping local forces through Mutual Security Program grants and large Military Assistance Advisory Groups. With South Korea and Taiwan transitioning into vibrant democracies with breathtaking economic development during the 1980s and

1990s, direct US support declined, although regular interactions and occasional sales of weapon systems maintained the close relationships. Unfortunately for relations, after 9/11 the US Army repeatedly deployed to the Middle East brigades from the 2nd Infantry Division based in South Korea, as well as the US-based (but Pacific-focused) 25th Infantry Division. Moreover, the few Army units remaining in theater were often called on to support counterterrorism missions, such as the ongoing deployments in the Philippines to counter Abu Sayyaf and Jammah Islamiyah.

Recent efforts to shift US military resources to East Asia, which is the most economically dynamic and strategically important region of the world, offer the US Army a tremendous opportunity to support national policy and aid long-time allies.[2] In the near future, the US Army must expand its engagement with South Korea and Taiwan as the military capabilities of North Korea and China increase in range and lethality. The Army can play a vital role in improving and accelerating the professionalization of allied land forces and assisting with their creation of a more capable reserve system and a volunteer regular army. Examining the current state of allied landpower in East Asia requires understanding the major successes of force modernization there, and provides insights into the greatest challenge for the next ten years—the manpower policies and military reserve system in Taiwan and South Korea.

2001–2016: Force Modernization and Modularity

After 9/11, both Taiwan and South Korea closely studied the US Army and its rapid organizational and doctrinal changes. The US Army's structural transformation from divisions to modular brigades brought to the surface latent advantages in maneuverability and firepower for efficiency and flexible deployment.[3] After adopting many of these templates, the Republic of China Army (ROCA, Taiwan) and Republic of Korea Army (ROKA, South Korea) are both smaller and better equipped than in 2001. In both nations, a force structure based around infantry divisions supported by obsolete M48 tanks and towed artillery transitioned to a brigade-centered force equipped with more capable armor (South Korea) or the equivalent of Stryker brigades (Taiwan).

In Taiwan, beginning in the late 1990s, defense officials began discussing a downsizing from 430,000 toward a more mobile force of 250,000–280,000 personnel. In the early 2000s, Taiwan began an ambitious program to transition from an infantry- and armor-based force built around twenty-four divisions into a more mobile brigade-centric force. By 2005, the division level reorganized the ROCA into thirty-five brigades that reported directly to the corps headquarters.

Taiwan's other major focus was to improve the technological capabilities of its armored and combat aviation assets. In 2000, Taiwan had sixty AH-1 Cobra helicopters, seventy to eighty aging UH-1 Huey helicopters, and a small number of OH-58 Kiowa armed scout helicopters. Since 2006, Taiwan's army has placed orders for sixty UH-60M Blackhawks and thirty AH-64D Apache Longbows, together with associated training and observation helicopters.[4] The total cost of these purchases was roughly $6 billion (US).[5] This allowed Taiwan to create three independent combat aviation brigades. Their armored forces have been streamlined as well, with the storage of many M41 and M48 tanks and the introduction of newer, more mobile systems. The CM-32 Yunpao is replacing heavy tracked equipment. It is an eight-wheeled armored vehicle in multiple configurations, including armored gun, mortar carrier, infantry squad, and command versions. The program began in 2002 after careful analysis of the strengths and weaknesses of the US Army Stryker and included improvements, such as a V-shaped hull and stronger armor. Up to 1,500 CM-32s are planned for production, a number that will equip all of Taiwan's Infantry Brigade Combat Teams (IBCTs).[6]

South Korea has pursued a similar defense modernization plan that drew heavily on US Army models and concepts. In 2005, South Korea announced the Defense Reform Plan 2020 (DRP 2020), which would reshape the ROKA into a smaller, more mobile force. During the 1980s and 1990s this force structure included 670,000 personnel in nineteen infantry divisions, which were mostly useful for linear defense, but with limited ability to maneuver.[7] Under DRP 2020, South Korea has taken steps to decrease its force strength to 495,000, a reduction of 125,000 from the late 1990s. This drawdown is planned to continue, with South Korean army forces projected to reach 387,000 in 2022.[8]

South Korean modernization also focused on improving combat aviation assets. In 2006, Korea Aerospace Industries began a joint venture with Eurocopter to begin development of a large-scale production run of approximately 245 light transport/utility helicopters.[9] While contract and bureaucratic delays have slowed the program and increased the price, production of the KUH-1 Surion has slowly allowed for the replacement of aging UH-1 Huey helicopters. In addition, South Korea purchased thirty-six AH-64E Longbow helicopters, valued at over $3.5 billion, with all helicopters attaining operational status in early 2017.[10]

South Korea also has invested billions of dollars to improve the mobility and firepower of its forces. It has funded acquisitions of the follow-on to the

K1 tank, the K1A1, and begun development of the very expensive K2 Black Panther.[11] During the 2000s, South Korea also produced more than eight hundred units of the K9 155 mm self-propelled howitzer, capable of multiple round simultaneous impact (MRSI) firing. In addition, the K21 infantry fighting vehicle entered production in 2009, with roughly one thousand planned to be acquired.

Another commonality between the two nations is that both South Korea and Taiwan have developed an army-centric ballistic missile defense system. In Taiwan and South Korea, political leaders have made difficult political choices to integrate their defense systems into a broader US missile architecture, and in both countries their army services have retained command and control of BMD systems.

US leaders have also supported missile defense systems, and the ability of Army offensive missile systems to complicate opponents' planning and undertake long-range precision strikes. At the October 2014 AUSA meeting, Secretary of Defense Chuck Hagel noted that US Army capabilities in long-range precision-guided missiles, rockets, artillery, and air defense systems are part of the "rebalance" to Asia, and are an area of great opportunity for the United States, Taiwan, and South Korea.[12] General Vincent Brooks, commander of US Army Pacific, was even more explicit in the April 2014 edition of *Army Magazine,* writing, "Opportunities being explored include: procurement and employment of ground-based anti-ship missiles for use in coastal defense and the interdiction of warships."[13] Private US think tanks have argued that US Army missile systems enjoy advantages in "survivability, sustainability and persistence" that complement and sometimes surpass Navy and Air Force systems.[14] Improved integration of missile assets and sensor networks would boost allied capabilities, and also assure local partners because US land assets demonstrate that the US commitment is durable.[15]

Taiwan first ordered US Patriot missiles in 1993, after Chinese DF-15 missile units were detected across the Taiwan Strait. These units did not arrive until after the 1996 Taiwan Strait crisis, and only in 1997 was Taiwan able to deploy three Patriot missile units equipped with PAC-2 Guidance Enhanced Missiles. In May 2004, Taiwan made a formal request for six PAC-3 firing units and for an upgrade of the three PAC-2 Plus firing units to that higher level capability. The extremely high price tag for these purchases, with none of the production being sourced from local Taiwanese partners, led to serious political disputes that slowed the acquisition program. Eventually these issues were resolved, and between 2008 and 2011 Taiwan spent more than $6 billion to acquire over 450 PAC-3 missiles and the related AN/MPQ-65 radar sets and launcher stations.[16] In addition, Taiwan developed an integrated sys-

tem of command and control, long-range early warning radars, and information distribution systems at a cost of over $2.5 billion.[17]

Taiwan has also made investments in offensive army missile forces.
In 2010, it agreed to purchase ninety-six Army Tactical Missile System
(ATACMS) missiles for its existing inventory of M270 launchers in a deal
valued at over $400 million. However, this deal was vetoed by the United
States.[18] In response, Taiwan has devoted considerable resources to developing its own missiles and it now deploys its locally produced High Mobility Artillery Rocket System (HIMARS)-type wheeled system.[19] Taiwan has
also taken steps to develop longer range missiles that could potentially conduct counterbattery strikes. In particular, the Hsiung-Feng IIE missile is road
mobile and reported to be capable of an eight hundred-kilometer range with
a two hundred-kilogram warhead, although details and production numbers
are deliberately unclear in order to not be perceived by China as a provocation.

Korean participation in missile defense activities has been more recent.
The United States has had one Patriot battalion in Korea since 1994, and
an additional battalion arrived in 2004 equipped with the more advanced
PAC-3 model.[20] The "Sunshine policy" of Presidents Kim Dae-jung (1998–
2203) and Roh Moo-hyun (2003–2008) slowed Korean deployment of
missile defense systems. It was not until 2006 that South Korea began an
indigenous Air and Missile Defense System (KAMD), which it initialized by
acquiring Patriot PAC-2 missile defense systems from Germany and AEGIS-
equipped ships from the United States.

After the election of pro-US Lee Myun-bak in 2008, and the 2010
Cheonan sinking and the shelling of Yeonpyeong Island, South Korean accelerated its missile defense efforts. In 2013, South Korea requested the United
States' assistance in upgrading its existing Patriot batteries. In June 2014, US
and South Korean Patriot batteries were able to conduct joint training for
the first time and were able to successfully transfer data between US Army
and ROKA equipment.[21] In July 2014, the Korean Ministry of Defense
announced that between 2014 and 2018, roughly 14 percent of the defense
budget would be spent on missile defense, with a mixture of US equipment
purchases and indigenous production.[22] In November 2014, 136 PAC-3 missiles were approved for sale, along with associated computer and networking
support, in a package totaling $1.4 billion.[23] The deployment of a Theater
High Altitude Air Defense (THAAD) unit to South Korea is indicative of a
shift in South Korean thinking toward the utilization of existing US Army
capabilities.

Like Taiwan, South Korea has also sought to develop an offensive missile capability through a mixture of United States' purchases and indige-

nous missile production. In 2002, South Korea purchased over two hundred ATACMS missiles, deploying them in 2004.[24] In 2008, South Korean arms manufacturer Hanwha obtained the license to produce longer range missiles for the M270A1 MLRS system.[25] South Korea is also independently developing a system with a range of 160 kilometers, more than double the range of the US-produced MLRS rocket.

The expenditure of billions of dollars on US helicopters, missiles, and sensors allows for significantly greater capabilities by linking together regional partners with broader US efforts. Although it is likely that Taiwan and South Korea will continue to develop some longer-range offensive missile systems that the United States cannot supply, the developments of the past decade are overwhelmingly positive and a reflect a high degree of confidence in US Army equipment and technology.

Challenges Ahead: The End of Conscription and Neglected Reserve Forces

Overall, the past decade has seen tremendous improvements in the land forces of Taiwan and South Korea, which have improved their firepower and combat aviation abilities. In the next decade, the biggest challenge for US Army strategic landpower partners South Korea and Taiwan will be demographic and social. In effect, the conscription systems that both nations have used for the past sixty-five years cannot continue to supply sufficient manpower. Like the US Army in the 1970s, Taiwan and South Korea are finding that designing and fielding new weapons systems is relatively easy compared to reforming the personnel system and attracting high-quality volunteers.

Social and demographic issues will challenge Taiwan and South Korea for two reasons. First, declining birthrates as each country became wealthier have resulted in a sharp decline in the age cohort available for military service. South Korea is currently ranked 220th out of 224 countries in its birthrate, with only 8.26 births per 1,000 people in 2014. Taiwan is not much better, at 216th, with 8.55.[26] This means that South Korea's yearly cohort of eighteen-year-old males will decrease from 360,000 in 2010, to 265,000 in 2020, and to 209,000 in 2030, reducing the manpower pool by roughly 40 percent.[27]

Second, and more important, the transition to a volunteer-based military is struggling to gain social support due to tensions within society, especially from younger members, who view the military with hostility. Increasingly large portions of society now view military service, either voluntary or through conscription, as an unfortunate waste of time that delays education and careers. The strict and coercive discipline used in South Korean and Taiwanese army units is no longer socially acceptable, heightening ill will.[28]

Both South Korea and Taiwan are finding that the only way between this Scylla and Charybdis is to expand the reserve training system, which they hope can provide sufficiently trained manpower without expanding the active duty force. The post-9/11 experience of the United States highlights the need for large numbers of adequately trained soldiers to provide support for combat operations and to perform a variety of labor-intensive tasks, such as area security. The US Army has been very successful in integrating reserve elements into the Army Force Generation process, and during Operation Iraqi Freedom and Operation Enduring Freedom these units provided commanders with the required forces despite a relatively small Regular Army.[29]

Reserve-type forces in Taiwan and South Korea would be incredibly valuable for a wide variety of missions. In Korea, the North Korean special operations forces (SOF) threat creates a demand for large numbers of rear security personnel. Similarly, since the easing of travel restrictions between Taiwan and China in 2008, there has been a rapid increase in cross-straits travel, and Taiwanese defense analysts are increasingly concerned about the ability of Chinese SOF to attack a broad series of targets across the island in any future conflict.[30] Both countries also face the threat of ballistic missile strikes that would require civil defense precautions. Reserve forces are also increasingly seen as having a vital role in responding to natural disasters. While earthquakes, storms, and mudslides are nothing new, the aging populations and extreme urban density in both South Korea and Taiwan, coupled with rising expectations of government efficiency, make reserve soldiers important for noncombat duties.

Current reserve force policy in Taiwan and South Korea is radically different from the recent US experience with its Reserve Component, where elements are routinely deployed and expected to perform missions alongside Regular Army units. Both South Korea and Taiwan maintain systems that include eight years of military service in the reserves after the period of conscription. In Taiwan, personnel on the army reserve list are mobilized every two years (four times during their reserve service) for refresher training. In an average year, roughly 140,000 reservists in Taiwan fulfill this biannual requirement (out of 2.6 million potential reservists).[31] The training consists of less than a week of marksmanship and other combat and disaster relief training.[32] This process has remained unchanged since the 1960s, when the reserve muster process was designed for a much slower operational tempo that allowed time for retraining and unit formation within a sixty- to ninety-day period.[33] In both Taiwan and South Korea, no equipment or permanent staff of officers and sergeants are assigned to reserve units. In time of crisis or war, reserve units would be created by aggregating personnel from computer database listings, but without prior coordination, retraining, or significant support by active component units; the operational capability of these units is doubtful.

After taking office in 2008, President Ma Ying-jeou approved a plan to transition Taiwan to a volunteer active duty force, and men would only be required to complete a four-month basic military training course, followed by reserve duty. A major roadblock for developing a volunteer force is the increasing antimilitary sentiment within society. In particular, public hostility has risen between 2002 and 2011. During that period four thousand soldiers were injured or killed while on active duty, and over three hundred soldiers committed suicide.[34]

The steady erosion of public support for the military on Taiwan reached a breaking point in the summer of 2013, when the death of Corporal Hung Chung-chiu led to massive street protests. Corporal Hung had entered the ROCA as a draftee, had served for eighteen months, and was due to end his service in one week, but he was detained for carrying a camera-equipped cell phone in a sensitive security area. Subsequent reports noted that Hung had a difficult relationship with his superiors and suggested that his detention was a form of payback.[35] While in detention, Hung was forced to perform strenuous exercises during a period of extremely hot weather, and he died from heat stroke two days before his scheduled discharge. On 3 August 2013, a massive protest of 150,000 people in front of the Presidential Office Building in Taipei sought to pressure legislators to protect soldiers. Four days later the military justice system was abolished and judicial authority transferred to civilian courts in peacetime.[36] A civilian court subsequently found thirteen military personnel guilty of various charges and sentenced Hung's company commander to eight months in prison.[37]

As a result of the Hung case and the broader declining trust, the transition to a volunteer-based force was dealt a serious setback. Polling showed that the military's public image had fallen from 72 percent positive in 1999 to only 31 percent by July 2013, and the number of people with a "strongly negative" impression of the military rose from 2 percent to 18 percent in the same period.[38] In August 2013, Taiwanese officials reported that the military recruitment goal of 28,531 would not be met and that only 4,290 personnel had voluntarily joined the military in 2013.[39] In response, the target date for the transition to a volunteer force has been repeatedly delayed.[40]

In South Korea, distrust of the army has been rising after a series of incidents involving conscripts. The use of physical punishment is often linked to a rise in suicide rates among soldiers; in 2011 the South Korean army reported ninety-seven suicides, up 30 percent since 2006.[41] In contrast to Taiwan, soldiers in South Korea have often responded violently to abuse. On 13 May 2015, a South Korean reservist doing his two days of annual training shot and killed two soldiers before committing suicide. During his active duty service, the soldier was monitored because he "failed to adapt to the barracks life," and a suicide note found in his pocket stated a desire to "kill them all," referring to his military superiors.[42] In another case, a conscript NCO killed five fellow soldiers before leading authorities on a two-day manhunt.[43] In 2011 a South Korean marine killed four fellow marines he claimed bullied him, leading President Lee Myun-bak to remark, "Some young people, who grew up in freedom, seem psychologically unable to adjust to a different environment in the military."[44] Since 2006, the South Korean Ministry of National Defense has organized campaigns to limit the abuse of conscripts and junior members of the military, and has regularly prosecuted sixty to seventy officers a year for abusing subordinates.[45]

The biggest increase in anti-military feeling in South Korea occurred in May 2014, when Private Yoon Seung-joo died after a period of beatings while in detention. Ultimately, sixteen officers were disciplined and Army Chief of Staff Kwan Oh-Sung was forced to resign.[46] The sergeant responsible for Private Yoon's squad received forty-five years in prison from a military court, and other members of the squad were also sentenced for their role in Private Yoon's death.[47] Although the severe punishment appears to have limited calls to end the military justice system, as was done in Taiwan, the case continues to resonate in South Korea.

One result of the anti-military feeling is that although most Korean citizens agree with some sort of civil responsibility for national defense, finding volunteers to develop a long-serving professional force is difficult. According to Korean analysis, switching to a US Army-style "all-volunteer force" would result in an army of less than 300,000, which would be insufficient to deter North Korea.[48]

The US Army experience in creating highly capable National Guard forces that are both rooted in local communities and capable of fulfilling military tasks is a viable template for Taiwan and South Korea. A National Guard-type force would allow for the development of more experienced (and older) local forces that also are able to perform security and disaster relief, all while potentially limiting the social distance between society and the military.

Conclusion

The position of the US Army in northeast Asia has been strengthened in the past fifteen years due to the force modernization of the Taiwanese and South Korea armies. Key Asian allies are struggling to balance their identity as vibrant democracies with military requirements. East Asian demographic and social trends are a significant problem, and the US Army must increase its efforts to assist in the transition to volunteer forces in South Korea and Taiwan. Existing policies, such as the Foreign Area Officer (FAO) program, attendance of Taiwanese and South Korean officers at US professional military education schools, and deploying Reserve units to East Asia, are all effective methods of engagement but have not been adequately supported. The challenge for the Army is to provide the increased resources and senior leader support to expand and strengthen these existing programs so that they are able to bolster our partners during this difficult transition period. Fifteen years into the "Pacific Century," US Army policies that focus on Eastern Europe and the Middle East risk slighting the long-term security and stability of vital allies in the most economically dynamic region of the world.

Notes

1. Army Pacific Command, *U.S. Army in the Asia Pacific: Ensuring Stability and Security* (Washington, DC: Army Quadrennial Defense Review Office, November 2013), foreword.

2. Joint Chiefs of Staff, "National Military Strategy of the United States of America," (Washington, DC: Joint Chiefs of Staff, 2015), 9; President of the United States of America, "National Security Strategy" (Washington, DC: The White House, 2015), i, 24.

3. William M. Donnelly, *Transforming an Army at War* (Washington, DC: Center of Military History, 2007), 79–81.

4. Defense Security Cooperation Agency, Transmittal Number 09-03, "UH-60 Blackhawk Helicopters," 29 January 2010.

5. Shirley Kan, "Taiwan: Major U.S. Arms Sales since 1990," Congressional Research Service, 3 March 2014, 59.

6. Huang Tai-lin, "Thumbs Up for New Armored Vehicle," *Taipei Times,* 12 January 2005; Republic of China, Ministry of National Defense, CM-32 Clouded Leopard wheeled armored vehicles, http://www.mdc.idv.tw/mdc/army/cm32.htm (accessed 28 September 2015).

7. Andrea Savada and William Shaw, *South Korea: A Country Study* (Washington, DC: Library of Congress, 1992), 283.

8. South Korea, Ministry of National Defense, 2014 Defense White Paper, 80.

9. Defense Industry Daily, "Surion: Eurocopter's Korean KHP/KUH Helicop-

ter Deal," 28 January 2015, http://www.defenseindustrydaily.com/korea-approves-eurocopters-khp-helicopter-deal-02325/ (accessed 16 September 2015).

10. Defense Security Cooperation Agency, "Republic of Korea (ROK) AH-64D APACHE Attack Helicopters," http://www.dsca.mil/major-arms-sales/republic-korea-rok-ah-64d-apache-attack-helicopters (accessed 1 October 2015); Gabriel Dominguez, "South Korea Completes Deployment of 36 AH-64E Apache Helos," 27 January 2017, http://www.janes.com/article/67283/south-korea-completes-deployment-of-36-ah-64e-apache-helos (accessed 25 May 2017) .

11. Tamir Eshel, Defense Update, "Korea to Bolster Its Land Forces with 100 New Black Panther Tanks by 2017," http://defense-update.com/20141229_korean_black_panther_tanks.html#.Vg1Vspc4Gvk (accessed 1 October 2015).

12. Secretary of Defense Chuck Hagel, "Remarks Delivered to the Association of the United States Army," 15 October 2014, http://www.defense.gov/News/Speeches/Speech-View/Article/605618 (accessed 16 September 2015).

13. General Vincent Brooks and Lieutenant Colonel Charlie Kim, "U.S. Army Pacific Makes Major Moves to Face Regional Challenges," *Army Magazine* 64, no. 4 (April 2014), 36.

14. Eric Lindsey, "Beyond Coast Guard Artillery: Cross-Domain Denial and the Army," Center for Strategic and Budgetary Assessments, 29 October 2014, 5; RAND, *The U.S. Army in Asia, 2030–2040* (Santa Monica, Calif.: RAND, 2014), 88–90.

15. Evan Montgomery, Testimony before the US-China Economic and Security Review Commission, 1 April 2015.

16. Defense Security Cooperation Agency, Transmittal Number 09-75, "Patriot Advanced Capability-3 (PAC-3) Firing Units, Training Unit and Missiles," 29 January 2010; Kan, "Taiwan: Major U.S. Arms Sales Since 1990," 58–59.

17. Ibid.

18. Richard Fisher, "The Story That Should Have Been," *Taipei Times,* 10 January 2011.

19. Lu Jianming, "An Introduction to the New Multiple Launch Rocket System Thunderbolt-2000" (Taipei: Ministry of National Defense, 2012).

20. Franklin Fisher, "Deployment of Patriot Missile Battalion to S. Korea Is Complete," *Stars and Stripes,* 1 December 2004.

21. Heather Denby, "U.S. South Korean Patriot Crews Seal the Gaps in Combined Air Defenses," 16 July 2015, http://www.army.mil/article/152437/US__South_Korean_Patriot_crews_seal_the_gaps_in_combined_air_defense/ (accessed 5 October 2015).

22. Eun-jung Kim, "Mid-Term Defense Program Focuses on Missile Defense Against North Korea," *Yonhap News,* 16 January 2014.

23. Defense Security Cooperation Agency, Transmittal Number 14-52, "Republic of Korea-Patriot Advanced Capability (PAC-3) Missiles," 5 November 2014.

24. *United States Arms Control and International Security Policy Handbook* (Washington, DC: International Business Publications, 2012), 252.

200   Eric Setzekorn

25. Gordon Arthur, "Artillery Systems 'Boom' in Asia," *Defense Review Asia*, 31 March 2014.

26. CIA World Factbook, "Birthrate," https://www.cia.gov/library/publications/the-world-factbook/rankorder/2054rank.html.

27. Joo-Sung Jung and Mye Sohn, "Korea's Military Service Policy Issues and Directions for Mid- and Long-Term Development," *Journal of Korean Defense Analysis* 23, no. 4 (December 2011): 477.

28. Yuan, Li-Cheng, "Recruitment and Retention in Taiwan's New All-Volunteer Force," *Res Militaris: Ergomas*, 5 (November 2017): 5–8.

29. John Sloan Brown, *Kevlar Legions: The Transformation of the U.S. Army, 1989–2005* (Washington, DC: Center of Military History, 2011), 280–281, 433–441.

30. Wu Shang-su, "Taiwan's Continued Conscription: An Unresolved Problem," 23 September 2015 (Singapore: RSIS Commentary, 2015), 2.

31. Republic of China, Ministry of National Defense, "2013 National Defense Report," 152.

32. Ibid., 208–209.

33. Ibid., 77–84.

34. "What to Make of the Nation's Military," *Taipei Times*, 19 July 2013.

35. "Vendetta Alleged in Death of Army Corporal," *Focus Taiwan News Channel*, 16 July 2013, http://focustaiwan.tw/news/aipl/201307160042.aspx.

36. Chris Wang, "Military Judicial System Altered," *Taipei Times*, 7 August 2013; Republic of China, Office of the President, "jun shi shenpan fa xiuzheng," 13 August 2013, http://www.president.gov.tw/PORTALS/0/BULLETINS/PAPER/PDF/7099-1.pdf. (accessed 25 May 2017).

37. Taiwan Taoyuan District Court Press Office, "Hung Chung-Chiu Sentencing Decision," 7 March 2014, http://tyd.judicial.gov.tw/newsDeta.asp?SEQNO=152219 (accessed 20 May 2017).

38. TVBS Poll Center (Minyi diaocha zhongxin), "Poll: Hung Chung-Chiu Case and Public Opinion, Conducted July 24–25, 2013," 25 July 2013, http://home.tvbs.com.tw/poll_center (accessed 15 May 2017).

39. "Military Tries Measures to Enhance Recruitment," *Taipei Times*, 22 August 2013; Lawrence Chung, "Lack of Interest Hits Recruitment Plan," *South China Morning Post*, 29 December 2013; Republic of China, Ministry of National Defense, "2013 National Defense Report," 183–185.

40. Republic of China, Ministry of National Defense, "Quadrennial Defense Review 2013," 88; Chris Wang, "Date for All-Volunteer Military Delayed," *Taipei Times*, 13 September 2013.

41. ABC News [Australia], "Fresh Suicides Spark Concern Over Military Service," 12 August 2014, http://www.abc.net.au/news/2014-08-12/an-south-korea-military-suicides/5666658 (accessed 17 September 2015).

42. Oh Seok-min, "3 dead, 2 Wounded in Shooting at Seoul Military Camp," *Yonhap News*, 13 May 2015.

43. Choe Sang-hun, "South Korea Hunts for Army Shooter," *New York Times,* 21 June 2014.

44. Choe Sang-hun, "A Korean 'Sacred Duty' Harbors a Dark Side," *New York Times,* 30 July 2011.

45. Park Si-soo, "Bizarre Military Assaults Persist," *Korea Times,* 29 September 2011.

46. "Army Chief of Staff Offers to Resign as Government Vows to Make Example of Offenders in Yoon's Death," *Naver,* 5 August 2014, http://news.naver.com/main/read.nhn?mode=LSD&mid=shm&sid1=100&oid=001&aid=0007053036 (accessed on 5 October 2015).

47. "Soldiers Jailed Over South Korean Bullying Death," 30 October 2014, http://www.bbc.com/news/world-asia-29828761 (accessed 29 September 2015).

48. Jung and Sohn, "Korea's Military Service Policy Issues and Directions for Mid- and Long-Term Development," 481.

12

ISIS's Projection of Landpower in Iraq

Ibrahim Al-Marashi

On 29 June 2014, Abu Bakr Al-Baghdadi, standing on the pulpit of the al-Nuri mosque in Mosul, declared the caliphate of ISIS. Three years to the day, Iraqi forces captured the remains of that mosque, destroyed by ISIS as they retreated, after a grueling nine-month battle for the city. The question remains as to how ISIS managed to seize so much territory in the first place, and how it endured three years in Iraq. While ISIS eventually lost control of its capital, Raqqa, in Syria, in October 2017, and Mosul by the end of 2017, its endurance for three years despite the vast coalition arrayed against it is the explanatory aim of this chapter, within the context of the organization's projection of landpower.

The ISIS phenomenon in Iraq and the inability of the Iraqi state to resist it was predicated on the former's use of landpower and the Iraqi government's inability to maintain a disciplined, cohesive standing army to resist it. Notwithstanding the eventual victory in Mosul, the Iraqi state does not enjoy a monopoly on the use of force, or in this case landpower, which institutionally has become decentralized and contested. A chapter on the Iraqi perspectives on landpower is problematic, as there are several military forces that emerged as the Ba'athist-era military collapsed in 2003, including the Iraqi state, but also the various substate actors or militias, and ISIS itself. As Michael O'Hanlon writes, "Put differently, in contemplating the character and scale of future warfare, the enemy gets a vote, too."[1] ISIS not only voted in the future direction of landpower, it served as an innovator as well. ISIS effectively employed landpower, initially leading to the rise of militias to counter it and forcing the Iraqi military to fight for close to three years to obtain victory.

ISIS and Landpower

ISIS's June 2014 offensive into Mosul and the resulting collapse of the Iraqi military occurred suddenly, yet these events were more than a decade in the making, a product of the collapse of the Iraqi military inherited from the Ba'athist state. ISIS's leadership is opaque, and understanding the motivation and rationale of this group requires some deductive analysis in explaining how the former Iraqi military elite under Saddam Hussein joined ISIS as a vehicle to reassert power. After 2003, these former officers might have coordinated their activities by joining some of the other short-lived Iraqi insurgent groups, organized during periods of incarceration, or perhaps they were isolated individuals who joined ISIS. Regardless of pre-ISIS affiliation, members lacked post-2003 options to join a military mobilization that would enable an eventual political comeback. The Ba'athism of the deposed Iraqi old guard held no promise of raising a mass-mobilization army to reassert power. Former Iraqi military officers had joined another insurgent group, *Jaysh al-Rijal al-Tariqa al-Naqshabandi* (The Men of the Naqshabandi Order), led by the last remaining high-ranking official from the Saddam era, Izat al-Duri, but this group did not offer the potential that ISIS did. Al-Duri's insurgency fused Sufism with Iraqi Sunni nationalism, but did not mobilize as many fighters as ISIS would.

Jordanian Abu Mus'ab al-Zarqawi established Al Qa'ida in Iraq, the precursor of ISIS, which consisted in 2003 primarily of foreign Muslim fighters. It slowly incorporated more Iraqis during the insurgency, essentially evolving into a de facto organizational shell for former Iraqi career military and intelligence officers under Saddam Hussein. In order to regain the power they lost after 2003, the Iraqi officers in ISIS mobilized Iraq's Arab Sunni population. The Coalition Provisional Authority disbanded Iraq's armed forces in 2003, and its subsequent de-Ba'athification policies denied job prospects to the suddenly out-of-power Sunni minority. While most insurgent groups collapsed after the 2007 Surge, ISIS survived,[2] even after the death of its founder, al-Zarqawi.

When it conquered Mosul in 2014, ISIS's command structure included a preponderance of Iraqis in leadership positions, including veteran officers of the Iraqi military under the Ba'ath rule.[3] Based on their last names, most of ISIS's leaders are Iraqi Arab and Turkmen Sunnis with military or security-related careers.[4] They are all relatively obscure figures, as is Abu Bakr Al-Baghdadi, its self-declared caliph. With the exception of al-Baghdadi, none of ISIS's leadership were religious clerics.

For the officers to have risen in the ranks during Saddam's rule, they would have professed the secularism of the Ba'ath party. Those who later joined ISIS are either genuine "reborn Muslims," becoming more religious during Saddam Hussein's faith campaign of the nineties,[5] or some of these officers might have become converts during their post-2003 incarceration in

Camp Bucca and genuinely believe in the religious outlook of ISIS.[6] Other officers, perhaps cynically, sought to manipulate the power of faith.[7] Nonetheless, if the interests of these former Iraqi officers were taken in aggregate as a constituency of ISIS, they benefitted from the Salafi religious veneer of the movement, which commanded a devoted religious following among Syrian and Iraqi fighters, in addition to foreign fighters from Europe and other areas of the Middle East. From a landpower perspective, it was the ideology of ISIS that allowed former Iraqi officers to create a cohesive standing army.

For the former Iraqi military officers in ISIS, their primary objective was securing territory on which to establish a state. ISIS and its professed Salafism was the rational choice for a religious ideological motivation to regain power, in that it could rally a critical mass of Sunni fighters in both Iraq and Syria against Shi'a-dominated states. The anti-Shi'ism embedded in ISIS's Salafism served as a potent mobilizer for both local Sunni communities and Sunnis living beyond Iraq and Syria to combat the Shi'a governments of Al-Asad in Damascus and Maliki in Baghdad. These religious volunteers in turn served the agenda of the former Iraqi military officers, enabling the Iraqi constituency in ISIS to seize territory, forming an anti-state against the Iraqi and Syrian governments. ISIS and its Iraqi commanders had successfully harnessed the energies and devotion of local Sunnis and a transnational Sunni wing, which bore the brunt of the heavy fighting and were willing to die in combat suicide operations.

For the former Saddam-era loyalists and career military officers, individually, or as a group, they most likely calculated that restoring their former control of all of Iraq was impossible given that Shi'a and Kurdish political elites had succeeded in entrenching their power over the respective governments in Baghdad and Irbil (the capital of the Kurdistan Regional Government [KRG]). In the post-2008 landscape, ISIS served as the most viable vehicle for these former officers to reassert their power in the Iraqi areas in which they had originated, such as Mosul, Ramadi, Fallujah, Rawa, Hit, and Tikrit.[8] While these officers of the Saddam Hussein regime might have lost control over Iraq, through ISIS they could capture and rule a larger Arab Sunni heartland in between the upper Euphrates and Tigris Rivers. These rivers fan out in separate directions north of Baghdad, creating a landmass referred to historically as the Al-Jazira, a quasi-island enveloped by these water arteries.

This geographic area in both Iraq and Syria had been home to a predominantly Arab Sunni population. The capital of ISIS, Raqqa, is located in the Syrian part of the Euphrates, and the group's first major foothold in an Iraqi urban center was Fallujah, another Euphrates town, which had capitulated to

ISIS control in January 2014. A rapid series of attacks into northern Iraq followed the offensive into Mosul on 9 June 2014, as ISIS seized several towns and cities, including Tikrit, securing two major urban centers on the Tigris flank of the Al-Jazira region. The location of the two rivers north of Baghdad and ISIS's ability to rule predominantly Sunni coreligionists within Al-Jazira essentially determined the borders of its caliphate.

Significant literature has been devoted to the ideological differences between Al Qa'ida and ISIS. Al Qa'ida had historically been selective in recruiting its adherents, seeking to serve as a vanguard of a global Muslim awakening rather than a mass mobilization force. Thus, the ISIS split from Al Qa'ida around this time ultimately hinged on the different strategies. ISIS prioritized seizing power and territory within Iraq and Syria and immediately declaring a caliphate, and thus the strategy of the former Iraqi officers differed from the global jihadist agenda of Al Qa'ida, contributing to their eventual split in 2014. What gave these Iraqi officers "buy-in" into the ISIS vision was its potential to raise an army, which in turn would allow these Iraqis to recapture the areas from which they originated.

Transnational Terrorism

ISIS projected its presence beyond the Middle East in a series of terrorist attacks in Paris in November 2015. This first coordinated attack in Europe resulted in around 130 casualties and attacks in Brussels followed in March 2016 aimed at its subway system and international airport. It appeared counterintuitive, then, that ISIS would engage in transnational terrorism based on the argument that ISIS's priorities were defending the land they seized in Iraq and Syria. The mission of ISIS suggested that it would have little interest in ordering or inspiring attacks in Europe or the United States, as opposed to Al Qa'ida, which envisioned such attacks as its primary function. Terrorist attacks abroad demonstrated how ISIS could bring urban-style guerrilla war attacks to the European metropolis but raised the question of their strategic benefits to ISIS in its local military campaign for survival on the Syrian-Iraqi front lines.

The ISIS landpower perspective reconciles this transnational strategy with its local agenda of securing territory in Iraq and Syria. ISIS's military forces, while commanded by career Iraqi military officers, depended on a devoted religious following among foreign fighters from Europe and the Middle East. ISIS's transnational Sunni fighters from Europe and the greater Islamic World served as its most effective shock troops.[9] One group estimated that close to thirty thousand foreign fighters had served in ISIS ranks, a significant percentage of its fighting cadres.[10] ISIS's urban guerrilla-style attacks sought to inspire more foreign fighters to move to the actual Islamic State and fight for it. For those who could not travel to Iraq and Syria, overseas attacks served as a means for sympathizers to conduct violence, declaring allegiance to the Islamic State in light of actually moving there. Their willingness to die in suicide car bombings on the front lines against Iraqi land forces proved essential to ISIS combat operations. Iraqi forces resisting ISIS indicated that these vehicle suicide bombings were its most effective tactic.[11] However, in the final battle for Mosul's old city, the narrow, winding alleyways proved a disadvantage to both ISIS and the Iraqi ground forces. Not only did this terrain make it impossible for the Iraqi ground forces to deploy heavy armor, but it precluded ISIS from using the vehicle suicide bomber in its final defense.[12]

Notwithstanding the heavy armor captured from the Iraqi military in June 2014, ISIS made its most rapid advances with decentralized, fast-paced, small units consisting of highly mobile trucks, seizing territory up to the outskirts of Baghdad in little more than a week. ISIS consolidated its control of territory in both Iraq and Syria due to its cohesive land force and the disarray of the numerous state and substate actors involved in the military campaign against it. Several nations had engaged their air forces against ISIS in both Iraq and Syria, ranging from token attacks by the air forces of Arab states such as Jordan, Saudi Arabia, and the UAE to more sustained American, British, French, Russian, and Iranian involvement. An alliance had formed, but a divisive one, and their competing agendas and end games had given ISIS respite.

The Role of the Shi'a Militias

In 2014, the post-2003 Iraqi Security Forces (ISF) had collapsed in the defense of the nation, resulting in a security vacuum that led to the resurgence of the Shi'a and Kurdish militias. After the fall of Mosul, both Baghdad and the KRG demonstrated a lack of political will in coordinating their land campaigns in combating ISIS. Tensions were further exacerbated when Kurdish forces, the Peshmerga, secured the disputed city of Kirkuk, which lay outside of the KRG's jurisdiction, to preempt ISIS from seizing it, as the Iraqi military had all but collapsed. While Kirkuk was saved, ISIS forces came dangerously close to the KRG capital of Irbil in August 2014. It was American support, particularly airpower, which played a defining role in its defense.[13]

Iraqi Shi'a parties joined Kurdish and Arab Sunni politicians calling for Maliki's resignation, blaming his divisive rule for the debacle. Iraq's top Shi'a cleric, Grand Ayatollah Ali Sistani, even called for Maliki to step down, albeit subtly, in a Friday sermon.[14] Haydar Abbadi, a more conciliatory candidate within the ruling Da'wa party replaced Maliki.[15] Abbadi inherited an array of political, social, and economic challenges, ranging from rebuilding Iraq's land forces to managing the agendas of Iraq's competing neighbors and the United States in combating the ISIS threat.

During the ISIS offensive in the summer of 2014, Sistani also issued a religious ruling calling for the defense of Baghdad and other sacred Shi'a sites in Iraq. After Sistani's call, volunteers swelled the ranks of these militias, augmenting their numbers, while the militias' leaders maintained a parallel political presence in the institutions of the Iraqi state, often serving as ministers. By the time Maliki resigned and Abbadi assumed power, a myriad of militias (often with differing agendas and loyalties) had emerged to combat ISIS. In theory, these militias were supposed to subordinate their loyalties under a new formal government institution, *al-Hashd al-Sha'abi*, or the Popular Mobilization Unit (PMU) Forces.

The Shi'a militias became invaluable to the defense of the Iraqi state, as the United States had to retrain what remained of the ISF. The ISF, and its most elite unit, the Counter-Terrorism Service (CTS), had been trained to deal with the contingencies of the Iraqi insurgency that erupted from 2003. During those years, Iraqi insurgents primarily employed hit-and-run tactics against US forces and the ISF, tactics typical of a guerrilla war meant to wear down the resolve of the enemy. As a result, the US training mission had focused on ensuring Iraq's new army could deal with guerrilla warfare. However, ISIS evolved into a landpower force that could capture and hold cities, which required retraining the Iraqi military forces in sustained urban combat, fighting street by street, building by building. The need to transform the Iraqi army from counterinsurgency operations to urban combat explained why it was not in a stage of combat preparedness to be deployed on the front lines after the fall of Mosul, creating a security vacuum that the Peshmerga and the PMU filled. Given the collapse of the ISF in the defense of Mosul and Tikrit, and the time the United States needed to retrain them in these tactics, the defense of the government in Baghdad became dependent on paramilitary forces, which supplemented—if not supplanted—the regular army during this intrastate conflict.

Estimates indicated that the Shi'a militias' numbers ranged anywhere from 60,000 to 120,000 fighters, while the Iraqi military after the fall of Mosul had dwindled to only 50,000 reliable forces. While those numbers are larger than ISIS's estimated fighting force of 30,000 to 80,000, the PMU were not organized into a permanent, standing army, and the entire total had never been mobilized at the same time for a single battle.[16] In the early phase of the conflict, the PMU essentially served as shock troops, used for frontal assaults on cities, and then moved on to the next battle. Until the Iraqi military was ready to confront ISIS in ground assaults, the Iraqi state did not have enough reliable ISF soldiers to be garrisoned at a base for long periods to control the surrounding areas, explaining how cities like Ramadi in the Anbar Province would later fall to ISIS in May 2015. This retraining process had its first success against ISIS when the ISF retook Ramadi in December 2015. During the time required for training, there would be a token ISF presence deployed on the front lines in certain battles, but they could not combat ISIS without tandem operations with the PMU.

The US and Iranian Roles

Even before the rise of ISIS in 2014, Iran had played a role in creating, training, and arming an array of Shi'a militias, enhancing its regional influence. After the ISIS offensive, Qassim Soleimani, commander of the Qods Force of the Iranian Revolutionary Guards, was often seen on the Iraqi front lines with these Iraqi Shi'a militias, such as Kata'ib Hizballah, which is on the DoS's list of terrorist groups.[17]

In June 2014, just a few days after the fall of Mosul, David Petraeus, the former commander of US forces in Iraq and the architect of the Surge, issued a warning about America's siding with the Iraqi Shi'a militias, with the headlines declaring, "Petraeus: U.S. Must Not Become the Shi'a Militia's Air Force." However, Petraeus's admonition would go unheeded. The US Air Force would become the Shi'a militias' air force because at that juncture there was no Iraqi air force or army of which to speak. Given America's aversion to "boots on the ground" in Iraq, Washington would have to rely on the PMU, and the PMU would have to rely on American airpower.

The United States formerly engaged in the military campaign against ISIS in August 2014 in the form of air strikes, targeting ISIS land forces as they came dangerously close to the KRG capital in Irbil. Another one of Washington's objectives was targeting ISIS land forces on the verge of conducting a wholesale massacre of the Iraqi Yezidi minority trapped on Mount Sinjar.[18]

However, due to the constraints of domestic politics, the Obama administration had been hesitant to increase the number of American "boots on the grounds" beyond the few thousand advisors retraining the Iraqi military. This aversion to increasing the number of ground forces was alluded to during his January 2015 State of the Union speech when he stated: "Instead of getting dragged into another ground war in the Middle East, we are leading a broad coalition, including Arab nations, to degrade and ultimately destroy this terrorist group."[19] In the first months of the air campaign, coalition air-power prevented ISIS from expanding and massing large military formations in open terrain, stalling its territorial momentum, allowing Shi'a militias to mobilize to defend Baghdad and its environs. However, throughout the duration of the air campaign, ISIS continued to consolidate its position in urban centers in both Iraq and Syria, melting into the urban fabric among civilians to avoid being targeted. It maintained enough financial resources to sustain its core organization and replenish its arms.

Essentially the air campaign bought time for Iraqi land forces to hold the front lines, with both American and, paradoxically, Iranian assistance. The Iranian and Shi'a forces had successfully defended the city of Samarra, site of the sacred Shi'a Al-Askari shrine, the destruction of which in 2006 set off Iraq's civil war. The PMU also took control of smaller ISIS-held towns, in the Diyala Province for example, indirectly benefitting from American air strikes that had targeted ISIS in the vicinity.[20] From this point onward, the Shi'a militias, Iran, and the United States maintained an uneasy, de facto alliance against ISIS, yet the tensions in that alliance would emerge during Iraq's battle for Tikrit.

The Battles for the Anbar and Salah al-Din Provinces

The battle for Tikrit in the Salah al-Din Province that began in March 2015 was the second attempt to dislodge ISIS from the city. Iraqi forces had tried to retake it in the summer of 2014 but had been repulsed, incurring heavy casualties in the process.[21] The second time proved just as deadly for Iraqi forces, with the campaign losing momentum after three weeks due to the relatively high casualty count as the Iraqi military, affiliated Iraqi Shi'a militias, and a small Sunni militia failed to expel ISIS fighters ensconced in the urban terrain.[22] As soon as the battle stalled, tensions within the American-Iranian arrangement also came to the fore. Initially, Iran and the United States appeared to have come to an informal agreement on keeping American air strikes out of the battle for different motivations. Iran and its affiliated militias sought to seize Tikrit without any American air support, so they could claim credit for the victory. The United States was willing to let the Iranian-led Iraqi Shi'a militias conduct the attack without its participation, first, because the Iraqi prime minister was not responsible for ordering the campaign, and thus did not request American air support, and second, its eventual failure would demonstrate that the militias could not succeed with their urban land campaigns without this air cover, much to the later chagrin of Iran.

This strategy caught Abbadi off guard, and in order to assert government control over the campaign he had to negotiate between the United States and Iran. He sought to recast the battle for Tikrit as a national one while reigning in the abuses conducted by the Shi'a militias against the civilian Arab Sunni population, as had happened after the militias' victories in Diyala and in villages south of Baghdad. The militias, most likely on Iran's order, boycotted the battle when Abbadi requested that the United States conduct air strikes against well-entrenched ISIS positions. The militias complained in public statements then that America would steal their glory and victory, but the introduction of American air power supporting the PMU and elements of the ISF finally expelled well-entrenched ISIS fighters from Tikrit in mid-April 2015. However, the May 2015 fall of Ramadi, capital of the nation's Anbar Province, soon undermined this victory. It also demonstrated that ISIS could wage simultaneous offensives on two distant fronts when it seized Palmyra in Syria.

Unlike the fall of Mosul in 2014, the fall of Ramadi was not a surprise attack, but rather a drawn-out ISIS campaign, lasting sixteen months.[23] The ISIS capture of Ramadi exposed the landpower problem the Iraqi state faced, as it did not have enough military forces to invest in the defense of the city, either with larger numbers of the conventional military forces or the more battle-hardened militias. Immediately after the fall of Tikrit, members of the Shi'a militias were deployed to Ramadi to deter further ISIS advances, demonstrating the state's reliance on these paramilitary forces in an emergency, as the ISF had ultimately faltered in the defense of the city.

By December 2015, after several months, the ISF captured ISIS's headquarters in Ramadi, utterly devastating the city in the process. This battle took longer than Tikrit, which was captured in a month.

As of October 2015, the ISF had reached the Albu Farraj area in the north of Ramadi, and three months transpired before a final assault commenced to penetrate the center of the city by the end of December. The slow pace of the campaign was most likely due to the preparations of the Iraqi forces for the final push and the government's efforts to do so with minimal civilian casualties.

While Abbadi had deployed the Shi'a militias successfully in the fight for Tikrit, he had hesitated in mobilizing them in the defense of Ramadi out of deference to a predominantly Arab Sunni city, whose citizens would have objected to the presence of these Shi'a forces on its streets.[24] Whereas the battle for Tikrit primarily featured the PMU, the battle for Ramadi involved the ISF, along with token irregular tribal Sunni levies. The composition of the Iraqi military forces during the battle for Ramadi included the national

ISF with the CTS, formations from the 8th Iraqi Army Division, the local police, and the Iraqi air force.[25] For the first time, Iraqi Air Force pilots flew F-16 combat aircraft against ISIS positions. Their participation might have been token in comparison to American-piloted air strikes, but the fact that there was an Iraqi Air Force to speak of during this battle was significant. Prior to the ISIS campaign into Iraq in 2014, the Iraqi Air Force consisted of a fleet of Cessna propeller planes outfitted with Hellfire missiles to target ISIS ground targets.

By June 2016, the Iraqi military declared victory in Fallujah against ISIS. Like Ramadi, the battle for Fallujah involved the ISF and militias. To allay fears that the PMU would take the predominantly Arab Sunni city, Abbadi announced that they would play a supporting role, and not participate in the assault on the city's center. The bargain was that if the militias were held back, the United States would increase the tempo of its air strikes, as it did in Ramadi. In both cases, American air power was contingent on sidelining the PMU. In Washington's view, the PMU's potential to alienate Sunnis in Fallujah took precedence over the military effectiveness of the militias. Also, like in Ramadi, it was the CTS and a thousand Arab Sunni tribal fighters that led the assault into the center of Fallujah, capturing ISIS's urban headquarters. Regardless of whether it might have taken longer for Iraq's formal military to achieve this aim, or whether it could result in burnout for the overworked CTS, Washington still prioritized the political value of having the national Iraqi army secure the urban centers of Ramadi and Fallujah over deploying the PMU.

The Iraqi Lessons on Landpower on the Eve of the Mosul Battle

The military dynamics that led to the recapture of Ramadi and Fallujah marked a transformation of the institutional military capacity of the Iraqi state as it prepared to recapture Mosul. In the two cities in the Anbar Province the ISF developed a doctrine for urban combat and "rehearsed" for the battle of Mosul. This development was significant in that until this battle it had been substate actors, such as the PMU, benefitting from US air support, which deprived ISIS of territory. The ISF role in Ramadi and Fallujah was not just a battle for a city, but for the Iraqi state to project to its public the military capacity of the national army. The role played by the national Iraqi landpower in expelling ISIS from these two cities had implications for the symbolic realm, creating an inclusive sense of Iraqiness. With the liberation of these two cities, the Iraqi military, featured prominently on the Iraqi state news channel, Iraqiya, was depicted as an institution that represented the national aspirations of Iraq. Any Iraqi would have known after these victories that the nation's fighting forces were still divided among Kurdish Peshmerga, PMU, and Sunni tribal militias. Yet, the government went to great efforts to highlight the role of the official army in the liberation of these cities. For Abbadi's legitimacy, the Iraqi army's victories served as a testament of his ability to preside at the helm of the remains of the national military, claiming a national victory since it was the Iraqi army, and not the PMU, that dealt the final blows to ISIS on the streets of Ramadi and Fallujah.

The ISF's willingness to incorporate fighters from local Arab Sunni tribes in recapturing both Anbar Province cities also served as a means for the state to perpetuate its narrative of inclusiveness. The number of Arab Sunni volunteers did not swell the numbers of ground forces significantly. The deployment of Sunni tribal fighters was most likely for domestic public consumption, given that the Anbar Province is predominantly Arab Sunni. Ostensibly their presence served as an attempt to downplay sectarian tensions when primarily Shi'a fighters took the majority Sunni town of Tikrit. By incorporating Arab Sunnis into the PMU, Abbadi deflected criticism of his overreliance on sectarian militias. This inclusion also removed the onus on Abbadi to constitute a separate Arab Sunni "National Guard," as Arab Sunni politicians had called for, so as to have a local force akin to the Kurdish Peshmerga in Anbar Province. The Shi'a parties in the Iraqi government had been resistant to the idea, most likely out of the consideration that if it were to allow the formation of a National Guard, it would give Iraq three separate paramilitary forces: the Kurdish Peshmerga of the KRG, the PMU, which itself was divided into numerous factions, and a third autonomous Arab Sunni force. While Abbadi made token efforts to arm the Arab Sunni tribes in Anbar, the central government gained control of their fighters combating ISIS by embedding them within the Shi'a-dominated PMU. Given that the PMU was controlled by the office of the prime minister, the state sought to claim that the militias functioned as an inclusive national landpower force, rather than a sectarian one.[26]

The ultimate victory in Mosul demonstrated successes in developing Iraq's land forces since its disaster in 2014. However, existing accounts from the battle of Mosul also indicate challenges ahead for the reform of the Iraqi land forces. One reporter imbedded with the Iraqi version of a SWAT team locked in the battle for the city noted the lack of coordination among the forces involved, including the CTS, the Iraqi 9th Division, the federal police forces, and the United States providing air support.[27] On the other hand, the CTS, otherwise known as the "Golden Division," previously had been derogatorily referred to as former Prime Minister Maliki's "private army." The US military training presence in Iraq contributed to its transformation. During the battle for Mosul the force reformed itself, enduring most of the urban combat, and emerged as one of the few professional, inclusive Iraqi military institutions.[28]

Conclusion

The offensive against ISIS demonstrated that the era of the traditional conscript army of Iraq that emerged after its independence in 1932 and was disbanded in 2003 had ended, replaced by an array of Iraqi paramilitary forces combating ISIS, itself a paramilitary force. Such divisions explain why ISIS survived for three years in Iraq despite being outnumbered. Divisions within Iraq's government and security forces, further divided among the Kurdish Peshmerga and Shi'a militias, had hampered the Iraqi state's capacity to organize a coherent political and military campaign against ISIS.

Until the final victory of Iraq's national land forces in Mosul, an amorphous coalition of the United States, Iran, Iranian-supported militias, and the Kurdish Peshmerga proved successful in depriving ISIS of territory. The PMU and Peshmerga became a pillar of American policy, achieving Washington's war aims in a much shorter time span. After the 2014 defeat, the Iraqi military, despite the US-led training effort, was not in an immediate position to retake urban centers without the support role of the militias. The Iraqi paramilitary units allowed this campaign to unfold a lot faster. Washington realized that the PMU would be central to any assault on the urban centers in Ramadi or Fallujah, whether they played a support role or took the city themselves, as in Tikrit in April 2015. The PMU and Iran also learned their lesson on the need of American air support to defeat ISIS in urban combat. America, Iran, and the PMU were locked in an informal alliance due to a paradox. The United States' hesitance to deploy landpower in Iraq necessitated its dependence on militias that could provide motivated forces, regardless of ideological affinities.

The American approach to combating ISIS in Iraq revealed the limitations of standoff warfare and how domestic considerations placed constraints on the United States' use of landpower. As ISIS is defeated, an Iranian-US battle for influence over the Iraqi state will ensue. The only advantage the United States has in Iraq in terms of ground forces is its five thousand-strong military advisory mission and the prospects of arms sales. Iran, on the other hand, by investing in building up Iraq's land forces, has been able to carve a land corridor for its ground forces stretching from Iran to the Iraqi-Syrian border, then continuing to Lebanon, providing a contiguous conduit for

Teheran's proxy on the Mediterranean—Hizballah.[29] Iraq could take advantage of American arms, but Iran's ability to invest in creating power on the ground will help keep Baghdad firmly within Teheran's influence.

Notes

1. Michael O'Hanlan, *The Future of Land Warfare* (Washington, DC: Brookings 2015), 3.

2. Mapping Militants Project, "Islamic State," Mapping Militant Organizations, Stanford University, 4 April 2016, web.stanford.edu/group/mappingmilitants/cgi-bin/groups/view/1.

3. Sarah Childress, "Who Runs the Islamic State?" PBS, 28 October 2014.

4. "Most of Islamic State's Leaders Were Officers in Saddam Hussein's Iraq," *Washington Post,* 4 April 2015.

5. Liz Sly, "The Hidden Hand Behind the Islamic State Militants? Saddam Hussein's," *Washington Post,* 4 April 2015.

6. Terrence McCoy, "Camp Bucca: The US Prison that Became the Birthplace of Isis: Nine Members of the Islamic State's Top Command Did Time at Bucca," *The Independent,* 4 November 2014.

7. For a debate on the religiosity of ISIS, see Samuel Helfont and Michael Brill, "Saddam's ISIS? The Terrorist Group's Real Origin Story," *Foreign Affairs* (12 January 2016), and Amatzia Baram, "Saddam's ISIS: Tracing the Roots of the Caliphate," *Foreign Affairs* (8 April 2016).

8. See Ibrahim Al-Marashi and Sammy Salama, *Iraq's Armed Forces: An Analytical History* (London: Routledge, 2008).

9. Sly, "The Hidden Hand Behind the Islamic State."

10. The Soufan Group, "Foreign Fighters: An Updated Assessment of the Flow of Foreign Fighters into Syria and Iraq" (8 December 2015).

11. Anand Gopal, "The Hell after ISIS," *The Atlantic* (May 2016).

12. Asa Fitch and Ali A. Nabhan, "Islamic State Turned Desperate in Mosul Fight, Iraqis Say," *Wall Street Journal,* 13 July 2017, https://www.wsj.com/articles/islamic-state-turned-desperate-in-mosul-fight-iraqis-say-1499986902?mod=e2fb.

13. Kenneth M. Pollack, "Iraq: Understanding the ISIS Offensive Against the Kurds," Brookings Institution, 11 August 2014, http://www.brookings.edu/blogs/markaz/posts/2014/08/11-pollack-isis-offensive-against-iraq-kurds.

14. Ali Mamouri, "*Kayf najaha al-sistani biizaha Maliki*" ("How Did Sistani Succeed in Ousting Maliki?") *Al-Monitor,* 20 August 2014, www.al-monitor.com/pulse/originals/2014/08/iraq-sistani-democratic-ways-successors-maliki.html#ixzz31gLdUFfl.

15. Doug Stanglin, "Iran, Saudis Pressure al-Maliki by Backing Rival PM Bid," *USA Today,* 12 August 2014.

16. The 60,000 figure comes from the Kurdish news portal Rudaw, rudaw.net/english/middleeast/iraq/180520155. The 120,000 figure comes from the BBC,

http://www.bbc.com/news/world-middle-east-32349379. The number of Iraqi military personnel comes from Kenneth Katzman and Carla E. Humud, "Iraq: Politics and Governance," Congressional Research Service, 16 September 2016, 12. There are no reliable figures for the number of ISIS fighters.

17. Bureau of Counterterrorism, "Foreign Terrorist Organizations," DoS, http://www.state.gov/j/ct/rls/other/des/123085.htm.

18. "ISIL Beheads Syria Troops and US Aid Worker," *Al-Jazeera*, 16 November 2015, http://www.aljazeera.com/news/middleeast/2014/11/isil-beheads-syrians-us-aid-worker-2014111683932604856.html.

19. The White House, Office of the Press Secretary, "Excerpts of the President's State of the Union Address," 21 January 2015, www.whitehouse.gov/the-press-office/2015/01/20/excerpts-president-s-state-union-address.

20. Katzman and Humud, "Iraq: Politics and Governance," 19.

21. Alissa J. Rubin and Suadad Al-Salhy, "For Iraq, Debacle in Tikrit as Forces Walk into Trap Set by Militants," *New York Times*, 16 July 2014.

22. Hayder al-Khoei, "Why 'Emotional' Battle for Tikrit Will Defeat ISIS," CNN, 4 March 2015.

23. Hassan Hassan. "The ISIS March Continues: From Ramadi on to Baghdad?" *Foreign Policy* (19 May 2015), foreignpolicy.com/2015/05/19/ramadi-is-the-canary-isis-islamic-state-iraq/.

24. Al-Marashi, "If ISIL Is Defeated in Ramadi," *Al-Jazeera*, 24 May 2015, www.aljazeera.com/indepth/opinion/2015/05/isil-defeated-ramadi-150521140832955.html.

25. Al-Marashi "How Iraq Recaptured Ramadi and Why It Matters," *Al-Jazeera*, 3 January 2016, www.aljazeera.com/indepth/opinion/2016/01/iraq-recaptured-ramadi-matters-160103061219164.html.

26. Hayder al-Khoei, "How to Reclaim Iraq's Ramadi from ISIS," Royal Institute of International Affairs, 19 May 2015, www.chathamhouse.org/expert/comment/17705.

27. Alex Mogdelson, "The Desperate Battle to Destroy ISIS," *New Yorker* (6 February 2017), http://www.newyorker.com/magazine/2017/02/06/the-desperate-battle-to-destroy-isis.

28. Michael Knights and Alex Mello, "The Best Thing America Built in Iraq: Iraq's Counter-Terrorism Service and the Long War Against Militancy," *War on the Rocks*, 19 July 2017, https://warontherocks.com/2017/07/the-best-thing-america-built-in-iraq-iraqs-counter-terrorism-service-and-the-long-war-against-militancy/.

29. Tim Arango, "Iran Dominates in Iraq after U.S. 'Handed the Country Over,'" *New York Times*, 15 July 2017, https://www.nytimes.com/2017/07/15/world/middleeast/iran-iraq-iranian-power.html?smid=tw-share&_r=0.

PART IV

The US Army as a Landpower Institution

13

Stryker Brigade Combat Team vs Future Combat System

An Institutional After Action Report on Innovation in the Transformation Decade

David Fastabend

The After Action Report (AAR) is a respected tradition within the US Army, and a key dimension of training robust landpower capabilities. The Army perceives straightforward self-assessment to be a tactical-level training technique of the Operating Force—the portion of the Army that conducts operations. The Army can with equal legitimacy apply honest self-assessment to the forecast and development of landpower capabilities in the Generating Force, or the "Institutional Army" that generates and sustains strategic landpower.[1] This "Institutional AAR" assesses the ability of the Army to generate landpower during the period 1999 to 2009, contrasting the successfully fielded Stryker Brigade Combat Team (SBCT) with the ill-fated Future Combat System (FCS). This is in every sense an AAR, vice a comprehensive history.[2] It reflects a partial perspective, admittedly shaped by my personal participation in the Army's transformation during this era, my work at the Army's Training and Doctrine Command's (TRADOC) "Future Center,"[3] my observations as Multi-National Force-Iraq C3, and finally as Director of Strategy, Plans, and Policy (DAMO-SS) on the Army Staff.[4]

The Transformation Decade: 1999–2009

The US Army encountered immense institutional challenges and evolved significantly during the decade 1999–2009, a period I have designated "The Transformation Decade." Such designation is admittedly arbitrary: transformational events occurred before 1999 and after 2009. Some might suggest, for example, that Army transformation began with General Gordon Sullivan's digitization focus or even General Carl Vuono's initiatives, which formed a foundation for Sullivan's direction.[5] But the Army's transformational efforts gained a famous milestone—and the overt "transformation" label—in October of 1999. The new CSA, General Eric Shinseki, declared the beginning of "Army Transformation" in his speech at the Association of the United States Army (AUSA) annual conference. In 2009, Secretary of Defense Robert Gates directed the effective cancellation of the FCS, the Army's signature landpower development endeavor of the Transformation Decade. Although the Army continued to adapt, it generally did not perceive or describe post-2009 adjustments as "transformative."[6] Why did the Institutional Army meet its strategic landpower innovation objectives for the SBCT, but not for FCS?

The classic opening to every AAR is the question: "*What was supposed to happen?*" Although there is no universally accepted answer when the task is to transform the Army to ensure the availability of ready and relevant strategic landpower, an analysis can decompose that question into five institutional innovation challenges:

- Forecasting the Environment. Did the Army accurately forecast the Operating Environment (OE)[7] that shaped these programs?
- Defining the Problem. Did the Army effectively (and compellingly) define the operational problem(s) the programs should solve?
- Aligning the Innovation Approach. Was the institutional innovation model properly aligned to Army institutional realities?
- Exploiting and Mitigating Process. Were the programs able to leverage institutional process while mitigating process limitations and pitfalls?
- Leveraging the Human Dimension. Did the program properly account for the human factors of leadership, politics, complexity, and culture?

Forecasting the Environment

Considering the significant time required to develop effective, integrated combined arms (in other words, the combination of the Army branches' capabilities to achieve a desired effect), an institution's ability to effectively forecast the future operational environment is a fundamental requirement for landpower capability development. The Army consistently recognizes that it cannot predict the future but must try to—as Michael Howard (and current CSA General Mark Milley) remind—"not get it too far wrong."[8] This AAR leverages contemporary history to compare the environmental forecasts near the beginning of the Transformation Decade with its actual outcomes.

A useful starting point is the National Intelligence Community (NIC) estimate of 2000.⁹ "Global Trends 2015" accurately identified globalization as an ever more powerful driver of international events, with an increase in the significance of nonstate actors and the impact of information technology and biological sciences. It predicted the growing power of China and the declining power of Russia; if one accepts the premise that recent Russian assertiveness reflects the desperate reaction of a declining power, this assessment was also accurate. As a practical projection for the development of strategic landpower, however, the 2000 projection of Russia in inexorable decline was inaccurate. At a minimum, Russia has played well a weak hand.

There were other "misses": Global Trends 2015 allowed that a US economic downturn was possible, vastly understating the financial collapse of 2008. It also incorrectly forecasted the potential for collapse in China and did not foresee its regional adventures in the South China Sea. Predictions inaccurately projected the United States as an ever more preponderant and unchallenged superpower. It forecast a United States hamstrung by increasingly unavailable energy resources, and an increase in the power of OPEC. The most egregious error was one of omission: the failure to imagine 9/11 and the subsequent wars in Iraq and Afghanistan.

Within the context of the National Intelligence Estimates, the Army was making its own forecasts. Army future "war-gaming," heavily influenced by the perceived risks of its reliance on preexisting air and sea ports of debarkation in the Gulf War, accurately projected extensive enemy use of anti-access and area denial (AA/AD) strategies.¹⁰ TRADOC foresaw adversary investments in missiles and air and missile defense capabilities to reassert local air dominance. Adversaries developed concepts aimed at deterrence and/or the achievement of "strategic preclusion" in a crisis, as well as responding rapidly in future wars. Unlike the NIC, the Army did not downplay the possibility of great power conflict in the coming decades, and in fact featured an invasion of Ukraine by a resurgent Russia in its 1997 winter war game.¹¹

The operational environment forecasts decisively shaped the SBCT and FCS innovation efforts. As an institution, the DoD in 1999 believed that it was entering—and could take advantage of—an extended "strategic pause."¹² The SBCT program was viewed as an interim solution for this near-future, strategic pause. Influenced by Balkan deployments, the Army estimated that this pause might include extended stability operations and a need for both speed in response and protected mobility (the ability to protect platforms and people while maneuvering) against nonstate actors. The SBCT program forecast an operational requirement for a medium force with protected tactical mobility in mid- to low-intensity conflicts—and that projection corresponded to initial deployments in the wars of 9/11. As US adversaries adapted in the latter part of the Transformation Decade, the inadequacy of the Stryker's protection became apparent, but its initial deployments were successful and added to the momentum of a program in production.[13]

Throughout the Transformation Decade, FCS was still in design, and designed for an operational environment quite at odds with operations from 1999 to 2009. This more distant, future operational environment featured a different threat: a peer competitor using high kinetic energy weapons that could outpace projected improvements in armor protection. FCS, therefore, had a systemic approach to protection that traded significant armor protection for upgraded intelligence, agile off-road mobility, and speed. This approach was a poor match for the actual operational environment, where persistent indigenous adversaries could threaten road-bound US forces with unsophisticated yet robust IED threats. Regardless of the accuracy of the FCS long-term operational environment forecast, at the time of its termination in 2009, reality in Iraq and Afghanistan was far removed from the premises that underpinned the FCS program. The inability of the program to deliver a protection solution to the IED threats of 1999–2009 was a significant factor in the decision to terminate it.[14]

The operational environment's projection for both the SBCT and FCS programs incorporated a primacy on the value of speed in crisis response, as well as the requirement—in the case of the FCS program—to circumvent predictable points of entry, such as large airfields and deep, large-capacity ports. The speed premium, however, was not evident in the Army's build-up in either Iraq or Afghanistan, nor was a significant AA/AD challenge encountered in the Transformation Decade. Speed and access challenges loom very large in Army thinking today, but it was not properly identified, as the future of the FCS program hung in the balance at the end of the Transformation Decade. Unlike the SBCT, the FCS program incorporated several premises on anticipated future technology. These technology trends were not wrong, but they were consistently overoptimistic with respect to schedule, particularly in light of the program's initial, accelerated goals.

Defining the Problem

Effective innovation does not mysteriously emerge and then seek problems to solve; innovation reacts to problems, and there is no more important innovation task than to define the problem. Moreover, this is not simply a "needs" statement, but rather it entails recognition of relevant context, a compelling narrative, measurable and achievable goals, and effective marketing.

Context

For the Stryker, the context was compelling and undisputed. At the time the Army announced the Stryker program, the Army had just demonstrated an armored force response shortfall during its recent Kosovo deployment. But timing is everything. The 1999 Stryker initiative itself became the context for the FCS initiative the following year, at which time the Army had to justify the need for both systems, and then after 9/11 explain the requirement for additional transformation. The urgencies of current operations during the Transformation Decade muted three things: the need for future capabilities; the desirability of air mechanization (armored vehicles that were readily air-deployable); and the future vulnerability of passively armored systems to kinetic energy threats.

Narrative

The relevant context made for an effective SBCT narrative, reinforced by the rapid fielding and the overall success of initial operations in Iraq. The narrative was widely accepted, and evolved only on the margins. The FCS narrative was far more complicated, much less evidence-based, and, as the Army attempted to develop the FCS, repeatedly changed. Initially, all operating units would field FCS. As the program gained definition, the FCS label was restricted to a limited—but undefined—number of future Army brigades. When the program costs mounted and forecasts of Initial Operating Capability (IOC) moved further into the future, the Army attempted to reinforce the relevance of the program by declaring an intent to field some FCS capabilities to the entire force. Most importantly, the armor protection problem the Army encountered with IEDs in Iraq was completely counterintuitive to the systemic approach to protection embodied in the FCS program. This undermined the apparent relevance of the program as a landpower solution to the Global War on Terrorism (GWOT) and rendered the FCS narrative extremely problematic.

Goals

Both programs had clear and ambitious goals, with associated metrics to improve landpower projection, although the efficacy of the goals for each program remain debatable. The utility of the strategic deployment of a brigade anywhere in the world within five days was a confusing metric during a decade when speed of strategic response was not an evident requirement for forces repeatedly rotating to Iraq and Afghanistan. The tactical metric of C-130 "deployability" drew scrutiny as ill-conceived from an employment perspective, although there was widespread understanding that the metric was intended to limit growth in platform size and weight. The weight goals were far more ambitions for the FCS program, which initially aspired to the deployability of the Stryker while retaining the mobility, lethality, and survivability of the heavy tank. As the program advanced, engineering tradeoffs pushed the weight metric beyond the C-130 air-capability size—thereby undermining the deployability goals. The significant difference was that the SBCT goals were technically achieved, but the FCS goals changed every few years, undermining faith in the program.

Marketing

Innovators compete for limited resources. For SBCT, the marketing was measured, and there was even an overt attempt to downplay the effort. The original "SBCT" was the "IBCT"—the *Interim* Brigade Combat Team—because General Shinseki did not want external audiences to perceive Stryker as the ultimate goal of his transformation effort.[15] On the FCS side, the Army had too many marketers, and too much hubris. With an Objective Force Task Force stood up in the Pentagon, Assistant Secretary of the Army for Acquisition, Logistics, and Technology (AASALT) overseeing the program, and TRADOC continuing to reinforce the effort with war-gaming and conceptual work, it was difficult to coordinate the Army's message. In addition, the unfortunate conflation of program goals with aspirational conceptual ideas like the Quality of Firsts—"See First, Understand First, Act First, Finish Decisively"[16]—left the FCS program vulnerable to devastating critiques. These ideas—adequately caveated in concept documentation—were toxic when migrated over to marketing efforts, particularly during a period when landpower challenges in Iraq and Afghanistan were anything but an illustration of the "quality of firsts."[17]

Aligning the Innovation Approach

The alignment of Army institutional realities can be assessed from multiple perspectives: innovation "champions," innovation in command and control, war-gaming, experimentation, and prototyping. Each perspective generates partial insights into success or failure.

Innovation Champions

Robert Kocher, a former DARPA program manager and CEO of Ideal Innovations, Inc., has suggested that effective institutional innovation needs a "trinity" of champions: a visionary, a competent project management professional, and an informed inventor.[18] Shinseki was the visionary for both these efforts, and subsequent CSAs during the Transformation Decade readily adopted his vision. The Army after Shinseki's tenure also had to adapt during two wars, which proved a fatal undermining of the FCS. Both the Stryker and FCS had effective program managers, although the wide-ranging FCS program imposed an unprecedented demand for project management talent across the Army. TRADOC was the "informed inventor" for the SBCT operational and organizational concept, and it combined an appreciation of near-term operational requirements with the potential of readily available platform solutions. The front-end invention and conception for the FCS initially came from DARPA (with Army collaboration) between 1998 and 2002, but the scientists and technologists of DARPA were not necessarily informed on military matters. They understood the potential of the science but were less cognizant of the emerging operational environment, particularly the IED threat.

Integration and Scope

Both programs used the same approach—a unit-based, combined arms design—to integrate Doctrine, Organization, Training, Materiel, Leadership, Personnel, Facilities, and Policy. The SBCT program facilitated integration via a common chassis selection supporting a set of existing platforms, and the Army further committed to using only existing systems at the subplatform level. The maturity of the selected platform made immediate engineering change proposals readily feasible, most famously in the addition of "slat armor" to the Stryker platform before it deployed to Iraq. The FCS program, however, had to contend with an unknown future platform and a plethora of notional subsystems, including a cutting-edge approach to software design.[19] The FCS air mechanization mode demanded operational airlift means that the other services had little interest in fielding. The FCS program presented an integration challenge that was several orders of magnitude greater than that of the SBCT.[20]

Innovation Command and Control

The difference in innovation command and control approaches between the two programs was significant. For the SBCT, a minimalist approach devolved implementation generally to a focused task force led by very effective individuals who oversaw the change, albeit with routine and earnest oversight and interest from senior Army leadership. For the FCS, the scale of the effort was unprecedented, and the Army explored new approaches to include its first employment of a Lead System Integrator (LSI). The immaturity of the underlying technologies required active and continuous participation of multiple major commands: Army headquarters; ASAALT; Army Materiel Command; and TRADOC. Always a daunting prospect given the scale of those commands, the simultaneous demands of two ongoing wars added a lot of strain to innovation command and control.

War-Gaming, Experimentation, and Prototyping

Neither the SBCT nor the FCS program evolved in the classic pattern wherein a concept is rigorously explored in war-gaming and tested in experimentation before decisions are made to definitize requirements and develop, test, and produce the platform.[21] The SBCT effort moved very quickly to prototype field trials at Fort Knox and platform selection. Numerous surrogates were used for training of the initial Stryker Brigade Combat Team. Such extensive prototype application was not feasible for the FCS program: given the immaturity of the associated technologies, prototypes—where available—were consigned to the subsystem or device level.

War-gaming and experimentation proceeded in parallel with platform development for the FCS.[22] The Army's Unified Quest war-gaming scenarios during the Transformation Decade employed both Stryker and FCS brigade types, and the Army explored detailed simulation of FCS systems at various TRADOC locations. War-gaming repeatedly surfaced potential issues—and doubt—about the feasible rates of deployment for FCS brigades (compared to the stated Army deployability goals). Participants also doubted the feasibility of the FCS's improved "situational awareness" and reduced armor protection. Although some believe the Army failed to give adequate credence to these war-gaming and experimentation insights, critics tend to forget that these insights were generally oriented on the *feasibility* of the FCS requirements, vice their *suitability*. The FCS requirements were already incorporated into a Program of Record, albeit as an act of technological faith, or at least a very aggressive estimate. Requirement feasibility was explored and tested within the material development process and not readily amenable to alteration from war-gaming results, which evaluated whether the FCS requirements—if achieved—would be suitable for our operational purposes.

Exploiting and Mitigating Process

Process is unavoidable in large-scale institutional innovation: without it, change is transient and limited in scope. At the same time, most institutional processes, such as requirement definition, research and development, budgeting, and scheduling, aim to facilitate stability and routine—factors not directly conducive to transformation. Both the SBCT and FCS efforts faced the challenges of simultaneously leveraging the institutional change process while mitigating its inherent limitations.

Requirements Definition

Both the SBCT and the FCS had an unfortunate similarity with respect to requirements. At the AUSA speech of October of 1999, the Stryker program was merely an aspiration, and in fact a surprise to the Army Staff with no defined requirement, no program, no budget. One year later, again at AUSA, the FCS program was another October surprise. Requirements were developed subsequent to the initiative announcements, and although out of sequence, both requirements documents were extraordinary—one for simplicity, the other for complexity. The Stryker requirements document was finalized in a joint effort of TRADOC and ASAALT in a conference at Fort Monroe in January of 2000, only a few months after the initial AUSA announcement. In what one participant still describes as "the most painful meeting experience of my life," the entire requirements document was reviewed with senior TRADOC leadership, who rigorously constrained the platform requirements to conform with the operational concept, insisted on a uniform platform solution wherever available, and limited subsystem components to currently available systems. This discipline generated a relatively simple, executable program.[23] The only exceptions—due to lack of availability among available platforms—were the Artillery Vehicle, the Mounted Gun System, and the Nuclear, Biological, and Chemical Reconnaissance System. Interestingly, none of these nonstandard platform requirements survived as solution components of the SBCT.[24]

    The FCS requirements process leveraged some initial conceptual work executed by DARPA during the period 1998–2000. The development of the requirements document was much more deliberate and—upon its completion in 2002—constituted perhaps the most comprehensive Army requirements document. It included 525 O&O requirements leading to 13,000 program requirements, and attempted the first ever "requirements definition" of a network. The FCS requirement's complexity represented the ambition of the program, but it is reasonable to wonder if it scaled beyond the limits of what the standard acquisition process could tolerate.[25]

Acquisition Scheduling

General Shinseki was a man driven by a well-founded appreciation for both the potential—and the inertia—of the institution he loved. He was determined to achieve "irreversible momentum" before institutional drag dissipated the energy of his ambitious goals.[26] For the SBCT, he was successful in realizing this initiative from idea to initial fielding within his term as CSA. The SBCT executed the standard acquisition process at breakneck speed given the scope of the program. With a requirements document completed in January of 2000, the Request for Proposal was released in May of that year. The contract was awarded in November of 2000, and the first vehicles were available for testing in November of 2001. Spring of 2003 saw the first fielding of a SBCT.[27]

He was even more ambitious for the scheduling of the FCS. Conceived in the conceptual work of DARPA, the agency ran the acquisition for the Army until 2002, to include selection of the Army's first Lead System Integrator (LSI), a task that went to Boeing. Although the feasibility timeframe initially described by DARPA was 2020, General Shinseki believed that any initiative that could not produce a result within the period of the budget POM (Program Objective Memorandum) had no hope of funding; therefore, the FCS's Initial Operating Capability was set at 2007. There was another restructuring in 2005 to project a series of technology spinouts and a 2017 implementing concept. These necessary scheduling adjustments reflected the complexity and cost of the program, but inevitably led to "program expectation failure" in an environment when pressing near-term operational requirements in Iraq and Afghanistan overrode concerns for future warfare.

Research and Development

Research and Development (R&D) demands were not significant for the SBCT due to the Army's commitment to an existing, common platform solution and already available subsystems. In contrast, the R&D requirements of the FCS program are legendary.[28] Forecasting the development schedule of these cutting-edge technologies—many of them codependent on each other—was exceptionally problematic.[29]

Budgeting/Affordability

When the October 1999 AUSA speech announced the SBCT effort, the Army budget already had been submitted. Subsequent to the speech, the Army Staff (including Ray Odierno, a future CSA) initiated a rapid process to amend the Army budget to include the termination of thirty ongoing programs to pay for the initial Stryker effort. Estimation of the cost of the FCS program, on the other hand, was quite problematic, given the immaturity of the technologies. As the program evolved, cost estimates rose, and as the Army struggled to meet the burgeoning requirements of two wars, it became increasingly difficult to justify the expense of an unaffordable and delayed FCS program.[30]

Leveraging the Human Dimension

Although most would acknowledge the role of human creativity in the innovation process, there are several other key aspects of human interaction at play for large-scale institutional change.

Emotional Intelligence

For the leadership of large-scale institutional innovation, emotional intelligence—the ability to manage the anxiety of change and operate in an ambiguous environment—is essential. For the initial SBCT standup effort, the Army found in General James Dubik a leader extremely gifted in this attribute. Designated as the Deputy I Corps Commanding General for Transformation, one of his early tasks was to present—as an infantry officer—at the annual Armor Conference and explain why the Army was inactivating an armor brigade in order to build an infantry capability. He pressed for immediate turn-in of the inactivating armor brigade equipment, long before the arrival of the new platforms, in order to "take away the old so there was nothing to cling to." He then took the leadership on a "conversion junket," a tour of all the TRADOC schools that were developing the SBCT, followed by crafting a professional development plan focused on training and leadership. He reduced Army internal cultural barriers by explaining to the initial SBCT cadre that they would "think like SOF; fight like Rangers; move like Armor."[31] The FCS leadership also was gifted with emotional intelligence. The scale and distribution of the FCS program across the Institutional Army, however, was far less amenable to influence by personal leadership.

Leadership Commitment

Leadership commitment was strong for both programs; both initiatives received frequent and recurring attention from senior Army leadership. General Shinseki was able to achieve "irreversible momentum" for the Stryker program, but the ambitions of the FCS program made generation of anything like irreversible momentum impractical. It is possible, moreover, that his attempt to accelerate the program by imposing overly ambitious implementation goals actually damaged the FCS program.[32]

As CSAs, Generals Peter Schoomaker and George Casey readily adopted Shinseki's vision. The challenge, however, was that his successors also inherited the post-9/11 wars. By 2005, the FCS program—although supported by subsequent CSAs—was no longer the priority project of the Army, and transformation was not the priority project of DoD. The impact of the concurrent demands of the GWOT was relentless. It is possible that if the ephemeral "strategic pause" foreseen at the start of the Transformation Decade had actually materialized, then the FCS program flaws would have been corrected. But by 2009 the Army had been at war for eight years in a counterinsurgency operations environment that bore scant resemblance to the requirements of the FCS program. The Army's internal senior leader commitment to the program did not extend to the leadership of the DoD.

Complexity

Complexity challenges institutions in many dimensions: comprehension, communication, adaptation. Any comparison of the SBCT with the FCS is inherently unbalanced: the former was simpler and far easier. "Off the shelf" acquisition, either "GOTS" (Government Off the Shelf) or "COTS" (Commercial Off the Shelf) is—in the estimate of a combat developer involved in both programs—"always at least an order of magnitude less demanding than a new start."[33] It is arguable that the SBCT effort took the current acquisition process to the limits of feasibility, and that the FCS program, with its multiple, ambiguous, and moving components, was at a level of complexity that current processes could not address, even when augmented by external resources like an LSI.

Political Positioning

As the SBCT program rapidly evolved from concept to fielded units, the Army made several decisions that reinforced political support for the program. This was particularly evident in the stationing decisions for the initial units: Washington (Norm Dicks, House Appropriations Subcommittee Defense), Alaska (Ted Stevens, Chairman, Senate Appropriations Committee), Hawaii (Dan Inouye, Chairman, House Appropriations Committee), and US Army National Guard Pennsylvania (John Murtha, House Majority Leader and House Appropriations Subcommittee Defense). Political positioning for the FCS was less fortunate in that, with DARPA's selection of Boeing as the LSI, the program became associated with a long-term target of Senator John McCain, the Senate Armed Services Committee Chairman. Moreover, the future stationing of FCS Brigade Combat Teams, still under development and still unassigned, could not be used to shape congressional support.

Culture

There was widespread acknowledgment across the Army's "tribes" (branches) that the infantry had a mobility problem that should be addressed and that the SBCT appeared to address it. As an armor officer, General Shinseki reinforced his commitment by eliminating an armor brigade to operationalize the initial unit. The FCS program intended to address a long-term deployment problem for the heavy force, but the armor community doubted the legitimacy of that problem, and the infantry foresaw little benefit in the FCS. Within the defense industry community, most of the combat vehicle industry was content with the SBCT decision and focused initially on the potential FCS procurements. With the selection of Boeing as the LSI, however, the legacy landpower defense industry saw Boeing as an unwelcome interloper entering its landpower industry space. This left Boeing with a set of well-established defense industry competitors actively courting congressional and DoD stakeholders on landpower program constraints and priorities, and with some doubt about how well the FCS addressed them.[34]

What Have We Learned?

The most significant AAR insight is that successful innovation must address the inexorable link between the operational environment, the operational concept, and the capability solution. For solutions that encompass platforms, there is another set of key linkages—the tradeoffs between lethality, mobility, protection, quantity, and cost. The less ambitious SBCT program was able to address those platform trades and was a reasonable match for the operational demands of Iraq and Afghanistan. The accelerated FCS program was too ambitious and could not solve the platform trades. Its future conceptual idea of air-mechanization was painfully discordant with the force protection realities of the ongoing operations in Iraq and Afghanistan. The FCS failed in particular because of physical constraints and fiscal infeasibility in the program of execution.

Have we learned that it is impossible to simultaneously fight two wars and prepare for future conflicts with the current volunteer force? Though perhaps not impossible, it is nonetheless daunting. Army senior leadership tenaciously struggled throughout the Transformation Decade to retain a focus on the future while sustaining support to multiple demanding operational requirements across the globe. The decision to terminate the FCS was an external one imposed on the Army's senior leadership.[35] Were it not for the simultaneous wars and urgency of current operational requirements, the Army and DoD might have had the patience to adjust and refine the FCS program.

The legacy of the program's failure, however, is a distinct suppression in institutional appetite for large-scale transformation. Today, the SBCT appears to be the high-water mark of large-scale institutional capability development, and the FCS is viewed as "a transformation too far." Army capability modernization ideas rarely expand beyond the platform level, and those platform modernizations in turn are largely a string of frustrated efforts.

This failure is not without consequence. Army tactical superiority in the landpower domain is decreasing. Recent operational experiences in Gaza and east Ukraine illustrate near-term operational threats that would challenge current US Army formations.[36] The United States has pressing operational gaps with respect to mobile protected firepower, such as active protection against high-end antitank guided missiles and rocket-propelled grenades,[37] counterbattery systems that can find and destroy rockets at least out to ninety kilometers, counter-unmanned aerial systems, counter-rocket defenses, and counter-high-end air defense systems for Army aviation.

Ironically, the FCS operational environment parameters that seemed so irrelevant at the time of the program's termination are now at the top of America's national list of strategic concerns: peer competitors, formidable adversarial AA/AD capabilities, and the technical limits of passive armor. The Army must be able to conceive of threats across time, adapting the current force, while evolving the programmed force and innovating in anticipation of future threats.[38] For Army modernization as a whole, the Transformation Decade was also a "Lost Decade." Resources—both money and time—were put into the FCS that did not produce a fielded system. The lost opportunity was a series of legacy equipment modernizations and perhaps less ambitious programs that might have mitigated current Army vulnerabilities. There is no small irony in the reality that the Army's current degradation in tactical superiority is partially due not to a lack of ambition and vision to prepare for the future, but to an ambitious future vision that proved to be beyond its grasp.

Notes

1. Generating Force: "The generating force consists of a wide array of Army organizations whose primary mission is to generate and sustain the operational Army's capabilities for employment by joint force commanders." *TRADOC Pamphlet 525-8-1,* TRADOC Generating Force Study, 17 May 2010.

2. For an excellent history of the FCS program, see in particular the RAND Study: Christopher G. Pernin, Elliot Axelband, Jeffrey A. Drezner, Brian B. Dille, John Gordon, Bruce J. Held, K. Scott McMahon, Walter L. Perry, Christopher Rizzi, Akhil R. Shah, Peter A. Wilson and Jerry M. Sollinger, *Lessons from the Army's Future Combat Systems Program* (Santa Monica, Calif.: RAND Corporation, 2012), http://www.rand.org/pubs/monographs/MG1206.html.

3. The Army Capabilities Integration Center (ARCIC) was originally named the Future Center.

4. My personal observations are supplemented by extensive interviews from the spring of 2015 with Lieutenant General James Dubik (Ret.) and Lieutenant General Joseph Yakovac (Ret.), both of whom participated in the Stryker and FCS efforts. I am also indebted to careful reviews by Major General William Hix (DAMO-SS, Army Staff), Robert Simpson (TRADOC ARCIC contractor), and Scott McMichael (former TRADOC employee.)

5. Insights from correspondence with Major General William Hix.

6. Many other important initiatives ensued in the Transformation Decade: refinements to concepts and doctrine, the modular redesign of the Army, development of the Army Force Generation Model, and—most importantly for the Stryker and FCS initiatives—the wars in Iraq and Afghanistan. The SBCT and FCS efforts happened in a dynamic and challenging period.

7. The Operating Environment (OE) is a defined document or set of documents within the field of Joint and Army capability development.

8. Sir Michael Howard, "Military Science in an Age of Peace," *RUSI, A Journal of the Royal United Services Institute for Defence Studies* 119 (March 1974): 3–9.

9. "Global Trends 2015: A Dialogue About the Future with Nongovernment Experts," NIC 2000-02, paper approved for publication by the National Foreign Intelligence Board under the authority of the Director of Central Intelligence, prepared under the direction of the National Intelligence Council, 13 December 2000.

10. Army After Next (AAN) work coined these as "Operational Exclusion Zones."

11. Major General William Hix, review notes.

12. PBS *Frontline* interview with General Eric Shinseki, The Future of War, 2000, http://www.pbs.org/wgbh/pages/frontline/shows/future/interviews/shinseki.

html. General Shinseki was cautious about the notion of "strategic pause," but willing to use it as one of the arguments for advancing Army Transformation.

13. Observing initial SBCT deployments in Iraq as MNF-I C3, I noted that for several months Stryker units did not experience combat casualties due to IEDs or RPGs—a consequence of their stand-off RPG "cages" as well as an operational employment concept that allowed them to travel great distances rapidly, arriving in an area before insurgents had time to seed the terrain with IEDs. As the SBCT's time in combat extended and insurgents increased the size and density of their IED weapons, these initial advantages diminished. Nonetheless, the initial operational experiences reinforced the momentum of an ongoing program.

14. I heard this argument several times from the Office of the Secretary of Defense as they moved to direct the termination of the FCS program.

15. Personal input from Strategic Studies Group advisors to General Shinseki in 1999.

16. The Quality of Firsts was a convenient shorthand for the potential benefits of emerging technologies, frequently employed by TRADOC in war-gaming and conceptual work in the late 1990s and early 2000s. For example, the Army Transformation Wargame 2001 booklet, 22–27 April 2001, http://www.tradoc.army.mil/tpubs/misc/ArmyTransformationBooklet.pdf.

17. "The Quality of Firsts" is frequently cited as evidence of technology hubris in critique of the FCS program.

18. Robert Kocher is CEO of I3: Ideal Innovations, Inc.

19. The cutting-edge approach to software design included the System of Systems Common Operating Environment (SOSCOE). A SOSCOE has a layered "toolset" of infrastructure services that provided a service-oriented architecture operating environment for FCS applications. "System of Systems Common Operating Environment (SOSCOE) Support to Net Centricity" briefing by Mark Uland, Deputy Chief Architect, FCS LSI Boeing Inc., 1 March 2007.

20. Interview with Lieutenant General Yakovac.

21. It is fair to say that this "classic pattern" is rarely adhered to.

22. Major General Hix points out that AAN and Transformation Wargames preceded the Unified Quest war-games. These contributed to the conceptual basis for the FCS.

23. Interview with Lieutenant General Yakovac.

24. Ibid.

25. Ibid.

26. Michael D. Formica, "Building Irreversible Momentum" (chapter 5), in *Army Transformation: A View from the U.S. Army War College,*" ed. Williamson Murray (Carlisle, Pa.: Strategic Studies Institute, 2001), 129–158.

27. Interview with Lieutenant General Yakovac.

28. John D. Moteff, Congressional Research Service Science and Policy Research Division, "Defense Research: A Primer on the DoD's Research, Development, Test and Evaluation Program," updated May 5, 1998.

29. Interview with Lieutenant General Yakovac.

30. Ibid.

31. Interview with Lieutenant General Dubik.

32. This is the consensus of all interviewees for this project.

33. Scott McMichael, member of the TRADOC DCSDOC / Future Center / Army Capability Integration Center during both the SBCT and FCS efforts.

34. Interview with Lieutenant General Yakovac

35. Pernin et al., *Lessons from the Army's Future Combat Systems Program.*

36. Dave Johnson at RAND has several excellent presentations describing "war in the middle" and the lethality of current hybrid threats.

37. If one examines the Russian T-14 tank, for example, it appears to be a significant threat—with an Active Protection System, built on a universal chassis system designed for thirteen combat vehicle variants, and with a central information control system, all like the FCS. There is some conjecture that the Russian claims for the T-14 are exaggerated, but there will be 2,300 of these deployed to Russian forces by 2025.

38. Major General William Hix, review notes.

14

On Headquarters

Use and Abuse of Army Operational Headquarters (and Contracting) from 2001 to 2015

John A. Bonin

> To enable superior headquarters to retain control over subordinate
> ones, a regular system for transmitting information from the top
> down, from the bottom up, and laterally among the subordinate
> units is indispensable and must naturally become more complex as
> the state of art advances.
> —Martin van Creveld, *Command in War*

The US Army since 9/11 has had to face the harsh reality that the complexities of the employment of landpower in modern warfare requires large headquarters staffs.[1] However, the leaders of the DoD and the Army are often at odds with that reality, as the United States frequently seeks to retain combat units at the expense of "unnecessary overhead." In addition, the Army found itself wholly unprepared for these headquarters to contract for the unprecedented level and complexity of support utilized in recent military operations.

Background

The US Army is not only organized into distinguished tactical units, such as the 75th Infantry (Rangers), the 3rd Cavalry (Brave Rifles) or the 173rd Airborne Brigade, but also famous operational headquarters, such as the 1st Infantry Division, the XVIII Corps, or Third Army. In addition, during World War II the Army employed named "theater army" headquarters in each major theater of operations to provide direction and planning for the employment of subordinate field armies, corps, and divisions for its respective supreme allied commander. These theater armies frequently performed "sequel planning," removed from the grind of current combat operations.

Unfortunately, the Army has not always valued all of these headquarters as key components to the employment of landpower.[2]

Likewise, since its inception in 1775, the Army has utilized commercially provided services and civilians in direct support of military operations. From laundresses in the Continental Army to the tens of thousands of foreign civilian laborers in World War II, Korea, and Vietnam to the numerous contracted workers in support of recent operations in USCENTCOM, contractors have always been a part of the force regardless of official documentation.[3] Before 1999, the Army published limited doctrine and policy regarding contingency contracting and contractors on the battlefield, and it lacked a larger contract support construct as documented today across various Army and joint doctrine, organization, training, materiel, and personnel products. Generally, military leadership considered contract support as nothing more than a limited headquarters' augmentation capability to support Army forces. The past decade-plus of war has provided significant insights that challenge that previously accepted view of what is today called operational contract support.

Prior to 9/11, the US Army's active component consisted of a mature ten-division structure essentially still based on the Reorganization Objective Army Divisions construct from the early 1960s.[4] Echelon above division headquarters' structure reflected recent experience and consisted of four corps and five army service component commands (ASCCs), which was the new designation for the historic theater army headquarters supporting five geographic combatant commands (US Army Europe [USAREUR], US Army Pacific [USARPAC], US Army South [USARSO], Third Army/US Army Central [USARCENT], and Eighth Army supporting US Forces Korea).[5] The Army's contingency contracting capabilities included a limited force of about 250 deployable uniformed military contracting positions. The Army assigned these individuals to various operating force headquarters at all echelons, as well as to specialty commands, but without central oversight.

Under the Army of Excellence (AOE) of the 1980s and 1990s, the Army designed corps and division headquarters primarily to serve at the intermediate tactical level under a higher Army, joint, or multinational staff. The Army considered corps headquarters capable of serving as a supporting Army Force (ARFOR) and operational Joint Task Force (JTF) headquarters, but did not believe division headquarters could serve in the same capacity. Only XVIII Corps had recently served as a JTF, in Panama in 1989 during Operation Just Cause. While the Third and Eighth Armies were both capable of serving as a supporting ARFOR and as an operational headquarters supervising multiple corps, the other ASCCs were not. During Operation Desert Storm, the

Third Army/USARCENT had directly commanded V and VII Corps, but the USCENTCOM commander, General Norman Schwarzkopf, had elected to command operations himself without a separate land component commander to integrate ground operations.[6] However, in 1999, after Task Force Hawk in Kosovo experienced command and control challenges, the CSA, General Eric Shinseki, required ASCC or corps headquarters to also be capable of serving as a joint force land component command (JFLCC).[7]

Early Stages of Operation Enduring Freedom and Operation Iraqi Freedom

Although Marine Corps General Anthony Zinni, the previous commander of USCENTCOM, had declared Third Army the joint force land component command in June 1998, Third Army had never been assigned the personnel required to enable it to function as such.[8] Third Army/USARCENT habitually operated split command posts, with its "main" officially at Fort McPherson, Georgia, subordinated to US Army Forces Command (USFORSCOM), and a small Coalition JTF forward command post located in Kuwait exercising daily operational control of forces assigned to Operation Desert Spring. On 9/11, ARCENT existed as a low priority organization and was manned at about 55 percent authorized strength, or only five hundred personnel. The headquarters has been redesigned based on Desert Storm experience into "modules" that allowed for the deployment of either a small or main command post or even a full "Main and Rear." In addition, the headquarters had the ability to maintain a "Sanctuary Module" in Georgia that provided critical staff functions not needed forward through reach-back capabilities. This structure allowed USARCENT to have the necessary functions present in Egypt for Exercise Bright Star on 9/11, and to redeploy directly into Kuwait by 13 November 2001.[9]

On 20 November 2001, USCENTCOM commander General Tommy Franks gave Lieutenant General P. T. Mikolashek, the commanding general of Third Army/USARCENT, his mission for Operation Enduring Freedom (OEF) as follows: "Coalition Forces Land Component Commander directs and synchronizes land operations to destroy Al Qaida and prevent the re-emergence of international terrorist activities within Coalition/Joint Operations Area-AFGHANISTAN and supports humanitarian operations in order to create a peaceful and stable environment within AFGHANISTAN."[10] Because the Third Army/USARCENT lacked an operational command post, the Coalition Forces Land Component Commander (CFLCC) had to employ the 10th Mountain Division headquarters to Karshi-Khanabad

Air Base, Uzbekistan, as its forward element. By February 2002, additional personnel from across the Army and planners from subordinate theater-level commands, other services, and coalition partners resulted in some 1,200 total (if untrained) personnel manning the Third Army headquarters at three primary sites, including some 140 joint augmenters and 167 personnel from 10th Mountain Division headquarters.[11] For Operation Anaconda, the 10th Mountain Division, lacking half of the division headquarters earlier deployed to the Balkans and without either assigned assistant division commander, reformed into CJTF-Mountain to conduct the first major ground operation of the War on Terror from 2–18 March 2002.[12]

The command structure in Afghanistan remained complicated. In December 2001, the UN-sanctioned International Security Assistance Force (ISAF) began arriving in Kabul in accordance with the Bonn agreement to secure the Afghan capital. ISAF later formally became a NATO unit and expanded outside of Kabul. On 31 May 2002, in a move indicative of the long-term US military commitment to Afghanistan, the XVIII Airborne Corps headquarters under Lieutenant General Dan McNeill deployed to Bagram Air Base, Afghanistan, as CJTF-180 headquarters and assumed control of US-coalition operations, as well as supporting troops in Pakistan, Tajikistan, and Uzbekistan. General Franks made this change because he wanted a more senior officer with a larger headquarters staff in Afghanistan to consolidate the growing international coalition forces under a single command reporting directly to him.[13] Consequently, command relationships were realigned, with USARCENT still responsible for the support of all Army forces in the USCENTCOM area of responsibility (AOR), and TF Mountain as the intermediate tactical headquarters and ARFOR for CJTF-180. This change also allowed the CFLCC staff in Kuwait to better focus on the conduct of planning potential land operations against Iraq. On 2 September 2002, Lieutenant General David McKiernan replaced Lieutenant General Paul Mikolashek as USARCENT and CFLCC commanding general at Camp Doha in Kuwait.[14]

For Operation Iraqi Freedom (OIF), USARCENT/CFLCC headquarters again expanded, to over 1,500 total personnel including allies and joint personnel, with Marine Corps Major General Rusty Blackman as chief of staff. Vice CSA General Jack Keane filled Third Army with many of the best and brightest of the Army's senior officers to maximize their service in the most important phases of the operation.[15] Third Army, as CFLCC for OIF, commanded almost 300,000 US and coalition ground forces, including not only the operational forces under V Corps and I Marine Expeditionary Force, but also nine major theater supporting organizations totaling some

56,000 personnel.[16] USARCENT unencumbered V Corps as the senior Army maneuver headquarters to focus on the significant operational challenges of defeating the bulk of the Iraqi army and seizing Baghdad. By 1 May 2003, Lieutenant General William Wallace, the V Corps commander, had over 130,000 troops in almost five divisions: 1st Armored Division, 3rd Infantry Division, 4th Infantry Division, Task Force Falcon (2nd Brigade, 82nd Airborne Division), and 101st Air Assault Division, as well as numerous V Corps troops.[17] Unfortunately, due to lack of policy guidance and the tyranny of conducting immediate actions, USARCENT was unable to conduct detailed planning for the occupation of Iraq, as had been performed by the European Theater of Operations US Army staff for General Dwight Eisenhower in World War II.[18]

Combined Joint Task Force-7

After eliminating Saddam Hussein, the US Army assumed grave risk with its headquarters in Iraq. The large and general officer-filled CFLCC, built around the Third Army headquarters, had been the principal planning organization for the stability phase of the operation and was scheduled to take charge after seizing Baghdad. USCENTCOM, however, deemed it too big for the desired end-strength of US occupation forces. The USCENTCOM chief of staff told Army historians that "Franks and others were interested in lowering the size of the military footprint in Iraq in line with prewar planning for a very brief period of military operations after toppling Saddam Hussein."[19]

But establishing Combined Joint Task Force-7 (CJTF-7) using the V Corps headquarters proved problematic. A Baghdad division commander noted that V Corps was not suited to the mission and observed that the forces in the capital were "a bit adrift," engaged in what was "a bit of almost discovery learning" as they transitioned from maneuver elements in a grand fight to governing a fractious capital city.[20] V Corps lacked the more senior and joint-experienced personnel the task required. V Corps/CJTF-7, now commanded by newly promoted Lieutenant General Ricardo Sanchez, tried to bring order to a complex insurgency in a large country beset by disgruntled Ba'athists, Shiite militias, restless Sunni tribes, and Al Qa'ida cadres, all vying for power and chafing under the coalition's presence. To become mission capable, Sanchez's organic corps headquarters built up slowly from an original authorized strength of 280 toward a required strength of 1,328 over a year's time. General officer strength went from three to nearly twenty "on hand" in roughly the same period.[21] Essentially, serving simultaneously as

CJTF, CFLCC, ARFOR, and the intermediate tactical headquarters forced CJTF-7 to perform too many tasks simultaneously at all three levels of war with an inexperienced staff and drove it to mission failure with Abu Ghraib and the burgeoning insurgency. As Lieutenant General William Wallace stated in *On Point II*: "You can't take a tactical HQs [V Corps] and change it into an operational [level] headquarters [CJTF-7] at the snap of your fingers. It just doesn't happen. Your focus changes completely, and either you are going to take your eye off the tactical fight in order to deal with operational issues, or you are going to ignore the operational issues and stay involved in the tactical fight."[22]

The US Army has an inherent responsibility to plan and prepare for post-conflict activities, even if not specifically directed. DoD Directive 5100.01 commands the US Army to not only defeat enemy ground forces, but also "seize, occupy, and defend land areas" and "occupy territories abroad and provide for initial establishment of a military government pending transfer of this responsibility to other authority."[23] From this experience, Lieutenant General McKiernan observed, "You have to put as much effort into the back end of the campaign as you do to the front end."[24]

While costly in number of staff, the landpower reality required splitting CJTF-7 into strategic and operational parts. USCENTCOM created a de facto four-star subunified command, Multi-National Force-Iraq (MNF-I), and a three-star operational headquarters, Multi-National Corps-Iraq (MNC-I). MNF-I as a four-star headquarters could better focus on external complex political-strategic issues dealing with US interagency partners, the Interim Iraqi Government, other US military headquarters, conducting detainee operations, etc. Meanwhile, MNC-I, as the de facto CFLCC for Iraq, could better focus internally on combat operations.[25]

Support for the Global War on Terrorism increased use of contracted support by headquarters, as the Army had been designated as the service responsible for most service contracting in Kuwait, Afghanistan, and Iraq. The continual introduction of nonstandard, commercial equipment, unexpectedly large commercial logistical support requirements (an estimated 80 percent of services provided via contracted support), and military force-cap restrictions of simultaneous operations in Afghanistan and Iraq quickly overwhelmed the limited ability of the Army's military contractor structure to properly plan and manage this support. This resulted in an approximate 1:1 ratio of deployed military to contractor personnel. Furthermore, the high level of contract support revealed major deficiencies in the contractor personnel and in the Army's competency in writing and executing complex contract instruments. Additionally, and most importantly, the lack of clear leadership direction due to the ineffective "dual" operational unit command and poor Army Contracting Agency acquisition oversight proved disastrous. In hindsight, both the Army Contracting Agency and the Army operating force headquarters' leadership proved completely unaware of the serious contract support planning and management deficiencies of this dual command and acquisition oversight arrangement. These deficiencies not only led to challenges in planning and managing contracted support, but also to significant levels of contract fraud, waste, and abuse.[26]

Combined Forces Command-Afghanistan

In Afghanistan, the XVIII Corps redeployed in May 2003 after serving as CJTF-180. Secretary of Defense Rumsfeld now shifted US resources to Iraq, leaving Afghanistan as an economy of force stabilization and reconstruction effort. Initially, 10th Mountain returned to replace XVIII Corps as the headquarters for CJTF-180, responsible for all of Afghanistan and its own intermediate tactical headquarters. This arrangement caused a substantial loss of momentum against the Taliban. A reassessment by General John Abizaid, the new USCENTCOM commander, led in October 2003 to Major General David Barno's temporary assignment for the direction of the overall military effort, but with absolutely minimal personnel. Starting with just six staff officers, recently promoted Lieutenant General Barno leveraged the overworked subordinate division staff until he could eventual create and justify a joint manning document of some four hundred individual augmentees for his ad hoc Combined Forces Command-Afghanistan (CFC-A) by his departure in May 2005. In late 2006, the DoD inactivated the CFC-A, as NATO's ISAF headquarters assumed the overall military mission in Afghanistan with a four-star general.[27] However, as MNF-I and ISAF constituted multinational headquarters in order to lend legitimacy to US and NATO efforts, and were not specifically US Army headquarters, these entities may also have detracted from unity of effort. They increased in size as every coalition member sought placement of senior officers in these headquarters to protect respective national interests.[28] Unfortunately, the observations of many senior US officers of these large, inefficient coalition staffs would also color their subsequent views of the optimal size of actual US Army operational headquarters.

Modularity

Beginning in September 2003, CSA General Peter Schoomaker began to reorganize the Army to meet the requirements of the twenty-first century. Under the concept of modularity, the Army moved from a rigid hierarchical AOE structure to a more flexible and autonomous brigade combat team (BCT) structure no longer organic to a division headquarters. In addition, the CSA specified that the Army's operational headquarters would be focused on actual employment of forces, not home station training.

However, in January 2004, before the modular designs could be completed, Rumsfeld, as part of a discussion on Army growth, asked the Army leadership if it still had the same number of echelons as in World War II. He also asked: "What is the theater army? What is its relevance today? Who else can do that mission?"[29] The Army's response indicated that it had reduced its larger echelons of command from the five echelons above brigade or regiment in World II to three, as approved in current Army doctrine, and was considering reducing to only two echelons above brigade. The theater army remained one of these as essential to providing landpower to combatant commanders. While the size of Army forces since World War II had decreased, the complexity and strategic significance of Army operations at the theater level had increased.

Modular corps and division headquarters provided the command and control structure into which capabilities-based BCTs and multifunctional or functional support brigades could be organized to meet geographic combatant commanders' (GCCs) requirements. Division headquarters, envisioned at over eight hundred personnel, while primarily focused on the tactical war fight, had corps-level attributes and were capable of employment as JTF headquarters. Unlike the AOE, the larger modular division headquarters included all personnel actually working at the headquarters, organized by warfighting function, and manned with additional special staff, such as information operations, operations research/systems analysts, electronic warfare specialists, and strategists. Modular divisions could provide command and control for up to six maneuver BCTs and numerous multifunctional support brigades (or forces the size of a World War II corps).

Modular corps headquarters were also increased from around three hundred to over eight hundred personnel and were envisioned as being capable of providing command for up to five divisions with supporting troops, or forces the size of World War II field armies. In addition, the Army redesigned all theater headquarters to serve at the operational level based on the recent model of USARCENT/CFLCC. With a design strength of some 1,100 personnel, these headquarters not only had a main command post but also a corps-like operational command post (OCP). Informed by the challenge of CJTF-7, all types of modular division, corps, and army headquarters were robust enough to accept joint capabilities, such as from Joint Manning Documents or Standing Joint Force headquarters elements. These headquarters also had organic capabilities, including signal support, to perform the functions required of a JTF, a JFLCC headquarters, or a multinational headquarters, such as a CFLCC.[30] Consequently, modularity increased not only the US Army's total number of operational headquarters, but also their organic capabilities to function as JTFs and JFLCCs. In addition, the remaining non-operational ASCCs were converted to operational theater armies.

Much of the intent of modular headquarters design was codified not only in Army doctrine but also in Army regulations. *Army Regulation 10-87: Army Commands, Army Service Component Commands, and Direct Reporting Units* (September 2007) recognizes the theater army as an ASCC, reporting directly to Department of the Army, and serving as the army's single point of contact for combatant commands. Geographic component commanders normally delegate operational control (OPCON) of Army forces to the ASCC. The secretary of the Army generally delegates administrative control (ADCON) to ASCCs for Army forces assigned to the GCC. In addition, the Army regulation specifies that a theater army, when directed by its combatant commander, would serve as a JFLCC/JTF.[31]

2009 Revised Army Operational Concept (AOC)

In 2009, at the height of the Iraqi Surge, CSA General George Casey modified modularity to reduce numbers in operational headquarters in order to grow numbers of BCTs. He reduced the robust theater army "4.2 design" with some 1,066 spaces to the "5.4 design" of some 700 spaces, including only a small contingency command post (CCP) of some 96 personnel and not the much larger OCP. This resulted in retaining V Corps and not merging it into USA-REUR as its OCP, and also not converting the Eighth Army into the OCP of USARPAC. But because of a new GCC, USAFRICOM, he converted the small Southern European Task Force (SETAF) two-star headquarters into US Army Africa (USARAF). The CSA also approved USARCENT's headquarters remaining at the larger design with its OCP until 2016 on the assumption that "peace" would have returned to the USCENTCOM's AOR.[32]

In this revised AOC, the corps (not the theater army) would become the Army's primary operational headquarters for command of land forces for major operations, including serving as a JTF or JFLCC-ARFOR. The reduced staff of the theater army would continue to provide: AOR-wide Title 10, ADCON, Army support to other services, and common-user logistics. In addition, it would serve as the Army executive agent for the combatant commander and other services, and for joint and Army forces operating within the AOR. The theater army could (with its CCP capability) directly command smaller scale contingency operations within the AOR that would be: limited in scale, scope, intensity, and duration; require immediate response; or provide direction for the early phases of more complex/lengthy operations until relieved by a corps/division headquarters capable of mission command for sustained operations. In essence, the US Army without OCPs in the theater army headquarters would no longer have the capability to provide command for a multi-corps operation.[33] This would reduce Army landpower effectiveness.

Modular Headquarters in Operation

During Army operations from 2005 to 2011, robust modular headquarters performed extremely well. While a JFLCC had not always been clearly designated, MNC-I directly supervised most of the coalition ground combat forces (US Army, US Marine Corps, and coalition) conducting stability and reconstruction operations in Iraq. This mission rotated among several US Army corps headquarters until 2010.[34] Consequently, MNC-I served as the de facto CFLCC for MNF-I. In 2010, MNF-I converted to United States Forces-Iraq and absorbed I Corps, then serving as MNC-I, until OIF ended in 2011. In addition, as operations shifted to focus on Afghanistan during 2009, US forces there increased to more than 100,000. NATO's ISAF formed the ISAF Joint Command (IJC) as a corps-level command to manage the ground operations of the several division-sized regional commands. In July 2011, I Corps became the nucleus of the IJC and the de facto CFLCC for Afghanistan and other US Army corps headquarters subsequently replaced it in succession until 2013.[35]

Modular divisions have also successfully conducted challenging stability and counterinsurgency operations over large areas in both Iraq as multinational divisions and in Afghanistan as regional commands, while transitioning operational roles to their Iraqi and Afghani counterparts. The typical rotation and transition of modular brigades separate from their division headquarters complicated these efforts.[36] During the Surge of 2007, the modular 1st Cavalry Division headquarters had some ten BCTs and numerous other formations under its command, far exceeding the capability of an AOE division headquarters.[37]

While the Army reorganized its headquarters, the contracting force also reformed its processes. Due to gross contractual mismanagement and criminal behavior from 2001 to 2007 and the notorious performance of firms such as Blackwater, the secretary of the Army chartered the Commission on Army Acquisition and Program Management and Expeditionary Operations, commonly known as the Gansler Commission.[38] The high-level commission quickly conducted a very thorough review of contracted support in USCENTCOM operations and rapidly published its groundbreaking report in November 2007. Soon thereafter, Army leadership responded by expanding the contracting work force structure into a new Army Contracting Command subordinated to Army Materiel Command. However, already by 2007 the Army (and the DoD as a whole) had made significant progress in integrating operational contract support matters into all military operations. These improvements ranged from comprehensive doctrine, a new Army operational contract support skill identifier, new operational contract support courses, and the establishment of new general officer-led Army contracting commands and staff billets.[39]

Since 2001, the Army has conducted less visible but more strategic actions at the theater level. Since 2003, the Third Army/USARCENT served as the USCENTCOM JFLCC and ARFOR headquarters in support of US operations in Afghanistan, Iraq, and initially the Horn of Africa. More recently, the Third Army/USARCENT has focused on the conduct of Operation Spartan Shield across the Gulf region. With the creation of USNORTHCOM, the Army converted the Fifth Army, a nonoperational Reserve Component supervisory staff, into the operational US Army North. US Army North has employed its small command posts on numerous operations in the homeland, including Hurricane Sandy in 2012 and, more recently, as the theater-JFLCC for the numerous hurricanes of 2017. In addition, USARSO conducted humanitarian operations in Haiti after the earthquake in 2010, and the Eighth Army in Korea converted from an ASCC to a JTF-capable "legacy field army" placed under the administrative control of USARPAC while remaining under the operational control of US Forces Korea.[40]

In March 2013, as the war in Iraq ended and operations in Afghanistan continued, CSA General Ray Odierno, sent the CJCS a memorandum concerning improving Army-joint force capability. It acknowledged that during these long wars Army support had waned to GCCs, specifically for providing joint-capable headquarters. General Odierno intended to provide better support to GCCs by aligning a corps or division headquarters ready to serve as the core of a JTF or JFLCC with each GCC. The CSA also stated that he wanted GCCs to understand the Army's concept for supporting contingencies with the ASCC's CCP initially until a joint force-capable corps or division headquarters could arrive.[41]

Headquarters Reductions, 2013–2015

Beginning in 2013, the impact of the Budget Control Act resulted in the Department of the Army establishing Focus Area Review Groups to develop personnel reductions. While the DoD directed 20 percent cuts to headquarters staffs, CSA Odierno volunteered even more by upping the Army's headquarters reductions to 25 percent.[42] As V Corps had already been programmed for elimination as part of the Army's reduction, its loss did not count. The Army reduced all division and corps headquarters by some 25 percent, to 571 and 517 active duty Army spaces, respectively, with an associated Reserve Component detachment as recompense. Theater army headquarters retained the 5.4 design of some 700 spaces, but all were reduced by various percentages. The largest reductions were programmed for USAREUR at 40 percent (based on the assumption of a "reset" with Russia) and USARCENT at some 47 percent, counting its conversion from the previous more robust 4.2 design. The overall operational headquarters reductions saved some 4,400 spaces, or approximately a single BCT.[43] Most theater armies could no longer actually afford their CCPs and used those spaces to fill required positions at the main headquarters. Such arbitrary reductions to create efficiencies risk replicating the same lack of Army headquarters and staff effectiveness or readiness made so apparent at the outbreak of hostilities in World War II, Korea, the Persian Gulf, and, more recently, Afghanistan and Iraq.

Ironically, due to the increasingly dangerous global environment, many theater army headquarters have been operationally employed by their GCCs despite reductions. USARCENT first deployed an element back into Iraq in 2014 to face ISIS as CJFLCC-Iraq, then reconfigured as JTF-Inherent Resolve before being replaced by III Corps as its own staff disappeared.[44] USARPAC used its remaining CCP spaces to source the Theater JFLCC Coordination Center when in 2013 the USPACOM commander directed them to perform the TJFLCC mission.[45] In September 2014, "USARAF deployed its expeditionary command post comprising the remnants of the doctrinal contingency command post, which had been cut from ASCCs as part of force structure reductions," to form rapidly a command post to serve as the staff for Operation United Assistance combating Ebola in Liberia until replaced by the 101st Air Assault Division.[46] USAREUR also created a CCP from its internal personnel for duty in Eastern Europe while facing a resurgent Russia during Operation Atlantic Resolve. In 2015, the 4th Infantry Division replaced this ad hoc CCP with an under-strength command element.[47] A consequence of theater army headquarters and staff reductions has been their challenge to provide even austere CCPs on short notice, which has resulted in dramatically increased demand for allocation, if not assignment, of the now smaller and less capable Army corps and division headquarters after these elements also suffered reductions. Since late 2016, the Army has employed rotating National Guard division headquarters to provide required capability to supplement a reduced USARCENT headquarters in Kuwait.

Conclusion

Every American war has required the expansion of US Army operational headquarters to meet new exigencies, and the American wars since 9/11 have been no different. Lieutenant General David Barno (Ret.) notes, "Leadership of joint and combined organizations created in ad hoc fashion to execute complex political-military tasks requires a diversity of skills . . . [and] the US military has done little to address its institutional shortcomings in building wartime joint headquarters."[48] In 2010, the Rand Corporation published *Enhancing Army Joint Force Headquarters Capabilities,* which indicated the Army should anticipate that the demand for Army-provided JTFs in the future would remain high; that the process to identify and assign key personnel to JTF headquarters needs to be improved; and that the robust modular corps and divisions headquarters can provide the core of JTF headquarters for ground missions. But even these Army headquarters must be augmented and would need significant support from the other services and other government agencies.[49] Additionally, the 2015 National Defense University study *Lessons Encountered: Learning from the Long War* found that unity of command remains a relevant and key tenet in joint operations, but that unity of command seems to have been bypassed in the development of disjointed command and control structures in the wars in Iraq and Afghanistan.[50] A recent joint staff "Insights and Best Practices Focus Paper" adds that even in today's complex resource-constrained environment, the Army should "avoid the risk of ad hoc HQs."[51] An early 2018 Army experiment with a new echelon above brigade concept found significant shortfalls specifically with the design of theater army headquarters for anticipated peer adversaries.[52] In the 2015 Army Posture Statement to the Senate, Secretary of the Army John McHugh and General Odierno also warned:

> Unlike previous eras and conflicts, today's fast-paced world simply does not allow us the time to regenerate capabilities after a crisis erupts. Faced with a national crisis, we will fight with the army we have, but there will be consequences. Generating the army is a com-

plex endeavor that requires policy decisions, dollars, Soldiers, infrastructure and, most importantly, time. It takes approximately 30 months to generate a fully manned and trained Regular Army BCT once the Army decides to expand the force. Senior command and control headquarters, such as divisions and corps, take even longer to generate and train to be effective given the skill sets and training required of Soldiers manning these formations.[53]

As the Army continues adapting to the current environment, it should heed insights from the past sixteen years of conflict. As it restructures, the Army must ensure that it is not exacerbating the problem of employing landpower by eliminating headquarters capabilities. This includes contractors as part of the total force, for a properly planned uniformed-commercial force structure mix can provide the Army significant capabilities while employing its limited active duty sustainment structure to only initial deployments.[54] Balanced headquarters reductions or growth deserve the same careful analysis and consideration as proposals to eliminate or grow combat forces. No defense professional would arbitrarily direct services to cut 25 percent of their combat units without careful analysis, nor arbitrarily prevent headquarters growth. Operational headquarters and staff positions should be treated the same as combat units; after all, they are the brains that direct the teeth of the force, and hence enable the projection and success of US landpower.

Notes

Epigraph: Martin van Creveld, *Command in War* (Cambridge, Mass.: Harvard Univ. Press, 1985), 271.

1. Some of the ideas in this paper have already been presented by Dr. Conrad Crane and Dr. John Bonin in *War on the Rocks* on 27 October 2015, https://warontherocks.com/2015/10/the-next-task-force-smith-the-danger-of-arbitrary-headquarters-reductions/.

2. For a history of army headquarters above corps, see John A. Bonin, "Echelons Above Reality: Armies, Army Groups, and Theater Armies/Army Service Component Commands (ASCCs)," *Essential to Success: Historical Case Studies in the Art of Command at Echelons Above Brigade* (Fort Leavenworth, Kans.: Army Univ. Press, 2017), 251–265.

3. Some of the material on contracting was extracted from Gordon L. Campbell and Charles F. Maurer, "Contracting During the Global War on Terrorism," unpublished conference paper. See also "Overview: Contracting in War," unpublished material, Center of Military History, 1987.

4. For divisions, see John B. Wilson, *Maneuver and Firepower: The Evolution*

of Divisions and Separate Brigades (Washington, DC: Center of Military History, 1998), 423. While division headquarters had some 280 assigned personnel, they were dependent on hundreds of additional staff from across the division to actually man the headquarters in the field.

5. Department of the Army, *Field Manual 100-7, Decisive Force: The Army in Theater Operations* (Washington, DC: Headquarters, Department of the Army, May 1995), A-1. In addition, on 9/11 the Southern European Task Force (SETAF) in Italy was a small joint task force-capable headquarters primarily for small-scale contingencies assigned to USAREUR.

6. Gregory Fontenot, E. J. Degen, and David Tohn, *On Point: The United States Army in Operation Iraqi Freedom* (Fort Leavenworth, Kans.: Combat Studies Institute, 2004), 42.

7. John A. Bonin, *Unified and Joint Land Operations: Doctrine for Landpower,* Land Warfare Paper No. 102 (Arlington, Va.: Institute for Land Warfare, Association of the US Army, 2014), 7.

8. Ibid., 7; Fontenot et al., *On Point,* 42.

9. Department of the Army, Draft TOE 51-001A000, 1 January 1996; Holly Heilman, "Minutes of ASCC Working Group," 4–5 March 1998; Michael E. Linick, Army Service Component Command TOE Review, 8 February 2001, all in author's files.

10. Third Army/ARCENT, "Coalition Forces Land Component Command Brief," Operation ENDURING FREEDOM/NOBLE EAGLE Initial Impressions Conference, Carlisle Barracks, Pennsylvania, 27 August 2002.

11. John A. Bonin, *US Army Forces Central Command in Afghanistan and the Arabian Gulf during Operation ENDURING FREEDOM, 11 September 2001–11 March 2003* (Carlisle, Pa.: Army Heritage and Education Center Foundation, March 2003), 9.

12. Buster Hagenbeck, "Operation Anaconda," *Essential to Success: Historical Case Studies in the Art of Command at Echelons Above Brigade* (Fort Leavenworth, Kans.: Army Univ. Press, 2017), 94–96.

13. Bonin, *US Army Forces Central Command in Afghanistan and the Arabian Gulf,* 23.

14. Ibid., 26.

15. Richard D. Hooker Jr. and Joseph Collins, eds., *Lessons Encountered: Learning from the Long War* (Washington, DC: National Defense Univ. Press, September 2015), 65.

16. Fontenot et al., *On Point,* CFLCC Order of Battle, 1 May 2003, 441–448, 484–496.

17. Scott Wallace, "V Corps Command Decisions," *Essential to Success: Historical Case Studies in the Art of Command at Echelons Above Brigade* (Fort Leavenworth, Kans.: Army Univ. Press, 2017), 223–235; Fontenot et al., *On Point,* CFLCC Order of Battle, 1 May 2003, 454–484.

18. Hooker and Collins, eds., *Lessons Encountered,* 52–54. However, ARCENT's

chief of plans, Colonel Kevin Benson, did do a troop to task analysis that indicated a Phase IV requirement for some twenty combat brigades and 300,000 ground personnel. See also Donald P. Wright and Timothy R. Reese, *On Point II: Transition to the New Campaign; The United States Army in Operation IRAQI FREEDOM, May 2003–January 2005* (Fort Leavenworth, Kans.: Combat Studies Institute, June 2008), 70–80.

19. Wright and Reese, *On Point II,* 145.

20. Hooker and Collins, eds., *Lessons Encountered,* 65–66.

21. Ibid.

22. Wright and Reese, *On Point II,* 30.

23. DoD Directive 5100.01, *Functions of the Department of Defense and Its Major Components,* 21 December 2010, 30.

24. Wright and Reese, *On Point II,* 165.

25. Ibid., 171–175. MNF-I by May 2005 consisted of over ten general officers and over 1,200 staff members.

26. Two major studies were conducted on the general use of and reliance on contracted support at the height of USCENTCOM operations: a CSA-directed October to December 2008 G-4 (logistics directorate)-led "Use of Logistics Contractors in Support of Contingency Operations" study, and a CJCS-directed J-4-led "Dependence on Contractor Support" study. Both of these studies found most (75 percent or more) of the traditional uniformed military logistic and civil engineer support functions were contracted out in OIF circa 2008–2010. Note: Army contracting officers hold the military occupation specialty of 51C.

27. David W. Barno, "Economy of Force: Building a Headquarters for Afghanistan, 2003–2005," *Essential to Success: Historical Case Studies in the Art of Command at Echelons Above Brigade* (Fort Leavenworth, Kans.: Army Univ. Press, 2017), 237–246. See also David Barno, "Command in Afghanistan 2003–2005: Three Key Lessons Learned," in *Commanding Heights: Strategic Lessons for Complex Operations,* ed. Michael Miklaucic (Washington, DC: Center for Complex Operations, Center for Technical and National Security Policy, 2009); and John A. Bonin, "Afghanistan C2: A Doctrinal Critique," unpublished course material (June 2010).

28. Hooker and Collins, eds., *Lessons Encountered,* 14.

29. Secretary of Defense Donald Rumsfeld, "Snowflake: Questions for the Secretary of the Army and CSA," 15 January 2004, copy in the author's possession. The author helped provide the Army's response.

30. William M. Donnelly, *Transforming an Army at War: Designing the Modular Force, 1991–2005* (Washington, DC: Center of Military History, 2007), 63–78; See also Headquarters, US Army Training and Doctrine Command, Task Force Modularity, *Army Comprehensive Guide to Modularity,* vol. 1, version 1.0 (8 October 2004).

31. Department of the Army, Army Regulation 10-87: *Army Commands, Army Service Component Commands, and Direct Reporting Units* (Washington, DC: Department of the Army, September 2007).

32. Headquarters, Department of the Army, *Field Manual 3-93: Theater Army Operations* (Washington, DC: Department of the Army, 12 October, 2011), Introduction, x–xi.

33. Ibid. Also see Headquarters, Department of the Army, *Field Manual 3-94: Theater Army, Corps, and Division Operations* (Washington, DC: Department of the Army, 21 April 2014), 1–5.

34. Bonin, *Unified and Joint Land Operations,* 11.

35. Ibid.

36. See Robert L. Caslen, Gregory L. Boylan, and Thomas P. Gutherie, "The Operations Targeting and Effects Synchronization Process in Northern Iraq: A Case Study for a Division-Level Approach to Staff Organization, Leadership, and Decision Making," *Essential to Success: Historical Case Studies in the Art of Command at Echelons Above Brigade* (Fort Leavenworth, Kans.: Army Univ. Press, 2017), 103–118.

37. Daniel P. Bolger, *Why We Lost: A General's Inside Account of the Iraq and Afghanistan Wars* (New York: Houghton Mifflin Harcourt, 2014), 253.

38. The Report of the Commission on Army Acquisition and Program Management in Expeditionary Operations, titled *Urgent Reform Required: Army Expeditionary Contracting, (31 October 2007),* can be found at https://www.acq.osd.mil/dpap/contingency/reports/docs/gansler_commission_report_final_report_20071031.pdf.

39. Both DoD Instruction (DODI) 3020.41 and JP 4-10, *Operational Contract Support* (16 July 2014), require combatant commanders to plan for the proper integration of operational contract support in all military operations. In May 2010, Admiral M. G. Mullen, the CJCS, included instruction of operational contract support as a joint professional military education special area of emphasis. CJCS, "2010 Joint Professional Military Education (JPME) Special Areas of Interest (SAEs)," 17 May 2010, 7–9.

40. John A. Bonin, "Evolution of U.S. Army Service Component Commands/Theater Armies," unpublished US Army War College course material, 2 January 2015.

41. General Ray Odierno, memo for the CJCS entitled "Improving Army Joint Force Capability through Increased J7/Joint Coalition Warfighting Integration," 21 March 2013.

42. John M. McHugh and Raymond T. Odierno, "2013 Focus Areas," Department of the Army, 14 August 2013.

43. Headquarters, Department of the Army, *"The Evolving Role of the Corps and ASCCs,"* Slide 9-Time Phased Approach to Operational Headquarters Reductions, 25 September 2013.

44. James L. Terry, "US Army Central: Promoting Stability, Freedom of Movement," *Army* (October 2015), 184–185.

45. See S. J. Locklear, Memo for: Commanding General US Army Pacific; Commander, Marine Forces Pacific, subj: Initiating Directive-Designation of Theater Joint Force Land Component Commander and Deputy, 12 September 2013;

and Vincent K. Brooks, "U.S. Army Pacific: USARPAC Embraces Creativity, Transition," *Army* (October 2015), 114.

46. Darryl Williams, Charles C. Luke II, Matthew Koehler, and Christopher O. Bowers, "Operation United Assistance: The Initial Response—Setting the Conditions in Theater," *Military Review* (July–August 2015), 75; and Joint Staff, J7, Operation United Assistance (OUA) Study, Executive-Level Summary, Joint and Coalition Operational Analysis, 20 August 2015, slide 14. This study (Rec 3.7) also recommends the documentation of USARAFs CCP as the core of a rapid response joint headquarters.

47. Ben Hodges, "US Army Europe (Seventh Army): Allies Matter in a 'Strong Europe,'" *Army* (October 2015), 98–100; and discussions with Lieutenant Colonel Eric Hiu, USAREUR G5 Plans, 3 December 2015.

48. Barno, "Economy of Force," 246.

49. Timothy M. Bonds, Myron Hura, and Thomas-Durell Young, *Enhancing Army Joint Force Headquarters Capabilities* (Arlington, Va.: RAND Arroyo Center, 2010), xiv.

50. Hooker and Collins, eds., *Lessons Encountered*, 10.

51. Deployable Training Division, Joint Staff J7, "Insights and Best Practices Focus Paper, Forming a JTF HQ," September 2015, preface, 1.

52. Craig Berryman, "Unified Challenge 18.1 Seminar Executive Summary," Fort Leavenworth, Kansas, Department of the Army, Mission Command Battle Laboratory, 9 March 2018.

53. John M. McHugh and Raymond T. Odierno, "On the Posture of the United States Army," submitted to the Committees and Subcommittees of the United States Senate and the House of Representatives, 114th Cong., 1st sess., 5 March 2015, 4, https://www.army.mil/e2/rv5_downloads/aps/aps_2015.pdf.

54. The 2005 Congressional Budget Office study "Logistic Support to Deployed Forces" estimated the Army's total cost to perform a broad range of logistics functions associated with LOGCAP Task Order 59 in OIF using the organic force structure would have been up to 90 percent higher than contracted support provided by the LOGCAP contractor.

15

Integrating the Components
The Army National Guard within the Total Army
Jon Middaugh

America's wars have a habit of lasting longer than planners and politicians initially forecast. Often the conflicts also take on a different character than predicted. With those historical trends in mind, it seems wise to structure US military organizations to meet the possibility of fighting a longer and quite possibly different kind of conflict than the United States might have anticipated. Based mostly on research of developments since 2001, this chapter discusses factors that have assisted or inhibited the Army National Guard's ability to work with the Regular Army and provide strategic landpower capability, capacity, and flexibility for meeting the almost inevitable surprises of the future.[1]

In particular, the essay argues that closely integrating the components can produce an overall organization with more diverse skills for fighting across the range of military operations. Integrating also makes the Army more affordable for the nation and provides the all-volunteer organization with the flexibility needed to appeal to today's more fluid society. Other important advantages of maintaining a strong Reserve Component include its capacity for quickly delivering homeland security capability—whether for natural or manmade disasters—and the social connection it provides between the military and "Main Street" America. Such a connection provides our nation's landpower with the staying power and versatility to adjust to the fluxes of war.

Declining Budgets and Increased Integration, Early 1990s to 2001

The significant drop in US defense spending levels following the pullout of most troops from Iraq in 2011 rekindled memories of the period a quarter-century earlier when the Cold War ended and the military endured tremendous cuts associated with a supposed "peace dividend."[2] Although the shrinking budgets that corresponded with the collapse of the West's biggest rival, the Soviet Union, contributed to an intercomponent fight for resources, the Regular Army and Army National Guard nevertheless began participating together in multiple "peacekeeping" efforts throughout the world. But operations in Somalia and elsewhere proved more complex and enduring than political leaders originally envisioned. To help stabilize the Balkans, for example, the Clinton administration in 1995 initially projected a one-year commitment of US forces to implement the Dayton Peace Process. The quest for stability required additional time and manpower, however, and thus the originally named Operation Joint Endeavor extended ultimately to a nine-year commitment that prompted the Army to incorporate more Guard units into the task organization.[3]

For the first time since the Vietnam War, the Guard in 1997 deployed an infantry company to an operation. Virginia's Charlie Company, 3rd Battalion, 116th Infantry, completed its security mission effectively, but its radios were incompatible with those of adjacent Regular Army units and might have proved problematic had local Balkan tensions flared. Likewise, the Virginians' mobilization experience revealed significant shortcomings within the components' processes used to man, equip, and train a unit for its mission.[4]

The 49th Armored Division reached an integration milestone in early 2000 when it deployed from Texas to Bosnia. Its nearly eight-month peace-keeping mission as the lead element in Stabilization Force 7 marked the first time since the Korean War that a National Guard division headquarters had deployed overseas. Perhaps as significant, it was also the first time since Korea that a Guard division had commanded an active subordinate unit, which came from the 3rd Armored Cavalry Regiment.[5] The 49th Division's preparation benefitted from teaming with the 1st Cavalry Division, located nearby in Fort Hood, Texas, which assisted with predeployment training.[6] In Bosnia, the 49th leveraged its unit members' civilian skills to execute a complex mission while having far fewer troops than previous rotations and suffering no casualties. Its division engineer happened to be the assistant director of the Water Utilities Department in Dallas. Accustomed to working with competing interests on his hometown city council, Colonel Larry N. Patterson offered negotiation and technical guidance to nudge forward the process of revitalizing a key water system in theater.[7] The increased cooperation that Guard and Regular units practiced in Bosnia, as well as in support of a Multinational Force and Observers mission in the Sinai Desert, began to approach the Total Force ideal and former Army Chief of Staff General Dennis J. Reimer's call for "one team, one fight."[8] Following the 49th Division's return, the Army scheduled Guard divisions to fill six of its next seven command elements in Bosnia.[9] Some fifteen thousand guardsmen deployed to the Balkans, Sinai, Persian Gulf, or Haiti from 1994 through 2000.[10]

These deployments proved successful for the US Army and the nation. They provided operational relief for Regular Army units facing repeated overseas assignments despite being in an ostensible peacetime environment. In addition, the deployments gave invaluable experience to the Guard units going overseas and critical practice for the mobilization entities and processes that typically atrophy between wars. "The great thing was that the experience I had in Bosnia and all the things I got to do in a slow rhythm to deploy a unit overseas and back was such a huge help," noted one National Guard battalion executive officer whose unit, the 1st Battalion, 193rd Infantry, received an alert for Iraq shortly after it had returned from Bosnia in mid-2002. "It was almost like a trial run before the big game."[11] The Guard and Regular Army units working together on peacekeeping missions in the Balkans and elsewhere also gained valuable experience that could reduce tensions and stereotypes that often grow when organizations have limited exposure to each other. In summary, the use of guardsmen for overseas deployments fulfilled US landpower objectives for stabilizing regions, gave national military leaders more latitude for employing Regular Army units in other locations, and provided Guard leaders and mobilization stations with invaluable experience mobilizing.[12]

Operation Iraqi Freedom and Operation Enduring Freedom

The planners of Operation Iraqi Freedom (OIF) assigned the major ground combat objectives to Regular Army, Marine Corps, and United Kingdom units, with Army Guard maneuver units initially cast to play a minor supporting role. Guard infantry companies primarily were to execute security or "force protection" assignments in Iraq, Kuwait, or elsewhere in the region. These units' initial mobilization orders therefore authorized only incomplete portions of the parent infantry battalion's personnel and equipment authorizations in nonstandard configurations, usually without their Delta Company, mortars, or fire support teams, and sometimes without the Headquarters and Headquarters Company element. Presumably the planners thought the war would end quickly, but the enemy disabused the coalition of that notion rather quickly. By the summer of 2003, the 3rd Battalion, 124th Infantry, of the Florida Army National Guard, reconfigured but still without its Delta Company, mortars, or fire support team, joined the 1st Brigade, 1st Armored Division, in central Baghdad. With the war taking on a different shape than planners had envisioned, the Florida guardsmen began conducting cordon and searches, patrols, and other classic infantry missions that were assigned to the "Ready First" Brigade.[13]

Conforming to the pattern for most US wars, OIF lasted much longer and took on a different form than planners imagined. It required more land-power and for a longer time. In July 2003, North Carolina's 30th Armored Brigade therefore received its alert to ready for mobilization. By the follow-ing spring, the 30th as well as Arkansas's 39th Infantry Brigade and Wash-ington's 81st Armored Brigade had entered central Iraq just as Sunni and Shi'a insurgencies dramatically intensified. By the summer of 2004, New York's 42nd Infantry Division mobilized, and in early 2005 it relieved the 1st Infantry Division of command and control in Multi-National Division-North Central. After directing US efforts to bring stability and hold elections there, the New Yorkers handed their responsibilities to the 101st Airborne Division. The 42nd's deployment corresponded with the peak of the Guard's contribution to the maneuver fight.

The summer of 2005 saw eight Guard brigades serving, with some being "battle space owners" and others completing convoy security or theater secu-rity assignments.[14] One, Pennsylvania's 2nd Brigade, 28th Infantry, operated jointly with the marines in the Multinational Forces-West sector. Represent-ing nearly half the Army's combat power in Iraq at the time, the guardsmen's execution of the landpower mission allowed Regular Army brigade and divi-sional units refitting back home the time to complete modular transforma-tion. Many of the Guard brigades would see a second deployment between 2008 and 2010, although only the 30th Heavy Brigade Combat Team would serve as a battle space owner both times. Until 2007, most of the Guard brigades mobilized for about eighteen months in a Title 10 status (in other words, federally activated). However, the 1st Brigade, 34th Infantry, had served on active duty for a total of twenty-two months when it finished its assignment during the peak of the 2007 Iraqi Surge.[15] The war placed a heavy burden on the soldiers of Regular Army units that repeatedly deployed, but one can only surmise how many more divorces and suicides they would have had without the Guard maneuver brigades and other reservists' service.[16]

Guard units also executed combat support and service support roles dur-ing the entirety of OIF. Engineer, military police, and transportation units served throughout the theater. Like the rest of the military, they adjusted to the ubiquitous threat of Improvised Explosive Devices (IEDs) on a battle-field that partially blurred the traditional conception of combat and non-combat roles. These Guard units typically operated particularly well in the human domain, where they could exploit their range of civilian expertise to gain an operational advantage. In 2003, for example, one of the 4th Infantry Division's organic units operating in Diyala, the 588th Engineer Battalion, had command and control of Army National Guard engineer and military police units, as well as of Regular and Army Reserve units. The 588th's commander, Lieutenant Colonel William G. Adamson, leveraged the civilian skills that reservists brought with them and that were not commonly found in his organic companies from Fort Hood. One prominent example Lieutenant Colonel Adamson noted was the effort of an Army National Guard engineer lieutenant who proved instrumental in preserving Diyala's water supply, which was less than a week from running out. After many others had failed to find a means of delivering sufficient potable water for the province, Lieutenant Robert Small, whose civilian work was at a water processing plant in the Great Lakes region, assessed the situation and then worked with Iraqi engineers to get water flowing to the people.[17]

Guardsmen in maneuver units also regularly applied the skills they brought from their careers. Major Michael Lins, a staff officer in the 1st Brigade, 34th Infantry Division, which served in Iraq from early 2006 through mid-2007, was a mechanical engineer in the civilian world. After an Explosively Formed Projectile (EFP) killed one of the "Red Bulls" Brigade soldiers early in the deployment, Major Lins analyzed the blast effects and recommended a different maneuvering method for the vehicles in convoys. The brigade's units encountered several more serious IED blasts, but none caused a fatality.[18] In 2009–2010, Oregon's 41st Infantry Brigade also was conducting convoy security operations in Iraq. The brigade's senior NCO in the operations cell was Sergeant Major Ted Carlson, who had worked seventeen years as a driver for FedEx. After assessing the routes the brigade was running, he determined that they could be routed more efficiently and safely by applying principles he had learned at work.[19]

Similar examples of guardsmen applying their civilian skills occurred in Operation Enduring Freedom (OEF). One of the more well-known efforts centered on agricultural development teams, which typically used farmers from units in traditionally agricultural states, such as Nebraska or Missouri. During my own experience in an engineer battalion in Regional Command (RC) East in 2011, I regularly noted guardsmen translating civilian expertise to the military mission. One of our horizontal engineer companies included among its officers a licensed professional engineer who worked for his state's department of transportation, one lieutenant with a master's degree in construction management from Stanford and employed by a major construction firm, and a recent UC Berkeley civil engineer. The company commander for one of our vertical engineer companies, meanwhile, worked as a manager in a nuclear power plant in Nebraska. Moreover, while we mostly employed our battalion chaplain to counsel and minister to soldiers, we took advantage of his professional engineer certification. As a full-time civil engineer in the city of Salem, Oregon, the chaplain proved quite capable of assessing the road-worthiness of a bridge in eastern Afghanistan.

The guardsmen's skills applied as much to the interpersonal demands of the human domain as to technical problems. With their experience as state troopers, chiefs of police, businessmen, lawyers, or college administrators, Guard leaders from the company through the brigade or divisional level operated familiarly and effectively among local populations. One Regular Army MP battalion commander, tasked with rebuilding Baghdad's civilian police presence in 2003 after it had evaporated following the initial invasion, observed: "When you look back at the police stations that . . . got rebuilt . . . correctly, it was those National Guard companies . . . that set the standard. They had the experience. They were the cops and DEA agents that had been serving in those positions for 10, 15, 20 years . . . they were as good or better than any company I'd ever been around."[20]

Many of the Guard's field grade and general officers had extensive civilian experience back home interacting with town councils, managing large budgets, and focusing a town's energy on priority projects. In Iraq they applied these understandings to move along civilian reconstruction projects that would tie local Iraqis more strongly to the coalition's objectives.[21]

Compared to their Regular Army counterparts, reservists and their leaders may have been more accustomed to dealing with civilians, but they also were less experienced, and thus typically less effective, with their early efforts navigating some of the Army's new command and control equipment and processes or logistics systems. It is unlikely that many Army National Guard brigade or divisional leaders and staffs would on short notice have been able to direct their maneuver units as effectively as the 3rd Infantry or 101st Airborne Divisions did in the spring of 2003. The ability to coordinate rapid moving maneuver units and respond quickly to the dynamics of the battlefield requires more practice than many Guard leaders had at the time. When the 42nd Infantry Division mobilized, it needed to supplement its staff with Regular Army officers to complete some of the specialized tasks of a divisional staff. Especially early in OEF and OIF, it was also apparent that guardsmen were less comfortable with the systems for coordinating movements of troops and equipment into theater.[22] Army National Guard lieutenants frequently have less experience overseeing maintenance systems because much of the day-to-day maintenance activity in nondeployed Guard units is managed by a small number of full-time technicians. Thus, mobilizing Guard units benefitted from additional training they received from Regular Army logistics officers on how to leverage "026" reports and other essential maintenance documents.[23] It is important both to capitalize on the strengths of the Guard and to address and provide support for its weaknesses.

Organizational Culture

The positive impact of integrating the Army components suggest the potential gain that can come from bringing together people within organizations that at one time were segregated within the nation. America's schools, sports leagues, commercial establishments, and much else within society have benefitted from doing away with boundaries that through the middle decades of the twentieth century formally or informally excluded groups based on perceived limitations or differences. It is true that the military has a unique charge to protect the nation, and personnel or organizational changes must not fundamentally compromise its ability to do so. Certain opponents of integration within the military—whether integration of African Americans, women, or homosexuals—therefore have made arguments that incorporating the new members would fundamentally alter the ability to get the job done. However, all the military services have essentially been able to maintain a similar level of readiness as they integrated these cohorts into the broader family. Integration must be done sensibly, and there is a point when relying too much on a reserve force will run an excessive risk. But the contributions of guardsmen in different types of conflict, from WWI through OIF, show that their contributions are genuine. And along with the operational dividends, integrating the components would, as it has with other groups of citizens noted above, yield various sociocultural returns that will be discussed below.

Cultural biases within an organization can impede cohesion and teamwork. As a young enlisted soldier in the Regular Army of the late 1980s, I viewed the occasional guardsmen I encountered as less competent members of the overall team. Their longer hair, less crisp uniforms, and inferior equipment informed my (and some of my Fort Hood colleagues') views of the capability of the "weekend warriors." Conversely, in my subsequent quarter-century of service in the National Guard I observed certain guardsmen who viewed their Regular Army brethren as elitists who could not make it in the real world. It was common for guardsmen to have a "chip on their soldier" for real or perceived slights they received from members of the Regular Army. At times, I heard fellow guardsmen state they were treated as outcasts because they received what in their minds were harder or less glamorous tasks, although often their Regular Army brethren also had completed similar assignments. And even a decade and a half after 9/11, I am reminded of my own early career perceptions when I occasionally hear Regular Army members question the willingness or capability of guardsmen to fight. Such antagonistic or disrespectful attitudes from both components typically hinder teamwork.

On the other hand, deploying together can help bring about mutual respect, especially when leaders emphasize working as one team. Oregon guardsmen who served in Iraq in 2003 as part of the 101st Airborne Division appreciated Major General David H. Petraeus's comments that he saw only US soldiers rather than Regular Army or Guard members. Two years later the leaders of Arkansas's 39th Infantry Combat Team were similarly impressed by Major General Peter W. Chiarelli's insistence on mutual respect and equivalent performance expectations for all units serving as part of the 1st Cavalry Division in Baghdad.[24] As the executive officer for Oregon's 1249th Engineer Battalion in Afghanistan in 2011, I talked with a Regular Army company maintenance sergeant whose unit fell under our National Guard-led task force. According to the sergeant, guardsmen had provided the best support his route clearance unit had ever received. These comments simply reflected the battalion leadership's unequivocal commitment to all units' successful accomplishment of their missions. As Army components worked together in the decade and a half following 9/11, the experience occasionally prompted soldiers from one component to reaffirm their own negative opinion of the other. However, my research and observations suggest that quality leadership can go a long way in bringing out the best in each unit.

While the institution ought to strive to be "one Army," is it also still fair and appropriate to accept that Reserve and Regular Components typically do have some cultural differences? Regular Army enlisted soldiers usually are a bit younger than their Guard counterparts. Regulars transfer into new units more frequently, while Army National Guard sergeants can spend ten to twenty or more years working their way up within the same company or battalion. Regular units usually look more polished. In Afghanistan, for example, it was my observation that our Regular Army brethren typically practiced more for the few ceremonial events we executed together and thus looked a bit sharper with their drill and ceremony movements. Regular units have a broader cross-section of America represented within their ranks, while Guard units mostly reflect the rural or urban makeups of the American locales that surround them. On the other hand, guardsmen typically bring more of the country's productive skills into their units. As contractors, retail clerks, teachers, sheriffs, information technology specialists, mechanics, store managers, and much more, guardsmen, like the large democratic armies of WWI and WWII, are predisposed to bring "American ingenuity" to the battlefield. These skills, practiced by individuals and units used to accomplishing much with limited resources and time, can translate into innovative approaches.

Guard units not on active duty have far less time to practice together and thus typically perform more poorly than their Regular counterparts when completing the first iterations of complex collective training tasks. Regular troops also have more dedicated time for physical fitness training, including remediation efforts. But a number of elements, some intangible and some more resource dependent, can help to improve fairly quickly the initially weaker levels of collective training proficiency or physical fitness. Veteran NCOs, whose years within their Guard units allow them to know the strengths, weaknesses, tendencies, and potential of their soldiers, understand how to prioritize training efforts to focus on the most essential tasks. Regular Army transplants into the Guard, meanwhile, can instantly leverage their years of proficiency to raise understanding within their units. More resource-dependent solutions include money for procuring comparable equipment and for attending schools and training center rotations.

How might the above observations, if they fairly describe the cultural relationship between the two components, inform the discussion of integration? They suggest that leaders in both components must be able to assess the strengths and weaknesses of a particular unit and to avoid ascribing an opinion based mostly on preconceived biases. Leaders will recognize that the amounts of training time and familiarity with equipment are critical variables for any unit, and that an inexperienced unit with quality leaders can make great strides with a moderate amount of focused training opportunities. When leaders are open to seeing all soldiers as potential contributors to the same landpower team, then it helps subordinates to work together more effectively.[25] Besides leadership techniques, however, changing select structural elements also can promote more seamless integration of Regulars and reservists.

Suggestions for Integrating the Components

The Army's overall personnel system should be integrated so that soldiers can transfer between components with little or no administrative friction. At the beginning of the Iraq War, many Reserve Component soldiers experienced a long string of pay problems. For over a decade the Pentagon attempted to develop DIMHRS (Defense Integrated Military Human Resources System), but in 2010 Secretary of Defense Robert Gates cancelled the expensive and unsuccessful effort.[26] There have been some improvements, such as iPERMS (Interactive Personal Electronic Records Management System), but soldiers who transfer from one of the Army's components still encounter many incongruities between the Army, Army Reserve, and Army National Guard record-keeping approaches. A truly integrated personnel system would help retain talent across the Army at a time when individuals tend to shift jobs more than they did a generation or two ago. Complementing this idea is a retirement system that encourages "a continuum of service" and that would facilitate being able to move between components without encountering significant administrative obstacles.[27]

Indeed, cross-component exposure should be encouraged. Many Army Guard leaders have at least a few years of experience in the Regular Army. Often this includes attendance at the resident officer basic and advanced courses, and some bring the leadership habits that are ingrained when completing the Ranger course and serving in a Ranger unit. If we structure and employ the overall force so that Guard and Reserve units have adequate training and a meaningful purpose, then dedicated individuals with excellent training from the Regular Army who may not want to serve for twenty or more years will be more attracted to joining the Guard.[28]

One way to increase Regular Army awareness of quality Guard units is by aligning Guard and Regular units so they can train together. In the 1980s and 1990s there were many variations of this theme, including "Roundout" and "Roundup" brigades. Guard leaders who participated in such structures said their units benefitted from this training relationship.[29] There are likely other ways that deserve consideration. For example, it should be possible at times to allow a Guard maneuver battalion to join an active brigade preparing for and then executing a rotation at a Combat Training Center (CTC).[30] It also makes sense to try a few different parallel approaches to see what works depending on various geographical alignments between Regular and Guard units.

Even easier than aligning units would be allowing select Guard officers to be occasionally assigned as Regular Army company executive officers, battalion intelligence officers (S2s), or logistics officers (S4s). In a similar fashion, allow some Regular officers to serve as a commander or executive officer in a National Guard battalion, which would position that officer to have a mentoring role for many company-grade officers. When a Regular Army officer commanded one of the North Carolina Army National Guard's maneuver battalions in the early 2000s, he left a strong and positive impression on a good number of traditional Guard officers.[31]

Having the Regular Army integrated with the combat power in the Guard would presumably allow us to leverage the overall Army budget in multiple ways. Guard units could help save by having training sets that regionally aligned units share at training depots. Such savings within the operating force could then be channeled into the generating force so that Regular and Reserve Component soldiers alike would have more trainers at quality schools. Having an appropriately balanced portfolio of Regular and Guard maneuver brigades could also presumably lessen the demand on attendance at CTCs because a Guard unit would not be expected to train there as frequently as its Regular counterpart.

There are at least three additional ways that a strong Guard contributes significantly to national security and enhances the nation's ability to employ landpower effectively. First, the Guard's State Partnership Program adds to America's ability to engage regional allies or partners in key parts of the world, such as Southeast Asia, Africa, and Eastern Europe. Such partnerships can provide important political and military ties should it become necessary to deploy larger numbers of soldiers on the ground. Second, the Guard offers unmatched capability to respond to manmade or natural threats to the homeland. For example, guardsmen played a vital role in the hours, days, and weeks after 9/11. When Hurricane Katrina struck in late August 2005, the Army National Guard rapidly sent over forty thousand soldiers to assist in the Gulf region even while it had multiple brigades deployed overseas. This capability for on-demand response to threats throughout the homeland, meanwhile, comes at but a fraction of the Regular Army cost.[32] Finally, guardsmen can help display and thus communicate, at least partially, the importance of landpower to the nation as a whole. According to former Secretary of Defense William J. Perry and others, there is a wide gap of understanding between the American public and the American military.[33] With locations in about three thousand communities throughout the country, guardsmen provide one of the most ubiquitous military connections to society.

Regular Army brigades and divisions are needed for providing presence or an immediate punch if necessary for conventional warfare. Their number occasionally will require adjustment according to the threat. But if history is any guide, it makes sense to maintain an operationally relevant Guard that can deploy within a few months, because the country almost always has time to increase readiness before a maximum force is needed. In September 1940, fifteen months prior to Pearl Harbor, the country had instituted a draft in anticipation of conflict. As the military generated and deployed its combat power during Operation Desert Shield beginning in August 1990, over six months passed before the ground campaign of Operation Desert Storm began in February 1991. Prior to OIF, the national command authorities also had many months to accelerate readiness prior to initiating hostilities in March 2003. Given 90–120 days of preparation time, a typical Guard battalion or brigade should be able to adequately supplement its Regular Army counterpart in a maneuver operation.

For less kinetic actions that might require a large or at least extended landpower presence, the Guard soldiers' daily exposure to working with civilian populations and Guard units' effective performance in the Balkans, Sinai, and elsewhere suggest that it makes good sense to use them alongside or in rotation with active units. The Guard can be highly effective as an organization that allows the Army to extend its investment in training and experience in quality people who, either as individuals or in response to their spouse's wishes, simply may want to enter the civilian world after five or eight years instead of twenty. When these professionals enter the Guard, they then can better strengthen the connection between general society and the military. Having such connections might make a difference in congressional and public support for landpower the next time a war lasts longer than expected.

Notes

1. This paper focuses mainly on the connection between the Army National Guard and the Regular Army. Although the Army National Guard and Army Reserve together comprise the Reserve Component and share much in common, they also have some important differences. Among the latter are the differences in force structure, with the Army National Guard having the Reserve Component's maneuver brigades. The Guard and Reserve also have different roles with regard to domestic operations, and each uses some different administrative systems. For this paper, Guard, Army Guard, Army National Guard, and National Guard may be used interchangeably, although the National Guard also includes the Air National Guard.

2. Maurice R. Greenberg, "Trends in U.S. Military Spending," *Council on Foreign Relations* (15 July 2014), https://www.cfr.org/report/trends-us-military-spending.

3. R. Cody Phillips, *Bosnia-Herzegovina: The U.S. Army's Role in Peace Enforcement Operations, 1995–2004* (Washington, DC: US Army Center of Military History, 2005). In 1996, Operation Joint Endeavor was renamed Operation Joint Guard, which in 1998 became Operation Joint Forge.

4. Michael D. Doubler, *Civilian in Peace, Soldier in War: The Army National Guard, 1636–2000* (Lawrence, Kans.: Univ. of Kansas Press, 2003), 352–357; Steve Rader et al., *Mobilizing an Infantry Company: The Experience of Calling Up C/3-116th Infantry (Virginia Army National Guard) for Operation JOINT GUARD* (McLean, Va.: Science Applications International Corporation, 1998).

5. Kristin Patterson, "Bosnia Mission Catapults Texas Guard into Limelight," *National Guard* 52, no. 10 (October 1998), 28–29.

6. Center for Army Lessons Learned (CALL), "After Action Report SFOR-7: Citizen-Soldiers in Bosnia," Historians files, US Army Center of Military History.

7. Steven Lee Meyers, "National Guard Unit Adds Dimension to a Peacekeeper Role," *New York Times,* 18 June 2000.

8. General Reimer was CSA from 1995 to 1999.

9. National Guard Bureau, *Annual Review of the Chief 2001* (Arlington, Va.: National Guard Bureau), 44.

10. Doubler, *Civilian in Peace, Soldier in War,* 357.

11. Interview, Major Allen Skinner with Colonel Ronald Westfall, Combat Studies Institute, Fort Leavenworth, Kansas, 28 December 2010.

12. Phillips, *Bosnia-Herzegovina,* 38–41; Doubler, *Civilian in Peace, Soldier in War,* 352–357.

13. Lieutenant Colonel Thad Hill, "A Letter from Iraq; Army Guard Colonel Writes Home," *The On Guard* 32, no. 6 (June 2003), 3; Peter R. Mansoor, *Baghdad at Sunrise, A Brigade Commander's War in Iraq* (New Haven, Conn.: Yale Univ. Press, 2008), 70–71.

14. The eight maneuver brigades were the 278th Armored Cavalry Regiment (Tennessee), 256th Infantry Brigade (Louisiana), 48th Infantry Brigade (Georgia), 2nd Brigade, 28th Infantry Division (Pennsylvania), 56th Brigade, 36th Infantry Division (Texas), 29th Infantry Brigade (Hawaii), 116th Cavalry Brigade (Idaho), and 155th Armored Brigade (Mississippi). In addition, the 197th Field Artillery (New Hampshire) completed a security mission in MND-SE.

15. In 2007, Secretary of Defense Robert Gates issued a directive that called for total Title 10 mobilization periods of one year or less. These typically included from four to twelve weeks of time at a mobilization station depending on the type and size of the unit.

16. Gregg Zoroya, "More Army Guard, Reserve Soldiers Committing Suicide," *USA Today* online, 20 January 2011, https://usatoday30.usatoday.com/news/military/2011-01-20-suicides20_ST_N.htm. National Guard suicide statistics climbed particularly high in 2010, with 101 "confirmed or suspected" suicides that year, as opposed to 48 in 2009. For the Regular Army, 156 were reported in 2010 and 162 in 2009.

17. Interview, SFC Marc A. Mantini with Lieutenant Colonel William G. Adamson, 14 April 2004; telephonic interview, Lieutenant Colonel Jon S. Middaugh, with Major Robert D. Small, 24 February 2003.

18. Telephonic interview, Lieutenant Colonel Jon S. Middaugh with Colonel Eric D. Kerska (Ret.), 13 August 2015.

19. "Civilian Skills Prove Useful in Iraq Convoy Route Clearance," *Oregon Sentinel* 8, no. 3 (March 2010), 4; interview, Lieutenant Colonel Jon S. Middaugh with Major General Dan Hokanson, Salem, Oregon, 17 April 15.

20. Mark R. Depue, *Patrolling Baghdad: A Military Police Company and the War in Iraq* (Lawrence: Univ. of Kansas Press, 2007), 60–82.

21. Interview, Lieutenant Colonel Jon S. Middaugh with Brigadier General

Danny H. Hickman (Ret.), Wilmington, N.C., 21 July 2014; Staff Sergeant Jessie Rae Johnson with Master Sergeant John J. Schwartz, Logistical Supply Area Adder, Iraq, 23 June 2007; interview, Staff Sergeant Jessie Rae Johnson with Lieutenant Colonel Paul Zimmerman, Logistical Supply Area Adder, Iraq, 11 September 2006; interview, Staff Sergeant Jessie Rae Johnson with Major Jacob D. Kulzer, Logistical Supply Area Adder, Iraq, 19 June 2007.

22. Charles H. Briscoe et al., *Weapon of Choice: U.S. Army Special Forces in Afghanistan* (Fort Leavenworth, Kans.: Combat Studies Institute), 216–218, 371–373. A contributing factor for the ARNG's Special Forces mobilizing for the early period of OEF was that they wanted to deploy and therefore were reluctant to appear unwilling when the mobilization process seemed problematic or unclear.

23. Interview, Lieutenant Colonel Jon S. Middaugh with Colonel Darryl Daniels, Camp Robinson, Arkansas, 16 September 2014.

24. Marcus Allen Williams, "We're All One Army, Says General," *Oregon Sentinel* 1, no. 3 (winter 2003), 4; John R. Bruning, *The Devil's Sandbox: With the 2nd Battalion, 162nd Infantry at War in Iraq* (St. Paul, Minn.: Zenith Press, 2006), 34.

25. Ibid.; interview, Lieutenant Colonel Jon S. Middaugh with Major General Gregory Lusk, Raleigh, N.C., 23 July 2014; interview, Lieutenant Colonel Jon S. Middaugh with Major General Ronald S. Chastain (Ret.), Little Rock, Arkansas, 16 September 2014.

26. Tom Philpott, "Military Update: DIMHRS Program Dumped as a Disaster," *Stars and Stripes* online, 10 February 2010, https://www.stripes.com/opinion/military-update-dimhrs-program-dumped-as-a-disaster-1.99558#.WUbfC2jyvIU.

27. The military's "Blended Retirement System," set to be implemented in 2018, may complement soldiers' ability to move more seamlessly between components during their career. In addition, the Integrated Personnel and Pay System (IPPS-A) is designed to streamline the processing of paperwork across the three components.

28. Interview, Lieutenant Colonel Jon S. Middaugh with Major General Raymond F. Rees (Ret.), Arlington, Va., 17 December 2014; interview, Lieutenant Colonel Jon S. Middaugh with Brigadier General Ivan E. Denton, Arlington, Va., 19 March 2015; interview, Lieutenant Colonel Jon S. Middaugh with Brigadier General Ivan E. Denton, Arlington, Va., 19 March 2015; and interview, Lieutenant Colonel Jon S. Middaugh with Command Sergeant Major Brunk W. Conley, Fort McNair, DC, 4 December 2014.

29. Interview, Lieutenant Colonel Jon S. Middaugh with Brigadier General Danny Hickman (Ret.), Wilmington, N.C., 21 July 2014; interview, Lieutenant Colonel Jon S. Middaugh with Major General Gregory Lusk, Raleigh, N.C., 23 July 2014.

30. Combat Training Centers (CTCs), such as the National Training Center in Fort Irwin, California, and the Joint Readiness Training Center in Fort Polk, Louisiana, have large training areas and dedicated opposition forces (OPFOR) that provide tough, realistic training to the units that rotate in for several weeks to face them.

31. Interview, Lieutenant Colonel Jon S. Middaugh with Major Shane M. Evans, Fayetteville, N.C., 22 July 2014.

32. Rick Morrison, "Reserve Component Costs: A Relook," *Parameters* 44, no. 1 (spring 2014): 107–111. Estimated cost comparisons for different components in the Army are contentious and vary depending on a number of factors, including type of unit and anticipated deployment cycles. In general, Army National Guard units' personnel costs when not deployed are significantly lower, but upon mobilization they begin to approach those of the Regular Army. Overall costs for mobilizing units, especially those with large amounts of equipment, begin to approximate those of Regular Army units during the preparation for, execution of, and recovery from a deployment.

33. William J. Perry, "Foreword," xiii–xix, and Robert L. Goldich, "American Military Culture from Colony to Empire," 79–109, in *The American Military*, ed. David M. Kennedy (New York: Oxford Univ. Press, 2013).

PART V

Landpower's Influence on Society

16

Landpower and Humanitarian Assistance/Disaster Relief

Charles Luke, Chris Bowers, and Alex Willard

In the contemporary environment, strategic landpower's effectiveness rests on responsiveness and on a unique ability to resolve policymakers' most pressing security challenges. Sea and airpower advocates often point out that land forces' track record as a force of strategic decision since 9/11 is mediocre at best, particularly in direct combat roles. However, it is the land force component of the joint and interagency team that has provided the United States with decisive military interventions in noncombat operations over the past twenty years. Three case studies that demonstrate the potential decisiveness of strategic landpower during Humanitarian Assistance and Disaster Relief (HA/DR) missions are Operation United Assistance (OUA), the effort to curb the spread of Ebola in Liberia; Operation Unified Response (OUR), the military portion of relief efforts following the 2010 Haiti earthquake; and Operation Damayan, the US military response to Typhoon Haiyan in the Philippines.

HA/DR is the most "JIM" (Joint, Interagency, and Multinational) type of operation in which the US military takes part. During these operations, military forces support the US Agency for International Development (USAID) and work alongside multinational partners and nongovernmental organizations (NGOs). HA/DR operations are normally executed under short-notice expeditionary conditions that present the most challenging aspects of US military operations other than combat itself. These missions showcase American military capabilities around the world and communicate the value of strong partnerships with the United States. Finally, because HA/DR involves solving problems that have become top policy priorities for policymakers, it constitutes a decisive application of military power—particularly landpower.

Strategic Decision

The often-cited Clausewitz quote "War is simply the continuation of political intercourse with the addition of other means" applies as much to humanitarian assistance as it does to a kinetic operation, although he very clearly had traditional combat in mind.[1] As the American political consciousness is biased toward rapid, technologically enabled "wins," the value of military intervention in humanitarian assistance or other-than-combat engagements is often lost. But as President Barack Obama mentioned in his first visit to the Philippines following Typhoon Haiyan in 2013, nations assist their strategic partners for altruistic, practical, and political reasons regardless of the nature of the military response.[2]

Thucydides's *History of the Peloponnesian War* posits that fear, honor, and interest spur states into battle.[3] These same forces drive states to commit precious military resources to assist with sudden and unpredicted humanitarian disasters. Fear and honor are quintessentially human emotions; writ large on a state policy apparatus, they reflect that the decision makers themselves are human beings. These policymakers frequently view matters of fear and honor with the same importance as more tangible interests, such as economic opportunity or territorial integrity. Indeed, in a republic like the United States, the perceived fear and honor of the voting public often looms largest in policymakers' minds.[4]

Disasters often occur that so strongly appeal to voters' sense of fear or honor that for a time it supersedes policymakers' agendas and becomes a national political priority. Although political sound-bites never bluntly say so, the real desire among policymakers is for the disaster to recede from public awareness, which allows them to quickly return to more routine affairs. These same policymakers also wish to reap personal political benefits for successful leadership and action in a crisis, and national benefits such as a burnished reputation on the international stage.[5]

In addition to national strategic documents like the National Security Strategy, reviewing speeches, statements, and weekly addresses can spotlight the president's evolving policy priorities.[6] During the Obama administration, these revealed scores of engagements focused on disaster relief, as each event suddenly emerged on the world's stage.[7] Each of these is a communication opportunity the president is choosing to expend on a foreign tragedy rather than more enduring domestic and foreign policy issues. Presidential weekly addresses, in particular, are focused on strategic messaging to the American people and are an indicator of current policy priorities. They are broadcast via YouTube, radio, podcast, and the White House website. They generate fairly substantial viewership—the most viewed was the address First Lady Michelle Obama delivered about the Chibok girls kidnapping in 2014.[8]

The United States prioritized relief efforts in Haiti over other national security priorities and contributed over $1 billion as well as the organizational and military resources of a Joint Task Force (JTF). The presidential weekly addresses for two weeks after the earthquake remained focused, however, on domestic issues.[9] Similarly, the United States provided over $86 million in aid, as well as substantial military and civilian agency assistance, in the wake of Typhoon Haiyan in 2013, but a narrative of relief remained absent from subsequent presidential weekly address.[10]

On the other hand, Ebola became such a strategic priority in October 2014 that it monopolized the presidential weekly address two weeks in a row, on 18 and 25 October. It is notable that the president deviated from critical domestic political efforts, like job creation initiatives and minimum wage hikes, for half a month just prior to elections. This strongly indicates the extent to which Ebola emerged as a top-tier strategic issue for the US government.[11]

When such unforeseen disasters do occur, US politicians feel compelled to devote resources to what is at once an intrusive strategic problem and a potential policy windfall. The US military, as the single largest player within the interagency team, has routinely delivered strategic-level solutions in these situations. As these disasters predominantly occur on land, it is the US Army that steps into the role of enabling a rapid, decisive application of landpower to the emerging political problem. Clausewitz indicates this in his so-called secondary trinity. In it, the critical relationship exists between the "rational" government policymakers, the "passionate" populace, and the military, the latter of which will grapple with chance and uncertainty to execute the policy decision that was made to reflect the peoples' fears and desires.[12] In this way, HA/DR is military strategy at its purest.

Touting the Army's core role in HA/DR success is not meant to undermine the entire JIM team's contributions, which are immense. However, only the Army has the capability to provide rapid, large-scale logistics, medical care, security, and (perhaps most importantly) robust command and control to oversee and synchronize efforts.[13] The Army's capability in this type of operation is uniquely responsive to the particular nature of modern policy imperatives in the digital age.

Three case studies from the past two decades showcase this contribution. While more traditional land combat operations during the same period proved to be inconclusive and costly at the strategic level, HA/DR operations in Haiti, the Philippines, and Liberia were strategically decisive. They provided regional stability, fostered JIM relationships, improved external views of the United States, and, most importantly, provided aid to nations in dire situations.[14]

Haiti Earthquake, 2010: Immediate Landpower Response

On Tuesday, 12 January 2010, a magnitude 7.0 earthquake struck Haiti west of the capital of Port-au-Prince. Over the next month, the earthquake killed 100,000–316,000 Haitians and left several million homeless. Haiti is among the world's poorest states, hobbled by a long legacy of corruption and violence. Compounding this, the initial earthquake destroyed many Haitian government and NGO buildings, and killed several key leaders, including the head of the United Nations Stabilization Mission in Haiti (MINUS-TAH), Hédi Annabi. This crippled whatever initial response Haiti could have mounted on its own.[15]

Within hours of the earthquake, President Barack Obama pledged US support and directed USAID to lead a "whole of government" response. USAID established a response management team through its Office of US Foreign Disaster Assistance (OFDA). The US response to the 2010 Haiti earthquake was the largest HA/DR operation the US military ever conducted and the largest international humanitarian response to a natural disaster.[16]

The DoD Response

The DoD sent a warning order to USSOUTHCOM to prepare for HA/DR operations, and on 14 January the CJCS issued an order authorizing US military operations as part of disaster relief in Haiti. By coincidence, the USSOUTHCOM deputy commander, Lieutenant General Ken Keen, was in Port-au-Prince visiting US Ambassador Kenneth Merten when the earthquake struck. The physical presence of a general officer was an enormous boon to US responsiveness, just as it was in Liberia in 2014. Ambassador Merten and Keen immediately formed an impromptu communications node, relaying information between the Haitian and US governments.[17]

In addition to the requirements for life sustaining necessities, thousands of Haitians remained trapped in rubble and only had a short time to live. Any delay in US response would risk both lives and negative outcry from both domestic and international audiences. The almost complete destruction of Haiti's infrastructure made a quick response difficult, but it reinforced the demand for the US military's expeditionary logistics, medical, engineering, communications, and mission command capabilities.[18]

Lieutenant General Keen chose speed over the doctrinal process for determining requirements and tailoring forces.[19] Rather than rely on a humanitarian assistance support team from USSOUTHCOM to conduct an initial assessment, he relied on his judgment as JTF commander to request and prioritize capabilities. Keen directly coordinated with the US general officers who commanded units and capabilities the mission required, like the XVIII Airborne Corps command post, a Special Tactics squadron from the Air Force Special Operation Command 1st Special Operations Wing, and the Global Response Force from the 2nd Brigade, 82nd Airborne Division.[20]

The DoD order for Operation Unified Response unfolded in five phases.[21] Phase I focused on immediately saving lives, evacuating US citizens, and assessing more substantial requirements for follow-on phases. US military personnel strength peaked in this phase at about twenty-two thousand service members, and the JTF headquarters was co-located with the US embassy. Phase II focused on relief operations from early February until April and then shifted from immediate rescue efforts to providing care for internally displaced persons (IDPs). Phase III transitioned responsibility back to the Haitian government and included engineering efforts to improve sanitation in IDP camps.[22] The JTF deliberately omitted Phase IV (stabilization) due to MINUSTAH's success at keeping the peace and enforcing security, and instead transitioned directly to Phase V, recovery. By late May, the JTF reduced its force structure, prepared to hand over all relief duties to the Haitian government, and then declared the mission complete on 1 June 2010.[23] During those five months, the military was a guiding force in America's responsive, successful efforts to relieve suffering in Haiti.[24]

Responsiveness Brings Success

Some critical aspects of JTF-Haiti's success seem to be downright lucky, but may not be as random as they appear. Lieutenant General Keen's presence in Port-au-Prince at the time of the earthquake enabled rapid and clear communication with USSOUTHCOM and saved valuable time. Though this may appear serendipitous, general officers from Geographic Combatant Commands (GCC) and their service components spend a significant portion of their time "forward" in their areas of responsibility. Additionally, while Keen's decades-long friendship with the UN's MINUSTAH commander, Major General Floriano Peixoto Vieira Neto of Brazil, may also seem like fate, the military cultivates long-term relationships with partner nation military officers for just this reason. It was made possible through years of partner nation exchanges.[25] In fact, Captains Keen and Floriano Peixoto met in 1984 during a one-month Army-to-Army exchange in Brazil, and they maintained their friendship over the next twenty-six years through multiple professional assignments.[26]

The widespread dissemination of publicly releasable information also enabled rapid response, clear coordination, and operation success.[27] The JTF used the All Partners Access Network (APAN), an Internet-based coordination tool, to foster collaboration among a wide range of departments and organizations.[28] This was one of the most successful "lessons learned" from Operation Unified Response, and it was deliberately replicated four years later during Operation United Assistance.

USSOUTHCOM's ability to conduct a rapid staff reorganization, transitioning from a counter-narcotics model to a traditional model, resulted in the sound conduct of HA/DR operations.[29] The need for a senior staff to rapidly restructure itself occurred again in Liberia with OUA and the headquarters for US Army Africa. Army doctrine, namely *Field Manual 3-94: Theater Army, Corps, and Division Operations,* changed to reflect solutions to this challenge, but the lack of resources and institutional priorities has slowed implementation.

Finally, USSOUTHCOM had previously developed enduring positive relationships with USAID and OFDA because it usually responds to more HA/DR missions than other GCC's.[30] These organizational relationships were invaluable in Haiti, where the JTF commander personally coordinated resources.[31] Similarly, the personal relationships that Joint Forces Command-OUA (JFC-OUA) commanders Major Generals Darryl Williams and Gary Volesky built in Liberia were significant enablers for success.

Operation Unified Response was decisive in part because it assisted the Haitian people while minimally impacting other national policy priorities, delivering a political win. Within forty-eight hours of a devastating earthquake, large segments of the entire joint force, including the Global Response Force, an aircraft carrier, special operations forces, search-and-rescue reservists, and a wide array of other capabilities were in transit or already in Haiti.[32] The response's readiness, training, and perception benefits were readily apparent and no American lives were lost. The ability of HA/DR operations to hone readiness by exercising capabilities while exposing shortfalls, and to affect larger strategic issues of assuring partners and deterrence, was also displayed in Operation Damayan, America's response to Typhoon Haiyan.

Typhoon Haiyan: Landpower as Part of a Joint Solution

"The United States will continue to lead global efforts with capable allies and partners to assure access to and use of the global commons, both by strengthening international norms of responsible behavior and by maintaining relevant and interoperable military capabilities."[33] On 8 November 2013, Super Typhoon Haiyan made landfall in the central Philippines as a Category 5 storm. The Joint Typhoon Warning Center located at Pearl Harbor, Hawaii, considers Super Typhoon Haiyan (known in the Philippines as Yolanda) one of strongest cyclones on record for the North Pacific Basin. It struck an ill-prepared and environmentally fragile coastal region.[34] This monumental storm displaced 4.1 million people, killed 6,200, and affected 16 million people on the islands of Leyte, Luzon, and the Eastern Visayas.[35] As the powerful typhoon quickly overwhelmed the Philippine government, the US military and USAID responded by swiftly dispatching warships, helicopters, and personnel to assist in relief efforts.

The US government assigned USAID as the lead federal agency, with the DoD in a supporting role. On 9 November 2013, the Philippine government issued a request for humanitarian assistance to the US government. In response, USPACOM directed Marine Corps Forces Pacific to lead military relief operations in the Philippines, with the 3rd Marine Expeditionary Brigade serving as the mission command element on the ground. USPACOM also ordered the deployment of the USS *George Washington* and elements of Carrier Strike Group 5 to the Philippines.[36] USAID personnel had deployed to Manila prior to the emergency, and the MEB established the command operations center at the Villamor Air Base in Manila. USPACOM also deployed a JTF Augmentation Cell (DJTFAC), which proved a critical asset to the monumental task of organizing US, Philippine, and international response teams. The DJTFAC was instrumental in influencing the AFP and UN to an operational battle rhythm, armed with practiced joint expertise. The DJTFAC also leveraged the Joint Special Operations Task Force-Philippines capabilities already on Mindanao. The US military presence totaled more than 13,400 personnel, sixty-six aircraft, and twelve naval vessels. USPACOM's review of the typhoon response highlighted six lessons learned:

1. Immediate Request for Assistance and Forward Deployed Assets Saved Lives
2. Centralized Planning and Decentralized Execution Facilitated Coordination
3. Direct Planning to Ensure Command and Control is Part of COA Analysis
4. Establishment of the International Coordination Team (ICT) Syn-

chronized Effective International Support Through All Phases of
USPACOM Operations
5. Preplanned Scalable Force Packages Optimize HADR Support[37]

While the tactical planning centered on direct humanitarian assistance
support, the operational and strategic planning included transitional planning between military JTF structures that occurred throughout the response.
This included the establishment of JTF-505 on 16 November 2013 and its
disestablishment on 1 December. The transition between military headquarters and civilian agencies is critical and does not happen without extensive
planning. In humanitarian assistance response, the difficulties are multiplied,
as the military often is not the lead agency, yet is coordinating execution
and organization transitions with civilian and multinational counterparts.
While most of the response to the typhoon involved air and sea capabilities,
it was the landpower joint headquarters that was uniquely capable of leveraging interagency assets in humanitarian assistance.[38]

Although the value of military intervention in operations other than war
is often lost, the robust US response provides a clear case for the joint force
as a means of response to a natural disaster. As President Obama mentioned
in his first visit to the Philippines following the 2013 typhoon, "That's what
friends do for each other."[39] The typhoon and the joint response exposed the
military weakness of a major military partner in the Pacific region, expanded
access to the Pacific rim in an atmosphere of growing competition with
China, and exercised and validated the JTF command structure.

Typhoon Haiyan further highlighted the weakness of the Philippine
government and military in glaring terms. A "nuanced understanding of the
Philippines' structure of governance suggests how a combination of a weak
state, long time neglect of basic infrastructure, and chronic underinvestment
in the armed forces explains the absence of a swift and effective response to
the crisis."[40] Even as a long-term partner in the Global War on Terrorism, the
overall weakness of the Armed Forces of the Philippines in executing HA/DR
surprised many, including the Filipinos. Many of the Philippine military's
vessels and aircraft turned into paper ghosts and hangar queens.

Beyond any altruistic motivation, given the expansion of China in the
neighboring seas, the substantial US ability to project forces served a wide
range of military objectives.[41] The month before the typhoon landed, US
and Philippine security agreement negotiations stalled. For the United States,
an expanded agreement would mean a boost to President Obama's strategic
"Pivot to the Pacific," but Philippine critics were wary that an expanded military access agreement would undermine Philippine sovereignty. However, the

robust US response shifted Filipino public and official opinion and led the US and Philippine governments to sign the 2014 Enhanced Defense Cooperation Agreement.[42] Utilizing land forces in this HA/DR situation improved international relations and enabled strategic access for the US military.

Humanitarian assistance operations as a strategic tool have numerous benefits beyond the altruistic, as the US response to Typhoon Haiyan demonstrated. While bolstering good perceptions of the United States from a landpower perspective, humanitarian assistance operations identify partner nations' capabilities, expand military access, and exercise US joint headquarters. While often unpredictable for planning, humanitarian assistance operations are a key component to joint force contingency planning at the combatant command and national strategic levels.

Operation United Assistance: Countering "Fearbola"

In the summer of 2014, Ebola's rapid expansion in Liberia, Sierra Leonne, and Guinea spread fear within the United States and forced the Obama administration to treat it as a national security issue. Initial attempts to halt the virus failed, despite courageous efforts from NGOs and West African governments. In September, the US Centers for Disease Control and Prevention (CDC) predicted the worldwide infection of up to 1.4 million people by the beginning of 2015.[43] President Obama's decision to assist Liberia through a "whole of government" effort, but especially landpower, proved to be the turning point that quelled the disease from spreading across West Africa.

The US Response

On 16 September 2014, in a speech at the CDC, President Obama declared that Ebola was "spiraling out of control . . . and if the outbreak is not stopped now, we could be looking at hundreds of thousands of people infected . . . it's a potential threat to global security."[44] In light of these circumstances, the president directed a whole of government response, with USAID in its usual role as the lead federal agency, and he directed the DoD to support USAID. In August and September, USAFRICOM issued a series of warning orders directing component commands to begin planning. US Army Africa (USARAF) and the 101st Airborne Division began detailed contingency planning to support USAID and contain Ebola in Liberia, and focused energy across four primary "lines of effort": command and control, logistics, engineering, and medical support.[45]

The USARAF commanding general and a small force arrived in Liberia on the same day as President Obama's speech at the CDC and immediately began establishing the theater for operations. As more USARAF personnel arrived throughout September, they initiated contracts to provide for servicemen, received personnel and material, negotiated spaces for future bases, ordered supplies, and completed missions assigned from USAID. Meanwhile, in Italy, USARAF planners issued orders communicating with higher DoD headquarters and the 101st Airborne Division to ensure all organizations understood the ever-changing situation.[46]

On 25 October 2014, USARAF transferred command authority of the JFC, only thirty days after the secretary of defense officially designated the 101st Division for the mission, and the 101st immediately began expanding the footprint USARAF had established.[47] The 101st Division headquarters flexibly adapted to the HA/DR mission and quickly determined needed resources. But more importantly, it provided continuity for the mission.

While USAID was undoubtedly the lead federal agency, its Disaster Assistance Response Team members rotated in and out of Liberia every four to six weeks; many NGO personnel did the same. The JFC was the de facto organization in Liberia providing continuity for the whole of government mission. Leveraging best practices learned in Haiti four years earlier, it fostered communication by establishing and maintaining an unclassified, collaborative website, using APAN, the same network used during the Haiti earthquake response. This increased information flow and reduced confusion while allowing non-DoD organizations to readily access information about all of the JFC's ongoing efforts.[48]

The number of newly infected victims slowly decreased in October, and by March 2015 reports of new infections dwindled to zero.[49] On 9 May 2015 the World Health Organization declared Liberia officially free of Ebola.[50] Operation United Assistance built and logistically supported Ebola treatment units and the Monrovia Medical Unit, trained more than 1,500 health care workers, increased the speed of Ebola detection, helped the Liberian government target the virus's spread, and provided continuity among the US government interagency team. However, the true utility of this mission came from its unintended consequences.[51]

Strategic Result

OUA put 2,650 uniformed military personnel (about 95 percent Army) on six bases with hundreds of pieces of equipment offloaded at the country's primary airport and seaport.[52] Soldiers drove around the capital and flew deep into the country's interior while performing their tasks. Many pundits now point out, with the benefit of hindsight, that Ebola infection rates in Liberia were beginning to decline just before the first US personnel arrived as part of OUA and that the disease was firmly in decline well before most of the Ebola treatment units were constructed. But this ignores the almost universal perception in the near-panic environment of September and October 2014, when nearly all authorities were predicting catastrophic consequences without a robust US or international response. It also ignores the intangible but critical reassurance that the mere presence of US landpower provided to beleaguered Liberians during that time. Inside Liberia, American soldiers served as a living, breathing strategic messaging campaign against Ebola to the people deep in the country's interior who lacked educational and medical access. Outside Liberia, the military embodied the US government's resolve to defeat Ebola, showcased its dedication to provide assistance in disaster response situations, and eased domestic fears about the spread of the disease.

Captain Bill Zarwolo was born in Liberia, moved to America at a young age, and joined the US Army after college. He deployed with the 101st to OUA and visited his family in Liberia on multiple occasions. His perspective into both the worldview of Liberians and the mind-set of a US Army officer is truly unique. He believes Liberians were not initially receptive to information about Ebola because eating monkey meat, ritualistically burying their dead, and trusting local medicine men were all part of their culture. However, once they saw US military personnel and doctors in Liberia, they realized Ebola was real and understood they needed to be more receptive to health education.[53]

When Captain Zarwolo left Liberia in March 2015, his family told him they were sad to see the Americans leave. Other governmental and nongovernmental organizations remained in Liberia for many months after the military departed, but his family believed the presence of the US Army and America's commitment were synonymous. Organizations like Médecins Sans Frontières, the CDC, and USAID had worked courageously in Liberia even as Ebola spread with increasing speed over the summer and early fall of 2014, but it appears that the US Army's response to the Ebola pandemic proved strategically decisive because of the implicit informational power inherent in the deployment of 2,650 soldiers.

In the policy world, perception is reality. America experienced the media-driven "Fearbola" epidemic, an ill-informed but visceral dread of an Ebola outbreak in the United States that gripped the country, hijacking the Obama administration's election season messaging for half a month while the president and the rest of the US government grappled with this illusory foe. The continuing good news of progress from OUA—clinics built, international assistance pouring in, and most importantly Ebola infection rates plummeting—certainly played a role in quelling Fearbola and enabling policymakers to refocus on their primary agendas. Once again, US land forces were the key enabler granting strategic utility and success to policymakers. The Ebola response was so effective that in December 2014 President Obama decided not to name a replacement for "Ebola Czar" Ron Klain, who had been appointed during the "Fearbola" period.[54]

Beyond domestic concerns, destabilization in Liberia and West Africa influences US security strategy both directly and indirectly. A destabilized Liberian government has historically led to widespread violence and eventual American military intervention. Al Qa'ida and Boko Haram, active in other parts of West Africa, have a propensity for exploiting weakened political environments. Indirectly, a lack of American resolve for intervention sends negative messages during increasing competition with China in Africa. While perhaps impossible to tie directly to US military intervention in Liberia, the American military has since gained unprecedented access to Nigeria, Cameroon, and other neighboring countries with a now shared security view.

Conclusion

As demonstrated in Liberia, Haiti, and the Philippines, US land forces can provide a rapid capability for decisive intervention in HA/DR operations worldwide. Within a matter of hours, land forces as part of a joint and interagency team can begin to resolve emerging problems that threaten to dominate policymakers' priorities. This is particularly true when it comes to certain capabilities, such as engineering, common user logistics, medical support ashore, and especially mission command and headquarters command and control. In no other type of operation is the US military able so successfully to provide policymakers with strategic solutions.

The effects of successful HA/DR go beyond the country and forces directly involved. Results of rapid and effective HA/DR response include strengthened alliances, improved US regional and global standing, and a visible reminder to potential adversaries of the robustness of America's expeditionary military capabilities. The United States' rapid projection of significant power into the southwest Pacific when the nearby Chinese could not offer the same served as a strong example of US strength. HA/DR operations also offer a unique opportunity to exercise joint, interagency, and multinational interoperability in a noncombat environment.

Related to this, disasters and the response operations allowed analysis of both US and partner capabilities, and also demonstrated shortfalls of both, ultimately strengthening those forces for the future. This occurred in Haiti, when USSOUTHCOM had to radically alter its organization mid-operation, as well as in the Philippines, where host military capacity and government coordination capabilities were exposed as fundamentally lacking. Both operations in Haiti and Liberia demonstrated the value of a deployable service component headquarters with regional familiarity.

Landpower successes in HA/DR operations across the globe provided a strategic narrative of success despite the entanglement of long-term combat missions in the Middle East. They showcased the power projection, logistics, engineering, rotary wing aviation, and mission command capabilities inherent in US landpower and broadened individual and organizational experience beyond large-scale combat operations at a fraction of the risk. It is critical that HA/DR remain a robustly resourced core competency for American land forces, as well as for the larger joint force.

Notes

1. Carl von Clausewitz, *On War*, trans. Michael Howard and Peter Paret (Princeton, N.J.: Princeton Univ. Press, 1976), 87.

2. President Barack Obama, "Joint Press Conference," remarks by President Obama and President Benigno Aquino III of the Philippines in a joint press conference, Manilla, Philippines, 28 April 2014.

3. Thucydides, *The Landmark Thucydides: A Comprehensive Guide to the Peloponnesian War*, trans. and ed. Robert B. Strassler (New York: Free Press, 1996), 43.

4. According to the "selectorate theory" of Bruco Bueno de Mesquita and associates, the voting public decides whether or not to reelect a representative based on the representative's actions. Elected representatives' decisions on foreign policy issues directly lead to voters' responses to the decision and ultimately affect voters' choice to reelect the representative. Bruce Bueno de Mesquita, Alastair Smith, Randolph M. Siverson, and James D. Morrow. "An Institutional Explanation of the Democratic Peace," *American Political Science Review* 93, no. 4 (1999): 791–807. Reiter and Stam, Weeks, and Baum and Potter all explore the influence of public opinion on the decision for politicians to choose to go to war. They conclude that elected representatives are at least somewhat concerned with a war's outcome because of the potential negative public reaction (Reiter and Stam), that politicians associated with a losing war face increased risk of not being reelected (Weeks), and that the public will try to remove politicians with poor foreign policy records (Baum and Potter); Dan Reiter and Allan Stam, *Democracies at War* (Princeton, N.J.: Princeton Univ. Press, 2002); Jessica L. P. Weeks, *Dictators at War and Peace* (Ithaca, N.Y.: Cornell Univ. Press, 2014); Matthew Baum, and Philip B. K. Potter, *War and Democratic Constraint: How the Public Influences Foreign Policy* (Princeton, N.J.: Princeton Univ. Press, 2015).

5. This dynamic is clearly portrayed by Saundra Schneider in *Dealing with*

Disaster: Public Management in Crisis Situations (New York: Routledge, 2011), particularly 15.

6. The White House, "National Security Strategy," February 2015. This document specifically highlights efforts to "confront the acute challenges posed by . . . disease" and "stop the deadly spread of the Ebola virus."

7. The White House, https://www.whitehouse.gov/ (accessed 6 November 2015).

8. GovTrack Insider, "We Looked at Eight Years of the Republican Weekly Address," https://govtrackinsider.com/we-looked-at-eight-years-of-the-republican-weekly-address-5f4b3237674 (accessed 20 June 2017).

9. "Weekly Address: President Obama Vows to 'Collect Every Dime' of Taxpayer Funds that Helped Big Banks," The White House, Office of the Press Secretary, 16 January 2010, https://obamawhitehouse.archives.gov/the-press-office/weekly-address-president-obama-vows-collect-every-dime-taxpayer-funds-helped-big-ba (accessed 14 November 2018); and "Weekly Address: President Obama Vows to Continue Standing Up to the Special Interests on Behalf of the American People," The White House, Office of the Press Secretary, 23 January 2010, https://obamawhitehouse.archives.gov/the-press-office/weekly-address-president-obama-vows-continue-standing-special-interests-behalf-amer (accessed 14 November 2018).

10. President Obama did not mention Haiti once in his first Weekly Address following the 2010 earthquake. President Obama, "The President's Weekly Address," 16 January 2010, by Gerhard Peters and John T. Woolley, *The American Presidency Project,* http://www.presidency.ucsb.edu/ws/?pid=87398.

11. President Obama's weekly addresses on 18 and 25 October 2014 completely focused on messaging Ebola facts to the American public. The preceding weekly address (11 October) featured the president's case for raising the minimum wage, while the following weekly address (1 November) discussed the economic challenges of working women. President Obama's weekly addresses can be found at https://obamawhitehouse.archives.gov/briefing-room/weekly-address.

12. Clausewitz, *On War,* 89.

13. During President Obama's remarks on the Ebola outbreak at the Centers for Disease Control on 16 September 2014, he noted that "our forces are going to bring their expertise in command and control, in logistics, in engineering. And our DoD is better at that, our Armed Services are better at that than any organization on Earth."

14. Erik Brattberg, "The Case for US Military Response during International Disasters," http://thehill.com/blogs/congress-blog/foreign-policy/190954-the-case-for-us-military-response-during-international (accessed 17 March 2016).

15. P. K. Keen, Floriano Peixoto Vieira Neto, et al., "Relationships Matter: Humanitarian Assistance and Disaster Relief in Haiti," *Military Review* 90, no. 3 (May–June 2010): 91.

16. Gary Cecchine et al., "The U.S. Military Response to the 2010 Haiti Earthquake: Considerations for Army Leaders," (Santa Monica, Calif.: RAND Corporation, 2013), 43.

17. Ibid., 32.

18. Cecchine et al., "The U.S. Military Response to the 2010 Haiti Earthquake," xiv.

19. Lieutenant General Keen's inadvertent pre-positioning in Haiti, his personal relationship with the MINUSTAH commander, and the immediacy of the situation (Haitians trapped under building rubble) made this a unique, one-off situation where it made sense to ignore doctrinal methods to conduct HA/DR operations.

20. Department of the Army, *Command Post Organization and Operations, Army Training Publication 6-0.5* (Washington, DC: Department of the Army, March 2017). A command post is a unit headquarters where the commander and staff perform their activities. Commanders employ command posts to help control operations through continuity, planning, coordination, and synchronizing of the warfighting functions. Commanders organize their command posts flexibly to meet changing situations and requirements of different operations (1-1). The functions of a command post include: knowledge management, building and maintaining situational understanding, controlling and assessing operations, internal and external coordination, and various administrative tasks. Command post personnel, equipment, and facilities are arranged to facilitate coordination, exchange of information, and rapid decision making. A command post must effectively communicate with higher, subordinate, adjacent, supporting, and supported units and have the ability to move as required (1-8).

21. "Operation Unified Response: Support to Haiti Earthquake Relief 2010," SOUTHCOM, http://www.southcom.mil/newsroom/Pages/Operation-Unified-Response-Support-to-Haiti-Earthquake-Relief-2010.aspx (accessed 6 November 2015).

22. Cecchine et al., "The U.S. Military Response to the 2010 Haiti Earthquake," 40.

23. "Operation Unified Response: Support to Haiti Earthquake Relief 2010."

24. The Five Phase construct of Operational Planning is detailed in the Phasing section of Joint Publication 5-0. US Joint Chiefs of Staff, Joint Planning, *Joint Publication 5-0: Joint Planning* (Washington, DC: US Joint Chiefs of Staff, 11 August 2011). Cecchine et al. describe the phases of Operation Unified Response and accurately note that various military entities use somewhat different phase numbers and terminology to describe each phase. Cecchine et al., "The U.S. Military Response to the 2010 Haiti Earthquake," 37–43.

25. Keen et al., "Relationships Matter," 8.

26. Ibid., 4–5. The two officers had many relationship-building professional exchanges throughout their careers, including Captain Keen's one-month exchange in Brazil in 1984, Major Keen's graduating from the Brazilian Command and General Staff Course in 1987, Captain Floriano Peixoto's graduating from the US Army Infantry Captain's Career Course in 1988, Lieutenant Colonel Floriano Peixoto's teaching Portuguese at West Point in the mid-1990s, and both working together during Brigadier General Keen's time as the US Army South commander while Colonel Floriano Peixoto was in the Brazilian Army Staff G5 International Affairs Directorate.

27. Ibid., 9.

28. Cecchine et al., "The U.S. Military Response to the 2010 Haiti Earthquake," 46.

29. Ibid., 47.

30. Ibid., 51. The prevalence of hurricanes in the North Atlantic Ocean from June to November, combined with national and regional infrastructure challenges in the Caribbean and Central America, make SOUTHCOM's area of responsibility especially vulnerable to the effects of inclement weather.

31. Ibid., 34.

32. The Global Response Force (GRF) is a rapidly deployable force that is primarily composed of units from the 82nd Airborne Division, 18th Airborne Corps, and US Air Force mobility and strike platforms. General Martin Dempsey, the former CJCS, believed the GRF was a critical asset to ensure the United States' access anywhere in the world in a relatively short amount of time. The GRF is particularly useful strategic tool because it can quickly tailor itself and deploy for traditional direct action missions or HA/DR operations. Brigadier General Charles Flynn and Major Joshua Richardson, "Joint Operational Access and the Global Response Force," *Military Review* 93, no. 4 (July–August 2013): 38–44.

33. DoD, "Sustaining US Global Leadership: Priorities for 21st Century Defense," January 2012, 3, http://archive.defense.gov/news/Defense_Strategic_Guidance.pdf

34. Joint Typhoon Warning Center, "2013 Annual Cyclone Report," 15 February 2014, 3, http://www.usno.navy.mil/NOOC/nmfc-ph/RSS/jtwc/atcr/2013atcr.pdf (accessed 18 November 2015).

35. USAID, "Typhoon Yolanda/Haiyan Fact Sheet #21," 18 February 2014, https://www.usaid.gov/sites/default/files/documents/1866/philippines_ty_fs21_02-18-2014.pdf

36. Lieutenant Colonel Thomas Parker, Major Sean Carroll, Gregg Sanders, Lieutenant Colonel Jason King, and Imes Chiu, "An Inside Look into USPACOM Response to Super Typhoon Haiyan," Center for Excellence in Disaster Management and Humanitarian Assistance, February 2015, 7, http://ndupress.ndu.edu/JFQ/Joint-Force-Quarterly-82/Article/793262/the-us-pacific-command-response-to-super-typhoon-haiyan/.

37. Ibid., 7–10.

38. Ibid., 8–9.

39. Barack Obama, "US Philippine Joint Press Conference," The White House, 28 April 2014, https://www.whitehouse.gov/the-press-office/2014/04/28/remarks-president-obama-and-president-benigno-aquino-iii-philippines-joi (accessed 17 November 2015).

40. Richard Heydarian, "Philippines' Haiyan Tragedy: What Went Wrong?" *World Post,* 23 January 2014, http://www.huffingtonpost.com/richard-javad-heydarian/philippines-haiyan-typhoon-response_b_4283845.html (accessed 15 November 2015), 1.

41. Ibid., 1.

42. US Embassy in the Philippines, "Signing of Enhanced Defense Cooperation Agreement," US Embassy Manilla, 28 April 2014.

43. Lena Sun, Brady Dennis, and Joel Achenbach, "CDC: Ebola Could Infect 1.4 Million in Liberia and Sierra Leonne by End of January," *Washington Post*, 23 September 2014, https://www.washingtonpost.com/national/health-science/cdc-ebola-could-infect-14-million-in-west-africa-by-end-of-january-if-trends-continue/2014/09/23/fc260920-4317-11e4-9a15-137aa0153527_story.html?utm_term=.5b52529ab2c5.

44. Barack Obama, "Remarks by the President on Ebola," Centers for Disease Control, 16 September 2014.

45. Geographic Combatant Commands dedicate time and effort to contingency planning and preparation before crises occur so the command will be farther along in the planning process and better prepared to support partner nations in the event of a disaster. Geography and international relations affect the priority of these planning efforts. For instance, USSOUTHCOM spends effort on inclement weather and humanitarian assistance. USAFRICOM issued warning orders and key operational tasks based on presidential directives and initial planning considerations, not from any standing contingency plan to respond to an Ebola outbreak in West Africa.

46. Major General Darryl Williams, Lieutenant Colonel Matthew Koehler, Lieutenant Colonel Charles Luke, and Major Chris Bowers, "Operation United Assistance: The Initial Response-Setting the Conditions in the Theater," *Military Review* 95, no. 4 (July–August 2015): 79–81.

47. First Lieutenant Peter Koerner, "101st Airborne Division Assumes Ebola Response Mission in Liberia," 27 October 2014, https://www.army.mil/article/137002.

48. Steve Goins, *101st Airborne Division (Air Assault) Operation United Assistance Initial Impressions Report,* Center for Army Lessons Learned, http://www.globalsecurity.org/military/library/report/call/call_16-05.pdf.

49. World Health Organization Statement, "The Ebola Outbreak in Liberia Is Over," WHO website, 9 May 2015, http://www.who.int/mediacentre/news/statements/2015/liberia-ends-ebola/en/.

50. Ibid.

51. Goins, "Initial Impressions," iv.

52. Ibid., 30.

53. Captain Bill Zarwolo, US Army, telephone interview by the author, 15 October 2015. David Heymann, a professor of infectious disease epidemiology at the London School of Hygiene and Tropical Medicine and a veteran of several Ebola outbreak responses, reiterated the importance of public health education. He believes that "educating populations is the best way to prevent transmission in the community." Dick Thompson, "Ebola's Deadly Spread in Africa Driven by Public Health Failures, Cultural Beliefs," *National Geographic,* 2 July 2014, http://news.nationalgeographic.com/news/2014/07/140702-ebola-epidemic-fever-world-health-guinea

-sierra-leone-liberia/ (accessed 13 January 2017). The World Health Organization estimated that up to 80 percent of Ebola cases in West Africa were tied to traditional West African burying practices. World Health Organization, "Factors That Contributed to Undetected Spread of the Ebola Virus and Impeded Rapid Containment," January 2015, http://www.who.int/csr/disease/ebola/one-year-report/factors/en/ (accessed 13 January 2017).

54. Jennifer Harper, "Ebola Czar Ron Klain Already Planning to Exit the Obama Administration," *Washington Times,* 8 December 2014, http://www.washingtontimes.com/news/2014/dec/8/ebola-czar-ron-klain-already-planning-exit-obama-a/.

17

Willing and Qualified

Social and Cultural Considerations and the Generation of Landpower in the Global War on Terrorism

Jacqueline E. Whitt

The Army You Have

On 10 September 2001, the US military's force structure reflected a decade of post–Cold War personnel and manpower policies, shaped by the First Gulf War, global humanitarian and military interventions, and administrative decisions under Presidents George Herbert Walker Bush and William Jefferson Clinton. Trends toward more inclusive recruiting policies that had begun in the 1970s, with the inception of the all-volunteer force, continued; the services were actively recruiting a more diverse force to fill staffing requirements, and military pay and benefits and the promise of meritocratic promotions attracted women and racial and ethnic minorities to military service. Increased demographic diversity came at a cost, however, and concerns about gender integration led to the so-called "woman pause" of the 1980s.[1] Nevertheless, the "all-recruited" force was firmly in place by the end of Ronald Reagan's presidency. Although post–Cold War drawdowns aimed to reduce the overall active duty force by 25 percent between 1987 and 1997, the force's demographic diversity had increased (albeit unevenly) and seemed unlikely to return to pre-AVF levels of homogeneity.[2]

The military diversified even further after the terrorist attacks of 9/11 and in conjunction with the United States' landpower responses over the next fifteen years. These events created—perhaps unintentionally—political, social, and cultural space for significant changes in the composition and management of military force in the twenty-first century. Wartime personnel demands, the nature of the wars in Afghanistan and Iraq, and domestic politics all fundamentally changed the conversation about inclusivity in the armed forces, and eventually affected policies surrounding broad sociocultural issues in the military. These included socioeconomic status, ethnicity, gender, sexual orientation, and citizenship.

The United States went to war after 9/11 with the army it had, but that army has emerged (although not yet definitively on the other side) as quite a different force—one that looks more and more, or less and less, like the United States as a whole, depending on whom you ask and what you measure. These developments are politically coded: they represent either significant progress or dangerous social engineering, depending on the viewer's political position and analytical frame.[3] Sociocultural factors have become central to the recruitment, retention, training, and management of the all-volunteer force. Although shifts in policy and views of the ideal social and cultural makeup of military forces have largely been framed in terms of military effectiveness and military necessity, the consequences have been profoundly cultural as well. These policies have reaffirmed an explicit link between military service, civil rights, and citizenship.

Breaking the Army

Arguments about personnel and manpower policies emerged anew in the mid-2000s, when the DoD and its observers concluded that simultaneous wars in Afghanistan and Iraq, combined with overseas commitments in Europe and the Pacific, threatened to overstretch the military. Proponents of more inclusive policies argued that these policies would ease the apparent shortage of military personnel and were thus pragmatic responses to military requirements and conditions on the ground; opponents suggested that wartime was no time to introduce new policies whose effects were uncertain.

Both sides, however, agreed that the armed forces were in urgent need of willing and qualified service members—both new recruits and experienced troops. Actual counts of troop levels and requirements for the Global War on Terrorism (GWOT) vary by source.[4] The Congressional Research Service, using numbers from the Defense Manpower Data Center, estimates that in June 2001 roughly 28,000 US troops were deployed to USCENTCOM. In December 2008 there were 294,000, with approximately 181,000 deployed to Iraq and Afghanistan.[5] Public statements about the wars routinely used a boots-on-the-ground figure, which understated the total number of service members involved in an operation. Instead of the anticipated rapid drawdown within six months of the end of major combat operations in Iraq, troop requirements for Operation Iraqi Freedom (OIF) rose rapidly between 2003 and their peak in 2008. Operation Enduring Freedom (OEF) also required significant troop commitments.

As early as July 2003, Michael O'Hanlon, a fellow at Brookings, warned that the US Army was overstretched, with anticipated deployments putting on the Army a burden "roughly twice what is sustainable."[6] Jeffrey Record, a professor of history and strategy at the Air War College, wrote in December 2003 that "unanticipated US ground force requirements in postwar Iraq have stressed the US Army to the breaking point."[7] In 2004, journalist James Fallows noted that "the military's people, its equipment, its supplies and spare parts, its logistics systems, and all its other assets are under pressure they cannot sustain." Fallows concluded there was "no end to the emergency in sight" and that the situation, which had been "serious before the invasion of Iraq," was now "acute."[8] By 2007, forty-three of the Army's forty-four brigades had served at least one twelve-month tour in a combat zone.[9] The US Army missed its recruiting goals in 2005 for the first time since 1999. This shortfall was caused, in part, by a slowdown in enlistments driven by 9/11, by worsening news from Iraq and Afghanistan, and by a robust economy with low unemployment at home. The Associated Press reported on a Pentagon study warning that the Army was in "a race against time" and risked catastrophic institutional failure if the "ops tempo" was not slowed or other measures taken, such as expanding the force.[10] In July 2007, Lawrence Korb, a former assistant secretary of defense and a senior fellow at the Center for American Progress, testified before the House Armed Services Committee, where he quoted retired general officers Colin Powell and Barry McCaffrey, saying that the US Army was "broken."[11] The National Security Advisory Group at the Harvard Belfer Center produced a substantial report titled "The U.S. Military: Under Strain and at Risk" that echoed many of these conclusions.[12]

As the Army, in particular, struggled to meet its recruiting goals, leaders lowered accession standards and allowed for more conduct waivers to facilitate recruitment. The percentage of recruits who were high school graduates dropped (though it was still higher than in the population as a whole), and the number of "high-quality" recruits also declined, reaching a low point in 2007.[13] The Army insisted, officially, that it was not lowering standards, but was instead committed to looking at an individual's record and capabilities.[14] Then, in the rubble of the global financial crash in 2008 and the ensuing recession, alongside political promises that the wars in Iraq and Afghanistan would be winding down, military recruiting recovered and accession policies tightened back up.[15]

During this period, the landpower forces of the GWOT became less representative of the US population as a whole, increasingly hailing from specific parts of the country—namely the rural and suburban South and West. Whites were generally proportionally represented in the force, but Hispanics and Asians were generally underrepresented.[16] Analysts disagreed about the effects of socioeconomic status on military enlistment, though most concluded that low-income and middle-class households were overrepresented (the poorest quintile remained underrepresented, likely due to low educational attainment). The greatest proportional spike in post-9/11 enlistments, likely driven by a sense of patriotic duty, came from youth from the top quintile of household incomes.[17] Other analysts noted that the military was increasingly a "family business"; according to a 2013 US Army study, 80 percent of recruits had a "close family member" in the military and 25 percent had a military parent.[18]

In the midst of OIF and OEF, recruiting and retaining a landpower force that could execute both combat and nation-building missions was of utmost importance to senior policymakers, and this was the context in which discussions about who serves—and in what capacity and on what terms— took place. Decisions about recruiting, retention, and force structure were all related to the broad civil-military relationship in the United States and the question of whether (or to what extent) the military should be representative of the society it serves. Questions about pragmatism, representativeness, military necessity, and the American civil-military relationship were most acute when it came to policies regarding the integration of openly gay, lesbian, and bisexual (LGB) service members and women serving in combat.[19] Decisions made in the midst of war tended to be pragmatic ones that reflected the social, cultural, and economic realities of early twenty-first century America, and the language used in debates about these issues, as well as the eventual outcomes of these debates, demonstrated that military policy was driven by both concern for military effectiveness and readiness and by social, cultural, and political concerns.

Asking, Telling, and Serving: Lesbians, Gays, and Bisexuals in the American Military

Military service has been, in most times and in most places, a predominantly male endeavor and a key part of defining masculinity and manhood. In these single-gendered spaces, questions about sexuality are critically important. Norms and expectations have varied widely; while historians must take care when applying the modern idea of homosexuality to historical actors, it is clear that some members of military organizations across time and space have engaged in intimate behaviors that we might call homosocial, homosexual, or homoerotic.[20] In the United States military, service by openly homosexual individuals was formally banned only in 1945. Policies usually required the immediate discharge of a military member found to be homosexual or engaging in homosexual behavior.[21]

William Jefferson Clinton, the Democratic nominee for president in 1992 (and the eventual winner), pledged to change this policy and to enable LGB persons to serve openly in the military. Clinton's pledge met with substantial political resistance. The 1993 compromise (which went into effect in 1994) came to be known as the "Don't Ask, Don't Tell" (DADT) policy. According to the law, homosexuality was still banned in the military, but DADT changed how homosexuality would be policed and managed, essentially protecting closeted homosexual service members while still mandating discharge for openly gay service members. It was a compromise that suited almost no one. People across the political spectrum and within the military decried it as a fundamentally bad policy.[22]

Changes in public opinion enabled movement on the issue of DADT. According to Peter Singer, outright bans on service by homosexual people and policies such as DADT were fundamentally cultural and political decisions that were rooted in the prevailing public perception of gay people. Singer argues persuasively that in the years between 1993 and 2010 being gay became, quite simply, no big deal.[23] By 2010, 58 percent of Americans approved of allowing gay people to serve openly in the military; only 27 percent opposed it. Support was highest among Democrats, young people, and nonreligious groups, and it was lowest among people over sixty-five, self-identified conservative Republicans, and white evangelicals.[24]

While the broader social, cultural, and civil rights issues that the policy represented generally motivated advocates for repealing DADT, they pragmatically and politically emphasized military necessity—especially the armed forces' demonstrated need for qualified service members—as the primary reason the policy should be discarded. As Aaron Belkin, founder and executive director of the Palm Center, has argued, "in order for Congress to repeal DADT, political and military leaders, as well as the public at large, had to be convinced that allowing gay men and lesbians to serve openly would not harm the military."[25] Public opinion continued to shift toward repeal as the media publicized the honorable, willing service of gay and lesbian troops in the GWOT as well as DADT-related discharges of combat veterans and of military service members with specialized skills, such as language or medical training.[26] West Point graduate and Iraq War veteran Dan Choi became the public face for the repeal movement after he came out as gay on national television.[27] The fact that the number of DADT-related discharges decreased dramatically in the wake of 9/11 seemed to some observers to definitively indicate that the policy was homophobic and politically motivated, rather than based on military necessity or effectiveness.[28] Ultimately, the repeal of DADT occurred because of changes in public perceptions about homosexuality and a clear demonstration that military readiness, effectiveness, and cohesion could be maintained or strengthened by allowing open service by LGB individuals.

The repeal of DADT did not end discussions about sexual orientation, sexuality, and gender identity in the military, as the 2010 policy left in place the prohibition against transgender people in uniform. The push to move from LGB to LGBTQ (Lesbian, Gay, Bisexual, Transgender, and Queer) inclusion in the military continued. In 2016, the DoD moved swiftly to implement a policy allowing such service, revitalizing arguments about sex and gender in the US military.[29] The policy on transgender service members must take into account the complex relationship between sex, gender, and sexuality, and it also involves complicated questions about medical care. It differs from the debates about DADT and homosexuality because the total number of transgender people is far smaller than the total number of people who identify as gay, lesbian, or bisexual.[30] In real terms, such a policy is likely to have negligible effect on the generation of landpower in the coming years. Nevertheless, it is another important sociocultural conversation that can be traced, in part, to the political and military environment in the waning years of the wars in Iraq and Afghanistan.

Breaking the Camouflage Ceiling: Women in the American Military

Debates about the role of female service members in the twenty-first century military are, in many ways, more complex than the debates about sexual orientation because of the persistent questions about whether women can meet the physical requirements of combat. Nevertheless, the repeal of DADT offered several parallels and arguments for considering the full integration of women into the force.[31] In the era of the all-volunteer force, women's contributions to the staffing requirements of the military and to the defense of the nation have been unmistakable, but there were always limits on their service.[32]

In 1994, Congress replaced the "Risk Rule," which excluded women from serving in noncombatant positions that carried combat-level risks, with the "Direct Ground Combat Definition and Assignment Rule" (also known as the "Combat Exclusion Policy"), which prohibited women from being assigned to units below the brigade level whose primary mission was to engage in direct ground combat and stipulated four additional conditions under which women could be excluded from a position.[33] Throughout the 1990s, discussions about women in combat had remained academic, if impassioned.[34] But the unconventional nature of the wars in Iraq and Afghanistan, and the attendant overstretching of the forces' personnel resources, thrust the question of women's service in combat to the forefront of public debates about military personnel policies.

Observers' most common conclusion was that the Combat Exclusion Policy was difficult to apply in OEF and OIF, which blurred the lines between combat and noncombat assignments; maintenance and logistics units and military police, in particular, were difficult to place neatly in one category or the other.[35] Personal narratives from both men and women praised the grit, determination, smarts, and physical toughness of women serving in Iraq and Afghanistan. In fact, many accounts downplayed the significance of gender altogether, asserting that they had not noticed that a certain soldier was a woman, that female service members were actually categorized as other-than-female in comrades' minds, or that women—in uniform and with a little dirt on them—were hardly distinguishable from men.[36]

As combat operations in Iraq and Afghanistan changed, turning toward nation-building, stability operations, counterinsurgency operations, and counterterrorism missions, the Army and Marine Corps made pragmatic decisions about how to use women in the war zone. In both Iraq and Afghanistan, cultural and religious norms limited the range of interactions that male US troops could have with local women, so American and coalition women were employed to conduct searches, to train local women as law enforcement officers, and to accompany male (combat) forces on patrols or door-to-door sweeps in order to interact with local women. These women were not assigned to these units, only "attached" to them; over time, these programs became more regularized and formalized.

Two of these programs are of particular note. The Female Engagement Team (FET) program combined the Lioness Program (an effort to use female troops to conduct searches of women) and the Iraqi Women's Engagement Program (part of civil affairs work).[37] Other women were specifically sought out to serve with all-male special operations units, including Army Rangers and Navy SEALs. These efforts, known as Cultural Support Teams, required more rigorous selection and physical training of its female recruits, but filled many of the same expectations as FETs: women were to interact with local women and children during raids and missions, gather intelligence, and provide a stabilizing presence in the midst of chaos. The CST program gained some public notoriety with the publication of Gale Tzemach Lemmon's best-selling book, *Ashley's War*.[38] Both the FET program and the CST program (and the coverage of them) have been criticized from many sides. Feminist academics have pointed out the ways in which these programs essentialized gender and reinforced stereotypically feminine and masculine traits, while others have criticized the positive coverage given to such endeavors, questioning the efficiency, efficacy, and wisdom of placing women into combat situations.[39]

The fact that women were engaging in combat (and being injured, killed, or captured in combat) was brought to public attention when Iraqi forces captured Private First Class Jessica Lynch in an ambush during the Battle of Nasiriyah in March 2003. An initial report in the *Washington Post* portrayed Lynch as a hero who fought back against her attackers and captors, but both the Pentagon and Lynch dispute this version of events.[40] Lynch's capture and rescue sparked significant debate about the suitability and acceptability of placing women in (or even near) combat zones. Concern about female casualties, men's responses to female soldiers being captured or killed, and the possibility that servicewomen might be raped or assaulted if captured dominated these discussions. As Lynch's story fades into historical memory, several scholars have noted the ways that her femininity has been preserved and highlighted in narrations of the event: Lynch was not just a soldier, she was a *female* soldier, and she bore the weight of all that meant.[41]

Later in the war, the scandal at Abu Ghraib prison made another female soldier, Private First Class Lynndie England, the target of intense scrutiny, sparking more discussion about the expectations and behavior of women in war zones. PFC England was among the American soldiers charged with torturing and abusing Iraqi prisoners. According to Jennifer Lobasz, while liberal feminists used Lynch and England as examples demonstrating that "women as a group were neither less valiant nor more upstanding than men, and that connecting men with war and women with peace was no longer sustainable," these arguments were largely absent from media coverage, which instead used these two women to reinforce stereotypical and traditional gender roles, emphasizing Lynch's purported heroism and femininity and portraying England as ugly, masculinized, and "ruined."[42]

A different story about gender and war emerged out of Afghanistan, where Spartan conditions, extreme terrain, and near-constant fighting at remote combat outposts and even more remote firebases reified the idea of war as a peculiarly masculine undertaking. Sebastian Junger's account in *War* of a platoon's deployment in the Korengal Valley is instructive here. After identifying the diverse racial and ethnic makeup of the platoon, Junger emphasized the essential *maleness* they had in common: they were drug dealers, boxers, sons of soldiers—all men bored by civilian life. They crushed PT tests while hungover (or maybe still drunk). They flouted uniform regulations, and "toward the end of their tour they'd go through entire firefights in nothing but gym shorts and unlaced boots, cigarettes hanging out of their lips." And when they were not fighting insurgents, they fought each other—beatings and chokings were standard when someone joined or left the platoon, when it was someone's birthday, or just because they were bored. Junger contrasts this existence with that of the "Fobbits," who spent their entire deployments inside the wire at a forward operating base, such as the one at Bagram. One of the only women in the book (other than the wives, girlfriends, sisters, and mothers who signify sex and home) is a soldier from the 82nd Airborne who "was beside herself" and "screamed" at Junger for his appearance after returning from Korengal.[43]

In the United States, the debate about women in combat zones was lively in military, political, and media circles. The argument was generally framed as having two discrete sides: either all military roles should be open to women or the status quo should be maintained. Few seriously argued that women's participation in the military could be rolled back from current levels. Policymakers and military leaders undertook the Women in Service Review (WISR, 2011–2012) to consider seriously the issue of women in combat zones.[44] In January 2013, the DoD issued a memorandum eliminating the Direct Ground Combat Definition and Assignment Rule and directing the services to undertake a self-assessment of job requirements and qualifications. The services were to submit an implementation plan that would open all jobs to women by 1 January 2016, making requests for exemptions to this policy as necessary.[45] The services complied, beginning extensive studies, testing, and pilot programs.[46]

The most controversial study came from the US Marine Corps. Its widely publicized results suggested, fairly unequivocally, that all-male teams performed better at combat-related tasks than mixed-gender teams, and that women, even with additional training, were more prone to injury in combat conditions.[47] Other critiques came as the Army announced that two women were set to graduate from the elite Ranger School, with anonymous sources accusing the school's leaders of lowering standards to ensure that one of the women would graduate.[48]

In December 2015, as he summarized the results of the WISR review and announced the final DoD policy, Secretary of Defense Ashton Carter made it clear that the more inclusive policy had won the day, supported by manpower- and military necessity-driven arguments. He said, "Like our outstanding force of today, our force of the future must continue to benefit from the best people America has to offer. In the 21st century, that requires drawing strength from the broadest possible pool of talent. This includes women, because they make up over 50 percent of the American population. To succeed in our mission of national defense, we cannot afford to cut ourselves off from half the country's talents and skills. We have to take full advantage of every individual who can meet our standards." The service secretaries and chiefs from the US Army, Air Force, and Navy, as well as the commander of US Special Operations Command, put forward no career fields for exemption from the new requirements; the US Marine Corps requested some exemptions. Carter then confirmed the administration's decision to make all jobs open to qualified women by January 2016. No exemptions were granted.[49]

Since 2013, American military women have been recognized for a series of "firsts"—the first women graduated from Ranger School in August 2015; the first female lieutenants commissioned into the US Army's combat arms branches in April 2016; the first gender-integrated Infantry Officer Basic Course graduated in October 2016, the first enlisted women attended infantry school in early 2017; the first female Marine Corps officer graduated from the Armor Officer Basic Course in April 2017; and the first female officers graduated from the Marine Corps Field Artillery Course in May 2017. The first woman to graduate from the grueling Marine Infantry Officer Course did so in September 2017. While numbers of women graduating from Army schools have continued to rise, the Marine Corps numbers remain very low.

Rights, Citizenship, and Military Service

In addition to the political and pragmatic arguments to increase the generation of military landpower in the twenty-first century and to bring military policies into line with changing sociocultural norms and attitudes, the consequences of these policies for the broad civil-military relationship in the United States are also important. As the number of Americans who are both willing and qualified to serve has decreased and as the ideal of military service as a right for those who wish to serve has solidified, the exclusion of willing and qualified individuals from military service due to demographic characteristics or identities is now broadly (but not universally) understood as being antithetical to American values and ideals.[50] President Barack Obama articulated this idea in his 2010 State of the Union address: "I will work with Congress and our military to finally repeal the law that denies gay Americans the right to serve the country they love because of who they are."[51] This idea—that there is a right for qualified people to serve in the military—is not yet established in law or jurisprudence, but it represents a shift from the attitudes of the 1990s.[52] The 1993 DADT bill, for example, asserted, "There is no constitutional right to serve in the military."[53]

President Obama's reaffirmation of the essential connection between citizenship and military service—of service as both a duty and a right—harked back to a historical understanding of this relationship, and was an especially powerful statement in the era of the all-volunteer force, which recruited by emphasizing the instrumental and transactional nature of military service: its provision of benefits, attainment of skills, and possibility of professional advancement.[54] This connection between citizenship, military service, and civil rights had been made clear as early as 1863, in the Emancipation Proclamation, which, as Harvard president Drew Gilpin Faust reminded audiences in 2008, guaranteed slaves not only freedom, but also the right to military service in Union ranks.[55] Faust's venue added to the message, as she delivered it at Harvard's ROTC commissioning in 2008, three years before she presided over the official return of ROTC to Harvard's campus. Harvard and other elite American schools broke recruiting ties with the US military over the Vietnam War, and its conflict with ROTC continued in part because of the ban on open homosexual service.[56] Faust's speech signaled the university's position and her commitment to reengaging with the military should DADT be repealed.

In the post-9/11 era, the connection between citizenship, military service, and civil rights was equally clear for immigrants. Between 9/11 and 2016, nearly 110,000 service members were naturalized as US citizens via military service, which offers an expedited path to citizenship for resident aliens (green card holders).[57] Between 2008 and 2016, the US Army also opened up the Military Accessions Vital to the National Interest (MAVNI) program to allow select legal non-immigrant medical professionals and people with highly sought language capabilities to join the US Army and become naturalized citizens. The program was suspended in FY 2017 as the Army drafted new (and retroactive) protocols to account for security concerns about the program. Changes in policy also meant that green card holders could not enlist until security and background checks were complete (rather than simply being started), which delayed entry for some immigrants. The suspension resulted in more than one thousand recruits losing their legal immigration status, as many were in the United States on visas that would expire before their military accession could be completed.

Furthermore, these changes increased the waiting period for green card holders to become naturalized citizens to 180 days.[58] The integral connection between military service, citizenship, and civil rights has been no less important for women and LGBTQ people serving in the military. Representative Loretta Sanchez (D-CA) highlighted this rights-driven logic when she introduced HB-1928, titled the "Women's Fair and Equal Right to Military Service Act." Advocates for LGBTQ inclusion within the military initially framed their arguments in terms of citizenship and the right to military service by qualified individuals, although these arguments were less effective than pragmatic arguments about military effectiveness and readiness.[59]

Even during this historical moment of heated political debate about sociocultural issues within the military and rapid policy changes, the connection between citizenship, rights, duty, and military service holds fast.

Compare, for example, how public rhetoric often frames military veterans as deserving of societal obligations and reverence with how it frames military contractors or civilian interagency employees. There is a real difference in public attitudes toward these two groups, although both groups faced similar dangers and both were compensated for their work.[60] To be sure, this is not the only public narrative about veterans, and rhetoric that paints military service as a last-resort option for the economically disadvantaged or which suggests military veterans are unstable, psychopathic, and drug-dependent clearly work against the narrative of heroism and citizenship.[61] But these critiques are often coupled with a broader critique of the state and its obligations to service members and veterans—in this case, that the state has failed to adequately provide for those whom it asked (or coerced) to serve. In both instances, service members and veterans are central to the symbology and mythology of the state: systematic exclusion from full participation in this venerated group suggests a diminished identity as a citizen. Ronald Krebs concludes that even though the definition and semiotics of the "citizen-soldier" have changed in the twenty-first century, "wherever the link between service and citizenship is maintained, it lays the groundwork for claims-making."[62]

As the wars in Afghanistan and Iraq drew down, the US military, and particularly its landpower components, responded to significant shifts in military, cultural, and political attitudes toward the ideal social and cultural makeup of military forces. These shifts in policy have largely been framed in terms of military effectiveness and military necessity, but the consequences have been cultural as well. These policies have reaffirmed an explicit link between military service and citizenship and have opened the possibility of full participation in public life to a much broader constituency than was possible on 10 September 2001. Further discussions are sure to come as the United States navigates questions about religious accommodation, disability, mental health, past recreational drug use, family status, socioeconomic class, and other characteristics that may serve as discriminators or disqualifiers for military service.

Notes

1. Beth Bailey, "The All-Recruited Army," *America's Army: Making the All-Volunteer Force* (Cambridge, Mass.: Harvard Univ. Press, 2009), 172–197.

2. Albert H. Schroetel, "Military Personnel: End Strength, Separations, Transition Programs and Downsizing Strategy" (1993), cited in Maria C. Lytell et al., *Force Drawdowns and Demographic Diversity: Investigating the Impact of Force Reductions on the Demographic Diversity of the U.S. Military* (Santa Monica, Calif.: RAND Corporation, 2015), 13, https://www.rand.org/pubs/research_reports/RR1008.html. During this period, for example, representation of non-Hispanic black men decreased (primarily due to decreased enlisted accessions), while female participation rose from about 11 percent to about 15 percent. Lytell et al., *Force Drawdowns and Demographic Diversity*, 24–37.

3. Jacqueline E. Whitt and Elizabeth A. Perazzo, "The Military as Social Experiment: Challenging a Trope," *Parameters* 48, no. 2 (Summer 2018): 5–12.

4. For example, OEF, roughly synonymous with operations in Iraq, also included limited numbers of troops deployed to Djibouti, the Philippines, and Kyrgyzstan.

5. Amy Belasco, "Troop Levels in the Afghan and Iraq Wars, FY2001–FY2012: Cost and Other Potential Issues," Congressional Research Service R40682, 2 July 2009, 3–4, https://fas.org/sgp/crs/natsec/R40682.pdf.

6. Michael O'Hanlon, "Breaking the Army," Brookings, 3 July 2003, https://www.brookings.edu/opinions/breaking-the-army/.

7. Jeffrey Record, "Bounding the Global War on Terror" (Carlisle, Pa.: USAWC Strategic Studies Institute Press, 2003), 39, https://ssi.armywarcollege.edu/pdffiles/PUB207.pdf.

8. James Fallows, "The Hollow Army," *The Atlantic* (March 2004), https://www.theatlantic.com/magazine/archive/2004/03/the-hollow-army/302891/.

9. David R. Segal and Lawrence J. Korb, "Manning and Financing the All-Volunteer Force," in *Modern American Military*, ed. David M. Kennedy (New York: Oxford Univ. Press, 2013), 123.

10. Robert Burns, "Study: Army Stretched to Breaking Point," Associated Press, 24 January 2006.

11. Lawrence Korb, Testimony before House Armed Services Committee, 27 July 2007, https://cdn.americanprogress.org/wp-content/uploads/issues/2007/07/pdf/Korb_Testimony.pdf.

12. William Perry et al., "The U.S. Military: Under Strain and at Risk," National Security Advisory Group, Belfer Center, January 2006, http://www.belfercenter.org/sites/default/files/legacy/files/nsag_us_military_under_strain_january2006.pdf.

13. Fred Kaplan, "Dumb and Dumber: The U.S. Army Lowers Recruitment Standards . . . Again," *Slate* (24 January 2008), http://www.slate.com/articles/news_and_politics/war_stories/2008/01/dumb_and_dumber.html; "Army Lowers Bar for Recruits" *Miami Herald*, 5 October 2005, http://www.military.com/NewsContent/0,13319,78111,00.html.

14. C. Todd Lopez, "Army Has Not Lowered Soldier Recruiting Standards," US Army website, 5 May 2008, https://www.army.mil/article/8983.

15. Zubin Jelveh, "How the Recession Is Boosting the Military," *New Republic* (15 October 2009), https://newrepublic.com/article/70300/military-thanks -recession-boost-recruits.

16. Segal and Korb, "Manning and Financing the All-Volunteer Force," 114.

17. Ann Scott Tyson, "Military Recruiters Target Isolated, Depressed Areas," *Seattle Times,* 9 November 2005, and Tim Kane, "Who Bears the Burden: Demographic Characteristics of U.S. Military Recruits Before and After 9/11," Heritage Foundation, November 2005, http://www.heritage.org/defense/report/who-bears-the-burden-demographic-characteristics-us-military-recruits-and-after-911.

18. Mark Thompson, "Here's Why the U.S. Military Is a Family Business," *Time* (10 March 2016), http://time.com/4254696/military-family-business/.

19. Daniel P. McDonald and Kizzy M. Parks, eds., *Managing Diversity in the Military: The Value of Inclusion in a Culture of Uniformity* (New York: Routledge, 2013).

20. G. Dean Sinclair, "Homosexuality and the Military: A Review of the Literature," *Journal of Homosexuality* 56, no. 6 (2009): 701–718; Allan Bérubé, *Coming Out Under Fire: The History of Gay Men and Women in World War II,* Twentieth Anniversary ed. (Chapel Hill: Univ. of North Carolina Press, 2010); Leo Braudy, *From Chivalry to Terrorism: War and the Changing Nature of Masculinity* (New York: Vintage, 2010).

21. Peter W. Singer, "How *The Real World* Ended 'Don't Ask, Don't Tell,'" Brookings, 6 August 2008, 4, https://www.brookings.edu/wp-content/uploads/2016/06/08 _military_singer.pdf.

22. Russell Berman, "The Awkward Clinton-Era Debate over Don't Ask, Don't Tell," *The Atlantic* (10 October 2014), https://www.theatlantic.com/politics/ archive/2014/10/the-awkward-clinton-era-debate-over-dont-ask-dont-tell/381374/; Elaine Donnelly, "Defending the Culture of the Military," in *Attitudes Aren't Free,* ed. James E. Parco and David A. Levy (Montgomery, Ala.: Air Univ. Press, 2010), 249–292; Sharon E. Debbage Alexander, "A Ban by Any Other Name: Ten Years of Don't Ask, Don't Tell," *Hofstra Labor and Employment Law Journal* 21, no. 2 (2003): 403–436.

23. Singer, "How *The Real World* Ended 'Don't Ask, Don't Tell.'"

24. Pew Research Center, "Most Continue to Favor Gays Serving Openly in Military," 29 November 2010, http://www.pewresearch.org/subjects/gays-in-the-military/.

25. Aaron Belkin, *How We Won: Progressive Lessons from the Repeal of Don't Ask, Don't Tell* (New York: Huffington Post Media Group, 2011), 3; Nathaniel Frank,

Unfriendly Fire: How the Gay Ban Undermines the Military and Weakens America (New York: St. Martin's Press, 2009).

26. Pelin Sidki, "Discharged Under 'Don't Ask, Don't Tell,'" CNN, 10 November 2009, http://www.cnn.com/2009/US/11/10/vif2.dont.ask.dont.tell/index. html?_s=PM:US; "Army Dismisses Gay Arabic Linguist," Associated Press, 27 July 2006, http://www.nbcnews.com/id/14052513/ns/us_news-military/t/army-dimisses-gay-arabic-linguist/#.WUwONxPytsZ; "Report: More Gay Linguists Discharged Than First Thought," Associated Press, 13 January 2005.

27. Daniel Nasaw, "Don't Ask, Don't Tell: Army Veteran of Iraq Takes on US Army," *The Guardian*, 29 June 2009, https://www.theguardian.com/world/2009/jun/29/gay-veteran-us-army-choi.

28. Evelyn Nieves and Ann Scott Tyson, "Fewer Gays Being Discharged Since 9/11: 'Don't Ask' Ousters at Lowest Level Yet," *Washington Post*, 12 February 2005, http://www.washingtonpost.com/wp-dyn/articles/A17522-2005Feb11.html; Patrick Letellier, "Gays OK in Wartime," *The Advocate*, 27 September 2005.

29. DoD, "Transgender Policy," https://www.defense.gov/News/Special -Reports/0616_transgender-policy/.

30. James E. Parco, David A. Levy, and Sarah R. Spears. "Transgender Military Personnel in the Post-DADT Repeal Era: A Phenomenological Study," *Armed Forces and Society* 41, no. 2 (2015): 221–242.

31. Carla Crandall, "The Effects of Repealing Don't Ask, Don't Tell: Is the Combat Exclusion the Next Casualty in the March Toward Integration," *Georgetown Journal of Law and Public Policy* 10 (2012): 15.

32. Beth Bailey, "If You Like Ms., You'll Love Pvt.," in *America's Army: Making the All-Volunteer Force* (Cambridge, Mass.: Harvard Univ. Press, 2009), 130–171.

33. DoD memorandum, "Direct Ground Combat Definition and Assignment Rule," 13 January 1994.

34. See, for example, Martin L. Van Creveld, *Men, Women, and War: Do Women Belong on the Front Line?* (London: Cassell, 2001); Rosemarie Skaine, *Women at War: Gender Issues of Americans in Combat* (Jefferson, N.C.: McFarland, 1999); and Mariam G. Cooke and Angela Woollacott, eds., *Gendering War Talk* (Princeton, N.J.: Princeton Univ. Press, 1993).

35. Kristy N. Kamarck, "Women in Combat: Issues for Congress," Congressional Research Service R42075, 13 December 2016, 7, https://fas.org/sgp/crs/natsec/R42075.pdf.

36. Mark Thompson, "American Amazons: Hiding in Plain-Jane Sight," *Time* (28 January 2013), http://nation.time.com/2013/01/28/american-amazons-hiding -in-plain-jane-sight/.

37. Megan Katt, "Blurred Lines: Cultural Support Teams in Afghanistan," *Joint Force Quarterly* 75 (30 September 2014), http://ndupress.ndu.edu/Media/News/News-Article-View/Article/577569/jfq-75-blurred-lines-cultural-support-teams-in-afghanistan/; Michael Doidge, "Combat Multipliers: Tactical Female Engagement Teams in Paktika Province," in *Vanguard of Valor*, vol. 2, *Small Unit*

Actions in Afghanistan, ed. Donald Wright (Fort Leavenworth, Kans.: Combat Studies Institute Press, 2012), http://usacac.army.mil/cac2/cgsc/carl/download/csipubs/VanguardOfValorII.pdf; *Lioness,* directed by Meg McLagan and Daria Sommers (United States: Docurama, Cinedigm, 2008), DVD.

38. Gayle Tzemach Lemmon, *Ashley's War: The Untold Story of a Team of Women Soldiers on the Special Ops Battlefield* (New York: HarperCollins, 2015).

39. For the feminist critique, see Laura Sjoberg, "What's Wrong with FETs? Thoughts from Gendering Global Conflict," http://www.cupblog.org/?p=11799; and Keally McBride and Annick T. R. Wibben, "The Gendering of Counterinsurgency in Afghanistan," *Humanity: An International Journal of Human Rights, Humanitarianism, and Development* 3, no. 2 (2012): 199–215. For the conservative critique, see Martin Van Creveld, "Review: Ashley's War," 17 September 2015, http://www.martin-van-creveld.com/ashleys-war/.

40. 110th Congress, H. Rept. 110–858, "Misleading Information from the Battlefield: The Tillman and Lynch Episodes," https://www.congress.gov/congressional-report/110th-congress/house-report/858/1.

41. See, for example, Deepa Kumar, "War Propaganda and the (Ab)uses of Women: Media Constructions of the Jessica Lynch Story," *Feminist Media Studies* 4, no. 3 (2004): 297–313; Shannon L. Holland, "The Dangers of Playing Dress-Up: Popular Representations of Jessica Lynch and the Controversy Regarding Women in Combat," *Quarterly Journal of Speech* 92, no. 1 (2006): 27–50; and Laura Sjoberg, "Agency, Militarized Femininity and Enemy Others: Observations from the War in Iraq," *International Feminist Journal of Politics* 9, no. 1 (2007): 82–101.

42. Jennifer K. Lobasz, "The Woman in Peril and the Ruined Woman: Representations of Female Soldiers in the Iraq War," *Journal of Women, Politics and Policy* 29, no. 3 (2008): 305–334.

43. Sebastian Junger, *War* (New York: Twelve, 2010), 21–24, 43.

44. DoD, "Fact Sheet: Women in Service Review(WISR) Implementation," https://www.defense.gov/Portals/1/Documents/pubs/Fact_Sheet_WISR_FINAL.pdf.

45. DoD memorandum, "Elimination of the 1994 Direct Ground Combat Definition and Assignment Rule," 24 January 2013, https://www.defense.gov/Portals/1/Documents/WISRJointMemo.pdf.

46. US Army memorandum, "U.S. Army Implementation Plan 2016-01 (Army Gender Integration)," 5 January 2016, https://www.defense.gov/Portals/1/Documents/pubs/WISR_Implementation_Plan_Army.pdf.

47. https://www.defense.gov/Portals/1/Documents/pubs/WISR_Implementation_Plan_USMC.pdf; USMC Integration Plan Red Team Report, CSIS https://www.defense.gov/Portals/1/Documents/wisr-studies/USMC%20-%20Center%20for%20Strategic%20and%20International%20Studies%20Red%20Team%20analysis%20°f%20Marine%20Corps%20research%20and%20analysis%20°n%20gender%20integrat-1.pdf.

48. Susan Keating, "Was It Fixed? Army General Told Subordinates: 'A Woman

Will Graduate Ranger School,' Sources Say," 25 September 2015, http://people.com/
celebrity/female-rangers-were-given-special-treatment-sources-say/.

49. Ashton Carter, "Remarks on the Women-in-Service Review," as delivered,
Pentagon Press Briefing Room, Washington, DC, 3 December 2015, https://www.
defense.gov/News/Speeches/Speech-View/Article/632495/remarks-on-the-women
-in-service-review/.

50. Nolan Finney, "Pentagon: 7 in 10 Youths Would Fail to Qualify for Military
Service," *Time,* 29 June 2014, http://time.com/2938158/youth-fail-to-qualify-mili-
tary-service/; Council for a Strong America, "Ready, Willing, and Unable to Serve,"
http://cdn.missionreadiness.org/NATEE1109.pdf.

51. Barack Obama, "Address Before a Joint Session of the Congress on the
State of the Union," 27 January 2010, http://www.presidency.ucsb.edu/ws/index.
php?pid=87433.

52. Elizabeth Hillman has argued that there may be a constitutional connection
between the Second Amendment and a right to military service. Elizabeth Hillman,
"Heller, Citizenship, and the Right to Serve in the Military," *Hastings Law Journal*
60, no. 1269 (2009): 1269–1284.

53. 10 U.S.C. § 654.

54. See, for example, laments about the end of the ideal of the "citizen-soldier"
from Charles Moskos, "From Citizens' Army to Social Laboratory," *Wilson Quarterly*
17, no. 1 (winter 1993): 83–94; the series of articles in Elliott Abrams and Andrew
Bacevich, "A Symposium on Citizenship and Military Service," *Parameters* 31 (summer 2001); and David R. Segal, *Recruiting for Uncle Sam: Citizenship and Military
Manpower Policy* (Lawrence: Univ. Press of Kansas, 1989). See also a critique of this
narrative by Ronald Krebs, "The Citizen-Soldier Tradition in the United States: Has
Its Demise Been Greatly Exaggerated?" *Armed Forces and Society* 36, no. 1 (October
2009): 153–174.

55. Drew Gilpin Faust, address at ROTC commissioning, Cambridge, Massachusetts, 4 June 2008, text as prepared for delivery, http://harvardmagazine.com/
commencement/president-fausts-rotc-commissioning-speech.

56. Michael Winerip, "The R.O.T.C. Dilemma," *New York Times,* 26 October
2009.

57. Department of Homeland Security, US Citizenship and Immigration Service, "Fact Sheet: Naturalization Through Military Service," June 2017, https://
www.uscis.gov/news/fact-sheets/naturalization-through-military-service-fact-sheet.

58. Department of Defense, "Military Accessions Vital to National Interest
(MAVNI) Recruitment Pilot Program Fact Sheet," https://dod.defense.gov/news/
mavni-fact-sheet.pdf; Anita Hattiangadi et al., "Non-Citizens in Today's Mili-
tary: Final Report" (Alexandria, Va.: CNA, April 2005); Molly F. McIntosh and
Seema Sayala, "Non-Citizens in the Enlisted U.S. Military" (Alexandria, Va.: CNA,
December 2011); Alex Horton, "'It Looks like We're Afraid of Foreigners': Army
Turns Away Some Green-Card Holders," *Washington Post,* 18 October 2017.

59. Catherine Connell, "Right to Serve or Responsibility to Protect? Civil Rights Framing and the DADT Repeal," *Boston University Law Review* 95 (2015): 1015–1028.

60. Krebs, "The Citizen-Soldier Tradition in the United States," 166–167.

61. Amy Lutz, "Who Joins the Military?: A Look at Race, Class, and Immigration Status," *Journal of Political and Military Sociology* 36, no. 2 (winter 2008): 167–188; Office of the Undersecretary of Defense, Personnel and Readiness, "Population Representation in the Military Services: Fiscal Year 2014 Summary Report"; Got Your 6, "Dispelling Myths about Veterans," https://gotyour6.org/impacts/dispelling-myths/; Bryant Jordan, "Poll: America Values Vets but Stereotypes Them," 14 June 2012, https://www.military.com/daily-news/2012/06/14/poll-america-values-vets-but-stereotypes-them.html.

62. Krebs, "The Citizen-Soldier Tradition in the United States," 157.

18

Post-Traumatic Stress (Disorder) in the Post-9/11 World

Lawrence Tritle

Today they call it the "Invisible Wound." It was on the road to Ramadi in the summer of 2006 that Captain Smith received his first. The exploding IED threw him against the bulkhead of the Humvee. It hit like a ton of bricks. A blast from a cluster of perhaps three 155 mm artillery shells, several pounds of Semtex, and a couple butane canisters created an explosion of intense pressure and heat, the latter perhaps six or seven thousand degrees. A blast wave moving faster than the speed of sound, perhaps a thousand feet per second, and with a force of four hundred pounds per square inch—over one thousand times atmospheric pressure—generated a blast wind exceeding any produced by a hurricane, throwing people and objects violently into one another. Fast forward eight years. Now diagnosed with multiple and debilitating physical and psychological issues, the US Army that Captain Smith had served for nearly ten years released him with full disabilities to a life of uncertainty.[1]

A truism of war since the time of the Greek historian Thucydides is the unpredictability of war. Policymakers, political and military alike, too often imagine that the outcome of conflicts can be anticipated, even predicted. Such a view is folly. Israeli backing of Hamas to challenge the PLO and the rise of ISIS subsequent to the invasion of Iraq demonstrate this all too clearly. The trauma of war also presents a contrasting reality: war is, in the words of Hollywood director and infantry veteran Oliver Stone, "bloody and messy and totally horrifying, and the consequences are serious."[2] This continues to be true. Since the outbreak of the Afghanistan and Iraq wars in 2002 and 2003, a great deal has been learned about the nature of battle trauma. Most significantly perhaps, the July 2016 study published in *Lancet Neurology* demonstrates fully the damaging consequences of exploding IEDs and their powerful impact inducing post-traumatic stress (disorder), or PTS(D).[3] What follows focuses on the horrifying consequences of the experience of war since

9/11, and perhaps most important, what has been learned from the lessons, though surely not by all.

Battle Trauma before 9/11

Since antiquity, soldiers like Captain Smith facing the sharp end of the spear have suffered. Greek soldiers of the classical era, such as the Athenian Epizelus at Marathon (and Romans of the Empire), experienced episodes of "hysterical" blindness—what the American medical community (distinct from the United Kingdom's) more accurately defines as conversion disorder.[4] In the eighteenth century, sources report, soldiers suffered from "Nostalgia," a vague and troubling psychological malaise.[5] Religious, mythical, and folk explanations of these phenomena gave way in the modern era to more elaborate though certainly limited medical diagnoses. US Civil War combatants, as well as my father's Second World War B-24 pilot, knew of "Soldier's Heart"—hearts racing in excess of 130 beats per minute, and this months, even years after combat.[6] Discovered and popularized with the events of the First World War, "shell shock" acquired multiple meanings. The *Lancet Neurology* study explains shell shock as having symptoms ranging from the various forms of conversion disorder (for example, blindness or mutism) to other types of physical disabilities (such as loss of control of bodily movements).[7] These responses to battle trauma reappeared as "combat fatigue" in its Second World War incarnation, as evident in the long-suppressed John Huston film *Let There Be Light*. Recorded in military hospitals in 1946–1947, the film was not shown publicly until the 1981 Cannes Film Festival, and this only on the intervention of Vice President Walter Mondale.[8]

Medical and scientific understanding of the consequences of battle has grown enormously since the mid-twentieth century. By the end of the Second World War, psychiatrists had seen enough in the shattered lives of combatants to characterize psychic trauma as "gross stress reaction." This term became part of the first edition (1950) of what is now regarded as the bible of the American Psychiatric Association, the *Diagnostic and Statistical Manual of Mental Disorders* (*DSM*). At the outbreak of the 1968 Tet Offensive in Vietnam, however, reference to "gross stress reaction" had disappeared from the new *DSM-2*. It would not return until after the social and political upheaval of the Vietnam War with the appearance of *DSM-3* in 1980.[9] It was at this time that post-traumatic stress (disorder), or PTS(D), entered scientific as well as popular discourse, though agreement today regarding its reality as science or cultural construct is not universal.[10] "Nostalgia," "Soldier's Heart," "Shell Shock," and "Combat Fatigue" are all well-known terms defining exposure to battle. Seemingly different, each conveys similar realities of the life-changing experience of battle; these realities combatants and caretakers continue to experience today.

Battle Trauma, the Universalist and Presentist Debate

In a 2013 symposium at Loyola Marymount University dedicated to the "Many Faces of War," I related to one of the participants, a medical doctor, the strange story of Epizelus, an Athenian soldier at Marathon, who was struck blind amid battle, evidently remaining so the rest of his life.[11] The doctor was surprised to learn of this, as are many others who imagine that "hysterical blindness" is a response to the carnage of the world wars, not ancient Greece. Yet such a "modern" response as Epizelus's is true, and other examples of similar responses could be cited.[12] This well-known story illustrates the dilemma over the universality of war and its traumas, particularly in assessing the reality of battle trauma and what is popularly known as PTS(D). Those participating in this debate are divided into two camps: the "Universalists," who argue that this is a timeless human response to events, a view I accept, and the "Presentists," who deny this, arguing instead that PTS(D) is a phenomenon, a cultural construct, of the modern era, namely the late twentieth century.[13]

Detailed discussion is impossible here, but Epizelus's physiological response to the terror of battle—and its repetition in other places and times and people—argues for its universality. As the foregoing discussion shows, knowledge of science, neurology in particular, increases almost daily. Not so long ago, schizophrenia was believed to be "an intrusion of the dream state into the waking state." Today, schizophrenia is known to be about chemical imbalances in the brain, possibly the result of stress, which can be corrected.[14] The "modern" human brain is some 50,000 to 100,000 years old. It functions pretty much the same, but only recently has science begun to understand it and how it regulates the body, as our understanding of schizophrenia today makes clear.[15]

On the other side, the "Presentists" argue for the primacy of culture and society, seemingly unaware of the origins of this society. As Edward Wilson reminds us, "history makes little sense without prehistory, and prehistory makes little sense without biology."[16] To characterize PTS(D) as a cultural construct is overly simplistic: all cultures are the products of their societies, and societies—people—are the products of biology. To define PTS(D) then as a sociocultural construct is not a remarkable conclusion.

Today, in the early twenty-first century, the importance of uniting history and science is becoming increasingly clear, if for no other reason than telling the story of mankind from the present vantage point and not from that of the nineteenth century. In reviewing Daniel Snail's thought-provoking *On Deep History and the Brain,* University of Reading archaeologist Steven Mithen observes that in the future, students of history will need to become "scientifically literate," learning "a new set of impersonal actors"— chemicals such as dopamine, serotonin, and oxytocin. A dose of evolutionary biology and psychology, I think, would be no less useful. At the same time, Mithen adds, biologists and physiologists will have to become "historically minded," appreciating how human bodies and brains are the products of society and culture.[17]

The Battlefield Meets the Gridiron

When the World Trade Center towers fell on 9/11, there was broad though certainly limited understanding of the nature and extent of war's traumas. The stereotypic crazed Vietnam veteran of film and television, Rambo and Billy Jack—violent, occasionally rightly so, often high on drugs and drink— had certainly done much to publicize PTS(D), but not always happily. New battlefields with new battlefield traumas, particularly the IED, the "signature" weapon producing the "signature" wound of the Afghanistan and Iraq wars, soon led to thousands of casualties—catastrophic and visible physical injuries, but also those of the unseen psychic variety.[18] But in the new and undemocratic American Way of War, these wartime combatants encountered other injured players, but those of the sports variety and from the nation's football fields. Here amid growing awareness of the cumulative damage to the brain from concussion, casualties of America's newest battlefields met those of the gridiron. Today, concussions and their harmful effects on players, whether in football and other contact sports (including even water ballet), grip the attention of sports physicians. Trainers and especially helmet designers are hard at work to find ways to protect those on athletic fields from catastrophic injury.[19] The medical and scientific study of these injured players has done much to advance the understanding of both war's physical injuries and its psychological traumas.

Yet there were probably few who knew or understood why, for example, soldiers during both world wars could be killed by the concussive effect of exploding shells or mines when their bodies appeared uninjured.[20] Such mysteries began to be unraveled in the 1990s with the development of magnetic resonance imaging (or brain imaging). While this technology has opened a new field of medical and scientific research, it has also begun the first real understanding of the brain and its structures, and so its afflictions, Alzheimer's disease, and especially psychic trauma.

When General Sir Charles "Ted" Harington saw German officers sitting dead at their table at Messines, he attributed their deaths to "shock" or "windage." What actually happened is that the exceedingly fine fabric of the brain—neurons, synapses—were compressed, most likely by the volcanic force of wind and pressure exerted by the blast, and were fatally damaged as their brains struck the very hard shell of their skulls. Such tentative diagnoses have only become possible with the invention of magnetic resonance imaging. Discovery of this technology dates to 1971, with the first fMRI scans performed in 1990; the Nobel Prize for the technology's discovery dates to 2003, with the American College of Radiology White Paper on imaging safety to 2002–2004. Since 2013, development of "susceptibility weighted imaging" (SWI), an improvement on T_1 or T_2 imaging, enables medical personnel and others to evaluate diseases like Alzheimer's or traumatically injured brains, as from exploding IEDs.[21]

One of the great ironies of the Afghanistan and Iraq wars, then, is the coincidence of brain imaging technology and IEDs, the former allowing medical personnel to understand the wounds caused by the latter. A thorough study of psychic wounds and trauma from earliest times (certainly not possible here) would show how military medicine has moved from attributing wounds from the body to the brain. As Dr. Ronald Glasser (among others) has argued, the twenty-first century will be "the century of the brain" in this regard.[22] One such example is current research into the pituitary gland, the brain's master gland that regulates the endocrine system and the production of hormones critical to growth and development and so critical to the body's homeostasis. The size of a pea, the pituitary is attached to the brain by a slender stalk. Damage to it does not show up on brain imaging.[23]

The development of brain imaging technology makes clear the shortcomings of First World War medicine and efforts to understand what was then called shell shock.[24] Essentially, the limited instruments and technology of medical science then could not see or determine the full extent or complexity of neurological injuries caused by shellfire or explosions. In 1916 and 1917, British Army surgeon and neurologist Frederick Mott conducted postmortems of the brains of a number of soldiers, either killed outright or dying soon after without obvious injury. Examinations revealed hemorrhages within the white matter and corpus callosum, this penetrating the brain's subarachnoid space (the space between the arachnoid membrane and pia matter).[25] But this probably raised more questions than answers, with the result that what constituted shell shock remained as much a mystery as before.[26]

Because of brain imaging's development, current generations gain better understanding, though still somewhat limited, of head injuries suffered on the battlefield or the gridiron. A number of 2011–2012 postmortem studies of Iraq War veterans revealed injuries remarkably similar to those associated with the repeated but comparatively mild injuries associated with contact sports. This syndrome, defined as chronictraumatic encephalopathy (or CTE), is a neurodegenerative tauopathy (or tau pathology), characterized by "neurofibrillary tangles in neuroanatomical areas."[27]

The *Lancet Neurology* study now adds to this, revealing evidence of "astroglial scarring," a neurological response to injury as the brain repairs damaged structures. Perhaps most interesting, and significant, is that the study's control group of civilian cases, or individuals who did not suffer IED-type injuries, revealed no "astrogliosis pattern similar to the specimens from blast exposure cases." In other words, the astroglial scarring might well be regarded as a distinctive signature of a blast wound.[28]

The researchers also commented on previous findings that concluded that axonal damage was a factor in possible neuropsychiatric injuries.[29] Termed diffuse axonal injury (or DAI) and associated with impact-caused traumatic brain injury (TBI), as seen on the football field or from a battlefield IED, DAI is an injury that damages the very fine fibers carrying electrical signals from one brain cell to another, including the nerves of the spinal column.[30] Medical diagnosis is difficult, as axonal injury escapes current medical imaging technology.

What might be the implications of these clinical findings? Damage to the brain's pia matter could explain cerebrospinal fluid flow and headache; damage to U-fiber connections at the gray-white matter junction could influence cognitive dysfunction and damage to the structures lining ventricles, or part of the limbic system, which would influence short-term memory and sleep disorders. Additionally, the IED blast itself will have different impacts on the brain. Specifically, waves with high frequency and low amplitude disrupt structures with differing densities, while low frequency and high amplitude waves can strain others but differently.[31]

The specialists conducting the *Lancet Neurology* study reached the tentative conclusion that "data suggest an association between combat blast TBI and PTS(D). One case-control study showed that the number of combat mild TBIs with loss of consciousness (most due to blast exposure) positively correlates with PTS(D) severity, neurological deficits, and cognitive impairment."[32] While identifiable, biological abnormalities seem clear, there are gaps in the scientific literature characterizing these abnormalities and there is the possibility that the chronic blast TBI cases had "concomitant" PTS(D).

While there are certainly unknown factors in the case studies examined, the evident astroglial scarring may be enhancing or making CTE more problematic, as it interferes with the glymphatic system. This is a recently discovered function of the central nervous system that in effect eliminates waste products from the brain. If, for example, the elimination of tau protein is impeded, then individuals, such as those wounded by an IED, would become more susceptible to neurodegenerative disease. This in turn would be revealed in various behavioral and memory issues typically seen in those suffering from post-traumatic stress.[33]

In the post-9/11 world, incidents of high-explosive attack increasingly occur, injuring and affecting not only military personnel but civilians. It is imperative then to learn more about what happens to those individuals, as the *Lancet Neurology* study reveals a type of injury to the human brain previously undetected. As such injuries persist for years after the injury, understanding them becomes critical for all. Not only does proper medical understanding become crucial, but so do effective treatments (if these are possible, given the nature of the wounds). No less critical is the development of protective equipment for those in the military.

During the last ten years, Dr. Douglas Smith of the University of Pennsylvania Medical School has led a team of researchers in developing a fabric that changes color when hit by the concussive waves of a high-explosive, as produced by IEDs. The idea here is to aid field medics and hospitals in the early detection of the kind of brain trauma that can lead to post-traumatic stress.[34]

The Burdens of Battle: The US Army and Multiple Deployments

In 2007, Pulitzer Prize-winning author Rick Atkinson, citing a Pentagon report, argued that the IED was "the single most effective weapon against our deployed forces" in Iraq.[35] Unplanned by Al Qa'ida, Iraqi insurgents, or the American military, the IED was a game changer in terms of response technology (in other words, counter-IED technologies, such as electronic jammers or vehicle design) not to mention costs and so much more. More importantly perhaps, the human toll has been staggering. As a 2008 RAND study details, hundreds of thousands of American military personnel (and uncounted numbers of Iraqis and others) have suffered visibly or invisibly. Moreover, as outlined above, the injuries suffered from an IED, whether physical or psychic, are often life-ending or life-long.[36]

These realities are crucial to the concept of landpower, as landpower depends on manpower and the willingness of citizens to serve. Yet, increasingly the burdens of service fall disproportionately on the poorer and less affluent. The popular press and media often report that in the Western democracies today, including the United States, military service is most undemocratic, with less than 1 percent of the population serving in uniform (and even a smaller percentage serving in the combat arms—infantry, armor, and artillery). In their study *The Casualty Gap,* Douglas L. Kriner and Francis X. Shen demonstrate these realities.[37] The income differentials of casualties in Korea and Vietnam were 10 percent between top and bottom, and 15 percent in Iraq. Kriner and Shen note additionally that "the communities that have suffered the highest casualty rates in the Iraq War possess levels of college educational attainment that are almost 40% lower, on average, than those of communities that have not yet suffered a casualty."[38]

A particularly telling example of this can be seen in the casualties from the state of California since 9/11. The Internet site vetfriends.com lists the names and hometowns of the 548 Californians killed in Iraq and Afghanistan. Even a cursory survey shows that elite communities (those with affluent schools, libraries, simply put, opportunities), such as Beverly Hills and Brentwood-Bel Air in southern California and Los Altos Hills and Tiburon in northern California, have suffered no losses. On the other hand, nonelite, "working-class" communities (again, simply those with fewer resources), such as Bakersfield and Clovis in central California, and others like them, have suffered multiple fatalities.[39]

Kriner and Shen also analyzed the political and social impact of this casualty differential. Survey groups were polled to determine what level of casualties was acceptable in a time of war. One group (the control group) was given no additional information, a second was told that rich and poor communities suffered equally, and a third was told that poorer communities suffered significantly higher casualties than richer ones. The results of the poll? The group that was told that the poor suffered more favored a casualty rate 40 percent lower than the control group, while the group told of a shared sacrifice accepted a higher percentage of loss than the control group. It seems clear that citizens believe in a shared sacrifice in wartime, but as the California losses reveal, that simply is not the case for the American Republic today. Kriner and Shen conclude that those communities suffering casualty rates higher than the more affluent "hold systematically different opinions" and exhibit "different political behaviors," and as a consequence have less confidence in government and the political process.[40] Such attitudes are common among American veterans of the Afghanistan and Iraq wars, as I found in the comments of my own veteran students.

The creation of the all-volunteer force in the United States was a response to the military-political-social upheavals of the Vietnam War. The all-volunteer force feeds on the social-economic inequities uncovered and explained by Kriner and Shen. These may also explain the shocking suicide rate in the armed forces (of many who had never deployed to a combat zone) and the high-profile crimes of other service members in Afghanistan, such as Sergeant Robert Bales of the so-called Kandahar Massacre of 2012, and in Iraq, as exemplified by Private Steven Green and others in the 2006 Mahmudiyah rape and murders.[41] The multiple deployments that have become the norm of America's "Forever Wars" will only exacerbate these issues and the undemocratic divides behind them. Others will address this subject further. But it is clear that the IED and the multiple deployments of America's newest wars have exerted striking impacts on the American military establishment and the wider public. But few, certainly in the public at large, seem aware of these or their consequences for a democratic society.[42]

As Rick Atkinson reported the powerful consequences of IEDs, the US Army was reaching a breaking point from multiple deployments amid ongoing conflict in Afghanistan and Iraq.[43] While detailed consequences of IED psychic injury were poorly known, the linkage between these and PTS(D) was recognized to some extent. This was evident in the Army's developed protocols (and those of the armed services generally) to detect and treat personnel who either requested help or displayed symptoms of psychic injury or trauma.[44]

Despite such measures, the longstanding difficulty of recognizing the effects of the trauma of battle on its participants and dealing with it fairly have continued. This was made clear in the May 2017 Government Accountability Office (GAO) report regarding misconduct separations and PTS(D). Among other findings, the GAO determined that between 2011 and 2015 some 62 percent of those personnel separated for misconduct (nearly 100,000) had been previously diagnosed with PTS(D), TBI, or a related condition. Additionally, 23 percent of these received an "other than honorable" separation, a punitive discharge that makes them potentially ineligible for veterans' benefits.[45] The GAO report also found evidence that service members were sometimes not evaluated for PTS(D) or TBI, and others did not receive counseling regarding the consequences of a misconduct separation. It was also found that some Army and Marine Corps officers had not received training in recognition of TBI symptoms and had not followed established procedures in reviewing whether TBI was a misconduct factor.

Among its conclusions, the GAO study found that "the Army and Marine Corps may not always be adhering to their own policies and that monitoring of the policies—which could include a review of documentation, data analyses, or other oversight mechanisms—by DOD, Army, and Marine Corps is limited." Such shortcomings, as the GAO found, give little assurance that service members diagnosed with PTS(D) or TBI are receiving proper screening and counseling. Furthermore, the risk may exist that individuals are being discharged without adequate consideration of how such factors might affect their behavior, separation, or eligibility for VA benefits.[46]

Conclusions

Pulitzer Prize-winning scientist Edward O. Wilson observes that "nowadays, as polls have repeatedly shown, most people, at least in the United States, respect science but are baffled by it. They don't understand it, they prefer science fiction, they take fantasy and pseudoscience like stimulants to jolt their cerebral pleasure centers."[47] Only hinted at here is the reality that few people actually read science or otherwise follow its discoveries.

This unhappy but accurate assessment contrasts with the rapid pace of discoveries in modern science, including medicine. Almost daily we learn of new findings regarding the biochemical and physiological makeup of the human condition. The problem is that too few in the humanities pay attention to these, let alone the policymakers, civilian and military, who make the decisions to send young people downrange. No less problematic, scientists and researchers in the medical community focus on the recent past to explain the varied responses to battle.[48] No less overlooked is literature, whether that of ancient Greece, the world wars, or Vietnam, which record and preserve perhaps the truest voices of battlefield trauma and memory.[49]

Battlefield trauma has a long but relatively poorly understood history, which is now changing with science and technology. Sports trauma also has become better understood with the invention of brain imaging. Today's football fans should know the consequences of their cheers, though sadly most remain cheerfully ignorant of the damage of those hard hits on the field. So too political and military leaders should learn the implications of exposing their fellow citizens to the hazards of war and take appropriate steps to attempt at least to try and protect them. This becomes even more critical as the percentage of physically able young adults liable for military service continues to decline. Finally, writers of history should not only tell how contemporaries experienced and reported wartime trauma, but should interpret narratives in light of increasingly sophisticated scientific and medical knowledge.

Notes

1. "Captain Smith" is a pseudonym, but the events, traumas, and discharge experienced by this officer are real. Details of the hypothetical IED described here are drawn from Ronald J. Glasser, M.D., *Broken Bodies, Shattered Minds: A Medical Odyssey from Vietnam to Afghanistan* (Palisades, N.Y.: History Publishing Company, 2011), 149, and Sharon Baughman Shively et al., "Characterisation of Interface Astroglial Scarring in the Human Brain after Blast Exposure: A Post-Mortem Case Series," *Lancet Neurology* 15 (August 2016): 944–953, at 950.

2. Oliver Stone, in "Quotes for the Week," *Newsweek,* 13 October 1997.

3. Popularly defined as "post-traumatic stress disorder," the latter word is bracketed here deliberately. Therapists and counselors today at the West Los Angeles Veterans Administration facility believe "Disorder" is inappropriate, as it suggests something unnatural. In fact, the human body's response to trauma, especially the trauma of war, is anything but unusual or unnatural.

4. Further discussion in Lawrence A. Tritle, *From Melos to My Lai: War and Survival* (London: Routledge, 2000); Lawrence A. Tritle, "'Ravished Minds' in the Ancient World," in *Combat Trauma and the Ancient Greeks,* ed. Peter Meineck and David Konstan (New York: Palgrave Macmillan, 2014), 87–104.

5. See, for example, Hans Binneveld, *From Shell Shock to Combat Stress: A Comparative History of Military Psychiatry* (Amsterdam: Amsterdam Univ. Press, 1997), 3.

6. Jacob Da Costa was the Union Army doctor who diagnosed racing hearts as "Soldier's Heart" (see, for example, Alfred Jay Bollet, M.D., *Civil War Medicine: Challenges and Triumphs* [Tucson, Ariz.: Galen Press, 2002], 321). The pilot noted was John Fanelli of Shenandoah, Pennsylvania, details from a telephone conversation of April 2002.

7. The post–World War I study of Frederick Walker Mott, *War Neuroses and Shell Shock* (London: Henry Frowde and Hodder and Stoughton, 1919), led to the *Report of the War Office Committee of Enquiry into "Shell-Shock"* (London: His Majesty's Stationary Office, 1922). Shively et al., "Characterisation of Interface Astroglial Scarring," elaborates greatly the limited medical and scientific tools of the First World War era.

8. For post–World War II study of "combat fatigue," see, for example, Roy R. Grinker and John P. Spiegel, *Men Under Stress* (Philadelphia: Blakiston, 1945), and Binneveld, *From Shell Shock to Combat Stress.* For details on *Let There Be Light,* see Tritle, "'Ravished Minds' in the Ancient World," 100 n. 22.

9. This confirmed to me in a 1997 discussion with Dr. Chaim Shatan, one of the founding fathers of PTS(D). See, for example, his 1971 *New York Times* editorial, "Post-Vietnam Syndrome."

10. For critics, see Allan Young, *The Harmony of Illusions: Inventing Post-Traumatic Stress Disorder* (Princeton, N.J.: Princeton Univ. Press, 1995), and Ben Sheph-

ard, *A War of Nerves: Soldiers and Psychiatrists, 1914–1994* (London: Jonathan Cape, 2000).

11. The symposium was organized by L. Tritle. The companion volume to the "Many Faces of War" program is *The Many Faces of War*, ed. L. A. Tritle and J. W. Warren (Los Angeles: Marymount Institute Press, 2018).

12. An example from the Vietnam War came to light in 2014 when actual combat footage from the 1967 Dak To campaign (not lost but forgotten in archives) emerged. "Raw War: The Lost Film of Dak To" details an incident of hysterical blindness and deafness by a 4th Infantry Division soldier coming to the aid of others hit by North Vietnamese mortar fire. Though he recovered, the soldier related how he was struck blind and mute at the sight of his mangled friends. Film available on YouTube.

13. Note 18.10, above, references discussions of this position.

14. David Eagleman, *The Brain: The Story of You* (New York: Pantheon Books, 2015), 60–61; David Eagleman, *Incognito: The Secret Lives of the Brain* (New York: Pantheon Books, 2011), 211.

15. See Edward O. Wilson, *Consilence: The Unity of Knowledge* (New York: Vintage Books, 1998), 145 (brain development and age in *Homo sapiens*), 141–142 (culture and society).

16. Edward O. Wilson, *The Meaning of Human Existence* (New York: Norton, 2014), 9.

17. Steven Mithen, "When We Were Nicer," *London Review of Books,* 24 January 2008, 24–25, reviewing D. L. Snail, *On Deep History and the Brain* (Berkeley: Univ. of California Press, 2008). Note also the review by Jan D. Galla of Meineck and Konstan, *Combat Trauma and the Ancient Greeks,* in *Michigan War Studies Review* (2015-097), 1, also calling attention to this issue.

18. A 2008 study suggested that hundreds of thousands of US troops in these two theaters of operations suffer from traumatic brain injuries (TBIs) and PTS(D) resulting from combat. See further Terri Tanielian and Lisa H. Jaycox, eds., *Invisible Wounds of War* (Santa Monica, Calif.: RAND Corporation, 2008), xxi.

19. Ben McGrath, "Does Football Have a Future?" *New Yorker,* 31 January 2011, 41–51. The 2011 suicide of former NFL player Dave Duerson underlines the concern among players regarding the consequences of such a "contact" sport as football; see, for example, Alan Schwarz, "N.F.L. Players Shaken by Duerson's Suicide Message," *New York Times,* 21 February 2011, D1, 7. All this is now made clearer by the study of former NFL star Aaron Hernandez's brain following his April 2017 suicide. See John Branch, "On the Table, the Brain Appeared Normal," *New York Times,* 10 November 2017, B9.

20. World War I: James Terraine, *White Heat: The New Warfare 1914–18* (London: Sidgwick and Jackson, 1982), 237: German officers found dead sitting at a table, killed from the concussion of an underground mine at Messines near Ypres, 1917. World War II: James D. Hornfischer, *Neptune's Inferno. The U.S. Navy at Guadalcanal* (New York: Random House, 2011), 319: a naval officer killed aboard the USS

Atlanta in the naval actions around Guadalcanal. Other examples could be found easily: cf. the 1922 *War Office Committee of Enquiry into "Shell-Shock,"* 18, 33, 60, 103, 104, 110; another example is shown in "Raw War: The Lost Film of Dak To" (see note 18.12 above).

21. Well beyond the scope of this essay, for a brief discussion of fMRI technology see D. Theodore George, M.D., and Lisa Berger, *Untangling the Mind: Why We Behave the Way We Do* (New York: HarperCollins, 2013), 31. Shively et al., "Characterisation of Interface Astroglial Scarring," 31, notes that "physical damage to the human brain after blast exposure [cannot currently be detected] by "standard clinical neuroimaging techniques."

22. The author of one of the great Vietnam War books, *365 Days* (New York: George Braziller, 1971), Glasser notes this in *Broken Bodies, Shattered Minds,* 129.

23. See, for example, Dina Fine Maron, "Damage to Pea-Size Gland May Cause PTSD-Like Symptoms," *Scientific American* (13 July 2016), www.scientificamerican.com/article (accessed 3 November 2018).

24. Soldiers in the First World War were not equipped with metal helmets until 1916. In my possession are both British/American and German helmets of the era. With their simple cotton or fabric padding, these provided only comfort (and not much of that!) and certainly minimal protection against the concussive force of exploding shellfire or mines. Even today, the helmets worn by American soldiers provide little protection against IEDs. Survivors comment that an exploding IED rings the head like a bell, and they clearly know the inherent dangers. See Glasser, *Broken Bodies, Shattered Minds,* 149.

25. Mott, *War Neuroses and Shell Shock,* 37–67, with Shively et al., "Characterisation of Interface Astroglial Scarring," 344–345.

26. The limitations of medical science at the time call into question the usefulness of such studies for an understanding of shell shock in the First World War. Such work will remain only useful for study of the "history of history," or what R. G. Collingwood referred to as "second-order history." This is true as well for even current investigations that omit reference to the ongoing body of research into neurology and such related fields as endocrinology. See note 48 below for an example.

27. Shively et al., "Characterisation of Interface Astroglial Scarring," 945. Tauopathy is a neurodegenerative disease produced by the concentration or accumulation of tau protein (which performs a stabilizing function) in the brain's neurofibrillary networks. When these become defective, the result is a range of neurological problems, as associated with Alzheimer's disease for example.

28. Shively et al., "Characterisation of Interface Astroglial Scarring," 345–349, at 949.

29. Axons are nerve fibers that conduct electrical impulses away from the neuron cell's body. See Glasser, *Broken Bodies, Shattered Minds,* 162–164, 166.

30. Such damage might explain the strange and awkward gaits of British soldiers captured in Arthur Hurst's film *War Neuroses* (1918), available on YouTube and other Internet sites.

31. Shively et al., "Characterisation of Interface Astroglial Scarring," 950; Eagleman, *The Brain,* 39 (with photo), notes that brain cells are tightly packed against one another; this surely heightens IED impact.

32. Shively, et al., "Characterisation of Interface Astroglial Scarring," 951.

33. From the immense bibliography, I would recommend Judith Herman, M.D., *Trauma and Recovery. The Aftermath of Violence—From Domestic Abuse to Political Terror* (New York: Basic Books, 1992/1997); Zahava Solomon, *Combat Stress Reaction: The Enduring Toll of War* (New York: Plenum Press, 1993); Jonathan Shay, M.D., *Achilles in Vietnam: Combat Trauma and the Undoing of Character* (New York: Atheneum, 1994), xx (for a list of symptoms); and David Wood, *What Have We Done: The Moral Injury of Our Longest Wars* (New York: Little, Brown, 2016.

34. See, for example, R. Kaufman, "Blast Badge: Innovative Material Could Signal Potential TBI," *American Legion Magazine* 170, no. 3 (March 2011): 14. In December 2016, National Public Radio reported that the Pentagon had placed on hold a program to provide blast badges for the thousands of troops deployed in Afghanistan.

35. Rick Atkinson, "About Left of Boom: The Fight Against Roadside Bombs," *Washington Post,* 30 September 2007, www.washingtonpost.com (accessed 24 May 2017).

36. Tanielian and Jaycox, eds., *Invisible Wounds of War.*

37. D. L. Kriner and F. X. Shen, *The Casualty Gap: The Causes and Consequences of American Wartime Inequities* (Oxford: Oxford Univ. Press, 2010); see also the thoughtful review discussion by Thomas G. Palaima in *Michigan War Studies Review,* http://www.miwsr.com/2011-009.aspx.

38. Kriner and Shen, *The Casualty Gap,* 31. Readers should note that each chapter of their study includes a technical discussion detailing the evidence based on employment rates, rent or income, race, rural residence, and voting records, all this for casualties suffered in World War II, Korea, Vietnam, and Iraq, and recorded in the US National Archives or at the DoD (for Iraq).

39. This survey is in no way scientific, but the three instances of deaths from "elite" communities—Aptos, Los Altos, and San Marino—are all officers, including two graduates of the Naval Academy.

40. Kriner and Shen, *The Casualty Gap,* 6–7.

41. Since 2012, military suicides have been closely monitored (and widely reported in news media), and in 2016 suicides reached record highs for the seventh consecutive year. Among the observations noted in the DoD's *Quarterly Suicide Report* (first quarter, 2016) is that "research suggests that there may not be a direct association between suicide and deployment" (3), and that military suicides are but a reflection of the "whole-of-life" (1). The social-economic inequities discussed above contextualizes this issue and cannot be ignored. Discussion of the Bales and Green courts-martial can be found easily enough via the Internet.

42. See also Andrew J. Bacevich, *Breach of Trust: How Americans Failed Their*

Soldiers and Their Country (New York: Metropolitan Books, 2013), and Dexter Filkins, *The Forever War* (New York: Vintage, 2009).

43. As seen on the 16 April 2007 cover of *Time*: "Why Our Army Is at the Breaking Point." The essay title by Mark Thompson reads "What the War in Iraq Has Done to America's Army—and How to Fix It. A Time Investigation" (28–35). The article is followed by Anthony Suau's photo essay "Keeping up the Fight" (36–41).

44. Descriptive pamphlets and other literature were made available. One example is the brochure "Battlemind Training," prepared by the Walter Reed Army Institute of Research (WRAIR) in 2006. Personnel returning from combat duty received questionnaires asking about their mental health. The questionnaires were transparent and it was clear that certain responses would trigger delays in home leave or discharge for some, and barriers to advancement for others. Accordingly, "safe" responses could be anticipated and were too often given. See also Shannon J. Johnson et al., "The Psychological Needs of U.S. Military Service Members and Their Families: A Preliminary Report," American Psychological Association, February 2007, 40–41.

45. GAO 17-260, *DOD Health: Actions Needed to Ensure Post-Traumatic Stress Disorder and Traumatic Brain Injury Are Considered in Misconduct Separations* (May 2017); cf. Dave Philipps, "War Wounds Often Precede 'Misconduct' in Discharges," *New York Times,* 17 May 2017, A21.

46. GAO 17-260, *DOD Health*, 30–31.

47. Wilson, *Consilence,* 293.

48. See, for example, Stefanie Linden, *They Called It Shell Shock: Combat Stress in the First World War* (Solihull/West Midlands, UK: Helion, 2016). This study omits any reference to examples of battle trauma in the ancient world (blindness and other forms of conversion disorder) and modern neurological studies and postmortems, as discussed above. Neither is there any awareness of the debate over the "Universalist" and "Presentist" positions on the issue of human physiology and trauma.

49. See Tritle, "'Ravished Minds' in the Ancient World," 98, for more detailed treatment.

Epilogue

J. Casey Doss

As General Bolger wrote in the forward to this volume, "some problems cannot be solved by landpower." However, the dilemma, as he also argues, is that we cannot give up on landpower as an attribute of American power, because "people live on land, not in the skies or seas. . . . At some point, you have to take and hold the key ground. That takes landpower. And we must get it right." But as these essays aptly demonstrate, the American relationship to landpower is complicated. Taking and holding the key terrain is difficult and expensive, it is bloody, and it brings us face to face with the tensions inherent to American principles and actions in ways much more direct than seapower and airpower. The exercise of landpower stirs within the American psyche deep fears of despotism and the curtailment of liberty,[1] and the prospect of ever more incomprehensible levels of national debt. Despite massive investments in lives and resources, and the moral price of employing American landpower in foreign lands, there is no guarantee of success.[2]

So there are limits to what America can achieve, but, frustratingly, those limits are unclear. The hope that compels volumes such as this one is that we can learn from our recent unsatisfying conflicts, that through postmortem analysis we can identify the missteps, the poor decisions, and the misalignment of capabilities and requirements, so that we can better understand the limits of our military power and prevent similar missteps in the future. Perhaps, but we must keep in mind the unique problems we faced in Iraq and Afghanistan. That we lacked enough firepower at Tora Bora, or that de-Ba'athification was entirely counterproductive, or that we withdrew American forces prematurely from Iraq, to ruinous effect, tells us less about the specific policy, strategy, doctrine, or force structure choices future political and military officials should make than it reminds us of the role of contingency and chance in war. Each conflict is *sui generis,* despite our best efforts to impose pattern upon chaos. The use of landpower generates innumerable decisions and actions that in their sum whole are entirely unpredictable and will ultimately determine the outcome of the conflict. That we can recognize harmful consequential decisions in the past does not inoculate us against making harmful consequential decisions in the future, and it is always easier to determine the limits of our power after we have exercised that power than when we are in the moment and confronted with intractable national security problems.

Generals and strategists, guided by experience, training, and education, and in collaboration with national policymakers, attempt to negotiate these decisions and to place them into a unified framework, of course, but just as we should not overvalue tactical excellence and technological advantage, we ought not to expect that good military strategy will always solve our land-power problems. As we are reminded that technology is no panacea for combat's friction, so too should we recognize that strategy is no panacea for war's unpredictability and no substitute for poor policy decisions. At our best we can stack the deck in our favor, but only to a degree, and never determinatively. We thus return to policy, and the humility we should maintain when deciding to use landpower, often the best bad choice.

But after seventy-five years of a generally consistent interventionist foreign policy, we still do not fully understand our limits in employing landpower. Perhaps we can begin by recognizing our national ambivalence and antipathy toward landpower. On the one hand, we have overly optimistic expectations for what force can achieve and have militarized our foreign policy. On the other hand, we tend to back off from our use of force when the inevitable complications occur and it becomes clear that our expectations were unrealistic. We agonize over putting boots on the ground, but our foreign policy since 1945 has depended on it—or at least the credible possibility of doing so—to achieve our objectives. It does not help matters that our Greatest Generation myth disguises the deep anxiety that confronted wartime leaders, who worried not just how to defeat fascism, but also how to balance military power, internationalist organizations, and economic structures in its aftermath to build a new international order and prevent a third world war.[3]

In resolving these anxieties, the Roosevelt-Truman administration and its allies established a mixture of means to ensure stability and peace. First, they constructed international economic and trade structures to provide immediate relief to wartime deprivation, support reconstruction, and prevent harmful economic protectionism that could spark another global conflict. The idea that abundance prevents war is at the core of American foreign policy ideology. Second, the postwar architects established the UN as a credible collective security organization that could resolve international disputes, albeit at the expense of democratic principles through the establishment of the Security Council's veto power. Finally, and in line with the establishment of those veto powers, Roosevelt advanced the notion of the Four Policemen—the United States, Soviet Union, Great Britain, and China—to act as guarantors of peace within their respective regional spheres of influence.[4]

In the aftermath of the war, the Four Policemen quickly became two as China splintered into civil war and Britain faced the inexorable loss of empire. The UN initially became politicized in its Western orientation, and then "unruly" as decolonization swelled its numbers. It was left to the fraught power relationship established between the two remaining superpowers—which always greatly favored the West, given its economic reach and control of the global commons—to maintain an uneasy peace throughout the Cold War. The superpowers became hypersensitive to disruptions in the international order, and NATO and the Warsaw Pact supplanted the UN as credible collective security organizations while the arms race made inconceivable the consequences of major armed conflict and a nuclear exchange. Within this security environment, lasting throughout the Cold War, overwhelming American airpower and seapower both enabled power projection and ensured that the global commons remained open to enable economic interconnection and the global prosperity necessary for the peace which followed. Meanwhile, the Soviet Red Army's mass and deep operations potential kept the European landmass deadlocked.

In addition to the antipathy that shaped its employment, American landpower became Janus-faced, with two competing imperatives. First, Cold War logic dictated that American landpower should remain in a high state of readiness and forward deployed to deter communist expansionism and to fight "the big one" if necessary, dictating the fielding of large peacetime standing armies well-equipped and well-trained for maneuver warfare, a significant departure from American military practice to that point in its history. But while the United States and Soviet Union were clearly superpowers, their combined span of control was by no means absolute, and Cold War tensions intersected and bisected with the profound changes in the international order caused by decolonization. That emerging states both rejected and invited superpower patronage opened new spaces for the employment of landpower, as Cold War logic also dictated that American landpower project into these spaces to deny communist access. Thus the second imperative for American landpower was to police against communist activity in what became known as the Third World, leading to numerous ideological interventions.[5]

In this era of containment and deterrence, a zero-sum landpower dilemma developed. The more America employed landpower in internationalist adventures to police postcolonial spaces from communist expansion, the weaker it became as a deterrent force in the central theater of Europe. This first became clear to President Harry Truman in December 1950, as Britain's Prime Minister Clement Atlee convinced him to accept a stalemate in Korea and to reorient American landpower from Asia toward Europe and the Soviet Union at the height of the Korean War, to the understandable consternation of General Douglas MacArthur.[6] More consequentially, a generation later the commitment of American landpower to Vietnam from 1965 to 1973 led to a scarred and "hollow army" that had lost a generation of modernization while facing down the Soviets in Europe, compelling President Richard Nixon to pursue détente.[7]

Moreover, both the American public and the American military professional was uncomfortable with this policeman role, with its abstract ideological objectives and interconnection with economic development and modernization theories. It challenged the idealistic notion that war can be bracketed from peace, and that the processes of peace can be kept separate from the processes of war, as success in these operations was defined less by military control and more by sociopolitical outcomes.[8] And while the US was not without success during this period, such as in the Philippines against the Hukbalahap Rebellion, the catastrophic failure in Vietnam deeply discredited American landpower.[9]

Despite this dilemma, landpower nonetheless played a critical role throughout this interventionist period, and the more expansive American foreign policy became, the more dependent it became on landpower—yet, simultaneously, the more the United States tried to break its dependence on landpower, or at least to minimize its cost. A thread of continuity thus extends throughout the American employment of landpower since the Second World War. In such policies as the 90 Division Gamble, New Look, the Nixon Doctrine, and others, American administrations have tried to achieve their foreign policy objectives while minimizing their landpower commitment. This ambivalence toward landpower and these efforts to address the zero-sum tradeoff between interventionism and superpower deterrence resulted in compromises over outcomes. Thus the American concession of landpower dominance to the Soviets in the Second World War ensured that the Soviets would capture Berlin—if it was ever really in doubt as to who would have the honors, given the Red Army's sophisticated and well-resourced combined arms operations—firmly drawing the Cold War fault line through Germany. Similarly, as president, Eisenhower found that his overreliance on nuclear power limited his capacity to respond to Third World crises due to a lack of available landpower capability. And Nixon's reliance on regional proxies to allow for the retrenchment of American landpower failed to prevent the collapse of the Republic of Vietnam 1975 and helped push Iran into revolution in 1979, though it did help win the bigger prizes of détente and the normalization of relations with China.

It is possible that future historians will view the collapse of the Soviet Union as more significant for the use of American landpower than the searing events of 9/11. After the sudden Soviet downfall, Roosevelt's Four Policemen were now down to one, and NATO remained the sole credible collective security organization. Though the military brass attempted through the Powell Doctrine to remain focused on fighting a peer competitor, American landpower, for the time being at least, was unencumbered from the realistic fear of a major conventional conflict. Spurred on by democratic peace theories and a view of America as the "indispensable nation," projection of American landpower thus became increasingly ideological and hyperactive in an attempt to exploit Cold War victory. NATO enlarged into former Warsaw Pact countries throughout the 1990s, and the United States often employed force to stomp out the refuges of disorder and reaction left uncovered by the collapse of the Cold War.[10]

Nation-building thus reemerged as a core task for American landpower. Dubbed stability and support operations, the ideas behind it—and later that of American counterinsurgency doctrine—draw a direct ideological line from the modernization theories espoused by Walt W. Rostow in Vietnam, the relief, recovery, and reconstruction of Europe during and following World War II, and the food relief mission led by Herbert Hoover after World War I. Deeply embedded within these approaches to conflict resolution are liberalism's core precepts that economic abundance, growth, and social and political participation are the best inoculates to political instability and military conflict. War is often a consequence of the dysfunctionality of political, social, and economic systems, and the regeneration of those systems is the best antidote to war. Successful conflict resolution thus requires first an effective response to the immediate postconflict crisis, but then a longer—and ultimately more decisive—investment in the affected society and economy. Success is achieved when a "politics of plenty" replaces a "policy of need," and thus depoliticizes and demilitarizes the society, as middle-class comforts tame not only the revolutionary but the militarist as well.[11]

Thus, as military leaders hoped to use the post–Cold War period to achieve a generational leap forward in their capabilities to fight a major conflict against a future peer competitor, their political masters hoped to use landpower in this unipolar moment to accelerate liberalism's global expansion. Both efforts proceeded apace, but it soon became apparent through interventions in Haiti, Somalia, and Bosnia that superior and technologically advanced landpower capabilities did not guarantee successful outcomes in interventions. While military leaders hoped to lessen the bill of using landpower through revolutionary advances in military operations that could reduce the need for mass, investments in technologies meant to protect the force and keep troop requirements low did not have a direct correlation to military effectiveness in ideological interventions. Further, while militarily decisive in Desert Storm, operational excellence enabled by precision targeting and information dominance failed to achieve regional stability on its own accord, and the United States spent the better part of the decade searching for ways to force Iraq's President Saddam Hussein to conform to international norms of behavior.

9/11 thus accelerated processes already underway, and there is more continuity than discontinuity in the foreign policies of Presidents Bill Clinton, George W. Bush, and Barack Obama. The attacks on New York and Washington amplified the importance to American policymakers of the need to stamp out disorder, and the difference between Clinton's and Bush II's foreign policies is more of tone and emphasis than substance: a hyper-interventionist foreign policy became even more so. American landpower's role following 9/11 was thus to fight a global war for order first, and to modernize and prepare to fight a future competitor second.

The chapters in this volume have detailed many of the challenges, problems, and consequences in fighting these interventionist wars. In our efforts to understand the reasons why we have struggled in employing landpower in these conflicts, we too often focus internally on our landpower itself. We ask whether it is our military's way of war, or its doctrine and training, or even poor decisions by its leaders. Problematically, our thinking is run through with a positivist perspective that assumes we could have—or even should have—won these wars. And this is not to argue that these wars were necessarily unwinnable, but they were certainly not necessarily winnable, either.

Further, we too often overlook those we are exercising our power upon, and if we do, we make blanket generalizations about the complexity of the postmodern era and globalization as an explanation for our recent struggles in employing force.[12] Indeed, the world is complex—as are humans. It has always been so, this is nothing new. And perhaps we are, in fact, at a disadvantage because we have designed our premises of landpower on the notion of massive state-on-state conflict, and we find ourselves fighting opponents who organize differently.[13] Yet while globalization may have degraded the effectiveness of this state-centric approach to landpower, we must also consider that the places in which we have chosen to employ it matters as well. In considering the reasons for American landpower's reduced utility, it is worth reconsidering the policy choices driving its employment. Since World War II, our epochal dominance of the sea and air has enabled an ideological and interventionist foreign policy that has caused us to interact in new ways in new places against new actors. This has only accelerated in the aftermath of the Cold War and 9/11, yet we have never come to grips with the demands on landpower our postwar foreign policy has created. As the memory of that day in September fades—we will, after all, soon see the first cohort of enlistees and cadets born after the attacks—and we move out of this unipolar moment and back into an era of great power rivalry, perhaps the most significant consequence of our foreign policy will become clear when we come to understand the opportunity cost in modernization for our unsatisfying foreign adventures.

Notes

1. Jason W. Warren, "Liberty Paradox: The Failure of the Military System in Mid-Seventeenth Century New England," in *Drawdown: The American Way of Postwar*, ed. Jason W. Warren (New York: New York Univ. Press, 2016).

2. The author thanks Colonel Gian Gentile (Ret.) for his assistance with this epilogue.

3. While we can certainly trace the origin of the Cold War's fault lines through the Grand Alliance's interactions, the overwhelming shared desire of all parties was to prevent another global conflagration.

4. Historian Mark Mazower argues, in fact, that the postwar order and the UN were deliberately established to reinforce the geopolitical status of the Grand Alliance. Mark Mazower, *No Enchanted Palace: The End of Empire and the Ideological Origins of the United Nations* (Princeton, N.J.: Princeton Univ. Press, 2009).

5. For a compelling narrative of American and Soviet interventionism in the Third World during the Cold War, see Odd Arne Westad, *The Global Cold War: Third World Interventions and the Making of Our Times* (Cambridge: Cambridge Univ. Press, 2005).

6. William Stueck, *The Korean War: An International History* (Princeton, N.J.: Princeton Univ. Press, 1995), 131–138.

7. Jeremi Suri, *Power and Protest: Global Revolution and the Rise of Détente* (Cambridge, Mass.: Harvard Univ. Press, 2003).

8. Indeed, the recent counterinsurgency debates were a manifestation of this ongoing struggle to determine the proper employment of American landpower. See Elizabeth Bumiller, "West Point Is Divided on a War Doctrine's Fate," *New York Times,* 27 May 2012, https://www.nytimes.com/2012/05/28/world/at-west-point-asking-if-a-war-doctrine-was-worth-it.html.

9. The Soviet Union suffered a similar dynamic with its use of landpower to quell the Prague Spring. For the interconnections between American and Soviet landpower retrenchment in the late 1960s and early 1970s, see Suri, *Power and Protest.*

10. As Westad has demonstrated, the Cold War's bipolarity helped create these pockets of disorder.

11. For an example, see Elizabeth Borgwardt, *A New Deal for the World: America's Vision for Human Rights* (Cambridge, Mass.: Harvard Univ. Press, 2007).

12. See Headquarters, Department of the Army, *Training and Doctrine Command Pamphlet 525-3-1: The Army Operating Concept: Win in a Complex World* (Washington, DC: Government Printing Office, 2009).

13. Emile Simpson, *War from the Ground Up: Twenty-First-Century Combat as Politics* (London: Hurst, 2012.

Acknowledgments

This volume is dedicated to my graduate school adviser, the late Dr. John F. Guilmartin Jr., US Air Force lieutenant colonel (ret.) and professor of history at The Ohio State University. Although not a direct purveyor of landpower, he embodied the spirit of the best of America's fighting men and women of all services and was highly decorated for bravery. Lieutenant Colonel Guilmartin witnessed the disappointing results of American efforts in Southeast Asia, participating in the air evacuation of the American embassy in Saigon. He never lost faith in his country, however, and would applaud the reform efforts herein. As a professor, "Dr. G" was peerless in his wide and deep knowledge of history from the early modern to the postmodern eras, producing the classic book *Gunpowder and Galleys* as a standard in the study of early modern warfare. Even with such successes, he often sacrificed his own scholarship for the betterment of his thirty-six Ph.D. students and more than two hundred master's advisees, with over twenty going on to write academic books. The best way to turn around America's landpower fortunes would be to produce more leaders, scholars, and patriots in the mold of Dr. G.

I am indebted to Melissa Hammer and the editorial staff at the University Press of Kentucky for their time and guidance in bringing this project to a successful conclusion. I am indebted to John Bonin and Lawrence Tritle, who provided critical insight for this study. I am, as always, most grateful for my loving children, William and Alice.

The views expressed herein remain the contributors' own and do not reflect the views of the military services, military service colleges, the DoD, DoS, or the Intelligence Community.

Contributors

Ibrahim Al-Marashi, PhD, is an Associate Professor at California State University, San Marcos. He has recently coauthored *The Modern History of Iraq* and has forthcoming "Reconceptualizing Shi'ism and Notions of the 'Shi'a Crescent': A History of Intra-Shi'a Tensions in Iraq vis-à-vis the Islamic Republic of Iran before and after the 2011 Uprisings," in *Islamists and the Politics of the Arab Uprisings: Governance, Pluralisation and Contention,* ed. Hendrik Kraetzschmar and Paola Rivetti.

Mark Balboni, Major, US Army strategist, serves as the Chief of Concepts and Doctrine at the US Army War College. He has deployed four times since 9/11.

Daniel P. Bolger, Lieutenant General (Ret.), US Army, PhD, currently teaches history at North Carolina State University. Among a number of other military commands, he served as Commander, Coalition Security Transition Command-Afghanistan/NATO Training Mission-Afghanistan (November 2011–April 2013). Along with eight other books, Lieutenant General Bolger is the author of *Why We Lost: A General's Inside Account of Iraq and Afghanistan.*

John A. Bonin, Colonel (Ret.), US Army, PhD, is Professor of Concepts and Doctrine for the US Army War College. He has twice been the General of the Army George G. Marshall Chair of Military Studies and is the lead author of *Joint Publication 3-31: Command and Control of Joint Land Operations,* as well as author of *Unified and Joint Land Operations: Doctrine for Landpower,* published for the Land Warfare Papers, August 2014.

Christopher Bowers, Major, US Army strategist, served as a planner for US Army Africa from 2014 to 2016 and has published on hybrid adversaries and military operations in megacities.

James V. DiCrocco III, Lieutenant Colonel, US Army strategist, is the Director of the Defense Strategy Course for the US Army War College and has served for over thirty-two years, with three combat tours. He led the development of the *Planner's Handbook for Operational Design* and the *Commander's Handbook for Joint Support to Distributed Forces.* He is a PhD candidate at the University of Leeds, UK.

J. Casey Doss, Lieutenant Colonel, US Army, is the Deputy Director of the Army Museum Enterprise, Center of Military History. He has twice taught as an Assistant Professor of History at the United States Military Academy at West Point and has deployed four times post-9/11. He is a PhD candidate at George Washington University.

David Fastabend, Major General (Ret.), US Army, is an independent consultant and has served in various high-level leadership positions in the military and the defense industry. These include Vice President of AIS, Exelis (now Harris) and Director of Strategy, Plans, and Policy for the US Army. He is an influential strategist in the wars of post-9/11.

Edward A. Gutiérrez, PhD, is a graduate student at Boston College and the consulting historian for the state of Connecticut's *Remembering World War One* project. He is the author of *Doughboys on the Great War: How American Soldiers Viewed Their Military Service.*

Joel R. Hillison, Colonel (Ret.), US Army, PhD, is a Professor of National Security Studies at the US Army War College and an Adjunct Professor at Gettysburg College. He is the author of *Stepping Up: Burden-Sharing by NATO's Newest Members.*

Charles Luke, Major, US Army strategist, served as a lead planner for US Army Africa from 2013 to 2015.

Peter R. Mansoor, Colonel (Ret.), US Army, PhD, is the General Raymond E. Mason Jr. Chair of Military History at The Ohio State University. A veteran of two combat tours, he was a brigade commander in Iraq from 2003 to 2004 and later served as executive officer to General David Petraeus, commanding general of Multi-National Force-Iraq from 2007 to 2008. He is a leading voice in the counterinsurgency dialogue and the author of *The GI Offensive in Europe: The Triumph of American Infantry Divisions, 1941–1945*; *Baghdad at Sunrise: A Brigade Commander's War in Iraq*; and *Surge: My Journey with General David Petraeus and the Remaking of the Iraq War.*

Jon S. Middaugh, Colonel, US Army Reserve, is a historian at the Naval History and Heritage Command and previously worked at the US Army Center of Military History.

Lukas Milevski, PhD, is an Assistant Professor of strategy at Leiden University. He has published two books with Oxford University Press, *The Evolution of Grand Strategic Thought* and *The West's East: Contemporary Baltic Defense in Strategic Perspective.*

Gregory Roberts is a desk officer at the DoS and previously served as a historian on the CSA's Operation Enduring Freedom Study Group. His first book, *Police Power in the Italian Communes, 1228–1326*, is forthcoming in 2019.

Eric Setzekorn, PhD, is a historian with the US Army Center of Military History and an adjunct professor at George Washington University, where he teaches courses on strategy and Chinese history. He has published academic research on a wide range of issues relating to US military history, Asian (particularly Chinese) military history, and intelligence operations.

Frank Sobchak, Colonel (Ret.), US Army Special Forces, is a former Assistant Professor at the United States Military Academy at West Point. He served as the director for the CSA's Operation Iraqi Freedom Study Group, producing the Army's official operational-level history and study of the Iraq War. He is a PhD candidate at the Fletcher School of Law and Diplomacy.

Donald S. Travis, Lieutenant Colonel (Ret.), US Army strategist, PhD, served for thirty-one years in both the Active and Reserve Components and deployed to Iraq. He is the author of multiple scholarly articles on civil-military relations and teaches American Government at Gettysburg College.

Lawrence A. Tritle, PhD, is Professor Emeritus of History, Loyola Marymount University, and a US Army veteran, having served in Vietnam. He has written and edited numerous studies, including *From Melos to My Lai: War and Survival* and *The Oxford Handbook of Warfare in the Classical World.*

William Waddell, PhD, is an Assistant Professor of strategy at the US Air

Force War College and has served as a US Army officer in both Iraq and Afghanistan. He published *In the Year of the Tiger: The War for Cochinchina, 1945–1951.*

Jason W. Warren, Lieutenant Colonel, US Army strategist, PhD, has served as an Assistant Professor at both the United States Military Academy at West Point and the US Army War College, and has deployed to both Egypt and Afghanistan. He is the author of *Connecticut Unscathed: Victory in the Great Narragansett War, 1675–1676* and the editor of *Drawdown: The American Way of Postwar* and *The Many Faces of War.*

Paul Westermeyer is a historian in the History Division of the US Marine Corps. He is the author of *U.S. Marines in the Gulf War, 1990–1991: Liberating Kuwait* and *US Marines in Battle: Al-Khafji 28 January–1 February 1991.*

Jacqueline E. Whitt, PhD, is an Associate Professor of strategy at the US Army War College. She is the author of *Bringing God to Men: American Military Chaplains and the Vietnam War* and the podcast editor and producer for *WAR ROOM,* the online journal of the US Army War College.

Alex Willard, Major, US Army strategist, deployed with the 101st Airborne Division to Liberia from 2014 to 2015 and has published on several topics, including talent management and military interoperability.

Index